Encyclopedia of British Women's Writing, 1900–1950

Encyclopedia of British Women's Writing, 1900–1950

Edited by

Faye Hammill, Esme Miskimmin and Ashlie Sponenberg

Introduction, Selection and Editorial Matter © Faye Hammill,
Esme Miskimmin, Ashlie Sponenberg 2006
All entries © Contributors 2006

First published 2006 by
PALGRAVE MACMILLAN
Houndmills, Basingstoke, Hampshire RG21 6XS and
175 Fifth Avenue, New York, N.Y. 10010
Companies and representatives throughout the world

PALGRAVE MACMILLAN is the global academic imprint of the Palgrave
Macmillan division of St. Martin's Press, LLC and of Palgrave Macmillan Ltd.
Macmillan® is a registered trademark in the United States, United Kingdom
and other countries. Palgrave is a registered trademark in the European
Union and other countries.

ISBN-13: 978–1–4039–1692–1 hardback
ISBN-10: 1–4039–1692–6 hardback

This book is printed on paper suitable for recycling and made from fully
managed and sustained forest sources.

A catalogue record for this book is available from the British Library.

Library of Congress Cataloging-in-Publication Data
Encyclopedia of British women's writing, 1900–1950 / edited by Faye Hammill,
  Esme Miskimmin, and Ashlie Sponenberg.
     p.   cm.
  Includes bibliographical references and index.
  ISBN 1–4039–1692–6 (cloth)
  1. English literature—Women authors—Dictionaries.   2. Women authors,
English—20th century—Dictionaries.   3. English literature—Women authors—
Bio-bibliography—Dictionaries.   4. Women and literature—Great Britain—
Dictionaries.   5. English literature—20th century—Dictionaries.   I. Hammill,
Faye.   II. Miskimmin, Esme, 1973–   III. Sponenberg, Ashlie, 1974–
PR111E53 2006
820.9'928709041—dc22

                                                                   2005056623

10   9   8   7   6   5   4   3   2   1
15   14   13   12   11   10   09   08   07   06

Transferred to Digital Printing 2006

Contents

Acknowledgements

As this is a truly collaborative project on many levels, we are indebted to many people. Our thanks go first of all to Dr Louise Harrington, for untiring assistance with writing author, topic and bibliography entries, and to Dr Keir Waddington, for essential guidance in identifying contributors and for numerous entries on historical topics and in the history section of the bibliography.

Professors Rick Rylance and Phyllis Lassner read our book proposal with great care, and made many invaluable suggestions. Guidance on the list of historical topic headwords was generously provided by Dr Kevin Passmore, and we are grateful to Rob Gossedge and Lucy Thomas for advice about Welsh writers. We would also like to thank our editors at Palgrave: Emily Rosser for her enthusiasm for the project and support in the early stages, and Paula Kennedy and Helen Craine for taking over and helping us to bring it to completion.

We are especially grateful to contributors who took on substantial numbers of entries (Drs Nicola Beauman, Kathleen Bell, Jane Dowson, Alice Entwistle, Stacy Gillis, Mary Grover, Lesley Hall, Elaine Hartnell and Anthea Trodd), and also to those who were flexible about entry assignments, or stepped in at a late stage to provide entries (Dr Catriona Beaumont, Luanda Stannard, Jana Nittel, Dr Julia Jones, Dr June Hannam, Dr Terry Phillips and Professor Ben Fisher).

Sarah Thwaites assisted with the preparation of entries on E. Nesbit and Mary Elizabeth Braddon, and Dr Michela A. Calderaro provided references for the entry on Eliot Bliss. Helen Parfect very kindly helped with the preparation of the timeline.

Our friends and families have been enthusiastic about the project, and patient with all our stressful moments. We would also like, individually, to acknowledge our gratitude to one another, for mutual support, encouragement and inspiration over the period we have been collaborating. Three editors is an ideal number: after all, 'A threefold cord is not quickly broken' (Ecclesiastes 4:12).

Contributors

Richard Aldrich, Institute of Education, University of London, England
Ann Alston, Cardiff University, Wales
Marie Askham, Anglia Polytechnic University, England
Nicola Beauman, Persephone Press, London, England
Caitriona Beaumont, London South Bank University, England
Kathleen Bell, DeMontfort University, England
Kristin Bluemel, Monmouth University, USA
Erica Brown, Roehampton University, England
Sebastien Chapleau, Cardiff University, Wales
Laura Christie, Roehampton University, England
Gladys Mary Coles, University of Liverpool and Liverpool John Moores University, England
Stella Deen, State University of New York at New Paltz, USA
Jane Dowson, DeMontfort University, England
Alice Entwistle, University of the West of England, England
Robin Edward Feenstra, McGill University, Canada
Benjamin F. Fisher, University of Mississippi, USA
Jane Garrity, University of Colorado at Boulder, USA
Judy Giles, York St John College, England
Stacy Gillis, University of Newcastle, England
Rob Gossedge, Cardiff University, Wales
Deborah Gorham, Carleton University, Canada
Mary Grover, Sheffield Hallam University, England
Fiona Hackney, Falmouth College of Arts, England
Toby Haggith, Imperial War Museum, London, England
Lesley A. Hall, The Wellcome Library, London, England
Faye Hammill, Cardiff University, Wales
June Hannam, University of the West of England, England
Louise Harrington, Cardiff University, Wales
Jenny Hartley, Roehampton University, England
Elaine Hartnell, Liverpool Hope University College, England
Pam Hirsch, Newnham College, Cambridge University, England
Jennifer Holberg, Calvin College, USA
Kathy Hopewell, University of Wales, Bangor, Wales
Avril Horner, Kingston University, England
Peter Hunt, Cardiff University, Wales
Elaine Jackson, University of Birmingham, England

Maroula Joannou, Anglia Polytechnic University, England
Jill Jones, South Western Oklahoma State University, USA
Julia Jones, Roehampton University, England
Phyllis Lassner, Northwestern University, USA
Rodney Lowe, University of Bristol, England
Elizabeth Maslen, Institute of English Studies, University of London, England
Kiriaki Massoura, Northumbria University, England
Esme Miskimmin, University of Liverpool, England
Fidelis Morgan, Writer, London, England
Rebecca Munford, University of Manchester, England
Jana Nittel, Roehampton University, England
Chris Nottingham, Glasgow Caledonian University, Scotland
Alison Oram, University College Northampton, England
Sharon Ouditt, Nottingham Trent University, England
Deborah Parsons, University of Birmingham, England
Terry Phillips, Liverpool Hope University College, England
Gill Plain, University of St Andrews, Scotland
Sean Purchase, Cardiff University, Wales
Susan Rowland, University of Greenwich, England
Bonnie Kime Scott, San Diego State University, USA
Val Scullion, The Open University, England
Lisa Shariari, University of Essex, England
Dorothy Sheridan, Mass Observation Archive, University of Sussex, England
Anna Snaith, King's College, London, England
Ashlie Sponenberg, York College-CUNY, USA
Luanda Stannard, Nottingham Trent University, England
Lucy Thomas, Cardiff University, Wales
Anthea Trodd, Keele University, England
Henrietta Twycross-Martin, Institute of Continuing Education, University of
    Cambridge, England
Keir Waddington, Cardiff University, Wales
Diana Wallace, University of Glamorgan, Wales
Alison Waller, Nottingham Trent University, England
Leigh Wilson, University of Westminster, England
Joanne Winning, Birkbeck College, University of London, England
Gina Wisker, Anglia Polytechnic University, England
Tory Young, Anglia Polytechnic University, England
Sue Zlosnik, Manchester Metropolitan University, England

Introduction

> It seems there is a Plan on foot that Ned should be painted by Mr Reynolds who is the Painter à la Mode now. I declare I cannot see why Ned with his Carroty Locks should have his portrait made while my more Worthy Features should go down unrecorded to the Tomb. Have prayed Papa to permit me to be painted by Miss Reid who is also very Modish but he declares he has not sufficient money for two, which I vow is a Monstrous shame.
>
> Cleone Knox [Magdalen King-Hall], *The Diary of a Young Lady of Fashion in the Year 1764–1765* (1925)

When the hilarious journal of 'Cleone Knox' was published in 1925, experts were convinced it was a genuine eighteenth-century document, and compared it to Pepys's diary in importance. The resulting publicity made it a bestseller, and the discovery that it was a hoax was reported on the front page of the *Daily Express*. The perpetrator of this literary sensation, the 19-year-old Magdalen King-Hall, went on to a successful career writing historical novels. One of them, *The Wicked Lady*, has been filmed twice, and the 1945 version was the most popular film of its year in the United Kingdom. Yet despite her impact on her contemporaries, Magdalen King-Hall is not to be found in any literary dictionary or reference work. In preparing the entry on her work for this encyclopedia, it was necessary to collate and compare information from a whole range of print and internet sources, including historical maps of Ireland, genealogical websites, library catalogues and film databases.

We did not wish Magdalen King-Hall to remain 'unrecorded', or displaced by her literary brothers. She is one among many fascinating women authors who deserve to be restored to their formerly significant places in the literary culture of the early twentieth century. The provision of reliable information about such authors is among the primary aims of this encyclopedia. We were motivated also by a desire to stimulate interest (among readers, teachers and scholars) in this exciting era of women's literary history. By choosing a timespan which is narrow in comparison to that of other encyclopedias, we have been able to be more inclusive, to offer a very detailed picture of the range and variety of women's literary activity in this period, as well as an extensive survey of the secondary material in the form of an annotated bibliography. The other major purpose of this book is to anchor the women's writing of 1900–50 firmly in its literary, intellectual and historical contexts. We have devoted one-third of the main text to topic entries, giving accounts of genres, aspects of literary culture, periodicals, popular culture, social issues, politics, and historical events. There are, for example, entries on modernism, detective fiction, censorship, libraries, little magazines, consumerism, domestic technology, the Women's Movement, contraception, the Titanic, the Spanish Civil War, socialism and Mass Observation. The 72 topic entries have been supplied by a range of specialists, including historians, archivists and literary critics, and are designed to provide the kind of detail which will be most useful to scholars of women's writing. Cross-references (indicated in small capitals) direct readers to relevant topic entries, but it will also be helpful to consult the indexes at the end of the book.

The editors of this volume have all recently developed research and teaching projects on women writers in the early twentieth century, and have been confronted by the lack of an introductory or reference guide to the field. We have each had to consult dozens of different sources (literary dictionaries covering the whole of women's writing, monographs on a few authors, historical textbooks and so on) in order to gather the basic material needed to plan and execute our books and courses. This encyclopedia provides a starting point for students, lecturers and researchers interested in any aspect of women's writing in this period. Our entries are long enough to include valuable critical interpretation and quotation, but they also point readers towards more substantial discussions via the secondary references.

We have come up against the usual problems of definition and scope. The category 'British women writers 1900–50' sounded very precise, but proved of course to be quite enormous and very blurred around the edges. We had little difficulty, to be sure, in determining who qualified as 'women', but 'British' is notoriously awkward, and 'writer' almost equally so, while the date range adds a further complication. We have been generous in our interpretations of these terms. The only exclusions in terms of dates were writers whose careers were all but over by 1900, or who had only just begun in the late 1940s. All authors of British birth or parentage were considered eligible, even if they spent many years abroad (for example, Anna Kavan or Rumer Godden) and we have included numerous authors who were born outside the United Kingdom, but lived and wrote there for significant periods. Most of these are from the Republic of Ireland (such as Eva Gore-Booth or Kate O'Brien) or from Commonwealth countries (including Elspeth Huxley and Pamela Lyndon Travers). The majority of our author entries are on women primarily known for their fiction, poetry and drama, whether for adults or children, but we also include writers in other genres who had a significant impact on the literary–intellectual culture of the period. Amongst them are women best known as literary critics and scholars (Q. D. Leavis, Helen Waddell), editors and journalists (Lady Rhondda, Iris Barry), autobiographers and travel writers (Ethel Smyth, Freya Stark) or social activists (Beatrice Webb, Dora Russell). There are entries for 187 authors altogether, and information about a further 66 appears in the appendix of minor writers, which lists authors about whom too little is known at present to warrant a full entry.

Many difficult choices presented themselves as we drew up and revised the list of headwords and word lengths. A large proportion of our editorial decisions have been taken in consultation with our contributors, and their interests, expertise and wisdom have had a significant bearing on the final content and structure of this book. We are particularly grateful for their suggestions for additional, less well known writers for inclusion. Such 'rescued' writers have entries of 200 words, while entries for better known writers were set at 500 words. In most literary encyclopedias, entries vary significantly in length according to the editor's judgement of an author's significance. We have sought to avoid such hierarchical organization as far as possible, aware that the perceived importance of any writer can vary greatly over time, and between different readers and critics. Inevitably, there is a degree of arbitrariness in our 500/200 word division, but we have assigned the shorter length only to those writers about whom little information is available, or who, despite their intrinsic interest, had only a limited output or impact in Britain. Our list of 500-word entries includes a great many authors who would be firmly categorized as minor in a standard literary encyclopedia, or left out altogether, either because they are perceived as too lowbrow (for example, Ethel M. Dell and Florence Barclay), or because they fell out of fashion, despite being greatly admired during their lifetimes (such as Frances Cornford or Elizabeth Taylor). We hope our entries will stimulate further research into the very rewarding writings of these women.

It is not easy to compress complex topics and eventful literary careers into the space of a few hundred words: it is, we have decided, like trying to pack a large duvet into a small suitcase. Considering that our contributors have had to take such pains to keep within word limits, it would seem hypocritical to devote any further space to a mere introduction. Besides, we have just finished writing our own entries, not to mention the bibliography, timeline and appendix of minor writers, and each of us feels tempted to borrow a phrase appended by 'Cleone Knox' to a particularly lengthy diary entry: 'My hand is nearly off have wrote so much.'

F. H.

A

Abortion

Abortion, achieved, or at least contemplated, forms a significant motif in twentieth-century British women's writing. Pioneering fictional depictions appeared in Jean RHYS's *Voyage in the Dark* (1934) and Rosamund LEHMANN's *The Weather in the Streets* (1936). Novels, memoirs and biographies reveal common patterns: ineffective gin and hot baths, followed by useless medication, the quest for a contact, the expensive Harley Street operator, the dangerous backstreet abortionist.

Abortion was a criminal act under the 1861 Offences Against the Person Act, which did not recognize medical justifications: even so, a few doctors performed discreet operations, costing around £100. During the 1930s, women's organizations supported amending the law, and an Abortion Law Reform Association was formed. In 1938 a government committee was appointed to investigate the subject, while Aleck Bourne, a gynaecological surgeon, operated on a girl of 14 who had been gang raped, to test the law. This case figures in the background of Virginia WOOLF's *Between the Acts* (1941). His successful defence, that continuing the pregnancy seriously threatened her mental HEALTH, established important case law.

In 1967 an Abortion Act legalized abortion on physical or mental health grounds, under medical control, and taking into consideration social conditions. The anti-abortion lobby has so far failed to overturn this.

Suggested Reading

Brookes, Barbara. *Abortion in England, 1900–1967* (London: Croom Helm, 1988).
Hindell, Keith and Madeleine Simms. *Abortion Law Reformed* (London: Peter Owen, 1971).

Lesley A. Hall

Ackland, Valentine 1906–1969

Neglected poet, autobiographer, and long-term partner of novelist Sylvia Townsend WARNER. Born in London, Ackland began writing poetry in her adolescence. Like Townsend Warner, Ackland was deeply committed to the Communist Party, and later to left-wing politics. She produced a documentary on labourers' lives, *Country Conditions* (1936), and wrote for papers such as the *Daily Worker*. Ackland's poetry, the bulk of which was published posthumously in two collections, *The Nature of the Moment* (1973) and *Further Poems of Valentine Ackland* (1978), concerns itself mostly with themes of love, war, the spiritual, and the writing of poetry.

One of her most innovative poetic endeavours was the collaborative production of *Whether A Dove or a Seagull* (1934), with Townsend Warner. Published without attribution, the writers described the collection as 'both an experiment in the presentation of poetry and a protest against the frame of mind which judges a poem by looking to see who wrote it'. In 1949, Ackland wrote the moving autobiography *For Sylvia: An Honest Account*, detailing her early recognition of her LESBIAN sexuality, her relationship with Townsend Warner, which she regarded as the central event of her life, and her struggle with alcoholism.

Suggested Reading
Mulford, Wendy. *This Narrow Place: Sylvia Townsend Warner and Valentine Ackland: Life, Letters and Politics, 1930–1951* (London: Pandora Press, 1988).

Joanne Winning

Allingham, Margery 1904–1966

One of the most influential and experimental crime writers of the twentieth century. Allingham was devoted to her home in rural Essex, setting many of her novels there, and others in Suffolk and London. Her work explores both city and country deviance. Allingham created one of fiction's most enigmatic detectives, Albert Campion. His real name and background are purposefully left vague, but there is a suggestion that he is aristocratic. When he is encountered posing as minor royalty at the start of *Sweet Danger* (1933), the reader is likely to be puzzled. Campion proves to occupy a more habitual role of semi-detached spy for the British government, and he finds himself menaced by a characteristic enemy: a criminal gang operated by a capitalist mogul. Allingham's dark forces come from *within* modernity and so can only be defeated by forces from the margin. Myth and romance can be marshalled to preserve England, in the form of a treasure hunt in *Sweet Danger*, a sacred aristocratic trust in *Look to the Lady* (1931), and a shadowy ritual government in *Traitor's Purse* (1941). The latter novel is narrated by a Campion who has lost his memory so he literally does not know whose side he is on. Here, Campion's ambivalence towards the law is embedded in an experimental literary form.

Allingham's DETECTIVE FICTION is more than simply nostalgic, and does not set a mythical representation of the past against a corrupt present. Rather, it depicts a multi-layered world in which attachment to the past has a dark side, be it the witchcraft that almost extinguishes the heroine, Amanda, in *Sweet Danger* or the dead hand of a deceased painter's will in *Death of a Ghost* (1934). Tradition can be ossified into corruption, as demonstrated by the decayed heart of an established publisher in *Flowers for the Judge* (1936). Indeed, bonding with the past can warp a whole family, as in the mordant relations of

Police at the Funeral (1931), in which the rule of Victorian matriarch Caroline has resulted in murderous immaturity in her elderly offspring. Attachment to past hierarchies can be condemned in explicitly modern terms; in *Coroner's Pidgin* (1945), an autocratic aristocrat is described as 'like a beautiful, high powered car driven by an engaging maniac'. Even more bizarrely out of touch with their emotions is the indigent genteel family of *More Work for the Undertaker* (1949). For example, one elderly man's erotic obsession with his niece drives him to hysteria.

If Allingham's villainy is associated with modernity's worship of money, it is also a sign of masculinity in crisis. Crucially, the breaking point occurs when money is used to assert power – the result is murder, frequently followed by madness. Campion himself demonstrates a genuine ambivalence about masculinity and the law. Frequently contrasted to a friendly policeman who believes absolutely in his job, Campion is several times faced with the possibility of killing to protect either his friends or his country. The law appears an inadequate structure within the modern world.

Allingham's work evolved from mythical underpinnings through family psycho-dramas to spy stories. She invented the urban serial killer novel in *The Tiger in the Smoke* (1952), and her influence can be traced in the development of psychological crime fiction. In later life she suffered from undiagnosed manic depression.

Suggested Reading

Pike, B. A. *Campion's Career: A Study of the Novels of Margery Allingham* (Bowling Green, OH: Bowling Green State University Popular Press, 1987).

Rowland, Susan. *From Agatha Christie to Ruth Rendell: British Women Writers in Detective and Crime Fiction* (Basingstoke: Palgrave, 2001).

Thorogood, Julia. *Margery Allingham: A Biography* (London: Heinemann, 1991).

Susan Rowland

Appeasement

A British policy adopted between the wars towards Germany, based on pacification through the granting of concessions. Appeasement sprang from the conviction that Germany was not wholly responsible for WORLD WAR ONE. In 1919, the Treaty of Versailles imposed heavy reparation payments on Germany and limited her armed forces, terms seen by appeasers as punitive and unlikely to bring lasting peace. Throughout the 1920s, Britain sought revision in German repayments and reconsidered German rearmament, hoping to revitalize European business damaged by the war and reposition Germany as an ally rather than an enemy.

Nazism and Hitler's rise to power in 1933 challenged appeasement, although hopes that FASCISM would impede the spread of COMMUNISM westward offset

British hostility. Many appeasers believed that Nazism would reform, but the policy became increasingly unviable as accounts of persecution in Germany grew.

Appeasement was further compromised by the Munich Agreement (1938), when Britain, under the leadership of Prime Minister Neville Chamberlain, agreed to cede the Sudetenland in Czechoslovakia to Germany. Any hope that war could still be avoided disappeared when Germany invaded Poland on 1 September 1939. Appeasement ended and Britain declared war on Germany on 3 September.

Suggested Reading

Gilbert, Martin. *The Roots of Appeasement* (London: Weidenfeld & Nicholson, 1966).

Marie Askham

Ashford, Daisy 1881–1972

Juvenile author who wrote her major work, *The Young Visiters, or Mr Salteena's Plan*, in 1890, aged nine. Unpublished until 1919, it was then printed with its original idiosyncratic spelling. Still readily available, it has subsequently been staged (1920), made into a musical (1968), filmed (1984) and adapted for BBC television (2003). *The Young Visiters* is a true comedy of manners; the protagonist, Mr Salteena, is 'not quite a gentleman' but wants to become 'the real thing'. Rich in childhood values and misapprehensions about the adult world, it makes hilarious reading. We learn that, before travelling, 'Mr Salteena did not have an egg for his brekfast in case he should be sick.' Meanwhile, another character boasts that one of his 'ancesters' was 'really the Sinister son of Queen Victoria' and, on being interrogated about what this means, admits, 'I dont quite know'. Elsewhere in the story, the Prince of Wales wears a 'small but costly crown' and eats ice-cream.

Margaret Mary Julia ('Daisy') Ashford started her story-telling career at the age of four – dictating her earliest efforts to her father – and continued writing until she was 14. Other pieces were collected and published as *Daisy Ashford: Her Book* (1920).

Suggested Reading

Barrie, J. M. Preface to *The Young Visiters* by Daisy Ashford (London: Chatto & Windus, 1951) 7–13.

McMaster, Juliet et al. (eds). Annotated edition of *The Young Visiters* (Edmonton: Juvenilia Press, 1997).

Elaine Hartnell

Asquith, Lady Cynthia 1887–1960

Best known nowadays as a diarist, Lady Asquith was also a novelist, biographer, and anthologist. She was born at the family home, Stanway in Gloucestershire (one of the most beautiful small country houses in England) to Hugo and Mary Elcho, who were 'Souls', that is, they belonged to a group of close friends who in some ways anticipated BLOOMSBURY but were much more monied and less intellectual. Hence, Cynthia's pedigree was illustrious and she had a wide circle of interesting and influential friends. An acknowledged beauty, she was too quick-witted to settle for the comfortable life of a Tory country estate but instead in 1910 she married 'Beb' Asquith, a younger son of the Prime Minister, and began a life of reduced circumstances (given what she had been brought up to expect), cultivating her friendships, enjoying intense but platonic relationships with a succession of men, and bringing up three sons. One of the writers she 'midwifed' was D. H. Lawrence, who used her as a model in several short stories and drew on aspects of her life for the heroine of *Lady Chatterley's Lover*.

When the First World War broke out she began to keep a diary, which remains her most enduring work and deserves to be far better known. It mixes the momentous and the everyday in a fascinating and endearing fashion: for example, she wrote on 23 March 1918: 'The nightmare of the battle now raging oppressed me all day like a heavy weight. I have never been so haunted by the war and, as far as I know, Beb is in the neighbourhood of St Quentin where things seem to be worse...I felt very sick at heart. Stayed in for dinner and read *Women in Love*...Surely (Lawrence) is delirious...or do I know nothing about human beings?' The diary was criticized, for example by Leonard Woolf, because of 'the arrogant frivolity and futility of the aristocratic clique to which Lady Cynthia belonged'. But Leon Edel wrote: 'What comes through the often humdrum story is the deep suffering, the eternal ennui of the home front, a kind of killing of time as a means of insulation against the killing one couldn't shut out.' The diaries were published posthumously in 1968, with a foreword by Cynthia's close friend, the novelist L. P. Hartley.

In the 1920s she began to write articles to make money, because her husband had endured shell-shock in the trenches, and she soon turned to writing books. She was encouraged in her writing by J. M. Barrie, whose secretary she had become in 1918, but his possessiveness was as damaging to the Asquiths as it had been to the Llewellyn-Davies family on whom he drew for Peter Pan. In 1936 Cynthia published *The Spring House*, a semi-autobiographical novel about the war years, for which she had her diaries at hand; and in 1950 and 1952 two volumes of memoirs about her girlhood which are much quoted by biographers of her contemporaries.

Suggested Reading

Asquith, Cynthia. *Diaries, 1915–1918*, foreword by L. P. Hartley (London: Century, 1987).

Beauman, Nicola. *Cynthia Asquith* (London: Hamish Hamilton, 1987).

Nicola Beauman

Auden Generation

The term 'Auden Generation' (the title of Samuel Hynes's 1976 book on literature and politics in the 1930s) identifies W. H. Auden as the focal point of 1930s literature. In November 1937, *New Verse* published an Auden double number. This focus was sharpened by Robin Skelton's Penguin anthology, *Poetry of the 1930s* (1964), which identified Auden as the 'Master of the Period' and identified the characteristic poetic voice of the 1930s in a generation born between 1904 and 1916. This disadvantaged women poets, who often start publishing later in their lives; only four of the poets discussed individually in Dowson's *Women's Poetry of the 1930s* (1996) fit Skelton's dates.

Writers connected with the Auden generation often include: Louis MacNeice, Stephen Spender, Cecil Day Lewis, Christopher Isherwood, Rex Warner and Edward Upward, although Upward is most helpfully seen as a critical influence on Isherwood and, through him, on Auden. Members of this group associated with women writers and artists, including Rosamund LEHMANN, Naomi MITCHISON and Nancy Sharp, but male critics rarely acknowledge this connection.

The focus on the 'Auden Generation' prioritizes a narrow range of experience; the typical writer is seen as male, educated at public school and Oxford or Cambridge, with interests in the contemporary (1930s critics wrote of the 'pylon poets'). One characteristic style is impersonal, often offering a political or scientific view of people, places or events; at times this becomes exhortatory. The conversational style – best illustrated by Auden and MacNeice's 'Last Will and Testament' in *Letters from Iceland* (1937) – can tend to privilege an inner circle of readers. Marx, Freud and D. H. Lawrence are key influences.

Major political change, whether Marxist revolution or FASCIST counter-revolution, seemed imminent, leading writers to consider their moral responsibility. Connection with others was vital; Isherwood's narrator in *Goodbye to Berlin* (1939), preparing to lose kinship with ordinary people, concludes 'I am lost'. Love (both specific and general) is frequently evoked, often in parallel to historical events; in 'Fish in the Unruffled Lakes' (1936), Auden evokes love as a model of willing involvement.

Writers saw their own class position as problematic; MacNeice in *Autumn Journal* (1939) writes of public schools teaching 'complete conformity and / An automatic complacence'. However, as Janet Montefiore suggests, such critiques 'implicitly claim ... universal status for exceedingly privileged modes of social construction'.

Suggested Reading

Mendelson, Edward. *Early Auden* (London: Faber, 1981).
Montefiore, Janet. *Men and Women Writers of the 1930s: The Dangerous Flood of History* (London: Routledge, 1996).

O'Neill, Michael and Reeves, Gareth. *Auden, MacNeice, Spender: The Thirties Poetry* (Basingstoke: Macmillan, 1992).

Kathleen Bell

Ayres, Ruby M. 1883–1955

Dubbed 'Queen of fiction', Ruby Mildred Ayres was one of the most prolific and high-selling writers of popular ROMANCE, or as Mary Ellen Chase described it, the reading matter of the third-class railway carriage.

The daughter of an architect, Ayres married Reginald William Pocock, an insurance broker, in 1909, but had no children. She wrote approximately 150 novels, and was at her peak during the interwar years. Titles such as *A Gamble with Love* (1922), *The Second Honeymoon* (1918), *Brown Sugar* (1921), *The Remembered Kiss* (1918), *The Big Fellah* (1931) and *The Marriage of Barry Wicklow* (1920) were the staple of twopenny LIBRARIES. Ayres's stories were regularly serialized in popular WOMEN'S MAGAZINES such as *Woman's Weekly* and she was a regular contributor to the *Oracle, Daily Chronicle* and *Daily Mirror*.

Ayres described the kind of girl who might be reading her novels as 'young and romantic', 'a kind-eyed, sentimental under-housemaid'. Although her style was realistic romance, Ayres was aware of the importance of escapism in light fiction. She set out to entertain and viewed her writing as a craft, claiming pragmatically that romance could last if 'mixed with two most important ingredients – tolerance and a sense of humour'.

Suggested Reading

Mckibbin, Ross. *Classes and Cultures, England 1918–1951* (Oxford: Oxford University Press, 1998).

Vasudevan, Aruna (ed.). *Twentieth-Century Romance and Historical Writers* (London: St James Press, 1992).

Fiona Hackney

B

Bagnold, Enid 1889–1981

Novelist and playwright, best known for her children's book *National Velvet* (1935). Enid Bagnold, daughter of Major Bagnold, a Commander of the Royal Engineers, and Ethel Alger, was born in Rochester. She led something of a military childhood, spending part of it in Jamaica, where her father had a command, and part in Surrey, at a progressive school run by Mrs Huxley (mother of Aldous; niece of Matthew Arnold). Having been 'finished' in Paris and 'brought out' on Shooter's Hill she left home and took up lodgings in Chelsea, where she studied drawing with Walter Sickert. For a while she worked for Frank Harris, then editor of *Hearth and Home*, as a 'sort of journalist'. She became his lover, but was not in love with him. The love of her life was Prince Antoine Bibesco, who later married Elizabeth Asquith. With the outbreak of the First World War Bagnold worked as a VAD nurse at the large military hospital, the Royal Herbert, Shooters Hill. She published *Diary Without Dates* (1917), an impressionistic piece that comments on, among other things, the unfeeling nature of routine hospital procedures. Publication coincided with the exposure of such procedures in a French hospital: the book seemed to exemplify these and was the subject of a leader in the *Daily Mail*. Bagnold was instantly dismissed. After the war she joined the FANY (First Aid Nursing Yeomanry) and went to France as an ambulance driver, an experience that provided material for *The Happy Foreigner* (1920), her first novel. In the same year she married Sir Roderick Jones, head of the new agency Reuters. This inaugurated a new life as 'Lady Jones': hostess, wife, and mother to four children, but she reserved the mornings for her writing and remained in touch with the literary world: among her friends were H. G. Wells, Desmond McCarthy and Lady Diana Cooper.

National Velvet, the tale of a young girl who wins the Grand National, was made into a film starring a youthful Elizabeth Taylor. Other novels include *Serena Blandish* (1924), published under the pseudonym 'A Lady of Quality' out of deference to her father; *The Squire* (1928), which is about pregnancy; and *The Loved and Envied* (1951), which includes a portrait of Lady Diana Cooper. Bagnold was also an accomplished playwright. Her first play was *Lottie Dundass* (1943). *National Velvet* was made into a drama as well as a film; *Gertie* (1952) was a flop, but *The Chalk Garden* (1955) was an outstanding success in New York and London, and *The Chinese Prime Minister* (1964) was similarly acclaimed, although Bagnold was unhappy with the sentimentality of the London production. Roderick Jones died in 1962; Bagnold published her autobiography in 1969. Some correspondence is held at the Universities of Tulsa and Yale and there are photographs of her at the National Portrait Gallery.

Suggested Reading
Sebba, Anne. *Enid Bagnold: The Authorized Biography* (London: Weidenfeld & Nicholson, 1986).
Stoneley, Peter. 'Feminism, Fascism and the Racialized Body: *National Velvet'*, *Women: A Cultural Review*, 9.3 (Autumn 1998) 252–65.

Sharon Ouditt

Barclay, Florence 1862–1920

Author of ten popular novels and some shorter writings, there is a deeply evangelical tone to her work – though it tends towards the sentimental and romantic rather than the sternly didactic. Barclay's first novel, *Guy Mervyn*, was published anonymously in 1891 but only reissued posthumously in 1932, her daughter having made minor revisions to the original text. Herself daughter to one vicar and wife to another, one might expect Barclay's novels to be dismissive of supernatural phenomena. However, *The Upas Tree* (1912) is a kind of ghost story, and *Returned Empty* (1920) centres on a particular instance of reincarnation. Notable amongst Barclay's shorter writings is the domestic, pro-war novella *My Heart's Right There* (1914), based on the popular wartime song.

The novels are indeed romances: love stories about almost impossibly virtuous women and inherently chivalrous men from the upper-middle classes or aristocracy, the epitome of this romantic paradigm being *The White Ladies of Worcester* (1917). Begun in 1915, and the only one of her novels to be set in medieval England, the novel completely reinscribes, rather than deconstructing, the chivalric ideal. The idealized male–female relationships to be found in Barclay's novels are typically perfected by a shared growth in religious faith. For example, in *The Following of the Star* (1911), a wealthy and cynical woman proposes a marriage of convenience to an idealistic young clergyman so that she can simultaneously retain her home and finance his work in the mission field. The two fall in love, and the end of the novel indicates that they will continue to grow in love and faith together.

Barclay's plots are simple, being largely explorations of various moral dilemmas. Is it well for a man to declare his love to a married woman (*Guy Mervyn*)? Should a plain woman marry an artist who worships physical beauty (*The Rosary*, 1909)? Can a woman ever justifiably set aside the vows she has made as a nun (*The White Ladies of Worcester*)? Should a woman forgive the man who has tried to persuade her to leave her husband (*The Mistress of Shenstone*, 1910)? Such dilemmas resolved, the stories all have happy endings.

A number of the novels deal with unequal marriages of one kind or another. Most notably, several heroines are significantly older, wealthier or more morally responsible than their partners (*Through the Postern Gate*, 1911; *Guy Mervyn; The Broken Halo*, 1913; *The Upas Tree*). Such novels arguably have as their major theme male redemption through the offices of a good woman. Only in one book, *The Mistress of Shenstone*, is the heroine significantly younger, both chronologically and psychologically, than her first husband. However, the novel focuses on her widowhood, her growth towards maturity and her eventual second marriage to a man who will treat her as a woman rather than as a child. Florence Barclay died in 1920 but she was in print well into the 1950s. Her bestselling novel, *The Rosary*, was reissued in 2002, and complete texts of *The Rosary, The White Ladies of Worcester* and *My Heart's Right There* are available on the internet.

Suggested Reading

Anderson, Rachel. *The Purple Heart Throbs: The Sub-Literature of Love* (London: Hodder & Stoughton, 1974).

Anon. *The Life of Florence Barclay: A Study in Personality, By One of Her Daughters* (London and New York: G. P. Putnam, 1921).

Vinson, James. *Twentieth-Century Romance and Gothic Writers* (London: Macmillan, 1982).

Elaine Hartnell

Barry, Iris 1896–1969

Journalist and film archivist Iris Barry made a lasting contribution through her film preservation work at the Museum of Modern Art in New York, and her writing raised the status of CINEMA at a time when it was scarcely considered an art. Barry was born in Birmingham and, after spending time writing poetry in France, moved to London as a result of a correspondence with Ezra Pound. There she joined MODERNIST literary circles, published a novel, *Here Is Thy Victory* (1930), and had two children with Wyndham Lewis.

In 1923 she became the first British newspaper film critic, writing for the *Spectator*, and later the *Daily Mail*. Barry helped to set up the London Film Society, and published *Let's Go to the Pictures* (1925), in which she asserts that 'going to the pictures is nothing to be ashamed of'. After being fired from the *Daily Mail* over her request for a salary increase, Barry went to New York and was hired as the curator of the Film Library at MOMA in 1932, becoming its director in 1947. Her work there paved the way for the serious study of film history, saving many films that would otherwise certainly have been lost.

Suggested Reading

Barry, Iris. *D. W. Griffith: American Film Master* (New York: Museum of Modern Art, 1940).

Montagu, Ivor. 'Birmingham Sparrow: In Memoriam, Iris Barry', *Sight and Sound*, 39.2 (Spring 1970) 106–8.

Kathy Hopewell

Bellerby, Frances 1889–1975

Her poetry is imbued with a spiritual awareness encoded through the natural environment while her political SOCIALISM is more evident in her prose. Under her maiden name, M. E. Frances Parker, she published a collection of essays, *Perhaps?* (1927), and a novella, *The Unspoiled* (1928), before marrying John Bellerby, a Cambridge socialist economist, in 1929. They were involved in a voluntary organization for social WELFARE based on communistic ideals of shared income, as described in Frances's pamphlet *Neighbours* (1931). She published two novels, *Shadowy Bricks* (1932) about progressive EDUCATION, and *Hath the Rain a Father?* (1946), and also a volume of short stories, *Come to an End* (1939), but she abandoned an autobiography.

Several poems date from 1915, when her brother was killed in action; this bereavement and her own tragic misfortunes – a fall on Lulworth cliffs which left her a semi-invalid; her mother's suicide; marital and mental breakdowns – fuelled the vigour of Bellerby's poems of the Second World War. Her later poems shift their focus from people to locality, and many are about the West Country, where she moved in 1941. Her first volume, *Plash Mill and Other Poems* (1946), was followed by seven others, including a *Selected Poems* (1970), and two volumes consisting of single or double poems. Her papers are held at the University of Exeter.

Suggested Reading

Stevenson, Anne (ed.). *Selected Poems by Frances Bellerby*, with a biographical introduction by Robert Gittings (London: Enitharmon Press, 1986).

Jane Dowson

Benson, Stella 1892–1933

Travel writer, poet, and fiction writer, whose best known novel is *Tobit Transplanted* (1931). Stella Benson, daughter of Ralph Beaumont Benson and Caroline Essex, was born at the family seat, Lutwyche Hall, in Shropshire. Her mother was the younger sister of the author of *Red Pottage*, Mary CHOLMONDELEY. Owing to illness, which plagued her for all of her life, Benson's education was neither formal nor extensive, but she travelled a great deal in her childhood, in search of favourable climates. In 1912, convalescing following an operation on her sinuses, she travelled to Jamaica, where she began writing her first novel, *I Pose*. This is a fantastical, satirical tale of a militant suffragette and a gardener, published in 1915. Benson left home in 1913 to go and live and work among the poor of Hoxton in London's East End. There she made friends, set up a shop, worked for the Charity Organization Society and, when war broke out, became secretary to one of the workshops operated by the Queen's Work for Women Fund.

In July 1918 she set sail for America, and in California she made numerous friends and took on some work, including teaching for the University of California.

Her adventurous spirit took hold once more in 1920 and she set off for Hong Kong, via Honolulu and Japan. In Hong Kong she worked at a mission school teaching 50 Chinese and Eurasian boys. In China, she met Shaemas O'Gorman Anderson, whom she was later to marry (in 1921), but not before she had travelled to India and then back to England. Her married life was spent between China (where her husband had an administrative role), New York, and England.

Benson's reputation as a writer was growing (*Living Alone* was published in 1917, *This is the End* in 1919, *The Poor Man* in 1922, and a collection of travel articles, *This Little World*, in 1925), and the commissions were pouring in, but this did not always sit well with her role as a married woman in a community of ex-patriots. She was a lifelong feminist, and campaigned vigorously, for example, against child prostitution in Hong Kong, writing a League of Nations report on the subject. *Tobit Transplanted* brought her some celebrity when it won the PRIX FEMINA-VIE HEUREUSE and the A. C. Benson silver medal of the Royal Society of Literature. Other publications include further travel writings, *Worlds within Worlds* (1928), and the novels *Pipers and a Dancer* (1924), *Goodbye, Stranger* (1926), and *Pull Devil/Pull Baker* (1933). She died of pneumonia in China, with her final novel, *Mundos*, unfinished. Her *Poems* came out in 1935 and her collected short stories in 1936. Cambridge University Library hold her diaries and further papers; other papers are held by the British Library, and the New York Public Library. There is a watercolour of her by Julian Orde in the National Portrait Gallery.

Suggested Reading

Bedell, R. Meredith. *Stella Benson* (Boston, MA: Twayne, 1983).

Bottome, Phyllis. *Stella Benson* (San Francisco: Printed for Albert M. Bender, 1934).

Grant, Joy. *Stella Benson: A Biography* (London: Macmillan, 1987).

Sharon Ouditt

Bentley, Phyllis 1894–1977

Yorkshire author of REGIONAL novels, for which she is best known, as well as autobiography, crime fiction, and short stories. Bentley, born into a family with a long history in the textile industry, was educated at Halifax High School for Girls and Cheltenham Ladies College before obtaining an external degree from London University. She lived with her parents and worked briefly as a school teacher before leaving for London again to work in the Ministry of Munitions as a clerk during the First World War. In 1918, she published a collection of four stories, *The World's Bane*, which she had written during the war; this book and her early novels, *Environment* (1922) and *Cat-in-the-Manger* (1923), received respectable reviews but did not sell well. She began to make a name for herself as a successful regional novelist with *The Spinner of the Years*

(1928), set, as was almost all of her fiction, in a West Riding mill community. Arnold Bennett, J. B. Priestley, and Hugh Walpole enthusiastically reviewed the book. From the publication of *The Partnership* (1928), she began an affiliation with the publisher Victor Gollancz which lasted throughout her career.

Bentley was to spend most of her life in Yorkshire, financing her father's textile mill during the 1930s and, after the Second World War, caring for her ailing mother. Devotion to family often interfered with her writing career, and Bentley's autobiography, *O Dreams, O Destinations* (1962), describes the difficulties of the educated but financially dependent woman, tied to the family home. Vera BRITTAIN later portrayed Bentley as provincial, insecure and unfashionable, and attempted to help her friend gain confidence in London literary society. However, Bentley, who never married, took a lifelong interest in social issues in her Yorkshire community and seemed to have made this, rather than romantic success, a focus of her energies.

Bentley wrote in her autobiography: 'Unconsciously at first, but afterwards with deliberate intention, I have written a series of novels, 15 in all and three volumes of short stories, presenting the life of the men and women of the West Riding textile trade from the sixteenth century to the present day.' Bentley became a bestselling author with her 1930 novel, *Inheritance*, which fictionalized, through the story of the Oldroyd family, the history of the Halifax textile workers and her own mill-owning family from the Luddite rebellion through the Great DEPRESSION. The book received more than 500 reviews and was serialized for the radio and translated into eight languages. It led to a successful international lecturing career for Bentley and, along with the publication of her 1941 study *The English Regional Novel*, made her reputation as a regional writer. The Oldroyds reappeared in *A Modern* Tragedy (1934) and *The Rise of Henry Morcar* (1946).

Bentley's career continued into the 1970s, with publication in a variety of genres including the anti-fascist historical novel, *Freedom, Farewell* (1936), serialized for radio in 1977; several critical studies of the Brontës; the successful Miss Phipps crime stories; and children's television programmes. Leeds University awarded her an honorary doctorate in 1949, and she received an OBE in 1970.

Suggested Reading

Bishop, Alan. *Chronicle of Friendship: Vera Brittain's Diary of the Thirties, 1932–1939* (London: Gollancz, 1986).

Ford, Eric. 'Phyllis Bentley: Novelist of Yorkshire Life', *Contemporary Review*, 270.1573 (February 1997) 89–94.

Ashlie Sponenberg

Besant, Annie 1847–1933

Author, journalist, social reformer, Theosophist and advocate of home rule for India. Born Annie Wood in London, she married in 1867. Initially Anglo-Catholic, when her beliefs changed and she refused to attend communion, her clergyman husband ordered her to leave the marital home. Following their legal separation in 1873, he obtained custody of their children.

Becoming an atheist and freethinker, Besant joined the National Secular Society and worked with fellow member Charles Bradlaugh on the radical newspaper *The National Reformer*. She later joined the FABIAN SOCIETY and co-founded the Law and Liberty League and its journal, *The Link*. In 1888 she became involved with the successful Match Girls' Strike and in 1889 she was elected to the London School Board.

Meanwhile, on meeting Madame Blavatsky, founder-president of the Theosophical Society, Besant converted to Theosophy in 1889. In 1893 she moved to India, location of the Society's international headquarters, and was joined there by her children. She was soon deeply involved in Indian politics, for some time working alongside Gandhi. However, she retained her interest in trade union, SOCIALIST and women's SUFFRAGE issues in England. Her many publications include *The Gospel of Atheism* (1877), *The Laws of Population* (1877), *Why I am a Socialist* (1886), *The Ancient Wisdom* (1897), and *Man: Whence, How and Whither* (1913).

Suggested Reading
Besant, Annie. *Annie Besant: An Autobiography* (London: Fisher Unwin, 1893).

Elaine Hartnell

Bliss, Eliot 1903–1990

White Creole author of two novels, *Saraband* (1931) and *Luminous Isle* (1934). She was born Eileen Bliss in Jamaica, where her father, an English army officer, was stationed. She began writing as a child, and was educated at convent schools in England, rejoining her family in Jamaica in 1923. Two years later, Bliss moved permanently to England, and adopted the name Eliot in homage to T. S. Eliot and George Eliot. After taking a diploma in Journalism at University College London, she worked in publishing and then for a literary agent. Her first novel, *Saraband*, named for a stately seventeenth-century court dance, is told from the perspective of an imaginative young girl, Louie, who grows up in a Berkshire village and is later sent to a convent school. Louie's love of music and of natural beauty are intertwined in the many descriptive passages:

> The trees were now in their light green and hung down like a veil. New grass was springing up in patches, and among it purple and white crocuses; they always made her think of notes of music, crochets perhaps. Ivy ramped over the overgrown flowerbeds, where the stag-beetles lived and sometimes looked out among the dark leaves with their satanic faces.

Bliss's friends in the literary London of the 1930s included Anna WICKHAM, Dorothy RICHARDSON, Jean RHYS and Vita SACKVILLE-WEST. She subsequently moved to the East Coast of Britain, and then to Hertfordshire.

Suggested Reading

Calderaro, Michela A. 'To be Sexless, Creedless, Classless, Free. Eliot Bliss: A Creole Writer', *Annali di Ca' Foscari*, 42 (2003) 109–20.

O'Callaghan, Evelyn. ' "The Outsider's Voice": White Creole Women Novelists in the Caribbean Literary Tradition', *Journal of West Indian Literature*, 1.1 (October 1986) 74–88.

Faye Hammill

Bloom, Ursula 1892–1984

Author of over 500 books, who was initially encouraged to write by the well-known author and family friend, Marie CORELLI. Frequently working under pseudonyms (Lewis Essex, Mary Essex, Rachel Harvey, Sheila Burns, Deborah Mann, Sara Slone, and the imaginative Lozania Prole), Ursula Harvey Bloom authored novels, autobiography, and biography, worked as a journalist reporting for *Empire News* and *Sunday Dispatch*, and contributed fiction and features to WOMEN'S MAGAZINES.

Bloom's style was characterized by humour and imagination; drawing on her life experiences gave clarity and honesty to characters and situations. Titles include *The Great Beginning* (1924), *The Passionate Adventurer* (1936), *Our Dearest Emma* (1949), and *Parson Extraordinary* (1963), a biography of her father, the village Rector in Whitworth, Warwickshire, where Bloom grew up.

The financial independence that her writing brought enabled Bloom to leave an unhappy first marriage; she frequently advocated career rather than marriage for women and marriage as a partnership of equals. As she wrote in *Home Chat*: 'No career ever lets you down with the same hideous bump. A career gives you a dividend on what you put into it. Marriage is not so fair. A pair of blue eyes can dislocate it.' Bloom married her second husband, Charles Gower Robinson, in 1925.

Suggested Reading

Bloom, Ursula. *Sixty Years of Home* (London: Hunt & Blackett, 1960).

Melman, Billie. *Women and the Popular Imagination in the Twenties: Flappers and Nymphs* (London: Macmillan, 1988).

Fiona Hackney

Bloomsbury Group

An informal and intimate group of writers, artists, intellectuals, and friends, who met in the Gordon Square home of Leslie Stephen's children – Adrian,

Thoby, Vanessa (Bell), and Virginia (WOOLF) – in the Bloomsbury district of London, from around 1905.

The Bloomsbury Group, as it became known, emerged from the 'Thursday Evening' meetings attended by Thoby Stephen's Cambridge circle, Vanessa Stephen's 'Friday Club' and, from 1920, the 'Memoir Club'. Although the boundaries delineating its membership are somewhat fluid, in addition to the Stephen siblings the group included Duncan Grant, Clive Bell, Roger Fry, Leonard Woolf, John Maynard Keynes, Lytton Strachey, and Molly and Desmond MacCarthy. The painter Dora Carrington, the writers Vita SACKVILLE-WEST and Katherine MANSFIELD, and the diarist Frances Partridge were also involved with Bloomsbury at various stages.

While the Bloomsbury Group did not have a formal basis, its members shared what Clive Bell described as a 'contempt for conventional ways of thinking and feeling'. Rebelling against the artistic and sexual manacles of Victorian society, they discussed art and politics with broad-minded agnosticism. Their contemplations of truth and beauty were greatly influenced by the Cambridge philosopher G. E. Moore's *Principia Ethica* (1903) and, centrally, by his argument that 'the rational ultimate end of human progress consists in the pleasures of human intercourse and the enjoyment of beautiful objects'. The members of the Bloomsbury Group were united by their PACIFISM and became conscientious objectors in WORLD WAR ONE.

The candid environment of the Bloomsbury meetings provided a certain freedom for the hitherto cloistered female intellectual. As Virginia WOOLF recalls: 'From such discussions Vanessa and I got probably much the same pleasure that undergraduates get when they meet friends of their own for the first time...The young men...criticized our arguments as severely as their own. They never seemed to notice how we were dressed or if we were looking nice or not. All that tremendous encumbrance of appearance and behaviour... vanished completely.' However, Bloomsbury's sexual and intellectual permissiveness and snobbish exclusivity were derided by some outsiders. While F. R. Leavis attacked the coterie's amateurish elitism, D. H. Lawrence, erstwhile associate of the group, notoriously dreamed of the Bloomsbury 'black beetles'. Representing an important strand of British MODERNISM, the Bloomsbury Group has exerted a lasting influence on aesthetics, philosophy, and gender politics, as well as political and economic theory.

Suggested Reading

Marsh, Jan. *Bloomsbury Women: Distinct Figures in Life and Art* (London: Pavilion, 1995).

Rosenbaum, Stanford Patrick. *The Bloomsbury Group: A Collection of Memoirs, Commentary, and Criticism* (Toronto: University of Toronto Press, 1975).

Rebecca Munford

Blyton, Enid 1897–1968

Bestselling CHILDREN'S author, responsible for the creation of the cartoon character 'Noddy in Toyland' as well as many series of adventure novels featuring groups of middle-class children, such as the 'Famous Five'. Blyton started her literary career by publishing poems and fairy stories in the 1920s. A trained teacher, she focused some of her early works on practical classroom aids. For many years she wrote a column for *Teacher's World* and was the sole author of a magazine, *Sunny Stories*, between 1937 and 1952. During the 1930s she produced junior versions of myths from ancient Greece, Arabia, and Arthurian Britain. She also wrote plays.

It was not until *The Secret Island* (1938) that the Blyton adventure series was born, and the first of the 'Famous Five' appeared as *Five on a Treasure Island* (1942). Other series include the *Circus* series, starting with *Mr Galliano's Circus* (1938); *The Secret Seven*, about a crime solving club; the *Adventure* series, which required the presence of 'secret serviceman' Bill Cunningham; and the *Mystery* series with the 'Five Findouters', Fatty (a minor Sherlock Holmes), Larry, Daisy, Pip, and Bets. School series begin with *The Naughtiest Girl in the School* (1940), set in a co-educational establishment. It was joined by a more traditional school, *First Term at Malory Towers* (1946). In typical Blyton style, the moral structure of the stories is made explicit by the headmistress: 'I count as our successes those who learn to be good-hearted and kind, sensible and trustable, good, sound women the world can lean on.' The Arthurian reference in 'Malory' signifies a literal quest for virtue.

All Blyton stories build on a group of middle-class children who form a close-knit team. Their insularity provides a safe space, in part explaining their popularity, but those of another class or another nationality are often slotted into stereotypical 'bad' roles. Frequently a series begins with anxiety over a newcomer to the group and whether he/she can be accommodated. The 'Famous Five' opens with harmonious siblings Julian, Dick, and Ann, encountering the tomboy Georgina, who only responds to 'George'. Sulky George has a secret, Timmy the dog, who has been banned by her father from their house. Blyton frequently includes animals with part-human qualities as a way of negotiating difference. Much of the fun of the *Five* books is in Timmy's limited yet decisive participation in adventures. Kiki the parrot fulfils a similar role in the *Adventure* series.

Typically setting her stories in the country or at the seaside, Blyton offers a taste of a child-governed utopia, in which safe, reliably nice children, are let loose to experience mystery and suspense, sure in the knowledge that they will succeed in righting the wrongs of the adult world. Blyton's audience could not get enough of these saviours, who play in the security of friendships and material comfort, but librarians and teachers worried about the effect of such a restricted palette for middle-class fantasy.

Suggested Reading

Givner, Joan. *Thirty-Four Ways of Looking at Jane Eyre* (New York: New Star Books, 1998).

Rudd, David. *Enid Blyton and the Mystery of Children's Literature* (Basingstoke: Macmillan – now Palgrave Macmillan, 2000).

Stoney, Barbara. *Enid Blyton: A Biography* (London: Hodder & Stoughton, 1974).

Susan Rowland

Boer War 1899–1902

'The' Boer War was actually the second of two wars (the first 1880–1), fought between the British and the Dutch settlers (Boers) of the Transvaal and the Orange Free State. The quarrel drew in troops and aid from other parts of the British EMPIRE, including Canada and Australia. Ostensibly about the rights of British subjects in South Africa, the acquisition of gold mines in the Boer states was undoubtedly a major consideration.

Initially successful, the Boers besieged British garrisons at Ladysmith, Mafeking, and Kimberley. However, reinforcements arrived in 1900, lifting the sieges and capturing the capital cities of the two Boer republics in that same year. Boer troops then moved to guerrilla warfare. The British response was to destroy Boer farms and to herd a quarter of the Boer population – mainly women and children – into concentration camps, where many died. The war ended in May 1902 with the Treaty of Vereeniging, the Transvaal and the Orange Free State thereby losing their status as Boer republics.

In Britain there was some popular support for the war. However, it was opposed by numerous leading Liberal politicians and members of the Independent Labour Party. Women writers who articulated – and published – their protests about the conflict included South African novelist Olive Schreiner and English social reformer Emily Hobhouse, who publicized the sufferings of the imprisoned Boer women.

Suggested Reading

Hobhouse, Emily. *Report of a Visit to the Camps of Women and Children in the Cape and Orange River Colonies* (London: Friars Printing Association, 1901).

Pakenham, Thomas. *The Boer War* (New York: Random House, 1979).

Schreiner, Olive. *An English South African's View of the Situation* (London: Hodder & Stoughton, 1899).

Elaine Hartnell

Book Clubs

The book club was an early twentieth-century innovation in the distribution of books via new channels. Early British clubs were modelled on the successful US Book of the Month Club, begun in 1897. Publishers and authors benefited from the publicity and discussion the clubs generated, whilst the public gained discounted prices and the expert introductions often included within cheaper club editions. Book clubs were also the subject of scholarly debate; Q. D. LEAVIS aligned the middlebrow reader with clubs, reviewers, and other popular sources of guidance in reading tastes. E. M. Delafield's heroine, the Provincial Lady, is a subscriber to the Book-of-the-Month Club and the Book Society, and although she does not always approve their choices, she endorses the book club system, and defends it against the criticism of her aristocratic neighbour Lady B., who is 'always so tiresomely superior about Book of the Month, taking up attitude that she does not require to be told what to read'.

The Times Book Club was, in 1904, the first club established in Britain, and membership was offered as part of the annual subscription fee to *The Times*. Members could borrow books from the Club LIBRARY and were offered retired library titles at reduced rates, a practice which controversially violated the mandates of the NET BOOK AGREEMENT. Booksellers objected to the new competition as subsequent clubs, such as the Readers' Union and Reprint Society, offered reprints or below-net prices to competitors. The Times Book Club library included works by Margery ALLINGHAM, Daisy ASHFORD, Mrs Belloc LOWNDES, Eliot BLISS, Naomi MITCHISON, Dorothy WHIPPLE, and Virginia WOOLF amongst many other women writers.

The founding of the Book Society in 1929 introduced the book club in what became its more traditional form: new books were sold by post in cheaper club editions to subscribing members. Book Society choices included works by many women writers and were regarded as an important source of publicity: Woolf's *Flush* was an early Book Society choice in 1933, and despite highbrow disdain of club lists, her diaries record her disappointment when *The Years* was not nominated five years later.

In 1935, Victor Gollancz's SOCIALIST Left Book Club began the practice of selling titles published only for the club and not available in bookshops, another manner by which subscription clubs offended traditional booksellers. The LBC was unique in providing cheap editions of polemical texts by established writers of the British Left to a wide audience of often self-educated sympathizers. Members also received the *Left Book Club News*, a newsletter featuring announcements of upcoming publications, articles on current events, and meeting times of organized neighbourhood reading groups. Books were recognizable by their orange and black cloth covers; titles included travelogues of journeys to the Soviet Union, sociological volumes on the British population, and anti-Fascist polemics. Christina Foyle, of London's Foyle's bookshop, established the Right Book Club in reaction to the proliferation of left-wing titles. Her publications featured blue and black covers. The club allowed nationalistic and conservative writers a voice which Foyle believed had little chance of expression in the climate of the 1930s literary Left.

In 1939, the Book Club Proposition, which established that more than one year had to elapse between the publication of trade and club editions, was reached in order to reduce the effect of book clubs on the trade. Despite the perceived threat of the popular subscription club, John Feather estimates that, at most, 5 per cent of total book sales were generated by clubs in this period.

Suggested Reading

Feather, John. *A History of British Publishing* (London: Routledge, 1988).

Laity, Paul. *The Left Book Club Anthology* (London: Gollancz, 2001).

Ashlie Sponenberg

Bosanquet, Theodora 1880–1961

Author of a novel, literary critical work, reviews, and poetry. She attended University College, London, where she attained a B.Sc., but her ambitions soon became literary. Learning that Henry James required a secretary, she immediately taught herself to type and began working for him in October 1907. Following James's death in 1916, Bosanquet embarked on her own literary career.

With Clara Smith, she co-wrote a novel, *The Spectators* (1916), which, while rather unsatisfactory, makes clear the authors' familiarity with many of the recent movements in art and ideas, from Futurism to PSYCHOANALYSIS. She went on to publish an account of James's working methods for the Hogarth Press, *Henry James at Work* (1924), and two studies, *Harriet Martineau: An Essay in Comprehension* (1927) and *Paul Valéry* (1933). Bosanquet's companion was Viscountess RHONDDA, founder of the magazine *Time and Tide*, and, as well as contributing reviews and poetry, Bosanquet acted as its literary editor (1935–53) and as a director (1943–58). Her diaries, kept throughout her life, offer an interesting account of the literary world during the period, and are held in the Houghton Library, Harvard.

In the 1930s Bosanquet began to practise automatic writing, and believed she had made contact with a number of literary figures, including James. The voluminous archives of her automatic writing, held in the Society for Psychical Research Archive, University Library, Cambridge, are a poignant testimony to both her ambition and her sense of eclipse by male literary figures.

Suggested Reading

Edel, Leon. *Henry James: A Biography, Volume 5: The Master* (London: Rupert Hart-Davis, 1972).

Thurschwell, Pamela. *Literature, Technology and Magical Thinking, 1880–1920* (Cambridge: Cambridge University Press, 2001).

Leigh Wilson

Bottome, Phyllis 1882–1963

A prolific and popular radical author in her own day, but now largely forgotten. As a young woman she suffered from tuberculosis and spent some years in the mountainous sanatorium areas of Switzerland, France, and Italy. She returned to England on the eve of the First World War, joining the war effort by taking on relief work for Belgian refugees and also assuming a writing post under John Buchan at the Ministry of Information. Both activities, organizing personal aid and using her writing skills, would become hallmarks of Bottome's lifelong commitment to social and political causes. Her novels of this era, *Secretly Armed* (1916), *A Certain Star* (1917), and *A Servant of Reality* (1919), are all about the homecoming of wounded soldiers and former prisoners of war and the separate role of women responding to war's havoc.

In 1920 Bottome went to war-ravaged Vienna with her husband, Ernan Forbes-Dennis, who, after being badly injured during the conflict, took up a job in the diplomatic services. Bottome's experience of WAR WORK in Britain served her well as she aided Viennese activists in organizing food and medical services. Her European fiction was based on her experiences there, and the force of her social and political involvement led her to create plots that predict the fate of European civilization through her representation of the plight of the Jews. She explored relationships between the Jewish origins of Christianity and the rejection and persecution of the Jews. Her 1924 novel, *Old Wine*, for example, charts the fall of the Austro-Hungarian Empire at the end of WORLD WAR ONE. Startlingly prescient, it traces the increasingly systematic persecution of Jews back to the destabilized populace of Central Europe.

In 1938, her novel *The Mortal Storm* was at first resisted by the British, but then became a blockbuster on both sides of the Atlantic. It dramatized the rise and consequences of Nazism with trenchant psychological, sociological and historical analysis. It was made into an MGM movie as part of a cycle of anti-Nazi feature films produced between 1939 and 1941. Her psychological analysis of political events was influenced by her adherence to the views of Alfred Adler, who argued that people's political behaviour was shaped by their particular historical and social circumstances. She wrote the authorized biography of Adler, returning to Austria to complete her research, and remaining in Vienna until three days before Hitler's troops entered on 11 March, 1938.

On her return to Britain, Bottome campaigned tirelessly for Jewish refugees, refusing to accept the arguments that cast Jewish refugees as an economic threat and potential fifth column, and excoriating government policies of severely limiting Jewish immigration as xenophobic. *Formidable to Tyrants* (1941) attests to the quiet fortitude of the English people and especially the courage of women, such as those who served in the naval service and ambulance corps; and her novel *London Pride* (1941) depicts a working-class family's valour as the symbol of solidarity and survival under siege. She also lectured and wrote about international relations and political responsibility, from the broad perspective of having lived in Vienna in the early twenties and then in

Munich from 1931 to 1933. Later in her life, after several visits to Jamaica, she turned her political and literary attention to anti-colonial struggles. Her 1950 novel *Under the Skin* plots racial tensions from the end of WORLD WAR TWO to the end of EMPIRE. Her deep commitment to social justice made her aware that the battle against racial persecutions was not over, but had to be fought as a global struggle against the remnants of imperial domination. She therefore falls into a small group of British women writing the narratives of the end of Empire.

Suggested Reading

Lassner, Phyllis. 'A Bridge Too Close: Narrative Wars to End Fascism and Imperialism', *Journal of Narrative Theory*, 31.2 (Summer 2001) 131–54.

Lassner, Phyllis. '"On the Point of a Journey": Storm Jameson, Phyllis Bottome, and the Novel of Women's Political Psychology', in Antony Shuttleworth (ed.), *And In Our Time: Vision, Revision, and British Writing of the 1930s* (London: Associated University Presses, 2003) 115–32.

Pam Hirsch

Bowen, Elizabeth 1899–1973

Novelist and short-story writer, increasingly seen as a significant prose stylist. Elizabeth Bowen was born into the Anglo-Irish Ascendancy and lived at Bowen's Court, her family's home in County Cork, until she was six years old, when her father suffered a mental breakdown. Bowen and her mother moved to England, living on the Kent coast until her mother died in 1912. When she was 20, Bowen settled in London and wrote the short stories which would be published as *Encounters* (1923). Bowen married in the same year, lived in Oxford and London, and inherited Bowen's Court in 1930. She went on to publish six more collections of stories, ten novels, and a number of non-fiction works. Often called 'strange' and 'odd' by critics, her representations of loss, homelessness, and the need for love have an immense capacity to disturb.

Bowen constructs intense, often claustrophobic worlds where the strange alchemies and contradictory yearnings of human relations are followed to their often violent end. An inheritor of the Jamesean sense of the dense space between self and other, her work often focuses on an innocent young girl in a network of people, usually the occupants of one house, and the strangely violent impact of such innocence on a dissembling world compromised and marked by the past. In what is often regarded as her greatest novel, *The Death of the Heart* (1938), a naïve girl's demand for love shatters the carefully ordered lives of her relations, and at the end forces a choice which, while apparently banal, powerfully exposes the corruption and moral emptiness of the adult world.

One of the most important short story writers of the twentieth century, Bowen wrote with insight of the demands of the form. Her stories stretch beyond the social scenes of her novels into the supernatural, as in the disturbing

'Look at All Those Roses' (1941) and the eerie 'The Demon Lover' (1941). The effect of her writing is always created by bringing together high and popular forms, where the texture of consciousness and human relations learned from Austen and from MODERNISM is melded with Irish Gothic, fairy-tale, and thriller.

Bowen writes of the upper classes, and her style repeats their preference for the beautiful, the elegant, the restrained. The omniscient narrator of her pre-Second World War novels is ironic and witty, with a well-bred yet cutting tone. In later novels, this narrator disappears to be replaced by a less certain voice. In *Eva Trout* (1968), Bowen's last novel, the protagonist's perplexed and childlike relation to the world is echoed in parenthetical narrative interventions, and the narrative flow is chopped up by letters, untrustworthy and self-interested.

While Bowen's fictional work has always remained in print and popular with general readers, her critical reputation has waxed and waned. Eluding critical categories, by the 1980s her work had disappeared from the attention of the academy. Bowen was an Anglican Tory who rejected feminism, but it was feminist critics who revived interest in her, particularly in her writing from or about the Second World War, such as *The Heat of the Day* (1949). More recently, Irish studies have included her work and poststructuralists have seen it as uncannily prescient of concerns around the instability of meaning and the problems of language.

Suggested Reading

Bennett, Andrew and Nicholas Royle. *Elizabeth Bowen and the Dissolution of the Novel: Still Lives* (Basingstoke: Macmillan, 1994).

Ellmann, Maud. *Elizabeth Bowen: The Shadow Across The Page* (Edinburgh: Edinburgh University Press, 2003).

Lee, Hermione. *Elizabeth Bowen* (London: Vintage, 1999).

Leigh Wilson

Braddon, Mary Elizabeth 1835–1915

The 'uncrowned queen' of the sensation novel, best known for her melodramatic *Lady Audley's Secret* (1862). Ranked alongside Wilkie Collins as co-inventor of sensation, Braddon had a prolific writing career, producing over 80 novels, 120 short stories, and numerous plays, poems, and essays, as well as editing and contributing to magazines. Self-critical, she wrote to her mentor and admirer Bulwer Lytton that speed cost quality, remarking: 'I have never written a line that has not been written against time.'

London-born with an Irish mother and Cornish solicitor father, whose deviancy ended their marriage, Braddon always aspired to be a writer. In order to earn money to support her mother, she controversially took to the stage under the name Mary Seyton, but retired from acting in 1860 to focus on writing. She met the publisher John Maxwell, editing his *Belgravia* and *Belgravia Annual* between 1866 and 1876. They cohabited, Braddon becoming a mother to his five children and to six of their own, and married in 1874 following the death of his first wife. Freed from the ostracism of her peers, she then became a social 'grande dame'. Continued commercial success provided the wealth and credibility to entertain the literati, and admirers of her work included Tennyson, Dickens, Thackeray, and Henry James.

Her first poetry appeared in the *Beverley Recorder* and *General Advertiser* (1857), and she began writing fiction soon afterwards. The Dickensian sensation novel *Three Times Dead* (1860) had to be rewritten before it sold effectively. Her first bestseller, *Lady Audley's Secret*, is a melodramatic tale of criminality and sexual passion. The protagonist, Lucy, seems angelic: 'Wherever she went she seemed to take joy and brightness with her.' But Lucy deserts her child, murders her first husband, and contemplates poisoning her second. Sensation novels *Aurora Floyd, John Marchant's Legacy* and *Eleanor's Victory* (all 1863), *Henry Dunbar* and *The Doctor's Wife* (both 1864), and *Birds of Prey* (1867) followed. *The Doctor's Wife* contains a satirical portrait of a male sensation writer reworking Flaubert's *Madame Bovary*, but Braddon's own plot recycling invoked accusations of plagiarism.

Braddon was a key originator of women's popular fiction, and her books were staples of the circulating LIBRARIES. Her ability to address topics of public concern and create intricately subversive plots, strong physical description, and multiple viewpoints maintained a socially diverse readership, though the sensation genre unnerved moralists. *Eleanor's Victory* (1863) featured one of fiction's first female detectives, and was followed by other crime fiction, including *Rough Justice* (1898) and *His Darling Sin* (1899). In 'The Good Lady Ducayne' (1869), Braddon presents an ageing socialite vampire who uses scientific procedures to bleed female companions and maintain youthful looks. Wolff claims *Joshua Haggard's Daughter* (1876), a tragedy, and *Ishmael* (1884), a HISTORICAL FICTION, as her masterpieces. Braddon's later work engaged with psychological realism: *Dead Love Has Chains* (1907), for example, concentrates on character rather than sensation, while *Rose of Life* (1905) is a novel of manners. *During Her Majesty's Pleasure* (1908) revisits some of the themes of *Lady Audley's Secret*, but shows the influence of altering literary fashions. She lived to see *Aurora Floyd* on film in 1913, but her final book, *Mary*, was published posthumously in 1916.

Suggested Reading

Carnell, Jennifer. *The Literary Lives of Mary Elizabeth Braddon: A Study of Her Life and Work* (Hastings: Sensation Press, 2000).

Pykett, Lyn. *The Sensation Novel from The Woman in White to The Moonstone* (Plymouth: Northcote House, 1994).

Wolff, Robert Lee. *Sensational Victorian: The Life and Fiction of Mary Elizabeth Braddon* (New York: Garland, 1979).

Gina Wisker

Brazil, Angela 1868–1947

Writer of nearly 50 novels for girls during the 'golden age' of the school story, as well as other children's stories, plays, poems, songs and articles. Brazil did not begin to write seriously until she was in her thirties and living with her unmarried brother and sister in Coventry. She produced *A Terrible Tomboy* (1904), followed by her first substantial school story, *The Fortunes of Philippa* (1906), which established the conventions of her romanticized schoolgirl adventures; 'hot friendships', daring slang, and a strong moral framework of loyalty and decency. She continued to write school novels throughout her career – the last being *The School on the Loch* (1946) – as well as contributing short stories to *Girls' Realm* and other periodicals.

Brazil was a member of the Natural History and Scientific Society and City Guild, as well as hostess to musical soirées and charity teas for orphan children. These interests are detailed in her autobiography, *My Own Schooldays* (1925), and inform her school stories. Several of her heroines pursue artistic or musical careers, and all enjoy rambling and forming secret societies such as 'The Fair Play Union'. The novels advocate patriotic duty, compassionate self-sacrifice, and an adherence to social structures as much as they encourage imaginative fantasies. Some critics have suggested that there are LESBIAN overtones in the ardent and often physical relationships between the girls.

Suggested Reading

Freeman, Gillian. *The Schoolgirl Ethic: The Life and Work of Angela Brazil* (London: Penguin, 1976).

Sims, Sue and Hilary Clare. *The Encyclopaedia of Girls' School Stories* (Aldershot: Ashgate, 2000).

Alison Waller

Brent-Dyer, Elinor M. 1894–1969

Author of almost 100 girls' stories, most famously the Chalet School series. Brent-Dyer, born Gladys Eleanor May Dyer, trained as a teacher and worked as a schoolteacher and governess throughout the 1920s and 1930s, eventually opening her own school in Herefordshire. She continued her literary career simultaneously, only becoming a full-time writer in 1948.

Her first book was *Gerry Goes to School* (1922), but it was after a visit to the Austrian Tyrol in 1924 that the idea for her most famous books was conceived. *The School at the Chalet* (1925), the first in the series, shows Madge Bettany setting up a girls' school in the Austrian Alps, with her tomboyish sister Jo as its first pupil.

Although criticized for its middle-class sensibilities, the series has been praised for its emphasis on religious equality, its celebration of an all-female community, and its political awareness: in *The Chalet School In Exile* (1940), one of the Austrian characters condemns the 'secret imprisonments, maltreating of Jews, and concentration camps' of the Nazi regime. The series totalled 59 books, from *The School at the Chalet* to *Prefects of the Chalet School*, published posthumously in 1970.

Suggested Reading
Auchmuty, Rosemary. *A World of Women* (London: The Women's Press, 1999).
McClelland, Helen. *Behind the Chalet School: A Biography of Elinor M. Brent-Dyer* (Swindon: Bettany Press, 1996).

Louise Harrington

Bridge, Ann 1889–1974
Pseudonym of Mary Dolling O'Malley (née Sanders), prolific and very popular author of novels with exotic settings. Before starting to write, Mary O'Malley, who came from an affluent family which suddenly lost its money, earned her living by working for a charity in Chelsea; she also became a member of the Ladies' Alpine Club, decoded German ciphers for the Admiralty, and, during the First World War, was a poultry farmer at the family home in Surrey, Bridge End, where she brought up three children. Her husband was a diplomat, and she accompanied him on his postings, using a pseudonym for her writing in order to give them both anonymity. In 1926 they travelled to Peking. Here, O'Malley learnt Chinese and explored the old Imperial City and surrounding countryside; her first novel, published in 1932, was called *Peking Picnic*. It was a great success (bizarrely, it was sometimes compared with *A Passage to India*), and the following year won the £3500 Atlantic Monthly prize, which provided an extremely welcome turnaround in the O'Malley family's financial circumstances. *The Ginger Griffin* (1934) and *Four-Part Setting* (1939) were also set in China; *Illyrian Spring* (1935) was set in Yugoslavia, giving an early boost to the Dalmatian Coast tourist industry and inspiring the Prince of Wales's 1937 cruise with Mrs Simpson; *Enchanter's Nightshade* (1937) was set in Italy; *Frontier Passage* (1938) in Spain; *The Portuguese Escape* (1958) in Lisbon; and so on.

All the novels combine travelogue with a portrait of isolated diplomats trying to understand the natives of the country in which they find themselves living. Homesickness for England is a running theme as is the loneliness of the wives (Ann Bridge's marriage was unhappy). Laura in *Peking Picnic* 'appeared to accept quite naturally, and without the smallest resentment the fact that [his] occupations left her husband with very little time or attention to spare for her or her interests; that she had to carry on their social life practically single-handed and fill in any leisure of her own as best she might'. The mystery, in terms of literary reputation, is why 'Ann Bridge' remains so popular. It is not difficult to see why she was read at the time her novels came out: she wrote easily and mellifluously, did not ask too much of her reader, and often used settings which provided her fiction with a bit of political grit. But why her 26 books have not been forgotten is less easy to define. Certainly, reprint publishers find that her name is constantly mentioned. Jennifer Uglow seeks to capture her appeal by describing *Illyrian Spring* as 'idyllic...an unusual mixture, at once romantic and tough, absurd yet realistic, escapist yet down-to-earth'.

Suggested Reading

Kellaway, Kate. Introduction to *Peking Picnic* by Ann Bridge (London: Virago, 1989) ix–xxii.

Uglow, Jennifer. Introduction to *Illyrian Spring* by Ann Bridge (London: Virago, 1990) ix–xviii.

Nicola Beauman

Brittain, Vera 1893–1970

Autobiographer, journalist and novelist, principally known for her feminist and anti-war memoir *Testament of Youth* (1933), which deals with the significance of the First World War from a woman's point of view. *Testament of Youth* is generally considered to be one of the major British literary productions concerned with the Great War, and is certainly the best known by a woman author. It was a bestseller both in Britain and North America when it first appeared, and it has enjoyed continued success.

Vera Mary Brittain was the daughter of a thriving Staffordshire paper manufacturer. She vividly describes her upbringing in *Testament of Youth*, explaining that her education was designed to fit her for 'provincial young ladyhood', but that she rebelled against conventional upper-middle-class patterns for women and instead successfully fought to achieve admission to university. Brittain entered Somerville College, Oxford, in 1914 and completed her first year, but then left Oxford for war service as a Voluntary Aid Detachment nurse. Her first book, *Verses of a VAD* , appeared in 1918. She returned to Oxford after the war, gaining a degree in history in 1921.

In addition to *Testament of Youth*, Brittain published more than 20 books and was a prolific journalist. The books include *Testament of Friendship* (1940), a memoir of her close friend and fellow writer Winifred HOLTBY; a second volume of autobiography, *Testament of Experience* (1957); nine novels and several works of social commentary. In the interwar decades, her journalistic pieces appeared in a wide variety of publications, ranging from the feminist weekly *Time and Tide* to *Good Housekeeping*.

Brittain was politically active throughout her life, both as a feminist and in the cause of peace. The peak of her feminist activity was in the 1920s and early 1930s, when she worked with the Six Point Group and the Open Door Council, two important interwar organizations. Her preoccupation with questions of war and peace deepened as the political situation worsened in the 1930s. In 1936, she became involved with the Christian pacifist Peace Pledge Union. As she would write later of her conversion to PACIFISM: 'I had come to see the enemy...as war itself.' During the Second World War, her courageous and outspoken criticism of the evils of war brought her opprobrium, but later earned her an important place in the history of British peace activism.

From her early struggles to escape the fate of 'provincial young ladyhood' to her subsequent achievements as a writer and social activist, Brittain was representative of the group of educated middle-class women who brought to fruition the goals of Victorian bourgeois feminism in the years following the First World War. Throughout her adult life she was sustained by feminist convictions and driven by a fierce desire to achieve personal autonomy. Brittain will be remembered as the author of *Testament of Youth*. She also deserves to be remembered for her struggles to achieve her feminist vision.

Suggested Reading
Berry, Paul and Mark Bostridge. *Vera Brittain: A Life* (London: Chatto & Windus, 1995).
Bishop, Alan with Terry Smart (eds). *Chronicle of Youth: Vera Brittain's War Diary, 1913–1917* (London: Gollancz, 1981).
Gorham, Deborah. *Vera Brittain: A Feminist Life* (Oxford: Blackwell, 1996).

Deborah Gorham

Broadcasting
The first half of the twentieth century brought many innovations in broad-casting technology and culture, from Marconi's first transatlantic airwave transmission in 1901 to the BBC's first London television service 35 years later. Radio signals were first used to transmit the human voice in 1902, and military interest helped the technology evolve so that, by 1910, ship-to-shore and air-to-ground communications were common. From the outset, the British government was concerned about the potential which the new technology would give enemies, and indeed members of the British public, to communicate in secret. In response, following upon the Telegraphy Act of 1869 (which gave the Post Office the monopoly of telegraph communications), in 1904 the Postmaster General was empowered to monitor and license airwave transmission, and British television licences are, to this day, purchasable through the Post Office.

In 1920, despite the reservations of military officials, the Marconi company was given permission to broadcast to the public as long as it did not interfere with military transmissions. Radio stations sprang up in London, Birmingham, and Manchester. Demand for frequencies increased until the Post Office inter-vened and, in 1922, invited the major broadcasters to join a monopoly, the British Broadcasting Company, which began its transmissions on 14 November. The Company became the British Broadcasting Corporation, or BBC, in 1927, with John Reith serving as its first General Manager from 1934.

Reith's belief in the independence and instructive power of radio set the tone for the BBC's early years of operation. Original programming included broadcasts that would appeal to multiple social classes: dance and classical music, educational programmes for adults and children, adaptations of novels, and sport. He instituted 'Reith Sunday', which allowed no broadcasts before 12.30 p.m. in order to encourage people to attend church; Sunday programming included classical music and 'serious' talks.

The BBC's potential for immediacy in news broadcasting caused concern for the national print press, and the Newspaper Proprietors' Association used its influence to get news transmissions forbidden before 7 p.m. for the first years of the BBC's operation. Reith's intended independence in news presentation was tested during the General Strike; because print journalists were also striking, the BBC became the country's main source for news, and Parliament pressured the BBC to present the government perspective, in a calm and even tone. Although the BBC today continues to avoid the influence of commercial interests, its relationship to government and the establishment causes ongoing conflict.

The British public quickly became keen radio listeners. Crissell reports that the number of radio licences issued increased from 80,000 in 1923 to one million a year later, and by 1939, nine million licences were being purchased annually. Radio sets varied in sophistication and expense: home-made crystal sets with headphones were available earlier in the century, while larger sets, designed to look like pieces of furniture, became more affordable from the late 1930s. Many radio entertainers, including women singers and comedians such as Gracie Fields, Elsie and Doris Waters, and Beatrice Lillie became celebrities. Demand for local programming helped shape the development of the Regional programmes that were in place by 1930; populist programming (including music hall relays and Britain's first radio soap, English Family Robinson, which began in 1938) also reflected the desires of the listening public. A weekly guide to programmes, *The Radio Times*, was established in 1923, and other NEWSPAPERS published daily broadcast schedules.

The BBC was a key source of entertainment and information during the 1930s and the Second World War. In 1932, Reith organized the EMPIRE Service in order to promote British cultural interests throughout the Commonwealth. From 1933, its funding was increased in order to combat the anti-English propaganda of English-speaking German stations. So that it might compete with similar broadcasts from Italian stations, the BBC began its own foreign language programmes in 1937; the first of these was the Arabic Service, and by 1943 the BBC was broadcasting in 45 languages. During the Second World War, national and regional services were combined to form a single Home Service, while in 1940 the BBC formed a second network, the General Forces Programme, to boost morale among servicemen and women in France. The BBC worked closely with the Ministry of Information during the war years to present coherent, reasonable and fact-based broadcasts, countering the emotionally charged, obviously propagandist Nazi and FASCIST radio. The smooth accents of the BBC, however, actually provided the British government with a subtle tool for the propagation and manipulation of public opinion. Story-telling was viewed as an especially appropriate (because not obvious) method for the presentation of the government perspective and many writers, including George Orwell, J. B. Priestley, and Dorothy L. SAYERS contributed patriotic programming to the BBC at the behest of the Ministry of Information.

Although the BBC began television transmission to a small number of privately owned sets in 1936, television programming ceased during the war and did not resume development until the late 1940s. By the early 1950s, television was a popular medium that competed with CINEMA and newsreels; once again, the establishment saw the potential of a new broadcasting tool to influence the public, with the coronation of Queen Elizabeth II in 1953 reaching an audience of 20 million on the two million television sets then owned in Britain. Despite the popularity of this new medium, British radio is considered to have enjoyed its Golden Age in the years 1945–60, when such enduring programmes as *Gardeners' Question Time*, *Woman's Hour*, and *The Archers* were first introduced.

Suggested Reading

Crissell, Andrew. *An Introductory History of British Broadcasting* (1997; rev. edn London: Routledge, 2002).

Piette, Adam. *Imagination at War: British Fiction and Poetry, 1939–1945* (London: Papermac, 1995).

Ashlie Sponenberg

Broughton, Rhoda 1840–1920

Author of many novels and short stories, Broughton's literary career extended from the 1860s to the year of her death. Toward the end of her life she remarked: 'I began by being the Zola and I have now become the Charlotte Yonge of English fiction.' Broughton was born in North Wales and grew up in a Staffordshire manor house. Breaking into the literary market with a serialized sensation novel, *Not Wisely But Too Well* (1865–6), and continuing with novels featuring naïve girls involved with profligate lovers of the Guy Livingstone stamp, Broughton nevertheless deftly depicted women's emotions, notably those arising when a woman desired an artistic career. She explored the conflicts occasioned by the Victorian conviction that marriage and domestic life were woman's destiny, and her acerbic humour enlivens such situations. Her work from the 1890s onward subsumes sensationalism to portrayals of characters' inner lives, culminating in subtly rendered family issues in her last completed novel, *A Thorn in the Flesh* (1916). Posthumously published, *A Fool in Her Folly* (1920) includes autobiographical elements of Broughton's own struggle as a writer. Her tightly crafted supernatural stories, some in the mode of her relative, Sheridan Le Fanu, continue to appear in anthologies and to attract readers. Broughton's later years were spent chiefly in Oxford and London, where she enjoyed the company of many intellectuals and became renowned for her sharp wit.

Suggested Reading

Fisher, Benjamin F. 'Twilight Stories, by Rhoda Broughton', in Frank N. Magill (ed.), *Survey of Modern Fantasy Literature* (Englewood Cliffs, NJ: Salem Press, 1983) 1989–91.

Wood, Marilyn. *Rhoda Broughton: Profile of a Novelist* (Stamford, CA: Paul Watkins, 1993).

Benjamin F. Fisher

'Brows' (highbrow, middlebrow, lowbrow)

The terms highbrow and lowbrow (literally referring to the distance of the hairline from the eyebrow) were coined in the nineteenth century by phrenologists to signify intellectual capacity, but with the enormous social upheavals of the twentieth century, distinguishing between heights of brow became allied to cultural attitudes towards class and gender.

Educational reforms (in particular the EDUCATION Act of 1870) increased the spread of literacy to all classes, leading to the rise of mass PUBLISHING, including high-circulation NEWSPAPERS, monthly story-magazines, and 'pulp' fiction. The practice of targeting certain types of literature at different groups intensified in the twentieth century. Periodicals such as the *Times Literary Supplement*, *The Criterion*, and the *New Statesman*, for instance, catered for highbrows; whereas publications such as *Peg's Paper* and *Tit-Bits* were aimed at a lowbrow readership, and achieved much higher sales. Challenging or serious books were available from Mudie's or Day's subscription LIBRARIES; but there was a plentiful source of formulaic romances, adventure stories, and the like at a cost of just two or three pence at newsagents and corner shops. Thus, while the authors who would later be seen as defining the literary zeitgeist of the early twentieth century such as Joyce, Eliot and WOOLF, were read by a tiny minority, books by Zane Grey, Edgar Rice Burroughs, Sax Rohmer, Ethel M. DELL and Ruby AYRES were read by millions.

Champions of high culture, such as F. R. and Q. D. LEAVIS, were convinced that the consumption of mass-market fiction would lead to a deterioration of moral fibre, and compared the enjoyment of such material to a drug habit. By the end of the First World War, highbrow culture had become synonymous with the literary experimentation now associated with MODERNISM. John Carey has insisted recently that modernism was in fact a conscious, hostile reaction to the rise of mass culture, and that modernist texts were designed to be too difficult for the mass readership of the day to understand and enjoy.

Modernist writers, however, occupied a complex position within the debate. Virginia WOOLF has long been held up as an icon of highbrow snobbery, but in fact her radical ideal of the classless intellectual, advanced in her *Common Reader* series (1925 and 1932), is the exact opposite of the hostile elitism of Q. D. Leavis. Similarly, in 'Surgery for the Novel – or a Bomb' (1923), D. H. Lawrence is equally dismissive of current highbrow and lowbrow incarnations of the novel, comparing 'the pale-faced, high-browed, earnest novel, which you have to take seriously', with 'that smirking, rather plausible hussy, the popular novel'.

Woolf's important statement on modernist aesthetics, 'Mr Bennett and Mrs Brown' (1924), defines the new fiction in opposition not to popular fiction, but to the socially responsible work of a group of novelists belonging to the middlebrow (a term that was coined later than high- and lowbrow, in the 1920s). Following the tradition of the realist novel, Hugh Walpole, Arnold Bennett, J. B. Priestly, Winifred HOLTBY, Mary WEBB, and Ethel MANNIN provided a more sober alternative to the thrills of popular fiction. The hugely successful Boots Library supplied these kinds of books to generally middle-class patrons, and publications such as the *London Mercury* and the *Daily Mail* (the first newspaper to have a column for women) were full of book reviews to guide the discerning but less adventurous reader.

Lawrence's characterization of the popular novel as a 'hussy' reflects a widespread and deeply entrenched association among cultural commentators between mass culture and women. ROMANTIC FICTION, following the formula consolidated by Ethel M. Dell in *The Way of an Eagle* (1912), became the archetypal feminine genre, and was increasingly downgraded as a consequence. DETECTIVE FICTION alone crossed the divide, being read by middlebrows and highbrows alike. Many of the exponents of the genre were women, such as Dorothy L. SAYERS and Agatha CHRISTIE, but it was considered to be a masculine form, and therefore had a higher cultural prestige than romance.

In the postwar years, the relationship between culture and the establishment altered. With the development of English Literature as a university subject under the guidance of F. R. Leavis and I. A. Richards at Cambridge University during the 1930s and 1940s, only those writers who had embarked on the modernist enterprise were accepted into the literary canon. Thus, modernism was and continues to be used to evaluate literature of this period, and in this way it would seem that the highbrows have won the day. At the same time, the fact that Woolf is the only female highbrow to retain a secure position within the canon, that many middlebrow novels by women are no longer in print, and that books read by millions of women are now forgotten, would suggest that the final effect of the battle of the brows has been to marginalize women, both as writers and as readers.

Suggested Reading

Carey, John. *The Intellectuals and the Masses: Pride and Prejudice Among the Literary Intelligentsia, 1880–1939* (London: Faber, 1992).

Cuddy-Keane, Melba. *Virginia Woolf, the Intellectual and the Public Sphere* (Cambridge: Cambridge University Press, 2003).

Light, Alison. *Forever England: Femininity, Literature and Conservatism Between the Wars* (London: Routledge, 1991).

Sinfield, Alan. *Literature, Politics and Culture in Postwar Britain* (Oxford: Blackwell, 1989).

Kathy Hopewell

Bryher 1894–1983

One of the most influential and well-connected of the female modernist writers, who produced a wide range of writings, including autobiographical fiction, historical novels, poetry, and literary and film criticism. Bryher's career is also notable for her contributions to the cultural production of modernism, both in financial and editorial terms. She began life as Annie Winifred Ellerman, daughter of a British shipping magnate and his common-law wife. In adolescence, she adopted the name of the wildest and most remote of her beloved Scilly Isles – the suitably androgynous Bryher. After encountering the first Imagist collection, *Des Imagistes*, in 1913, the trajectory of Bryher's career was set: her literary allegiances were to experimental modernism, Futurism, and Surrealism. After writing her first piece of precocious criticism, *Amy Lowell: A Critical Appreciation* (1918), Bryher orchestrated a meeting between herself and the Imagist poet H. D. which marked the beginning of a lifelong sexual and emotional relationship. She described the meeting in *Two Selves* (1923): 'A tall figure opened the door. Young. A spear flower if a spear could bloom. She looked up into eyes that had the sea in them, the fire and colour and the splendour of it. A voice all wind and gull notes said: "I was waiting for you to come." '

Bryher's auto/biographical fictions, *Development: A Novel* (1920), *Two Selves* and *West* (1925), are characterized by a mixture of realism and Imagist prose, and represent the complexities of early twentieth-century LESBIAN subjectivity. Bryher sought intellectual and medical discourses to understand her own identity, turning first to SEXOLOGY and then to PSYCHOANALYSIS. She began a friendship with Havelock Ellis in 1919 and met Freud in 1933. Bryher found, in psychoanalysis, a compelling narrative of human subjectivity in which she saw much potential for the alleviation of human suffering. Uniquely, she believed in the efficacy of analysis for all, and devoted time and money to opening up access to treatment and training

Together with Robert McAlmon, Bryher founded the Contact Publishing Company in Paris, which published prominent authors including LOY, RICHARDSON, Barnes and STEIN. Bryher then discovered the remarkable, emergent form of film, and in 1927, along with H. D. and Kenneth Macpherson, she founded the film journal *Close Up*. Bryher's writings on CINEMA express her belief that film is a unique cultural form through which political and social ideals could be mobilized. The *Close Up* group also produced three short films and one full-length feature, *Borderline* (1930), in which Paul Robeson appeared alongside H. D.

In the 1930s, Bryher ran the review *Life and Letters Today*, which continued to publish the most innovative writing throughout the Second World War. War itself focused Bryher's already politicized outlook and she used her money, influence, and residence in Switzerland to secure the escape of numerous Jewish refugees, including Walter Benjamin. Between 1952 and 1966, Bryher wrote nine historical novels, which are situated principally in the ancient histories of the Anglo-Saxons, Greeks, and Romans. In these novels, Bryher continued to express herself through a kind of literary cross-dressing, constructing male personas at the centre of each narrative. She wrote two works of non-fictional auto/biography: *The Heart to Artemis: A Writer's Memoirs* (1963) and *The Days of Mars: A Memoir, 1940–1946* (1972).

Suggested Reading

Donald, James, Anne Friedberg, and Laura Marcus (eds). *Close Up, 1927–1933: Cinema and Modernism* (London: Cassell, 1998).

Magee, Maggie and Diane C. Miller. *Lesbian Lives: Psychoanalytic Narratives Old and New* (New York: Analytic Press, 1996).

Winning, Joanne. Introduction to *Bryher, Two Novels: Development and Two Selves* (Madison: University of Wisconsin Press, 2000) v–xli.

Joanne Winning

Burdekin, Katherine 1896–1963

Author of over 20 novels, best known for her staunchly anti-fascist dystopia, *Swastika Night* (1937). Burdekin's writing is characterized by explorations of the disabling restrictions of gender categories and of the evolution of humanity, often considered in the setting of a future world.

Born Katherine Penelope Cade in Spondon, England, the youngest of four sisters, she was educated at Cheltenham Ladies' College and married Australian barrister Beaufort Burdekin in 1915. During WORLD WAR ONE Burdekin worked as a VAD nurse, an experience which inspired her sixth novel, the vigorously anti-war *Quiet Ways* (1930). She had two daughters and in 1920 moved with her family to Australia, where she began to write. Her first book, *Anna Colquhoun* (1922), was written, like the majority of her novels, in just a few months. Burdekin's marriage ended in the same year, and she returned to England to raise her daughters. In 1926 she met the female companion with whom she lived until the end of her life.

Burdekin's daughters provided the impetus for her only work for young readers. As a 'non-sexist' children's book, *The Children's Country* (1929), published under the name Kay Burdekin, was ahead of its time in depicting the adventures of two children in a liberating country without adults, where they escape the gender-laden assumptions of their own society. The utopian novel, *The Rebel Passion*, in Burdekin's own view her first mature work, was also published in 1929 under the same name.

It was the 1930s, however, that saw Burdekin at her most accomplished and prolific, her overwhelming concern at the threat of FASCISM, and its impact on women in particular, proving fruitful inspiration. *Proud Man* (1934), a novel which questions the 'natural' state of heterosexuality, saw the first use of her pseudonym, Murray Constantine; and the celebrated *Swastika Night* has been lauded as an important anti-fascist work and favourably compared with Orwell's *Nineteen Eighty-Four* (1949). Burdekin's frightening, futuristic portrayal of fascism sees Nazi ideology taken to its logical extreme. Women are used as breeding machines and allowed no other form of identity. As an enlightened male character reflects: 'The human values of this world are masculine. There are no feminine values because there are no women.'

Burdekin was keenly aware of misogyny in all its manifestations, becoming one of the first female critics of D. H. Lawrence. Indeed, although living a mainly solitary life and suffering bouts of depression, Burdekin was not isolated from the literary world, corresponding with Radclyffe HALL and H. D. as well as being acquainted with the Woolfs and Russells. *Venus in Scorpio* (1940), an historical novel about Marie Antoinette, was written with Margaret Goldsmith.

At times ambivalent about seeing her work into print (many novels remain unpublished), and working in a shoe factory, printers, and flour-mill during and after the war, Burdekin did not publish again in her lifetime. Thanks to the recovery of her *oeuvre* by feminist critics, however, the futuristic, utopian novel in which women rule the world, *The End of this Day's Business*, was published in 1989.

Suggested Reading

Patai, Daphne. 'Orwell's Despair, Burdekin's Hope: Gender and Power in Dystopia', *Women's Studies International Forum*, 7. 2 (1984) 85–95.

Patai, Daphne. Introduction to *Swastika Night* by Katherine Burdekin (New York: The Feminist Press, 1985) iii–xv.

Patai, Daphne. Afterword to *The End of This Day's Business* by Katherine Burdekin (New York: The Feminist Press, 1989) 159–90.

Luanda Stannard

Burnett, Frances Hodgson 1849–1924

While Burnett wrote several adult novels which tended towards sentimentality and are now largely forgotten, she is famous for her contributions to a golden age of CHILDREN'S LITERATURE, her most influential works being: *Little Lord Fauntleroy* (1886); *Sara Crewe* (1887), later rewritten as *A Little Princess* (1905); and *The Secret Garden* (1911).

Born on the edge of Manchester, Frances Eliza Hodgson lived there until she was 15, when the family emigrated to Tennessee. This move was the first of several, as Burnett repeatedly travelled between America and Britain, hence the transatlantic feel of her work. The family lived in relative poverty and Burnett, like many other female authors of this period, sought to earn money through writing potboilers for magazine publication.

Burnett came to fame when her adult novel, *That Lass o'Lowrie's* (1877), proved to be highly successful both in Britain and America, but it was after her play *Esmerelda* (1881) was poorly received that she began to write for children. *Little Lord Fauntleroy* was reviewed favourably by Louisa M. Alcott and was an immediate success. So influential was the story of the perfect boy, who was modelled partly on her younger son, that young boys (including A. A. Milne) across both Britain and America were dressed in velvet suits and had long curly hair. The book, though distinctly sentimental, further enhances the nineteenth-century notion of the beautiful innocent child, as Cedric reforms his aristocratic grandfather who had been 'so selfish himself that he had missed the pleasure of seeing unselfishness in others, and he had not known how tender and faithful and affectionate a kind-hearted little child can be, and how innocent and unconscious are its simple generous impulses'.

A Little Princess (1905), in typical Burnett fairy-tale style, follows the story of Sara's initial wealth to the death of her father and her plunge into poverty. Sara's inner nobility shines through – when penniless and hungry, she still gives up her hot cross buns to a starving street girl – and she is justly rewarded when her wealth is restored through a series of coincidences.

A similar degree of Romanticism is evident in *The Secret Garden*, as the children restore their health and happiness in the garden. The story, set in the midst of the Yorkshire Moors, displays strong links with Gothic novels such as *Wuthering Heights* and *Jane Eyre*, and it has also been suggested that it had a strong influence on *Lady Chatterley's Lover*.

The Lost Prince (1915) is the last of Burnett's successful books, although the plot is uncovered within the first few pages. *Editha's Burglar* (1818) is a long short story in which we see the re-emergence of Burnett's theme of the good child overcoming the corrupted adult. Fashions by this time were beginning to change, and her final adult novel, *Robin* (1922), received poor reviews. Nevertheless, Burnett's work remains popular and is frequently adapted for film and television.

Suggested Reading

Gerzina, Gretchan H. *Frances Hodgson Burnett: The Unpredictable Life of the Author of 'The Secret Garden'* (London: Chatto & Windus, 2004).

McGillis, Roderick. *'A Little Princess': Gender and Empire* (Boston, MA: Twayne, 1996).

Thwaite, Anne. *Waiting for the Party: The Life of Frances Hodgson Burnett* (London: Secker & Warburg, 1974).

Ann Alston

Butts, Mary 1890–1937

Experimental novelist, essayist, short-story writer, poet, and journalist, best known for her MODERNIST masterpieces, *Armed With Madness* (1928) and *Death of Felicity Taverner* (1932). Butts began her writing career with poetry, and its technical discipline clearly affected her fiction, which is lyrical, saturated with visual imagery, and filled with unfamiliar syntax and disconnected scenes. Butts's most formally innovative novel, *Armed With Madness*, combines free indirect discourse, first-person interior monologues, and omniscient third-person narration toward an exploration of her characteristic preoccupation with the Grail legend. Butts's texts also reflect the period's interest in the anthropological discoveries of Jane Ellen Harrison on primitive ritual and animism, nature cults, and matriarchal origins. Her work earned admiration from many of her contemporaries, such as Ford Madox Ford, Jean Cocteau, Robert McAlmon, May SINCLAIR, and Virgil Thompson. Butts published six novels, three volumes of short stories, two pamphlets, and dozens of reviews, articles, essays, and poems.

A great-granddaughter of Thomas Butts, who was a patron of William Blake, Butts grew up in her family home of Salterns in Poole Harbour, Dorset, surrounded by the Blake paintings now hanging in the Tate. Salterns became the imaginative centrepiece of Butts's life, inspiring her memoir *The Crystal Cabinet: My Childhood at Salterns* (published posthumously in 1937). Butts consistently emphasized the aristocratic nature of her familial pedigree, although later in life she became estranged from them and struggled with financial difficulties. Always preoccupied with notions of social status and material security, she was obsessed with acquisition because she believed in the auratic value of beautiful things – that is, their ability to legitimate the family's genealogical and geographical link to English territory.

Butts's other recurrent preoccupations include postwar shell-shock, erotic desire (particularly male HOMOSEXUALITY), sexual violence, sadomasochism, blackmail, extortion, addiction, environmental disease, black magic, the horrors of the nuclear family, and England's interwar crisis regarding the preservation of the countryside. Butts viewed nature as the basis for a spiritual reconstruction that is unattainable in the industrial squalor of urban life.

Nowhere in her writings is this more evident than in her conservative pamphlets, *Warning to Hikers* (1932) and *Traps for Unbelievers* (1932).

She married twice, first the Jewish writer and publisher John Rodker (in 1918), and later the British painter Gabriel Aitkin (in 1930), and she also had several passionate affairs with men and women, including Eleanor Rogers, a writer, and Mireille Havet, a cross-dressing protégée of Apollinaire who, like Butts, relished passionate sex, drugs, and writing. In 1916 Butts wrote: 'There is no such thing as man and woman – but there is sex – a varying quantity.' Her rejection of male and female is attributable to her disdain for repressive sex and gender roles, but it also speaks to her lifelong interest in invoking classical and mythical structures as ways of exploring alternatives to heterosexuality: 'Only in Homer have I found impersonal consolation – a life where I am unsexed or bisexed, or completely myself.' Hellenistic discourse provided Butts with a homoerotic tradition which enabled her to challenge dichotomized ideas about sexual identity, reminding us of other modernists such as H. D., Djuna Barnes, and Natalie Barney, who similarly invoke classical models to convey same-sex desire. All of Butts's original manuscripts are now in the Beinecke Rare Book and Manuscript Library at Yale University.

Suggested Reading

Blondel, Nathalie. *Mary Butts: Scenes from the Life* (New York: McPherson, 1998).

Garrity, Jane. *Step-Daughters of England: British Women Modernists and the National Imaginary* (Manchester: Manchester University Press, 2003).

Foy, Roslyn Reso. *Ritual, Myth, and Mysticism in the Work of Mary Butts: Between Feminism and Modernism* (Fayetteville: University of Arkansas Press, 2000).

Jane Garrity

C

Cannan, May Wedderburn 1893–1973

The first president of the Female Writers' Club and employed by Oxford University Press, she published poems, novels, and memoirs. *The Lonely Generation* (1934) is autobiographical, and *Grey Ghosts and Voices* (1976) consists of thinly disguised personal reminiscences. Her aspiration to train as an actress were thwarted by the First World War in which her fiancé, Bevil Quiller-Couch, was killed. The first-person pronoun which dominates the slim volume *In War Time* (1917) is sometimes personal but often ungendered and universalizing. She published two other poetry collections, *The Splendid Days* (1919) and *The House of Hope* (1923).

The selection in Catherine Reilly's VIRAGO anthology of war poetry represents Cannan's range. The rhythmic poem 'Rouen' records nostalgia for her nursing adventures in France, and athough it tends towards jog-trot Edwardian metres and patriotic consolations, 'Rouen' testifies to the excitement which WAR WORK provided. The grief expressed in 'Lamplight' or 'Since they have died' can seem awkwardly sentimental and uncritical of nationalistic propaganda, but documents how women internalized its pervasive rhetoric.

Suggested Reading

Fyfe, Charlotte (ed.). *The Tears of War: The Love Story of a Young Poet and a War Hero* (Upavon: Cavalier, 2000).

Jane Dowson

Carrington, Leonora 1917–

Surrealist writer and painter. Born in Lancashire to a wealthy family, Carrington attended the Chelsea School of Art and the Academy of Amédée Ozenfant in London. In 1937, aged 19, she eloped to Paris with the Surrealist painter Max Ernst. Her writings and paintings of 1937–40 share the themes of women conjoining with and transmogrifying into animals: in the short story 'As they rode along the edge' (1937–8), Virginia Fur 'has a mane of hair yards long and enormous hands with dirty nails', while in the tales 'The Oval Lady' (1937–8) and 'The Seventh Horse' (1941), horses figure as sexual consorts.

The German-born Ernst was arrested after the Nazi invasion of France, but was soon released and left for America, while Carrington, after being incarcerated in a Spanish psychiatric hospital, was granted asylum at the Mexican Embassy in Portugal, leaving for New York in 1941. Her flight from France and the nightmarish experience of the mental institution form the core of her books *Down Below* (1983) and *The Stone Door* (1978). She moved to Mexico in 1942, and remains one of Mexico's most celebrated artists.

Carrington's most famous work, *The Hearing Trumpet* (1977), is the story of 92-year-old Marian Leatherby, a resident of an old people's home, and is a feminist parody of medieval romance quests, murder mysteries, fairy-tales, and classical mythology. She was virtually unknown in her native Britain until a revival of interest in Surrealism in the mid-1980s reintroduced her work to critical attention.

Suggested Reading

Griffin, Gabriele. 'Becoming as Being: Leonora Carrington's Writings and Paintings 1937–40', in Griffin (ed.), *Difference in View: Women and Modernism* (London: Taylor & Francis, 1994) 92–107.

Suleiman, Susan Rubin. *Subversive Intent: Gender, Politics and the Avant-Garde* (London and Cambridge, MA: Harvard University Press, 1990).

Louise Harrington

Carswell, Catherine 1879–1946

Scottish writer and journalist, born Catherine Roxburgh Macfarlane in Glasgow. She studied music at Frankfurt and English at Glasgow University, although at the time women could not graduate. She married Herbert Jackson in 1904, and he tried to kill her upon finding out she was pregnant with their only daughter Diana, born in 1905. The marriage was eventually annulled in 1908. Catherine then returned to Glasgow and began her career as a journalist, drama critic, and book reviewer for the *Glasgow Herald*. In 1912, after her mother's death, she returned to London, where her daughter died of pneumonia in 1913. She lost her job at the *Glasgow Herald* when she secretly slipped in a positive review of D. H. Lawrence's *The Rainbow* in 1915.

After an affair with the married painter Maurice Greiffenhagen, she married Donald Carswell in 1915. In need of money she wrote two semi-autobiographical novels, *Open the Door* (1920), which was composed over five years, and *The Camomile* (1922), a *Kunstlerroman*. Renting a room opposite her house specifically for her writing, she produced *The Life of Robert Burns* (1930), *The Savage Pilgrimage* (1932) on the life of her close friend D. H. Lawrence, and *The Tranquil Heart* (1937), a biography of Boccaccio. Her partly finished autobiography, *Lying Awake*, was published posthumously in 1950.

Suggested Reading

Anderson, Carol and Ailenn Christianson (eds). *Scottish Women's Fiction, 1920s to 1960s: Journeys Into Being* (East Linton: Tuckwell Press, 2000).

Gifford, Douglas and Dorothy McMillan (eds). *A History of Scottish Women's Writing* (Edinburgh: Edinburgh University Press, 1997).

Laura Christie

Cartland, Barbara 1901–2000

Prolific author of over 700 romance novels; journalist, biographer, and playwright; and one of the bestselling novelists of all time. Cartland was born in Edgbaston and educated at Malvern Girls' College and Abbey House, Hampshire. Her family moved to Kensington in London after Barbara's father was killed in Flanders in 1918. Cartland married twice: she divorced her first husband, Alexander McCorquodale, in 1933 and married his cousin, Hugh, in 1936. Throughout her life, she was a passionate traveller, and her observations abroad enhanced the settings of her fictions.

Cartland's first published writings were anonymous gossip columns for such papers as the *Daily Express, The Tatler,* and Lord Beaverbrook's *Daily News.* In 1923, her first novel, *Jigsaw,* appeared; it was based upon her own experiences of Mayfair society and mimicked the styles of such popular ROMANTIC novelists as Ethel M. DELL. The book's chaste young heroine and wealthy hero overcome many obstacles before their happy ending and marriage are achieved in a standard Cinderella narrative from which Cartland never deviated throughout her career. Critical distaste for her formulaic, uncomplicated plots did not deter the fans who were attracted to her thoroughly researched Regency, Victorian, and Edwardian fantasies. Cartland insisted upon moral behaviours for her heroines; even such potentially spicy titles as *A Virgin in Mayfair* (1932) and *Say Yes, Samantha* (1975) contained no pornographic scenes. Her working style was also legendary. She dictated her short novels to secretaries and was capable of producing, as she did in 1976, up to 16 novels per year.

During the Second World War, Cartland began to undertake social and political activities. She served as Chief Lady Welfare Officer for Bedfordshire from 1941–5 and later founded the National Association of Health. She campaigned for better working conditions for nurses and midwives. Her interest in HEALTH and nutrition inspired such titles as *Be Vivid, Be Vital* (1956) and *Health Food Cookery Book* (1971).

Cartland also produced advice books for single and married women, and these imparted the domestic morality that determined the actions of her fictional heroines. In *You ... In the Home* (1946), a premarital guide for women, she asserts that 'there is no better or higher job for a woman than that of creating a home.' This wartime text, like her romances, expresses a conservative view of women's roles: 'A woman bending over a wash-tub, a woman singing as she baths her baby, a woman hanging a pretty picture on a freshly painted wall – three women working for their country, three women making history. It is hard to remember it always but it is the truth, for homes are the rock on which great Empires are built, and homes are created by the women who own them.'

Historical biographies, such as *Metternich: The Passionate Diplomat* (1964), and several autobiographies, including *The Isthmus Years* (1943) and *The Years of Opportunity: 1939–1945* (1948), are also comprised in Cartland's bibliography. A screenplay, *The Flame in Love*, was successfully produced for television in 1979. In 1992, Cartland was made a Dame of the British Empire. When she died, her estate contained 160 unpublished manuscripts, many of which will be released by the official Cartland website.

Suggested Reading

Diski, Jenny. 'Homage to Barbara Cartland', *London Review of Books* 16.16 (1994) 26–7.

Heald, Tim. *A Life of Love: Barbara Cartland* (London: Sinclair-Stevenson, 1994).

Ashlie Sponenberg

Censorship

The production of literary works during much of the twentieth century was strongly influenced by the climate of censorship, which was mostly informal and covert. Respectable PUBLISHERS, booksellers, and proprietors of LIBRARIES applied pressure on authors to avoid expensive and embarrassing prosecutions. Those producing and disseminating risqué materials tended to accept the occasional confiscation of stock, prosecution and fines as risks of doing business.

Though the 1857 Obscene Publications Act had not been intended to affect serious works of art, in 1867 Lord Justice Cockburn ruled, in Regina v. Hicklin, that the test of obscenity was its 'tendency... to deprave and corrupt those whose minds are open to such immoral influences and into whose hands a publication of this sort might fall'. Under this vague but potentially far-reaching rubric, moral policing organizations such as the National Vigilance Association prosecuted literature they considered immoral. There were several well-known prosecutions of works of science and literature. Although Charles Bradlaugh and Annie BESANT successfully defended their publication of the birth control manual *Fruits of Philosophy* (1877), Havelock Ellis was not even allowed to speak in defence of his *Sexual Inversion* (1898). Later volumes of his *Studies in the Psychology of Sex* were published outside Britain, a strategy also employed in the case of works such as Joyce's *Ulysses* and D. H. Lawrence's *Lady Chatterley's Lover*, which were then subjected to Customs bans on import. The arbitrary nature of the situation made publishers extremely cautious.

Plays accepted for performance by London theatres had to be licensed by the Lord Chamberlain, an unelected official of the Royal Household, under eighteenth-century legislation against political sedition. His Examiners of Plays seldom had any obvious qualifications and deployed mysterious and arbitrary criteria. Serious plays on contentious moral issues could thus often only be produced under 'club' conditions, limiting their audience. Theatre managements supported the system, as reducing the risk of prosecution. Films were regulated by the British Board of Film Censors, set up by the industry, again anxious to avoid prosecutions. Both theatre and CINEMA were thus subject to more systematic and organized censorship than books.

Roy Jenkins's Obscene Publications Act of 1959 brought in the defence of 'publication for the public good', the first test case of which was Regina v. Penguin Books, for publishing *Lady Chatterley's Lover*. In 1968 the Theatres Act abolished the Lord Chamberlain's powers, but the significance of individuals and groups in morally policing what other people might read or see continued well into the late twentieth century.

Suggested Reading

de Jongh, Nicholas. *Politics, Prudery and Perversions: The Censoring of the English Stage, 1901–1968* (London: Methuen, 2000).

Mitchison, Naomi. 'A Note on the Literary Decencies', *You May Well Ask: A Memoir 1920–1940* (London: Gollancz, 1979) 171–80.

Travis, Alan. *Bound and Gagged: A Secret History of Obscenity in Britain* (London: Profile Books, 2000).

Lesley A. Hall

Chartres, Annie Vivanti 1868–1942

London-born novelist, poet, and playwright of Italian and German-Jewish parentage. Vivanti's early career was influenced by the poet Carducci who wrote the preface to her verse collection, *Lyrica* (1890). Although English was her first language, she wrote much of her work in Italian, and her marriage to the Irish Sinn Fein patriot, John Chartres, serves to underline her cosmopolitanism. Her extensive travels are reflected in her novels, whose popular appeal should not blind the reader to their ultimate seriousness. Her first novel, *The Devourers* (1910), is a study of motherhood. This theme is taken up again in *Vae Victis* (1917), a tale of two Belgian women raped by German soldiers. Its ultimate celebration of the female body as a site of transgression is encapsulated by: 'She heard no other voice but that child-voice asking from her the gift of life, telling her that in the land of the unborn there are no Germans and no Belgians, no victors and no vanquished.' Her interest in the hybrid child recurs in *Mea Culpa* (1927), an anti-colonial novel set in Egypt, which reflects her independent, free-ranging spirit. Other works include *Zingaresca* (1918), a collection of stories and sketches, and *Naja Tripudians* (1921), an ironic postwar tale of innocence and corruption.

Suggested Reading

Merry, Bruce. 'Annie Vivanti', in Rinaldina Russell (ed.), *Italian Women Writers* (London: Greenwood, 1994) 441–6.

Parati, Graziella. 'Maculate Conceptions', *Romance Languages Annual*, 7 (1995) 327–32.

Terry Phillips

Children's Literature

It is perhaps not surprising that children's literature, the area of writing most dominated by women, is both the most culturally influential and most intellectually marginalized, nor that the standard histories of the subject have been written in terms of male 'landmark' writers judged by male-order literary standards. Well over half the writers of British children's books in this period, and eight of the 13 winners of the Carnegie Medal presented between 1936 and 1950, were women – yet historically they seem to exist in a shadowy parallel universe.

Three writers defined the 'first golden age' of children's books. Frances Hodgson BURNETT, especially with *The Secret Garden* (1911), demonstrated the symbolic power of the popular 'romance'; Edith NESBIT, in books like *The Wouldbegoods* (1901), attempted to establish an appropriate mode of address to a newly defined childhood; and Beatrix POTTER was equally revolutionary, with her ironic, dark humour.

Milne's 'Pooh' books are thought to epitomize the retreatist period between the world wars, but it was Rose ('there are fairies at the bottom of our garden') Fyleman, the person who first asked Milne to write for children, whose work is the apotheosis of the 'beautiful child' cult, as in collections such as *Gay Go Up* (1929). The nostalgic romanticism of the 1920s is now similarly out of fashion, and with it has gone the once huge reputation of Eleanor FARJEON, her complex, idyllic story collections such as *Martin Pippin the Apple Orchard* (1921) all but forgotten.

Fantasy that can stand beside that of Masefield or Tolkien can be found in the mystic-eccentric work of P. L. TRAVERS (*Mary Poppins*, 1934), or Alison UTTLEY (*A Traveller in Time*, 1939), while a unique attempt at social realism, perhaps 30 years ahead of its time, was Eve Garnett's *The Family from One End Street* (1937). One curiosity is that Richmal CROMPTON's 'William' books (from 1922) remain successful, while William's female counterpart, Evadne Price's Jane (ten volumes from *Just Jane*, 1928) has vanished. For similar reasons, perhaps, 'Hilda Richards's' Bessie Bunter was never as funny as 'Frank Richards's' Billy.

While the boys' school story genre was moribund, the girls' flourished with writers like Elinor BRENT-DYER (the Chalet School, from 1925), Angela BRAZIL, Dorita Fairlie Bruce (with her 'anti-soppist' Dimsie stories, from 1920), and Elsie J. Oxenham (the Abbey School, from 1920, and 'camp fire' novels). The 'Nesbit tradition' of the family story, now linked to children's careers, was continued by Noël Streatfeild (*Ballet Shoes*, 1934), and later by Elfrida Vipont (*The Lark in the Morn*, 1948).

The pervasive influence of women writers is demonstrated by the number of iconic characters who are better known than their authors, such as Milly-Molly-Mandy (Joyce Lankester Brisley, from 1928), Ameliaranne (Constance

Heward, from 1920, and others), Worzel Gummidge (Barbara Euphan Todd, from 1936), Rupert Bear (Mary Tourtel, from 1921, and others), and Little Grey Rabbit (Uttley, from 1929).

Generally unsung, but culturally highly influential, was Joanna Cannan, whose *A Pony for Jean* (1936) founded a genre – carried on most notably by her daughters, Christine, Diana, and Josephine Pullein-Thompson: like the school story, the pony story has a symbiotic relationship with reality.

Some highly topical series, such as Katherine Tozer's 'Mumfie' books (from 1935) have disappeared, and very few mainstream children's books survived the war; however, almost all of those which did are by women, notably Mary Treadgold's *We Couldn't Leave Dinah* (1941). Women can also be found among the pioneering picture-book makers, notably Kathleen Hale (Orlando series, from 1938).

Through all this, Enid BLYTON, the one-woman fiction factory, who had begun publishing in 1924, had covered virtually every genre. Reputed to be the only British author whose paper allocation was increased during the war (and her 'Mary Mouse' series was designed to be printed on off-cuts), she introduced three series – Noddy, the Famous Five, and the Secret Seven – in the late 1940s, which cemented her position as the most influential British woman writer ever.

From the 1950s onward, women have come to dominate publishing for children, and the most significant precursor of this – and symbolic of the power involved – was Puffin Books, edited by Eleanor Grahame from 1941 to 1961, which in later years saved its parent, Penguin Books, from collapse.

Suggested Reading

Cadogan, Mary and Patricia Craig. *You're a Brick, Angela! The Girls' Story, 1839–1985* (London: Gollancz, 1986).

Hunt, Peter (ed.) *Children's Literature: An Illustrated History* (Oxford: Oxford University Press, 1995).

Hunt, Peter, *Children's Literature: A Guide* (Oxford: Blackwell, 2001).

Peter Hunt

Cholmondeley, Mary 1859–1925

Novelist, short-story, essay and memoir writer, remembered primarily for her novel, *Red Pottage* (1899). Cholmondeley's reputation depends on this once controversial book. Its satiric depiction of the clergy caused public outrage which initially upset her. However, she later noted: 'when a witty bishop wrote to me that he had enjoined on his clergy the study of Mr. [Reverend] Gresley as a Lenten penance, it was not possible for me to remain permanently depressed.' Humour is a persistent feature of her ten novels and autobiography, *Under One Roof: A Family Record* (1918).

Mary Cholmondeley grew up in a country parsonage in Hodnet, Shropshire. The third of eight children, she took on responsibility for the family at the age of 16, and began writing stories for her siblings. She published her first short story anonymously in 1878 in *The Graphic*, and through recommendation from friend and novelist, Rhoda BROUGHTON, her first novel, *The Danvers Jewels* (1886–7), was published serially in *Temple Bar* and then in book form. Its suspense and intrigue echo Wilkie Collins's DETECTIVE novels. She gained popular acclaim with *Diana Tempest* (1893), its plot depending on four sensational attempts on the hero's life and ending conventionally with marriage. More substantially, the novel probes the contemporary stigma attached to old maids. The heroine, Diana, resembles Shirley Keeldar in Charlotte Brontë's *Shirley* (1849) in her deliberations about marriage.

In 1896, unmarried and in her early forties, Cholmondeley moved with her family to London. Her reputation as a writer changed dramatically with the publication of *Red Pottage*. Sales were prodigious, but having sold the COPYRIGHT, she made little money from the novel's success. It was reviewed by the *Spectator* as 'brilliant and exhilarating' (28 October 1899). As a clerical satire, it was compared to Brontë's work. Simultaneously, it was denounced from the pulpit as libellous.

Several interwoven narratives in *Red Pottage* vigorously attack hypocrisy. In one of these, the Reverend Gresley's self-righteousness as both patriarch and parson is exposed as risible, largely in the comic manner of Jane Austen's Mr Collins rather than George Eliot's Mr Casaubon. The narrator observes with asperity that Gresley's article on Modern Dissent attacks 'the great religious bodies who did not view Christianity through the convex glasses of his own mental *pince-nez*'. With illusions of moral superiority, he burns the only copy of a novel by his sister, Hester Gresley, just before publication. Passion, bitterness, and dramatic incidents ensue.

After *Red Pottage*, Cholmondeley's work gained scant recognition. She excels at the social comedy of manners, but later novels, including *The Prisoners* (1906), *Notwithstanding* (1913), and *The Romance of His Life* (1921), unevenly combine melodrama with a moralizing voice. She regarded Eliot with unqualified reverence, but her own tone is more priggish. Her writing is essentially late-Victorian and fell out of favour with the rise of MODERNIST literature. However, acute observation of children, women's friendship, family dynamics, and the wasted talents of unmarried women in her best work is a pleasure to read.

Suggested Reading

Colby, Vineta. ' "Devoted Amateur": Mary Cholmondeley and *Red Pottage*', *Essays in Criticism*, 20 (April 1970) 213–28.

Lubbock, Percy. *Mary Cholmondeley: A Sketch from Memory* (London: Jonathan Cape, 1928).

Showalter, Elaine. *A Literature of Their Own* (1977; rev. edn London: Virago Press, 1982).

Val Scullion

Christie, Agatha 1890–1976

One of the bestselling authors in English of all time, Agatha Christie dominated the clue-puzzle or 'cosy' DETECTIVE FICTION genre with her creation of
super-sleuths Hercules Poirot and Miss Marple. An intensely private woman,
Christie ironically endured a media frenzy when she mysteriously disappeared
in 1926. She divorced her unfaithful husband afterwards and eventually
married an archaeologist. In later life she clung to her strong Christian faith,
which can be traced in the attitudes of her fictional detectives.

First appearing as a Belgian refugee in *The Mysterious Affair at Styles* (1920),
fussy Poirot was a satire on the traditional English heroism discredited by
the war, and also represented a new focus on the domestic sphere as both
source of, and solution to, crime. Poirot's gossipy engagement with suspects
in a close-knit group is matched by a belief in intuition. Despite his gender,
Poirot constitutes a feminizing of the 'great detective' to a more familial,
relational mode.

In 1930 he was joined by Miss Marple in *The Murder at the Vicarage*. A deadly
combination of spinsterish nosiness and worldly knowledge, Miss Marple is
part sly satire on sexist devaluation of ageing women and part avenging fury.
Unsurprisingly, one of the novels about her is called *Nemesis* (1971). All of
Christie's detectives, including appealing young couple Tommy and Tuppence
Beresford, and ironic self-portrait crime writer Ariadne Oliver, stand firmly for
the justice of the law as aligned with the justice of God. The conservatism of
Christie's writing resides in her immense faith in detection and the law to right
wrongs. In her domain, the killer is unmasked and suitably punished, and the
world is returned to stability. The one exception is the famous *Murder on
the Orient Express* (1934), in which Poirot's discovery of the truth does not
result in action against the perpetrators, in the cause of a greater justice. However,
Christie's exception is signalled as unique in the subsequent *Appointment with
Death* (1938), in which Poirot insists that the execution of a monstrous tyrant
is not comparable to the mercy he showed on the Orient Express.

Christie's signature mode is summed up by Miss Marple's prescription for the
witches in *Macbeth*: 'I would have them three ordinary, normal old women . . .
and you would feel a sort of menace just behind the ordinariness of them.'
Christie's plots are focused on middle-class decay from within. Although the
poor, SERVANTS and foreigners may be easy suspects, such scapegoating is
decisively shown to be part of culpable racism and snobbery within the
English group, as in the fruitless attempt to implicate the Egyptians in *Death on
the Nile* (1937).

Crucial to Christie's critique is the self-conscious nature of her genre. From
the first her detectives quote other fictions to show the playful yet ritual
quality of the writing. Her parody can embrace the Gothic, as in *They Do It
With Mirrors* (1952), in which a mysterious mansion finally serves to validate

the instincts of the most 'feminine' inhabitant. Equally, viewing the country house as a self-referential fiction in *The Hollow* (1946) highlights how its backward-looking nature itself leads to violence. Agatha Christie is a conservative critic of modernity, cautiously in favour of incremental social changes for individual betterment.

Suggested Reading

Light, Alison. *Forever England: Femininity, Literature and Conservatism Between the Wars* (London: Routledge, 1991).

Plain, Gill. *Twentieth-Century Crime Fiction: Gender, Sexuality and the Body* (Edinburgh: Edinburgh University Press, 2001).

Rowland, Susan. *From Agatha Christie to Ruth Rendell* (Basingstoke: Palgrave Macmillan, 2001).

Susan Rowland

Cinema

Cinema, especially Hollywood movies, exerted a strong cultural influence in the first half of the twentieth century on British life, and on women's appearance, expectations, and prescribed roles. The early development of the moving image was led by British and European innovators, but in 1915 the American film industry relocated to Hollywood and organized itself into vertically integrated conglomerates which controlled all aspects of the movie business, including production, sales, publicity, distribution, and exhibition. By 1920, as a result of the commercial opportunities caused by Europe's involvement in the First World War, Hollywood studios dominated the world market, and 80 per cent of films shown in British cinemas were American. In 1927 the British government intervened and enforced a quota system, which required a proportion of films shown to be made in Britain. Unfortunately, one result of this was the production of numerous poor quality films (called 'quota quickies'), ironically often made by American companies located in Britain.

Hollywood's prime marketing device was the promotion of movie stars. Female stars have always functioned as idealized images of femininity, but these ideals were manufactured by a male-defined capitalist industry. Women, although central to the success of the movie business as stars, scriptwriters, costume designers, and so forth, have rarely exercised creative control, except in Hollywood's early years, when Lois Weber and Mary Pickford, along with a number of others, worked as directors or producers. Even in the silent era, there was a sexist polarization of female screen roles into either virgins or whores. Lillian Gish played childlike girls caught in the harsh world of Victorian values in films such as *Way Down East* (1920), while vamp roles, instigated by the sensational success of Theda Bara in *A Fool There Was* (1915), continued to colour the representation of the sexual woman. Flapper films, such as *It* (1925) starring Clara Bow and based on the novel by Elinor GLYN, portrayed a new sassy type of American girl, but sexual standards did not change. By contrast, the appeal of Greta Garbo was that of a sophisticated, sexually experienced European.

The lack of stars was one reason for the moribund state of the British film industry, but there was a flowering of intellectual debate about film in Britain in the mid-1920s. In 1927, *Close Up* appeared: an international journal focusing on the art cinema movements of Europe, and in general scorning Hollywood movies as artistically impoverished. *Close Up*'s investment in the European tradition resulted in the making of *Borderline* (1930), a unique film influenced by Soviet montage and German Expressionism, in which H. D. and BRYHER appeared alongside Paul Robeson. Bryher (the journal's financial backer), H. D. and Dorothy RICHARDSON all wrote regularly for *Close Up*. Bryher's interest in cinema was in its potential for social change, while Richardson's pieces discuss the cinema from the perspective of a female audience member, rather than critiquing films as an art. In a similar vein, Virginia WOOLF'S essay 'The Cinema', published in America in 1926, discovers many suggestive possibilities in the new cinematic visual language, but also expresses concerns about the passive quality of cinematic spectatorship.

During the 1930s, glitzy musicals provided escape from economic privation, and violent gangster movies were popular, while the Western kept the angel/whore dichotomy alive entering its heyday with *Stagecoach* (1939). Following the upheavals of the Second World War, however, more complex Hollywood representations of gender roles appeared. This was the era of screwball comedies in which the battle of the sexes was played out in verbal contests of wit by pairings such as Katharine Hepburn and Spencer Tracy. The postwar years were also the context for the rise of films noir. These were 'B' movies adapted from pulp fiction and featuring scheming, smart femme fatales, such as Barbara Stanwyck, star of *Double Indemnity* (1944). Stanwyck, along with Joan Crawford and Bette Davis, dominated Hollywood in the late 1930s and 1940s, and also starred in *Stella Dallas* (1937), one of the 'women's weepies' or melodramas which were watched by millions of women in the United Kingdom as well as the United States, during what Molly Haskell memorably describes as 'wet, wasted afternoons'. British film had something of a renaissance in the 1940s. David Lean's *Brief Encounter* (1945) was a highly successful, and quintessentially English, melodrama, and Gainsborough Studios supplied a femme fatale to match the American dames in Margaret Lockwood, who starred in *The Wicked Lady* (1946), based on the novel by Magdalen KING-HALL. Women also made an important contribution to the British DOCUMENTARY FILMS of the 1930s, 1940s, and 1950s.

Hollywood films form a record of the changing position of women through the years, although the mirroring process described by 1970s feminists such as Haskell is now regarded as too simplistic. Also outmoded is the somewhat puritanical reaction to Hollywood movies which second-wave feminists share with first-wave writers, and there is now a new willingness to accord importance to the history of women's pleasure in mainstream film.

Suggested Reading

Donald, James, Anne Friedberg and Laura Marcus (eds). *'Close Up', 1927–1933: Cinema and Modernism* (London: Cassell, 1998).

Haskell, Molly. *From Reverence to Rape: the Treatment of Women in the Movies* (New York: Holt, Rinehart & Winston, 1974).

Kaplan, E. Ann (ed.). *Women in Film Noir* (London: BFI, 1998).

Ryall, Tom. *Britain and the American Cinema* (London: Sage, 2001).

Kathy Hopewell

Cole, Margaret Postgate 1893–1980

FABIAN socialist and prolific writer of history, politics, biography, poems, short stories, novels, and crime fiction, often in collaboration with her husband, G. D. H. Cole. Cole was educated at Roedean School, Brighton, and read Classics at Girton College, Cambridge, under Jane Harrison. Her wide circle of literary and political acquaintances spread from George Bernard Shaw to T. S. Eliot and Ezra Pound. She and her husband were pillars of the FABIAN SOCIETY, where they met in 1918; it was dedicated to 'equality of opportunity' and the abolition of the 'economic power and privileges of individuals and classes'. Margaret Cole's writings on democracy and social reform concentrated primarily on marriage, EDUCATION, and Soviet Russia. Her contributions to feminist work include a collection of essays on careers for women entitled *The Road to Success* (1936); a series of biographical sketches, *Women of To-day* (1938); and, most famously, *Marriage, Past and Present* (1938).

Her only poetry book, *Margaret Postgate's Poems* (1918), is most notable for the war poems. (G. D. H. was a conscientious objector to the war.) 'The Veteran' and 'Praematuri' are reminiscent of Wilfred Owen in protestingly ironic vein; they were printed in *An Anthology of War Poems* (1930) and are included in Catherine Reilly's VIRAGO anthology of war poetry. Cole's biographies include the highly rated *Beatrice Webb* (1945).

Suggested Reading

Cole, G. D. H. *The Fabian Society: Past and Present* (London: The Fabian Society, 1942).

Cole, Margaret. *Growing Up into Revolution* (London: Longmans, 1949).

Jane Dowson

Communism

Social unrest and the Bolshevik Revolution in Russia in October 1917 paved the way for the establishment of the Communist International (Comintern) and the creation of new communist parties in other countries. This led to the formation of the Communist Party of Great Britain (CPGB). It was formed in 1920, reformed in 1921 with about 3000 members, peaked in the early 1940s with a membership of around 56,000, and then went into a decline (although it is still in existence). It never captured the centre stage of British politics, since working-class support in Britain was largely attracted to the Labour Party through the trade unions.

To overcome the lack of female participation in the first years, the Party set up a Women's Department under Helen Crawfurd (1877–1954), a former suffragette, and she edited a separate women's page in the official newspaper. The first CPGB women's conference was held in May 1924, with Crawfurd attending as the 'women's representative' on the Party's political bureau. She contributed enthusiastically to the task of drawing more women to the CPGB, in order to raise awareness among ordinary women about communism's quest for equal rights for all.

With the growing threat of FASCISM in Europe and Hitler's rise to power in 1933, the Comintern advocated a unity between all communist parties and social democratic parties to support the anti-fascist cause. The CPGB increased in popularity in Britain, being the only party to adopt an uncompromising stance towards the British Union of Fascists (BUF) and its leader Oswald Mosley. The Seventh Comintern Congress (July 1935) established a Popular Front against fascism, uniting the British Marxists with the Independent Labour Party and all other opponents of the common fascist enemy. The Popular Front Alliance had, however, failed by 1939, since the CPGB's policy at this time was often confused, contradictory, and highly dependent on decisions in Moscow. Stalin, concerned with his own territorial interests, had signed a ten-year treaty of non-aggression with Hitler in 1939, which made it impossible for the CPGB to remain within the Popular Front Alliance and yet be part of the international communist movement. The collapse of the Popular Front Alliance was also partly caused by socialist PACIFISTS, who disagreed with the necessary rearmament to combat fascism, and radical communists, who were disappointed by the interruption of the revolutionary process.

Suggested Reading

Thompson, Willie. *The Good Old Cause: British Communism, 1920–1991* (London: Pluto Press, 1992).

Worley, Matthew. *Class Against Class: The Communist Party in Britain* (London: I. B. Tauris, 2001).

Jana Nittel

Compton-Burnett, Ivy 1884–1969

Prolific novelist whose work was widely read and stylistically original. The eldest of seven children of Dr Jones Compton Burnett and his power-wielding wife Katherine (who inserted the hyphen into the family name), Ivy was educated privately and then gained a Classics degree at Royal Holloway College. Her father died in 1901 and her mother in 1911, after which she brought up her siblings until they mutinied in 1915 and set up house in London. Death repeatedly affected her family: her favourite brother, Guy, died in 1905, another brother, Noel, in WORLD WAR ONE, and her two younger sisters committed suicide by drinking veronal in 1917. After this, she lived for over 30 years with a female friend.

Compton-Burnett's Edwardian domestic dramas, always set in enormous, dilapidated old houses, centre on family tensions and crises including incest, obsession, blackmail, and murder. Yet she is not merely an inheritor of the sensation novel, much more a stylistic innovator. Her extraordinary ironic dialogues are mostly between the children in a household, who analyse adult actions with acute insight into pretence and cruel intent, processing thoughts resembling *Nouveau Roman* novelist Nathalie Sarraute's 'sous conversations'. Although critics have not acknowledged her as an experimental, MODERNIST writer, the conversations in her fictions also have affinities with Virginia WOOLF's characters' inner dialogues, but are more formal and staged, almost a Greek chorus of critical retort and comment. Woolf herself recognized Compton-Burnett's 'bitter truth and intense originality'. Compton-Burnett's novels are further characterized by a house-bound plottedness reminiscent of Agatha CHRISTIE, claustrophobic social situations, ironies, malice, and manipulative relationships. In her emphasis on social performance, she might be compared with Jane Austen, Barbara Pym, Henry Green, or Evelyn Waugh. Her characters are comic exaggerations who declaim with insensitivity and mutter critically. Plots incorporate the comedy and tragedy of domineering households, powerless children, tyrannical grandmothers, aunts, and fathers, and ignored but necessary servants.

Her first novel, *Dolores* (1911), was minor. Successful novels with dualist titles begin with *Pastors and Masters* (1925), followed by *Brothers and Sisters* (1929), and *Men and Wives* (1931). *A House and Its Head* (1935), about a tyrannical father, was Compton Burnett's own favourite, while *Daughters and Sons* (1937) portrays female evil in 85-year-old Sabine Ponsonby's domination of her family. Noted for its vivacious wit, *Manservant and Maidservant* (1947), a tale of 'below stairs', was successful in the United States as *Bullivant and the Lambs*.

Her most innovative novel, a *Father and His Fate* (1957), written entirely in dialogue, seems to conjure a listening presence. Miles Mowbray, the father, is a misogynistic, self-justifying, domestic dictator who, on the death of his wife, proposes to steal his nephew's young fiancée. Here, as elsewhere in Compton-Burnett, poor relations cannot change the vacuous self-justification of dictatorial household tyrants, sometimes stoically surviving or plotting together to take revenge. Family mealtimes are monstrous power games of ordered seating, bullying statements, hidden histories, and sensitivities outraged.

Her work adapted well to new media. In the 1960s, several radio plays and two television plays based on her novels were followed by a 1975 West End production of *A Family and a Fortune* starring Alec Guinness. Two TV documentaries followed in 1974 and 1984.

Suggested Reading

Dick, K. (ed.). *Ivy and Stevie: Ivy Compton-Burnett and Stevie Smith, Conversations and Reflections* (London: Duckworth, 1971).

Gentile, Kathy Justice. *Ivy Compton-Burnett* (London: Macmillan Education, 1991).

Spurling, Hilary. *Ivy: The Life of Ivy Compton-Burnett* (New York: Knopf, 1984).

Gina Wisker

Comyns, Barbara 1909–1992

Artist and novelist, best known for *Our Spoons Came from Woolworths* (1950), set in bohemian London during the 1930s. Comyns was born in 1909 in Warwickshire and, after a brief career as a cartoonist, married an artist by whom she had two daughters. They later separated and thereafter she earned her living as antique dealer, dog breeder, car dealer, cook, and writer. Comyns's first novel was published in 1947 and she went on to write ten more, four of which were republished by VIRAGO in the 1980s. Her most accomplished books are *The Vet's Daughter* (1959), which later became the musical *The Clapham Wonder; The Skin Chairs* (1962); and *The Juniper Tree* (1985). Their plots focus on abusive and controlling relationships, described vividly by a faux-naïve narrator. Blackly comic, these novels subtly combine literary realism with Gothic interludes and moments of magical realism. The influence of Ivy COMPTON-BURNETT and Stevie SMITH on Comyns's writing is clear, and the combination of lyricism and surrealism that marks her work has led one critic to describe her as 'Beryl Bainbridge on acid'.

Suggested Reading

Horner, Avril and Sue Zlosnik. *Gothic and the Comic Turn* (Basingstoke: Palgrave Macmillan, 2004).

Horner, Avril and Sue Zlosnik. 'Skin Chairs and Other Domestic Horrors: Barbara Comyns and the Female Gothic Tradition', *Gothic Studies*, 6.1 (May 2004) 90–102.

Avril Horner and Sue Zlosnik

Consumerism

British consumers spent more and more throughout the first half of the twentieth century. In spite of two world wars and recessions, there was overall expansion in most of the major sectors: general retail, HOUSING, leisure, and tourism. The growth in home ownership, for example, hit an all-time high in 1938–9, at 20 per cent of the population (reaching 30 per cent by 1951). Sport became steadily commercialized, the motor industry flourished, and British seaside resorts found increasing popularity, especially with the 'package holiday' phenomenon led by Butlins (first camp established in Skegness in 1936) and Pontins (first camp built in 1946).

Co-operative shopping outlets also sprang up throughout Britain, and by 1900 most of Britain's major towns and cities had at least one department store. It was during the interwar period that Britain's leading stores firmly established themselves as household names. By 1928, Woolworths had created some 280 outlets nationwide, endearing itself to working and middle-class consumers alike, largely through its mass production of cheap but useful commodities. In 1939, Marks and Spencer had 250 branches, and Liptons had 615, and all of these companies contributed to the erosion of Britain's local corner shop culture. Woolworths features in a number of middlebrow women's novels of the period, including Rachel FERGUSON's *The Brontës Went to Woolworths* (1931) and Barbara COMYNS'S *Our Spoons Came From Woolworths* (1950). These deal, to varying extents, with the gender and class issues raised by the huge popularity of the Woolworths chain.

Between the wars, the unprecedented variety and amount of commodities available in British shops resulted in a 20-fold rise in the use of hire purchase, and credit usage was also on the increase. Desirable products included a range of labour-saving domestic devices, such as the vacuum cleaner and the sewing machine, as well as clothes, cosmetics, and cigarettes. Broadly speaking, the purchasing power of women rose throughout the period, as did levels of disposable income for the population in general. Although the DEPRESSION (beginning in 1929) caused prices to fall, wages for those still employed did not fall at the same rate. The result was that the average purchasing power of Britons rose by around 24 per cent during the interwar years.

A link between national identity and consumer consciousness was encouraged by the various 'buy British' campaigns launched by advertisers. These held up Britishness as a hallmark of superior quality and integrity, even though by that stage 'buying British' also meant buying colonial or Dominion-produced goods, an idea promoted by the creation of the EMPIRE Marketing Board in 1926.

Suggested Reading

Benson, John. *The Rise of Consumer Society in Britain, 1880–1980* (New York: Longmans, 1994).
Cross, Gary. *Time and Money: The Making of Consumer Culture* (London: Routledge, 1993).

Humble, Nicola. *The Feminine Middlebrow Novel, 1920s to 1950s: Class, Domesticity, and Bohemianism* (Oxford: Oxford University Press: 2001).

Lunt, Peter and Sonia Livingstone, *Mass Consumption and Personal Identity* (Maidenhead: Open University Press, 1992).

Sean Purchase

Contraception

Discussions of contraception were largely taboo at the beginning of the twentieth century, even though it was not illegal. Available methods were condoms, female caps, chemical pessaries, withdrawal, an inaccurate safe period, early intrauterine devices (rare), and abstention. Marie Stopes broke the silence, arguing that smaller, better spaced, families meant improved maternal, child, and social HEALTH, as well as better husband/wife relations.

During the 1920s a vigorous movement established clinics, lobbied for birth control advice in local authority clinics (conceded, with limitations, in 1930), publicized the issue, and promoted research. In 1930 the National Birth Council Association (later Family Planning Association) co-ordinated existing activities. Though omitted from the National Health Service in 1948, birth control became increasingly respectable throughout the 1950s. The contraceptive pill was introduced in the early 1960s, and contraception became free under the NHS in 1974.

Continuing taboos limited explicit mentions in literary texts throughout the interwar period, although implicit assumptions about the possibility of preventing pregnancy were pervasive. Contraception and its problems featured as a significant thread in novels of the 1950s and early 1960s, until the advent of the Pill brought a higher degree of reliability and detached the practice of contraception from appliances about which many expressed squeamishness.

Suggested Reading

Leathard, Audrey. *The Fight for Family Planning* (London: Macmillan, 1980).

Szreter, Simon. *Fertility, Class and Gender in Britain, 1860–1940* (Cambridge: Cambridge University Press, 1996).

Lesley A. Hall

Cooper, Lettice 1897–1994

Prolific writer in several genres, and lifelong Labour Party supporter. Lettice Cooper was brought up in Leeds, and was the eldest of three children, all of whom eventually chose literary careers. Their father ran an engineering business and Cooper worked with him for several years after graduating from Oxford. She did not perceive her parents' marriage as happy, and was emotionally much closer to her father than to her mother. Several of Cooper's fictional heroines experience difficulty in their relationships with their mothers and it may have been this early experience of disharmony that led to her lifelong interest in Freudian PSYCHOANALYSIS.

Cooper's first novel, *The Lighted Room*, was published in 1925 and others followed regularly thereafter. In the interwar years, she also contributed occasional articles to *The Yorkshire Post*, and helped in a centre for unemployed people, an experience described in *We Have Come to a Country* (1935). She became the only Labour supporter in a staunchly Conservative household, and awareness of family tensions and difficult political choices are central to the success of *National Provincial*, written during 1937 when: 'Half England recognized that a war was coming, half refused to believe it.' Set in a fictionalized Leeds (renamed 'Aire'), the novel also dramatizes conflict within the Labour Movement itself.

National Provincial was inevitably compared with Winifred HOLTBY's *South Riding* (1936), and this may have been a factor in Lady RHONDDA's invitation to Cooper to come to London in 1939 to work on *Time and Tide*. Unlike Holtby, Cooper found her employer capricious and demanding and was glad to move to a wartime public relations post at the Ministry of Food. There she became friendly with 'George Orwell' and his wife, Eileen Blair, whom she commemorated as 'Ann' in *Black Bethlehem* (1947). Cooper's sister, Barbara, came to London during the war and they made their home together. Cooper also established a long-lasting friendship with Lionel Fielden, whose villa near Florence she regularly visited. Italy provides a setting for several of her later novels, notably *Fenny* (1953).

She developed her literary career in the years after the war, writing novels, biographies, short stories, and 15 children's books, as well as regular book reviews. She was one of five founder members of the Writers' Action Group, which lobbied successfully for the introduction of Public Lending Right in the 1970s, and in the late 1970s she also chaired the English Section of International PEN. Her last novel, *Unusual Behaviour* (1986), was published just before her ninetieth birthday.

Lettice Cooper wrote convincingly from within the individual consciousnesses of her characters and their families. She was also a precise observer of changing attitudes and anxieties within society. A character in *The New House* (1936) explained: 'Why there are people with 1930 minds and 1914 minds and 1890 minds living in the same house!' She returns to this idea in *Desirable Residence* (1980). The honesty and charity of her analyses distinguishes her work and gives a particular gallantry to the portraits (self-portraits?) of old age in her later novels.

Suggested Reading

Cooper, Jilly. Introduction to *The New House* by Lettice Cooper (London: Persephone, 2003) v–xvi.

Duffy, Maureen. Introduction to *The New House* by Lettice Cooper (London: Virago, 1987) vii–xv.

King, Francis. Introduction to *Fenny* by Lettice Cooper (London: Virago, 1987) v–ix.

Julia Jones

Copyright Act of 1911

The 1911 Copyright Act offered authors significantly improved legal protection of their work during their lifetimes and for 50 years after their death. It followed a series of similar acts dating back to 1710; the 1911 Act was updated from the previous Act of 1842, which had protected works for up to 42 years or seven years after death, whichever was longer. As well as books, the 1911 Act covered printed records, perforated music rolls, and sound recordings amongst other media. The Act stood until it was amended in 1956, when the United Kingdom joined the Universal Copyright Convention.

Ashlie Sponenberg

Corelli, Marie ?1850–1924

Bestselling novelist and journalist. Born Mary Mackay, probably the illegitimate daughter of valetudinarian scholar Charles Mackay and his mistress (later wife), Mary Mills, Corelli began writing to help keep her ailing father and ne'er-do-well half-brother. A contradictory personality, she alienated many, and her relationship with the press was one of mutual hatred. Yet she was also fêted by royalty. Hitherto, Corelli has been treated primarily as a 'personality' rather than as a writer, her work attracting surprisingly little critical attention considering her impressive sales and the diversity of her audience. Her greatest successes were her novels of the 1880s and 1890s, but she continued writing until her death and has never been out of print.

Corelli's novels frequently critique upper-class life. Titles such as *The Mighty Atom* (1895), which condemns secular EDUCATION, and *Jane* (1897), which offers a wry depiction of the London Season, are somewhat prim; but, in the main, never has a writer managed to so roundly condemn the sins of the upper classes whilst making them so fascinating. *Vendetta!* (1886), which recalls Dumas's *Count of Monte Cristo*, and *Wormwood* (1886), a tale of Parisian absinthe drinkers, are sheer melodrama. The former begins with the lines: 'I, who write this, am a dead man . . . dead by absolute proofs – dead and buried! . . . Yet . . . I live! . . . and even sorrow has left few distinguishing marks upon me, save one. My hair, once ebony-black, is white . . . .'

Meanwhile, in *The Sorrows of Satan* (1895), hell graphically manifests itself around its fictional sinners as they blindly eat and drink themselves unto damnation. This book also deals extensively and critically with the press and discusses the nature and responsibilities of authorship. It was thus widely regarded as an exercise in personal spleen. (*Review of Reviews* editor W. T. Stead dubbed it 'the sorrows of Marie Corelli'.) Undoubtedly, Corelli resented the fact that she never gained the critical acclaim she craved. However, in engaging with notions of the author and of the 'high–low' culture divide – *The Murder of Delicia* (1896) deals with similar themes – she was tapping into existing debates in the literary world of her day.

Likewise, exploiting *fin-de-siècle* interest in alternatives to mainstream Christianity, Corelli wrote extensively on metaphysical subjects. However, she was not consistent. For example, whilst *Holy Orders* (1908) might be classified as a Christian temperance novel, *Thelma* (1887) critiques low-church Protestantism, sentimentalizes Roman Catholicism, and sympathetically portrays a modern-day Viking who is ultimately fetched away to Valhalla by his own personal Valkyrie. Meanwhile, *The Master Christian* (1900) tells of the Christ-child returned to earth and *The Sorrows of Satan* is even more unorthodox, its narrative based on the non-canonical premise that Lucifer has long ago repented of the pride that caused his fall and that he can be restored to his former place in Heaven if sinners reject him. Several other novels share a comparatively coherent, semi-scientific religious/philosophical system, in which elements of Eastern religions are grafted onto Christianity. *Ziska* (1897) and *Ardath* (1889) deal with reincarnation, whilst novels about other worlds and other kinds of incarnation include *A Romance of Two Worlds* (1886), *The Soul of Lilith* (1892), *The Young Diana* (1918), *The Life Everlasting* (1911), and *The Secret Power* (1921).

Suggested Reading

Federico, Annette R. *Idol of Suburbia. Marie Corelli and Late-Victorian Literary Culture* (Charlottesville, VA: University Press of Virginia, 2000).

Masters, Brian. *Now Barabbas was a Rotter: The Extraordinary Life of Marie Corelli* (London: Hamilton, 1978).

Scott, William Stuart. *Marie Corelli: The Story of a Friendship* (London: Hutchinson, 1955).

Elaine Hartnell

Cornford, Frances 1886–1960

Winner of the Queen's Gold Medal for Poetry in 1959, she published eight poetry collections and two books of translated poetry between 1910 and 1960. These were out of print for many years until a new *Selected Poems* appeared in 1996 (Enitharmon). Frances Cornford was well known through numerous anthologies, extending from *The Oxford Book of English Verse* to *Some Contemporary Poets*, and a spectrum of journals encompassing *The Criterion*, *Time and Tide*, *The Listener*, and the American *Poetry: A Magazine of Verse*. In the absence of critical analysis, she has accrued credentials through her grandfather (Charles Darwin), father (Sir Francis Darwin), husband (Francis, a Fellow of

Trinity College Cambridge), or radical left-wing son, John. Her literary papers (British Library) are the best source of information about her ideas and connections. They record her conscious rejection of the disreputable abstractions and high diction of the Edwardian poets in favour of a naturalistic idiom, using rhyme and regular rhythm.

Spring Morning (1915) and *Autumn Midnight* (1923) were published by Harold Monro's The Poetry Bookshop Press, while *Different Days* (1928) was the first of the Woolfs' *Hogarth Living Poets* series. Accordingly, Cornford's techniques and subjects span both these GEORGIAN and BLOOMSBURY associations. 'Cambridge-shire', which registers her affinity with her home county, has the Georgian celebration of local landscape combined with the MODERNIST interplay between external impressions and unconscious imperatives. These are concentrated in the processes of memory. In some poems, the idioms are highly cultured, but often she was more successfully colloquial and chose popular forms such as ballad, epigram, and epitaph.

Belonging to a large family, Cornford frequently encountered death: after her mother died when she was 17, she suffered the first of three long depressions; in WORLD WAR ONE she lost several friends; her father died in 1925; her son was killed in the SPANISH CIVIL WAR; and her husband died along with other friends and relatives in WORLD WAR TWO, which provoked some of her finest poems. As in 'Grand Ballet', Nijinsky is one recurring symbol of the fine line between life and death or sanity and insanity. Her correspondence presents a cheerful compliance with the competing demands of her literary career and her five children, but her journal entries reveal a secret desperation. Cornford wrote to Virginia WOOLF that she was conscious of writing back 'through one's fathers' and was drawn to the ideal of androgyny articulated in *A Room of One's Own*. A 'pseudo-male' lyricism arguably both enervates and restrains Cornford's creativity, while she is most free in the poems which centre on conflicted female experience.

Suggested Reading

Dowson, Jane. *Women, Modernism and British Poetry, 1910–39: Resisting Femininity* (Aldershot: Ashgate, 2002).

Fowler, Helen. 'Frances Cornford', in Edward Shils and Carmen Blacker (eds), *Cambridge Women: Twelve Portraits* (Cambridge: Cambridge University Press, 1996) 137–57.

Raverat, Gwen. *Period Piece: A Cambridge Childhood* (London: Faber, 1960).

Jane Dowson

Crompton, Richmal 1890–1969

Novelist and creator of the enduringly popular 'William' series. The first William stories appeared in 1919, the last posthumously in 1970. Throughout these years, Crompton's schoolboy provided a comic commentary on the pretensions and pomposities of comfortable, middle-class, country-town life. William's first appearance coincided with that of another long-running comic hero, P. G. Wodehouse's Bertie Wooster. Both heroes, happy in their mildly disreputable hedonist pursuits, continually encounter the demands of representatives, usually female, from the respectable world. William struggles with a succession of do-gooders, organizers of social events with unrealistic expectations of boyhood, and also with his gushing manipulative blonde, Violet Elizabeth.

Crompton took children seriously: 'You must be able to see the world as the child sees it. To "write down" is an insult that the child quickly perceives.' The main targets of her comedy are the 'people to whom the expression on a child's face conveys absolutely nothing'. The first 'William' stories, however, appeared in the *Home Magazine*, a WOMAN'S MAGAZINE for family reading; the original target audience was thus primarily adult and female. Crompton developed exceptional skill in addressing these stories, which explore the contradictory stresses of childhood, to both adult and child audiences. William fiercely defends his freedom with the Outlaws, a secret society 'with few aims beyond that of secrecy', but sometimes seeks to control the adult world. He intervenes in the romantic entanglements of his flapper sister, Ethel, and his earnest student brother, Robert; while in *William the Conqueror* (1926), he recreates his home town as Stratford for a glamorous, lost American tourist.

Richmal Crompton Lamburn was born in Bury, a curate schoolmaster's daughter. Unlike William, she was an exemplary student, enjoying boarding school, and winning a scholarship to Royal Holloway College, where she studied classics from 1911 to 1914 and became an ardent SUFFRAGIST. She taught classics at Bromley High School until disablement by polio forced her retirement in 1923; thereafter, she concentrated on writing. In 1922 the first collection of stories appeared in book form as *Just – William*, and the William stories transferred from the *Home Magazine* to the *Happy Mag*, where they ran until 1940. In 1924 Crompton published *The Innermost Room*, the first of the adult novels that she wrote in tandem with William throughout her life, often producing a book in each genre in a year. These adult novels were mild family romances, focused seriously on the kinds of middle-class tensions and aspirations comically explored in the Brown family. Their failure to compete with William's overwhelming international popularity disappointed her. She lived quietly in Bromley, and continued to write William stories until her death, adapting them slightly to contemporary events, as in *William and the Evacuees* (1941), but essentially maintaining the secure, almost timeless 1920s world towards which William directs his relentless scepticism. They have often been dramatized for theatre, CINEMA, radio and television.

Suggested Reading

Cadogan, Mary. *Richmal Crompton: The Woman Behind William* (London: Unwin, 1987).

Cadogan, Mary and Patricia Craig. *You're A Brick, Angela: A New Look At Girls' Fiction, 1839 to 1975* (London: Gollancz, 1976).

Anthea Trodd

Cunard, Nancy 1896–1965

The image of Nancy Cunard as a hedonist and a 'negrophile' has eclipsed her standing as an intensely dedicated journalist, activist, editor, translator, poet, and publisher. Whilst the photographs Man Ray and Cecil Beaton took of her emaciated arms weighted with ivory bangles still circulate as evidence of the vogue for primitivism in 1920s Paris, and the fictions of Michael Arlen (*The Green Hat*, 1925) and Aldous Huxley (*Antic Hay*, 1923 and *Point Counter Point*, 1928) serve the myth of the 'roaring twenties', her industry goes largely unrecorded.

Cunard grew up in the rarefied atmosphere of her mother Emerald's artistic salons where she was introduced to writers, artists, and musicians. Her enthusiasm for literary introductions, which led to her status as a nexus for the transatlantic exchange of ideas, was perhaps nurtured at Emerald's parties; but, as the title of her first volume *Outlaws* (1921) indicates, her most vibrant verse was motivated by a desire to reject the values of her mother's society. She established the Hours Press to publish contemporary poetry and was allegedly the first to publish Samuel Beckett. Whilst her verse was criticized by Pound for merely imitating high MODERNISM, even the title of one of her better known poems – 'Sonnet in Five Languages: The Internationals' – indicates her dedication to formal innovation as a means of expressing egalitarianism. It is not widely known that she was the compiler of responses to the question 'Are you for, or against, Franco and fascism?' in *Authors Take Sides on the Spanish War* (1937). Fluent in French, German, Spanish, and Italian, Cunard was one of the first to translate Pablo Neruda.

A move to Paris in the 1920s consolidated her shift of interest from poetry to internationalism. Louis Aragon introduced her to ethnography and this, in combination with her relationship with Henry Crowder, her African-American lover, initiated what became a lifelong commitment to racial equality. In December 1931 she circulated a devastating public attack upon slavery, colonialism, and her mother's racism in a kind of Christmas card manqué: a pamphlet entitled *Black Man and White Ladyship*. Like the monumental *Negro* anthology which she edited (1934), this pamphlet has been dismissed as impassioned and unscholarly, but now its startling juxtapositions are valued as Surrealist collage. *Negro* was intended as an encyclopedia of black history and culture, and contains the writings of many significant writers and politicians including Zora Neale Hurston, Claude McKay, and Langston Hughes. It demonstrates the fearlessness of Cunard's opinions: an article by the esteemed leader of the National Association of the Advancement of Colored People, W. E. Dubois, is accompanied by Cunard's own critique. Copies of the anthology are scarce, and the only edited reprint (by Hugh Ford in 1970) is more celebratory of the editor than true to the multivocal nature of the original.

Because she devoted the rest of her life to political journalism for the Associated Negro Press as one of its few white contributors, most of Cunard's work – as yet uncollected – has been more widely read in black America than Europe. It is only now becoming known through the scholarship of feminists, chiefly Jane Marcus.

Suggested Reading

Chisholm, Anne. *Nancy Cunard* (London: Sidgwick & Jackson, 1979).

Young, Tory. 'The Reception of Nancy Cunard's *Negro* Anthology', in Maralou Joannou (ed.), *Women Writers of the 1930s: Gender, Politics and History* (Edinburgh: Edinburgh University Press, 1999) 113–22.

Young, Tory. 'Nancy Cunard's *Black Man and White Ladyship* as Surrealist Manifesto', in Robin Hackett et al. (eds), *British Women Write the 1930s* (Gainesville, FL: Florida University Press, 2004).

Tory Young

D

Dane, Clemence 1888–1965

Pseudonym for Winifred Ashton, novelist, playwright, and screenwriter, a well-known and accomplished member of London's literary and theatrical worlds between the wars. Dane was a forthright feminist, writing for *The Daily Express* in 1926 that: 'A woman who cannot drive a car, deal with a drunken man, speak in public and run a business and a home is getting to be as much a rarity as 50 years ago a woman who could not faint when she was proposed to.'

After studying art and acting briefly under the stage name Diana Cortis, Dane won success with her first play, *A Bill of Divorcement* (1921), which tackled the contentious topic of women's divorce rights, and had an impact on current thinking. Her first novel, *Regiment of Women* (1917), picked another controversial topic, LESBIANISM; it was a bestseller and an influence on subsequent lesbian fiction. It was reissued by VIRAGO as a Lesbian Landmark in 1995.

The array of media Dane worked in is impressive: film, TV, radio, stage – including musicals, biblical epics, costume dramas, and a large wartime pageant so popular it held up the London traffic. She adapted Shakespeare and Schiller for the radio, and Tolstoy for the screen (*Anna Karenina* with Greta Garbo in 1935). Her writing career spanned six decades from 1917 to 1964, during which she published 30 plays and 11 novels in a range of genres. She collaborated with Helen Simpson on crime novels, wrote HISTORICAL FICTION, and was an anthologist, editor, and essayist. She was also a member of the influential 'Great Five' Book Society Selection Committee founded by Arnold Bennett. Her poem 'Trafalgar Day' (1940) was an instant hit during the London Blitz. Dane's versatility extended to the visual arts: her oil painting and bronze bust of Noel Coward are in the National Portrait Gallery.

A miniature performance in itself, Dane's pseudonym suggests church, nursery rhyme, and saint; it matched her preoccupation with the twin issues of performance and the larger-than-life character. Described by a friend as 'in every way a big woman, large in stature, heart and mind', Dane specialized in portraying figures of sometimes ambiguous power. During the Second World War her patriotism prompted her to celebrate national icons such as Merlin, Robin Hood, Elizabeth I, and Nelson. *The Arrogant History of White Ben* (1939) drew on her reading of Hitler's *Mein Kampf* for a fascinating insight into evil charisma and crowd behaviour.

Dane revelled in the theatre and lived in Covent Garden, the heart of London's theatre-land, where she said she had 'a stall front row in the best theatre of all – the Garden itself' (then London's main fruit, vegetable, and flower market).

The best chapters of her knowledgeable reminiscences, *London Has a Garden* (1964), describe rehearsals and explore the processes of creating illusion and effect. She was Life President of the SOCIETY OF WOMEN WRITERS AND JOURNALISTS, won an Oscar for her screenplay for Alexander Korda's 1945 film *Perfect Strangers*, and was awarded the CBE in 1953.

Suggested Reading

Cameron, Rebecca. 'Irreconcilable Differences: Divorce and Women's Drama before 1945', *Modern Drama*, 44.4 (Winter 2001) 476–90.

Smithers, David Waldron. *'Therefore, Imagine...': The Works of Clemence Dane* (Tunbridge Wells: The Dragonfly Press, 1988).

Jenny Hartley

D'Arcy, Ella 1857–1937

Fiction writer and translator, remembered for her association with *The Yellow Book*. D'Arcy's parents were Irish, but she was born in London, brought up in the Channel Islands, and partly educated in France and Germany. She studied art, but when failing eyesight hindered her aspiration to be a painter, she began to write, first composing a novel about the Shelley circle, which she continued to circulate into the first decade of the twentieth century, though it was never published. She turned to the short story, and published several stories anonymously in magazines such as the *Argosy*. D'Arcy found her real place as a writer of bleak realistic fiction for *The Yellow Book*. Her work appeared in ten of its 13 issues, and she also unofficially assisted editors John Lane and Henry Harland. D'Arcy also published in *Queen, Century*, and *The English Review*. Her stories exhibit a worldly, cynical tone, and are typically centred in blighted love. Many of them are regionally based, drawing on the folkways and local colour of the Channel Islands, Normandy, and Antibes. They were collected in *Monochromes* (1895) and *Modern Instances* (1898).

In her short novel *The Bishop's Dilemma* (1898), a young Catholic priest, Father Fayler (a transparent name), is sent to a tiny parish, and there falls hopelessly in love with the companion to a wealthy, domineering old widow, who dictates to the church and community. Both priest and companion are banished by the Bishop to unpleasant destinations, and the young cleric will inevitably die in his unhealthy new surroundings, while the self-centred old lady and the well-circumstanced Bishop will live on contentedly. Similar themes concerning a monk or nun who briefly tries to reassimilate into worldly life but comes to grief (the monk suffers horrible tortures inflicted by a jealous, powerful husband) are found in two stories, 'Agatha Blount' and 'From the Chronicles of Hildesheim'. These both appeared in 1909 in the LITTLE MAGAZINE *The English Review*, which was then a new magazine desiring D'Arcy's avant-garde reputation to help get it off the ground.

Rampant sexuality, violence, and murder recur in D'Arcy's representations of love relationships. Although she was in her personal life very much a New Woman, D'Arcy's fiction explores tragedies brought about by selfish, arrogant, greedy females. Her fiction overall is certainly MODERNIST in its themes of fragmenting psychology. She attempted to publish biographies of Baudelaire and Rimbaud, and an anthology of the latter's writings, which publishers considered too daring. Her last publication, *Ariel*...(1924), a translation of André Maurois's biography of Shelley, met with mixed reactions from reviewers. D'Arcy died, impoverished, obscure, and senile, in a London charity home in September 1937, but interest in her writings has revived during the later twentieth century.

Suggested Reading

Fisher, B. F. 'Ella D'Arcy: A Commentary with an Annotated Primary and Secondary Bibliography', *ELT*, 35.2 (1992) 179–211.

Mix, K. L. *A Study in Yellow: The Yellow Book and Its Contributors* (Lawrence, KS: University of Kansas Press, 1960).

Benjamin F. Fisher

Daryush, Elizabeth 1887–1977

Formally innovative poet; translator. Educated privately in Berkshire and Oxford, Elizabeth Daryush married Ali Akbar, a Persian government official, in 1923 but had no children. Their three years in Persia informed her study and translations of Persian poetry. Elizabeth Daryush suppressed her first three books of poetry, written before her father, Robert Bridges, died in 1930. As Poet Laureate since 1912, his status and limited theories of syllabic metre seem to have restricted her experimentation; the following decade saw the development and discovery of her talents, with a new volume appearing almost annually. Negotiating with the strait-jackets of conventional metre and form, she was more adventurous than her father in achieving a natural rhythm. Her irregularities and elliptical syntax within the sonnet and other lyrical modes are strategies which illuminate the imperfection of experience and the misleading consolations of literary regularity. As she explains in her Preface to *Verses: Fourth Book* (1934), reprinted in the *Selected and Collected Poems* (1972, 1976), she used many five- and sometimes four-syllabled lines as well as blank verse.

Recognition of Elizabeth Daryush's metrical pioneering has been more consistent in America, where her poems have been included in many anthologies and received some critical attention. In Britain, she was rescued from several years' silence by Michael Schmidt, who published the last three editions in the 1970s and whose commemorative poem pays tribute to her personal and professional qualities.

Her preoccupation with the questions of freedom and identity, along with her frequent images of enclosure, connect Elizabeth Daryush to the nineteenth-century woman writer. Admittedly, there is some archaic diction, but she was increasingly colloquial and outspoken against the complacency of social privilege. In the much anthologized 'Still Life', the poise of the lines deliberately presents the suffocating sphere of an heiress whose 'unopened future' suggests as much closure as promise. Sensitivity to class differences is similarly suggested in 'Children of Wealth'. The nearest to a feminist impulse comes in the speaker's questions on a woman's slavery to her mirror, but frustratingly, she concludes that a woman should focus on the inner beauty of female virtue. More assertively, in 'When Your Work's Done, Banish It Behind You', women are advised to move on after they have spent themselves in bringing up children. Although her personal voice is often muted, Daryush seems most imaginative with these woman-centred explorations. She is at her most freely expressive in a rare dramatic monologue spoken by Persephone: this reworking of the archetypal silenced woman resonates with the conflations of history, myth, and modernity by other female poets.

Suggested Reading
Dowson, Jane. *Women's Poetry of the 1930s: A Critical Anthology* (London: Routledge, 1996).

Schmidt, Michael. 'For Elizabeth Daryush', *PN Review*, 14. 6 (1988) 44.

Winters, Yvor. 'Robert Bridges and Elizabeth Daryush', *American Review*, 8.3 (1936–7) 353–67. Repr. in Francis Murphy (ed.), *Yvor Winters: Uncollected Essays and Reviews* (London: Allen Lane, 1974) 271–83.

Jane Dowson

Delafield, E. M. 1890–1943
Novelist, short-story writer, essayist, and playwright, remembered today primarily for her witty *Diary of a Provincial Lady* series. An incredibly productive writer, in the 26-year period from the publication of her first novel in 1917 until her premature death in 1943, she produced at least one novel a year (29 in all); authored four books of short stories, three plays, and nine works of non-fiction; and published at least one article every week in a major magazine for about 15 years. A regular contributor to *Punch* and *Time and Tide* (of which she was also a director), in 1931, for example, she published 43 pieces in *Time and Tide* alone. In addition, she went on frequent lecture tours, made radio BROADCASTS, served as a Justice of the Peace, and was active in Women's Institutes. Her works, which focus primarily on the everyday lives of middle-class women, satirize not only the foibles of these middlebrow women, particularly the country gentlewoman, but also – and equally importantly – society's preconceptions of them as dull housewives or repressed matrons. Honest in their assessment yet

generous in tone, Delafield's works are characterized by dry wit, unpretentious prose, and a spirit of self-deprecation. As the Provincial Lady notes: 'Realise – not for the first time – that intelligent women can perhaps best perform their duty towards their own sex by devastating process of telling them the truth about themselves. At the same time, cannot feel that I shall really enjoy hearing it.'

Born Edmée Elizabeth Monica de la Pasture, E. M. Delafield (known as Elizabeth or E. M. D. to her friends) adopted her pseudonym as a play on her surname. Although she was later received into the Anglican Church, Delafield was raised a Catholic and educated with stringent discipline at convent schools. Trained only for the marriage market, she had an unspectacular debut in 1908. Although Delafield often harshly condemned the lack of opportunities for women and the exclusive emphasis on marriage in her novels, including *Consequences* (1919) and *Thank Heaven Fasting* (1932), she was left at the time with a profound sense of inadequacy and purposelessness. After a short, but painful, period in a religious order in Belgium, she joined the Volunteer Aid Detachment (VAD) in Exeter just before WORLD WAR ONE, and found a new life of freedom – both physical and monetary. This contributed to a confidence and a creativity that led to her first novel, *Zella Sees Herself* (1917), and to the adoption of her pseudonym. At the end of the war and after the production of three more novels, Delafield married Major Arthur Paul Dashwood OBE and, after two years in the Malay States, they returned to Croyle, Devonshire, where they had two children, Lionel and Rosamond, and she began to write in earnest. She would remain at Croyle the rest of her life, though she also eventually took an apartment in London (as did her Provincial Lady) where she would go to write.

Delafield worked diligently to craft her novels and was somewhat disconcerted at the popularity of the Provincial Lady series at their expense. Although virtually no scholarship has been devoted to these novels, their contemporary critical reception was generally encouraging. *The Diary of a Provincial Lady* began as a serial in *Time and Tide* in 1929 and proved so popular that it was published as a book in 1930. Three more followed – *The Provincial Lady Goes Further* (1932) (published subsequently in America as *The Provincial Lady in London*), *The Provincial Lady in America* (1934), and *The Provincial Lady in Wartime* (1940) – chronicling the heroine's eventual success as a novelist, her book tour to America, and her experiences during the so-called 'Phoney War'. Though important as humorous and well-paced comedies of manners, the diaries are also significant because of their subtle, satirical analysis of the material conditions of women's lives and the demands of their domestic lives during the 1930s. Unfortunately, despite continuing popularity with readers, Delafield is virtually unstudied by critics today and no good scholarly biography exists.

Suggested Reading
McCullen, Maurice L. *E. M. Delafield*. (Boston, MA: Twayne, 1985).
Powell, Violet. *The Life of a Provincial Lady: A Study of E. M. Delafield and Her Works* (London: Heinemann, 1988).

Jennifer Holberg

Dell, Ethel M. 1881–1939

Prolific ROMANTIC novelist active from 1912 and still reprinted in the mid-1950s. Educated at a private girls' school in Streatham, South London, Dell later moved to Kent. She enjoyed a close relationship with her sister, Ella, and in 1922, after the death of her parents, married Lieutenant-Colonel Gerald Tahourdin Savage of the Royal Army Service Corps. The union was happy; the couple had no children.

In 1933 Dell was still the most popular woman author in Ray Smith's Twopenny Library. When some titles were condensed and reissued in the 1970s' 'Library of Love', Barbara CARTLAND recalled her earlier responses: 'Her strong, passionate, often brutal heroes excited me...her very feminine and elusive heroines were everything I was brought up to think a woman should be.'

Dell's first novel, *The Way of an Eagle* (1912), was an immediate bestseller. In *Keep the Aspidistra Flying* (1936), George Orwell mocks the uneducated reader who 'don't never seem to get tired of *The Way of an Eagle*'. The 'eagle', the only officer ruthless enough to be trusted by his dying commander to kill his daughter before she is slaughtered or raped by Indian mutineers, saves his opium-befuddled charge because he can disguise himself as a native. Relying on her reading of Kipling, Flora Annie STEEL and others, Dell used India as backdrop for many of her narratives. It is not picturesque exoticism but the threat lurking in 'India the vampire!' that titillates. The hero can deliver the heroine from the alien environment because he can merge with it. In *The Lamp in the Desert* (1919), the hero succours the bigamous heroine in many native disguises. In both *The Lamp* and *Storm Drift* (1930), the scale of the British EMPIRE facilitates the poor communication which makes inadvertent bigamy possible, and in Dell's fiction, happiness is often sabotaged by the desire to protect a lover from complex truths.

Heroes such as the eponymous *Greatheart* (1921), or the ageing 'eagle' in *The Keeper of the Door* (1915), can be as patiently protective as Dell's own husband. However, more characteristically, men struggle to control a violence which, as in *The Knave of Diamonds* (1912), causes the heroine to thrill 'through and through'. Dell's cousins enjoyed counting her uses of 'passion', 'tremble, 'pant', and 'thrill'. Addiction to alcohol or drugs is often the source of violence, and the hero, too, often behaves like an addict, unable to control his lust. Though enervated by physical abuse and rape, the heroine is often sustained by devotion to an 'angel child' (not her own) and vaguely religious 'pluck'. Fears of violation shape the symbolism which structures each narrative and are reflected in such titles as *The Keeper of the Door* and *The Bars of Iron* (1916).

Dell wrote compulsively, producing over 30 novels and many short stories, and was also motivated by duty to her fans: *By Request* (1927) was aptly named. Though deploring lowbrow 'day-dreaming', Q. D. LEAVIS praised the 'magnificent vitality' of such authors as Dell and Florence BARCLAY, while Rebecca WEST admired the way Dell 'rode the Tosh Horse hell for leather'.

Suggested Reading

Anderson, Rachel. *The Purple Heart Throbs* (London: Hodder & Stoughton, 1974).

Dell, P. *Nettie and Sissie: A Biography of Best-Selling Novelist Ethel M. Dell and her Sister Ella* (London: Hamish Hamilton, 1977).

West, Rebecca. 'The Tosh Horse', in *The Strange Necessity: Essays and Reviews* (London: Jonathan Cape, 1928) 319–25.

Mary Grover

Depression

Economists define a depression as a period of economic hardship, more prolonged and severe than a recession, and characterized by high unemployment and falling output. The Great Depression of the 1930s is usually identified as the most widespread and serious of all depressions. Its crisis years were those immediately following the collapse of the New York Stock Exchange in 1929, but its causes can be traced back to the First World War and to the economic conditions of the postwar era. The prosperity of 1920s America was a fragile construct, and since large sections of society in both America and Europe lived in poverty during this decade, some historians read the whole interwar period as one of depression.

In the United States, wealth was extremely unequally distributed during the 1920s, with approximately 5 per cent of the population receiving one-third of all income, while 70 per cent survived on low wages. The market for the rapidly expanding range of CONSUMER goods was therefore limited, and overproduction, in combination with unrealistic credit levels, increasing stock-market speculation, and a badly regulated banking system destabilized the domestic economy. Further, high tariffs on imports to the United States caused a large imbalance between exports and imports, which meant that overseas markets for American goods shrunk, since foreign countries could only afford to buy them with the help of American loans.

The resulting Wall Street Crash wiped about 30 thousand million dollars from stock values in the first week, closed many banks, and forced American investors to recall foreign assets and discontinue loans for European reconstruction. Many central European countries, particularly Germany, had come to depend on American funds, and members of the public began a 'run on the banks', rushing to withdraw their investments before they were frozen. British banks had also made substantial loans to central European economies which were now collapsing, and this, combined with the existing budget deficit and the effects of the long-term decline of Britain as an industrial trading power, put so much pressure on the pound that the Gold Standard finally had to be abandoned.

Industrial concerns, no longer able to borrow, had to close or reduce their operations, and retail trade and agriculture also slumped. These factors led to high unemployment in many countries: it reached record levels of about 20 per cent worldwide, although by 1937 it had declined to 10 per cent. The most important effect of the Great Depression, however, was that in the worst-hit countries, in central Europe and South America, hardship made populations receptive to the rhetoric of far-right movements. In Germany, the Third Reich established itself as the force which would revitalize the economy.

In British writing of this period, the experience of poverty and the threat of FASCISM were central – and often connected – concerns. Unemployment in Britain was already high during the twenties due to high taxation and interest rates; in the thirties, it rose so far that benefits had to be severely cut. Unemployment was, however, unevenly spread – between 1929 and 1936, it averaged at around 30 per cent in Wales and 20 per cent in the north of England, but only 8 per cent in London and the south-east. The best known literary images of unemployment in the 1930s are found in novels such as George Orwell's *The Road to Wigan Pier* (1937), Walter Greenwood's *Love on the Dole* (1933), and J. B. Priestley's *English Journey* (1934), but many women writers also engaged with experiences of poverty and working-class life in the 1930s. They include Eve Garnett, author of the children's book *The Family from One-End Street* (1937), Eleanor RATHBONE, Kate ROBERTS, Ellen WILKINSON, Winifred HOLTBY, Ethel MANNIN and Lettice COOPER.

Suggested Reading

Kindleberger, Charles P. *The World in Depression, 1929–1939* (1973; rev. edn Harmondsworth: Penguin, 1987).

Miles, Peter and Malcolm Smith. *Cinema, Literature and Society: Elite and Mass Culture in Interwar Britain* (London: Croom Helm, 1987).

Smith, Malcolm. *Democracy in a Depression: Britain in the 1920s and 1930s* (Cardiff: University of Wales Press, 1998).

Stevenson, John. *British Society, 1914–45* (Harmondsworth: Penguin, 1984).

Faye Hammill

Detective Fiction (Golden Age)

The 'golden age' is shorthand for a predominantly British mode of crime writing that emerged during the period 1920–45. Although the sobriquet can be seen as contentious (as Stephen Knight has argued), the era was undoubtedly a golden age for women crime writers. Agatha CHRISTIE remains the most famous exponent of the form, but other key practitioners included Dorothy L. SAYERS, Margery ALLINGHAM, Gladys Mitchell, Patricia Wentworth and Ngaio MARSH. These women were all producers of what Knight calls 'clue-puzzle' narratives, but while this is certainly an appropriate structural description, like 'golden age' it cannot adequately convey the extent to which these novels are also fictional engagements with the anxieties and debates of the time. Both terms also elide the extent to which – beneath the generic template – these writers were fundamentally dissimilar.

Golden age fiction enjoyed considerable popularity, appealing in particular to the middle classes and intelligentsia, and it had a number of characteristic features. The crime committed is usually murder and there must be a contained community of suspects. Consequently, novels are seldom set in dynamic urban environments, but confined to such locations as villages, country houses, and colleges. The suspects emerge from the respectable middle and upper-middle classes, and although only one will be identified as guilty, all will have had both the opportunity and the desire to kill. The butler, however, could not have done it. Literally or metaphorically, the criminal must be one of the family, motivated by jealousy, greed, or revenge. The form thus presents a precarious civilization, constantly under threat from its own atavistic tendencies.

Since the community has been corrupted, a detective outsider is required to restore stability, and it is in the construction and development of this figure that some of the variety within the genre becomes evident. Agatha Christie produced two influential detectives, the retired Belgian policeman, Hercule Poirot, and the steely English spinster, Miss Marple. In the construction of detectives who were old and eccentric, Christie drew attention away from active agency towards a celebration of the more 'domestic' skills of observation and the reading of bodies, both living and dead. She also fundamentally undermined earlier conceptions of the popular fiction hero. By making her first detective an 'unmanly' man, a vain comical foreigner who is frequently misrecognized as foolish, Christie challenged the tradition of hyper-masculine imperial heroes epitomized by Sapper's 'Bulldog Drummond'. Light has argued that Christie was a distinctly modern writer, whose fiction responded to the trauma of the First World War with a refusal of seriousness, offering the pleasure of surface in place of the pain of depth.

Dorothy L. Sayers, by contrast, came to see the formula as one which permitted depth as well as surface. Her detective, Lord Peter Wimsey, was also initially presented as a somewhat ridiculous figure. However, as the novels progressed, Sayers moved away from the clue-puzzle formula, and Wimsey evolved into a complex hybrid of war veteran, scholar, and lover. This last characteristic broke the 'rules' of a formula that was meant to be more concerned with timetables than desire, but it also facilitated the introduction of Harriet Vane, who can be seen as a precursor of the contemporary feminist detective. Many of the later Wimsey novels give prominence to Harriet, foregrounding questions of moral responsibility and the position of women in a changing society. These contrasts indicate that the sub-genre comprises several radically different approaches to fiction, suggesting that the term 'golden age' is best understood as denoting not so much a formula as an historically specific nexus of generic experimentation.

Suggested Reading

Knight, Stephen. *Crime Fiction, 1800–2000: Detection, Death, Diversity* (Basingstoke: Palgrave Macmillan, 2004).

Light, Alison. *Forever England: Femininity, Literature and Conservatism Between the Wars* (London: Routledge, 1991).

Plain, Gill. *Twentieth-Century Crime Fiction: Gender, Sexuality and the Body* (Edinburgh: Edinburgh University Press, 2001).

Rowland, Susan. *From Agatha Christie to Ruth Rendell* (Basingstoke: Palgrave Macmillan, 2001).

Gill Plain

Dickens, Monica Enid 1915–1992

British novelist best known for her popular *Follyfoot* series of children's books (1970s), later successfully televised. Educated at St Paul's Girls' School, London, great-granddaughter of Charles Dickens, she resented her middle-class identity, and found inspiration for her first novel, *One Pair of Hands* (1939), whilst working as a cook and general servant, commencing as a wartime nurse in *One Pair of Feet* (1942).

Her prolific writings are reflections of her professional and personal experiences; at the heart of her fiction are human relationships in times of pressure, stress, and conflict. *My Turn to Make the Tea* (1951) depicts her time as a local reporter in Hertfordshire; *Cobbler's Dream* (1963) reflects her involvement in the RSPCA; and *Kate and Emma* (1964) results from her activities in the NSPCC. Her work for the Samaritans – she founded the first American branch in 1974 – shaped *The Listeners* (1970), continuing her focus on social issues such as urban poverty, child abuse, suicide, alcoholism, and the causes of crime. She contributed to *Woman's Own* for 20 years and published the third volume of her autobiography, *An Open Book*, in 1978.

Suggested Reading

Hartley, Jenny. *Millions Like Us: British Women's Fiction of the Second World War* (London: Virago, 1997).

Lane, Harriet. Introduction to *Mariana* by Monica Dickens (London: Persephone, 1999) v–xiv.

Jana Nittel

Documentary Filmmakers

Women filmmakers made an important, if barely acknowledged, contribution to documentary making in the 1930s, 1940s, and 1950s, widely considered the 'golden age' of British documentary. The relative obscurity of such pioneers as Mary Field, Margaret Thomson and Kay Mander can partly be explained by the fact that they worked in companies devoted to the production of scientific, instructional, and educational films, an overlooked and less glamorous aspect of the genre.

The documentary cinema of the 1930s provided women with opportunities denied them in the feature industry, where roles were more clearly defined within larger production teams. At Gaumont British Instructional, Mary Field, a history teacher, soon progressed from Education Manager to directing films for the *Secrets of Nature* series. Later she was joined by the zoologist Margaret Thomson who, after working in the GBI library, was given the opportunity to direct with a series on British ecosystems.

The outbreak of the Second World War brought greater opportunities for women as the documentary industry expanded to cope with government demand for propaganda and instructional films covering all aspects of the civilian and military war effort. Women were particularly prominent at companies such as Verity Productions, Realist, and the Shell Film Unit, where they scripted, edited, and directed films. Many of these films were concerned with women's roles, children, and the domestic sphere. They include Ruby Grierson's *They Also Serve* (1940), a paean to the unsung role of the housewife; Mary Francis's *Willing Hands* (1944), about the work of the WVS; and Budge Cooper's *Children of the City* (1944), on juvenile delinquency in Scotland.

Although few of the filmmakers would have described themselves as feminists, they tended to portray women and their concerns in a more progressive and less patronizing fashion than was usual. In Kay Mander's *Homes for the People* (1945), a deliberate strategy of examining the issue of house design through the eyes of ordinary female householders, was an implicit rejection of male approaches to mass HOUSING. Jill Craigie, one of the most avowedly feminist filmmakers of her generation, was later commissioned by the trade union NALGO, to make *To be a Woman* (1951), arguing the case for equal pay. Women, did not work exclusively on 'feminine topics': one of the ironies of wartime CINEMA is that they were required to make so many films on scientific, technical, and military topics. Louise Birt's *Fighting Allies* (1941), Margaret Thomson's *The Signs and Stages of Anaesthesia* (1944), and Anne Womersley's *Debris Clearance* (1944) are just a handful of the films made by women on subjects normally assumed to be the preserve of men.

In the immediate postwar years, commissions from the COI, local government, and international organizations, particularly on various aspects of reconstruction, enabled some women documentary makers to consolidate their careers, with

Mander and Cooper setting up successful documentary companies with their husbands (Basic Films and DATA). Among the notable films from this era are Cooper's *Birthday* (1945) on antenatal care; Thomson's *Children Learning by Experience* (1946) for the Ministry of Education; Craigie's documentary-feature *The Way We Live* (1946), about the reconstruction of Plymouth and *The Children of the Ruins* (1948), for UNESCO; Mander's *Clearing the Lines* (1951) made in Technicolor for the Marshall Plan, and *The New Boat* (1955) a parable of modernization set in an Indonesian fishing village. However, by the 1950s, with the closure of the government-funded Crown Film Unit and the general decline in demand for documentary, many women found it increasingly difficult to secure commissions and were unable to find equivalent positions of seniority in the feature film industry, where more sexist attitudes existed.

Suggested Reading

Haggith, Toby and Sarah Easen. 'Sisters of the Real', *Viewfinder: The Magazine of the British Universities Film and Video Council*, 46 (March 2002) 12–14.
Easen, Sarah. 'Mary Field', *Viewfinder: The Magazine of the British Universities Film and Video Council*, 55 (June 2004) 27.

Toby Haggith

Domestic Technology

In the first half of the twentieth century scientific knowledge, some of which had been accelerated by the needs of total war, was transformed into technology. This technology was not confined to factories or transportation but was also used in the domestic sphere. Domestic technology brought enormous benefits to women in their role as housewives. In 1900 only a small proportion of HOUSING was wired for electricity and had access to piped water. By 1950 more than two in three houses were supplied with electricity and the same number could rely on a clean water supply. These changes were to transform the work required to maintain comfort and order in the home. Electricity not only made it possible to heat and light homes but also enabled the proliferation of labour-saving devices designed to ease the burden of housework. Vacuum cleaners replaced carpet sweepers, dustpans, and brushes; refrigerators changed the way in which food was bought and stored; the heavy flat irons previously used gave way to electric irons; electric washing machines replaced mangles, possers, and scrubbing boards; and cast-iron stoves and ranges were replaced with easy-to-clean gas and electric cookers.

The provision of piped water, more than any other technology, produced significant changes. Constant hot and cold running water not only made it easier to keep the home clean and comfortable, improving HEALTH by combating diseases linked to polluted water and unsanitary conditions, but also led to new ways of organizing domestic space. A ready supply of water eliminated the back-breaking work of transporting water to where it was needed, and also made possible separate bathrooms and indoor toilets, which enabled new forms of privacy that in turn shaped the ways in which people understood their bodies in relation to others.

Domestic technology transformed not only the work required in running a home but the leisure activities that could, increasingly, take place within it. Radios and, after the Second World War, televisions and music systems, led to a growth in home-based leisure. Women of all classes benefited from the development of domestic technology. However, it was particularly working-class women, who had carried the burden of domestic work both in their own houses and, as SERVANTS, in those of their middle-class employers, for whom the improvements offered by domestic technology were greatest.

Suggested Reading

Bowden, Sue and Avner Offer. 'The Technological Revolution That Never Was: Gender, Class and The Diffusion Of Household Appliances in Interwar England', in Victoria De Grazia and Eileen Furlough (eds), *The Sex of Things: Gender and Consumption in Historical Perspective* (Berkeley, CA: University of California Press, 1996) 244–74.

Giles, Judy. *The Parlour and the Suburb: Domestic Identities, Class, Femininity and Modernity* (Oxford: Berg, 2004).

Judy Giles

Douglas, O. 1878–1948

Pseudonym for Anna Buchan, one of Hodder and Stoughton's 'Big Five' writers, and author of barely fictionalized celebrations of the Glasgow and Borders communities where her father was a Presbyterian minister. As is said of one of her heroines, Douglas is a 'grand praiser'. Despite its setting and episto-lary form, her first novel, *Olivia in India* (1912), has much in common with later books such as *Penny Plain* (1920) and *Eliza for Common* (1928), rejoicing, like them, in the love of the ludicrous and illustrating the dignity of unspectacular private grief. After the deaths of two brothers, one in the First World War, several of Douglas's novels deal with loss, and with war's disruption of the romantic plot. Douglas cautions her 'Gentle Reader' that the 'chronicle' of the wartime novel, *The Setons* (1917), is robbed of an ending. The precariousness of romantic desire is often eclipsed by the pleasures of spinsterhood: orchestrating the potentially anarchic energies of the young, decorating a house, and writing. Douglas herself never married.

In *Pink Sugar* (1924), Douglas dramatizes her awareness that her fiction might be regarded as sentimental. However, she escapes this, and likewise the censure directed at the Kailyard school by her brother, John Buchan, because of her irony, self-awareness, and keen ear for linguistic idiosyncrasy.

Suggested Reading

Dickson, Beth. 'O. Douglas', in Douglas Gifford and Dorothy McMillan (eds), *A History of Scottish Women's Writing* (Edinburgh: Edinburgh University Press, 1987) 329–46.

Forrester, Wendy. *Anna Buchan and O. Douglas* (London: The Maitland Press, 1995).

Mary Grover

Du Maurier, Daphne 1907–1989

Bestselling writer whose career spanned five decades. Daughter of the famous actor, Gerald du Maurier, and granddaughter of George du Maurier (Punch cartoonist and author of *Trilby*), du Maurier was educated in London and France. In 1929 she left London for Cornwall, hoping to establish a distinct and 'authentic' voice for herself. In 1932, she married Major Tommy 'Boy' Browning', and led the life of an army wife. Returning to Cornwall ten years later, she lived from 1943 until 1969 at Menabilly (a run-down mansion near Fowey), lovingly restoring it until evicted by its hereditary owners. She spent the rest of her life at its dower house, Kilmarth.

Du Maurier regarded Cornwall as her natural home, a view now endorsed by the heritage industry, although much of her fiction is not set there. A prolific writer, she is still widely regarded as a lightweight middlebrow novelist, although this view has been challenged by recent critical evaluations; her writing also includes biographies, plays, and short stories. Her work engages with questions of gender, identity, family, and history: novels such as *The Scapegoat* (1957) and *The Flight of the Falcon* (1965), for example, explore masculine identity in the context of a postwar Europe which carries the scars of its history. She was to struggle throughout her career with a belief that creativity was masculine.

Du Maurier's Cornwall is a Gothic landscape in which the past haunts the present. The influence of writers such as the Brontës and R. L. Stevenson is visible in her early Cornish novels, most notably *Jamaica Inn* (1936) and her most famous novel, *Rebecca* (1938), a complex and subtle exploration of feminine identity, adapted by Hitchcock for the screen in 1940. *My Cousin Rachel* (1951) is a Gothic story told by an insecure young man in which the roles of persecutor and victim in a sexually charged family relationship remain ambiguous. *Frenchman's Creek* (1941), an escapist fantasy involving cross-dressing and a refined pirate, helped to create her reputation as a writer of escapist ROMANTIC FICTION for women.

Always fascinated by her French roots, du Maurier wrote a number of books based on her family's history: *The Du Mauriers* (1937), *Mary Anne* (1954), and *The Glass Blowers* (1963). Her biography of her father was published in 1934, shortly after his death. Later in her career, in the 1970s, she wrote biographies of Branwell Brontë and the Bacon brothers.

Du Maurier wrote two successful plays: *The Years Between* (1945) and *September Tide* (1948), and also produced some memorable short fiction, much of which bears the mark of the uncanny. The most famous are 'Don't Look Now' (adapted for the screen in 1973) and 'The Birds' (its Cornish setting and characters abandoned in Hitchcock's 1963 film version).

Suggested Reading

Auerbach, Nina. *Daphne du Maurier, Haunted Heiress* (Philadelphia, PA: University of Pennsylvania Press, 2000).

Horner, Avril and Sue Zlosnik. *Daphne du Maurier: Writing, Identity and the Gothic Imagination* (Basingstoke: Macmillan – now Palgrave Macmillan, 1998).

Light, Alison. *Forever England: Femininity, Literature and Conservatism Between the Wars* (London: Routledge, 1991).

Avril Horner and Sue Zlosnik

E

Education

Education in the first half of the twentieth century was characterized by major legislation and reports and the achievement of secondary education for all, but differentiation along lines of gender and social class remained strong. The Balfour Act of 1902 established Local Education Authorities with powers to provide elementary and secondary schools and teacher training colleges. The Butler Act of 1944 created a Ministry of Education (in place of the previous Board), reorganized public education into three stages – primary, secondary, and further – and made provision for the raising of the school leaving age to 15 (implemented in 1947). Influential reports included those of Hadow on the Education of the Adolescent (1926) and the Primary School (1931). The Newbolt Report of 1921 was concerned with English teaching at all levels, from elementary and preparatory to university and adult. The report affirmed the centrality of English in schools, declaring that 'for English children no form of knowledge can take precedence of a knowledge of English, no form of literature can take precedence of English literature'. The third of its 105 recommendations advised: 'That every teacher is a teacher *of* English because every teacher is a teacher *in* English.'

Gender divisions were reflected in educational outcomes, participation rates and remuneration. Some 84.6 per cent of females born in the first decade of the twentieth century failed to acquire any significant educational qualifications, while only 6.1 per cent gained a professional qualification and 1.1 per cent a university degree. Of the 1940–9 cohort, 46.2 per cent were unqualified, 13.0 per cent achieved a professional qualification, and 5.4 per cent a degree. Corresponding figures for males were 71.4 per cent, 5.6 per cent, and 2.4 per cent for 1900–9; and 35.9 per cent, 17.9 per cent, and 9.7 per cent for 1940–9. In 1929–30 there were 12,921 full-time female and 32,682 male students in British universities. By 1950–1 these figures had risen to 19,483 and 65,831. At the former date 74.7 per cent of women students were studying Arts subjects. This percentage fell to 63.0 per cent in 1950–1. Over the same period the percentage of women studying pure science rose from 15 to 17 per cent and medicine (including HEALTH and dentistry) from 8.8 to 16.6 per cent. Throughout the first half of the twentieth century, women outnumbered men in the teaching force. Census returns for England and Wales in 1901 recorded 171,670 women and 58,675 men as teachers. Corresponding figures for 1951 were 182,409 women and 119,270 men. On average women teachers were paid about three-quarters of the salaries of their male counterparts.

Suggested Reading
Aldrich, Richard (ed.). *A Century of Education* (London: Routledge, 2002).
Gosden, P. H. J. H. *The Evolution of a Profession* (Oxford: Blackwell, 1972).
Halsey, A. H. with Josephine Webb (eds). *Twentieth-Century British Social Trends* (Basingstoke: Palgrave Macmillan, 2000).
Shayer, David. *The Teaching of English in Schools, 1900–1970* (London: Routledge & Kegan Paul, 1972).

Richard Aldrich

Edwards, Dorothy 1903–1934

Dorothy Edwards produced two major works – a collection of short stories, *Rhapsody* (1927), and a novel, *Winter Sonata* (1928) – both of which, like the work of many WELSH women writers, attempted to establish literary links outside of the cultural influence of England, particularly with the Russian novelists Turgenev and Dostoevsky. Although a socialist and a Welsh nationalist, Edwards – being educated, English-speaking, and living in a respectable suburb of Cardiff – found it difficult to actively engage with the Welsh-speaking working classes of the South Wales Valleys. Nor could she imbue her fiction with her ardent political beliefs. Similarly, she found her position as a woman difficult to reconcile with her status as a writer. She wrote in one of her short stories that: 'Women like sibyls, with strength like iron, do not exist anymore. Goddesses are now wisps of things.' When writing in the first person, she always assumed a male perspective.

Her subtle and perceptive prose was praised by critics and she was – briefly – welcomed into both the Garnetts's and BLOOMSBURY literary sets. However, forced into a dual role of protégée and nanny within the Garnetts's household, she found it impossible to write. In 1934 she returned to Cardiff and, after burning her letters and papers, she committed suicide.

Suggested Reading
Jones, S. Beryl. 'Dorothy Edwards as a Writer of Short Stories', *The Welsh Review*, 8.3 (Autumn 1948) 184–93.
Meredith, Luned. 'Dorothy Edwards', *Planet*, 55 (February/March 1986) 50–7.

Rob Gossedge

Empire and Imperialism

Terms described by Edward Said in *Culture and Imperialism* (1993) as the 'practice, theory, and attitudes of a dominating metropolitan centre ruling a distant territory'. *Empire* and *imperialism* should be distinguished from *colony* and *colonialism*, even though the categories are often used interchangeably. Strictly speaking, colonialism refers to the development of actual settlements on the dominated territory in question. In the history of the British Empire, territories such as North America, Australia, and New Zealand are referred to as former 'colonies', because they underwent large-scale immigration and settlement by Britons. By contrast, another major part of the 'empire', India, was not formally settled to this extent, but was administrated (and to all effects governed) by, and dependent on, Britain, and was therefore never technically a 'colony'. The same goes for other important parts of the empire, including the West Indies, areas of Africa, and Malaysia. The confusion partly arises from the fact that both sets of terms have come to define an aggressive form of territorial acquisition and power exerted over the peoples, cultures, lands, and languages, as well as the economic and natural resources of the subjugated nation. Left-leaning critics and commentators also identify a relationship between the aggressive forces of imperialism/colonialism and capitalism, especially when these forces combine to extend the given nation's export markets into another country or territory. Nowadays, the 'British Empire' is a term frequently used to cover all of the above definitions, and describes the entire history of British expansion throughout the world. It defines a long period of British supremacy and domination around the globe, the origins of which might be traced to the early British merchants who began trading in India in about 1608, or even further back to the beginnings of the Atlantic slave trade around 1562. Although this empire had effectively disappeared by the 1960s, the economic, political, social, cultural, and linguistic legacies the British left behind retain an immeasurable significance for the rest of twentieth-century history and beyond.

By 1920, the British Empire had grown to unprecedented proportions. It comprised Canada, parts of the West Indies and west Africa, a line of countries which all but connected Egypt to South Africa, parts of the Middle East including most of modern-day Iraq, India, Burma, areas of Malaysia and Borneo, New Guinea, Australia, New Zealand, and a series of islands and smaller territories throughout the world. Between 1900 and 1950, the organization of this empire had become increasingly complex. This is largely because most of its significant former colonies (by then referred to as Dominions), such as Canada (independent by 1867), most of the Australian territories (independent by 1855, federated by 1901), New Zealand (independent by 1856) and the South African Union (formed in 1910), had by this time all won some form of internal self-governance and autonomy from Britain. This new, more liberal and democratic relationship, renamed the British Commonwealth, only achieved official recognition and implementation with the passing of the Statute of Westminster in 1931. From then on, the Commonwealth alluded to a relationship between Britain and its former colonies technically defined by equal political and economic status. But it also, significantly, described a system of semi-independent nations still united by their common allegiance to the British crown, and this entailed a continued allegiance to British values. Such a commitment had crucial implications for the first half of the twentieth century and beyond, particularly because Britain still dominated the foreign policy of each former colony. During the two world wars, for example, Britain was able to draw upon the vast military and economic resources of the Commonwealth, and many Commonwealth citizens lost their lives fighting under the name of the British Empire. Although many commentators attribute the eventual disintegration of the British Empire to the crises generated before and by WORLD WAR ONE, events such as these also attest to that empire's continuing strength and influence throughout the globe. The war tested and to some extent verified the integrity and cohesiveness of the relationship between Britain and its empire. Britain actually gained more territory after the Great War, especially from the defeated empires of Germany and Turkey, and the decline of the empire only really began to take effect after the global upheavals generated by the Second World War and its aftermath. India, for instance, which had become Britain's famous 'jewel' in the imperial crown, only achieved formal political independence in 1947, after which it, too, was subsumed within the British Commonwealth.

The twentieth century was heralded by Britain's involvement in a more notorious war of Empire: the second BOER WAR (1899–1902) in South Africa between British forces and settlers of Dutch origin. The conflict represented the latest outbreak in the 'Scramble for Africa' campaigns, the last phase of large-scale European expansion waged across that continent from the 1880s onwards. On the domestic front, there were also continuing tensions with the IRISH QUESTION. Although Ireland had been subject to British settlement and rule for centuries, the Irish Home Rule Party eventually won an important victory in the creation of the Irish Free State (Eire) in 1922. Unfortunately for Ireland, any concessions granted by the British government during these years were themselves problematic. The question of Britain's relationship with Ireland came to be seen by pro-imperialist Britons as a benchmark for both the British Empire's world role and the start of its decline. In an age of both nationalism and imperialism, when so many European nations, like Ireland, Germany, Italy, and Russia, were striving to assert themselves on the world stage, Britain became increasingly concerned with preserving the way its own sense of nationhood was bound up in its Empire. It was therefore reluctant to surrender Ireland completely. This explains why Eire remained part of the Commonwealth for such a long period after these events, holding a similar status to Canada.

Published during a period which more or less oversaw both the rise and fall of the British Empire, British writing between 1900 and 1950 consequently exists in climactic years. By the turn of the century, the Empire had begun to resonate throughout British culture. Africa and India, in particular, found increasing representation in the novels and poetry of the day, especially in the work of writers like Rudyard Kipling, Joseph Conrad, and E. M. Forster. A series of gung-ho masculine adventure stories and comic books for boys also appeared, including *The Boys Own Paper* (first published in 1879) and the much shorter lived *Boys of Our Empire* (first published in 1902). The cultivation of imperial attitudes and Englishness in the nation's youth was further consolidated by the foundation of the Boys Brigade (1883), and the Boy Scout (1908) and Girl Guide (1912) movements in the prewar period. Meanwhile, the idea of empire began to permeate the nation's theatre, music, and music-hall entertainments for adults. It also became ever more visible through its promotion in CONSUMER advertisements, and in the increasing amount of foreign and exotic goods available throughout the British marketplace.

The relationship between the British Empire and women's writing between 1900 and 1950 is complex. On one level, as with men's writing, it is connected to the way in which notions of the nation state, nationalism, race, and the 'British' identity came to be perceived, or rather rearticulated in the period. Between 1901 and 1912, for example, some 63 per cent of all British emigrants moved to a Commonwealth territory, and most of these to the 'Dominions' of Canada and Australia. The ensuing sense of displacement, and its implications, are reflected in British women's writing. This is especially true of those women writing from these imperial margins, those encountering new cultures or 'colonial' identities, and also those moving back and forth between these margins and Britain. Writers like Rumer GODDEN, Katherine MANSFIELD, Elspeth HUXLEY, Jean RHYS, Flora Annie STEEL, Ngaio MARSH, and Eliot BLISS are all significant in this respect. Equally important is the manner in which these writers, all of whom are influenced by their relationship to the context of displacement and exchange, negotiate crucial factors such as gender, sexuality, work, marriage, the family, domesticity, the home, class, race, and the role of the 'imperial mother'. Other specifically British writers, whose work approaches and complicates many of these issues and problems in the domestic context, include Dorothy RICHARDSON, Sylvia Townsend WARNER, Mary BUTTS and Virginia WOOLF.

Suggested Reading

Garrity, Jane. *Step-Daughters of England: British Woman Modernists and the National Imaginary* (Manchester: Manchester University Press, 2003).

Harlow, Barbara and Mia Carter (eds). *Imperialism and Orientalism: A Documentary Sourcebook* (Oxford: Blackwell, 1999).

Marshall, P. J. (ed.). *The Cambridge Illustrated History of the British Empire* (Cambridge: Cambridge University Press, 1996).

Said, Edward W. *Culture and Imperialism* (London: Vintage, 1994).

Tylee, Claire M. *The Great War and Women's Consciousness: Images of Militarism and Womanhood in Women's Writings, 1914–64* (Basingstoke: Macmillan, 1990).

Sean Purchase

English Association

Founded in 1906 by a group of teachers and scholars, among them F. S. Boas, A. C. Bradley, and Sir Israel Gollancz, with the aim of developing English teaching and scholarship in schools, colleges, and universities. Presidents of the Association have been highly distinguished authors, academics, clergymen, and public figures, and in the period to 1950, they included Sir Edmund Gosse (1922), John Galsworthy (1924), and Sir Osbert Sitwell (1947). The first female President was Lady Ritchie (1912), but no other woman held the post until Clemence DANE in 1961. The English Association has gradually become an international organization which sponsors a wide range of events and publications.

Faye Hammill

Eugenics

The term eugenics – 'that science which deals with all influences which improve the inborn qualities of a race' – was coined by Sir Francis Galton in 1883; theories were initially based on pre-Mendelian assumptions of the unproblematic transmission of desirable and undesirable characteristics. In terms of policy, eugenics had two facets, 'positive' and 'negative': the 'fit' should reproduce themselves at (at least) replacement rate, while the 'unfit' should be discouraged from perpetuating themselves.

As institutionally embodied in the British Eugenics Education Society (founded 1907), eugenics appeared to reinforce male meritocratic values. However, ideas about 'breeding', good and bad, were miasmatically pervasive and not necessary correlated with the Society's pronouncements. Appeals to eugenics could be critically and subversively made against existing economic and social arrangements; for example, some feminists suggested that female mate-choice would improve a race degenerating under patriarchy. The term was often used very loosely: it was frequently inflected with neo-Lamarckian notions of inheritance of acquired characteristics, while strictly hereditary defects were frequently confused with congenital disorders, in particular those resulting from venereal diseases. Many examples of contradictory and unexamined uses of ideas about 'breeding' can be found in the literature of the time.

Eugenics is often assumed to have logically culminated in the excesses of the German Third Reich. This is only one story: the idea had a strong appeal across the political spectrum, given its association with modernity and the promises of science. What 'eugenics' meant in particular contexts and at specific moments, or to any given individual, varied enormously. Eugenic policies could cover a wide range: immigration restriction, premarital HEALTH examinations, sterilization of the 'unfit', research into birth control, legalization of ABORTION, and maternal WELFARE measures. During the 1930s, and possibly in response to what were perceived even then as the unscientific excesses of the Third Reich, there was a shift in British eugenic circles to a new 'reform' eugenics, as Mendelian genetics rendered the whole concept much more complex, and scientific developments in fields such as nutrition indicated the continuing importance of environmental factors.

Eugenics fell into disrepute because of the abuses of the Nazis, but recent developments in genetics have led to the recrudescence of notions that 'it's all in our genes', and suggestions that developments in prenatal screening and genetic engineering are reintroducing a crypto-eugenic agenda under the rhetoric of 'choice'.

Suggested Reading

Hall, Lesley A. 'Women, Feminism and Eugenics', in Robert A. Peel (ed.), *Essays in the History of Eugenics: Proceedings of a Conference Organised by the Galton Institute, London, 1997* (London: The Galton Institute, 1998) 36–51.

Kevles, Daniel. *In the Name of Eugenics: Genetics and the Uses of Human Heredity* (Cambridge, MA, and London: Harvard University Press, 1995).

Soloway, Richard A. *Demography and Degeneration: Eugenics and the Declining Birthrate in Twentieth-Century Britain* (Chapel Hill, NC: University of North Carolina Press, 1990).

Lesley A. Hall

Evans, Margiad 1909–1958

Pseudonym for the novelist, poet, and short-story writer, Peggy Eileen Whistler. Born in Uxbridge, London, to English parents she adopted a distinctly WELSH name after she underwent what she later described as a mystical experience while visiting relatives on the Anglo-Welsh border. Her fiction, beginning with *Country Dance* (1932) – a novel concerned with the divided love of Ann Goodman for two lovers, one Welsh the other English – consistently explores the themes of personal and political allegiances, divisions, and discord that are inherent in Evans's perception of Borderlands.

Her three later novels – *The Wooden Doctor* (1933), *Turf or Stone* (1934), and *Creed* (1936) – all received much praise from contemporary critics for their MODERNIST depictions of love, sex, illness, and death in restrictive moral environments. In nearly all her fiction she attempted to define Man's relation to God within a consistently bleak environment, only briefly relieved by intensely comic moments.

In 1950 she was diagnosed as epileptic and a few months later she gave birth to her only child. Her final work, the autobiographical *Ray of Darkness* (1952), understands these traumatic events as themselves belonging to the Border experience. They also contain some of the finest descriptions of epilepsy since the writings of Dostoevsky.

Suggested Reading
Lloyd-Morgan, Ceridwen. 'Portrait of a Border Writer: The Life and Work of Margiad Evans', *Planet*, 107 (October/November, 1994) 45–57.
Lloyd-Morgan, Ceridwen. *Margiad Evans* (Bridgend: Seren, 1998).

Rob Gossedge

Eyles, Leonora 1889–1960

Novelist, author of polemical texts and prolific journalist. Leonora Eyles's writing was an expression of her feminist and SOCIALIST convictions. She was born Leonora Pitcairn, to a well-to-do family of Staffordshire pottery owners, but an idyllic childhood was followed by poverty and hardship when her parents died and Leonora ran away from home and a stepmother she detested. Alone in London at the age of 18, she worked addressing envelopes and often went hungry, before answering an advertisement for domestic SERVANTS to go to Australia. Selling the few possessions left to her by her mother, she sailed in 1907 with only ten shillings to her name. In Australia she enjoyed the experience of working hard on the land, later writing that it was then that she changed from 'a timid-mouse sort of person to a fighter'. Her determination and independence (she resolved that no man would ever support her and, with some pride, wrote in 1926 'and no one ever has'), together with her writing ability, proved her salvation. Beating 500 others to a job writing charity appeals advertised in *The Times* was the beginning of Eyles's career as a professional writer.

During the First World War, she volunteered as one of 2000 women working on the munitions at Woolwich Arsenal. Then came an intensive period of journalism and book writing. Fiction, for her, was part of a political project, as exemplified by her first novel, the bestselling *Margaret Protests* (1919), the subtext of which was CONTRACEPTION. As a journalist, Eyles wrote for left-wing and women's publications including George Lansbury's *Labour Leader*, the woman's page of the *Daily Herald* and, under the pen name 'Martha', the women's page of *The Miner* in 1927. She became a widely read and respected agony aunt, with advice columns in WOMEN'S MAGAZINES such as *Modern Woman* in the 1920s and the popular weekly *Woman's Own* in 1932.

A relatively forgotten figure today, Eyles is perhaps best known for her documentary book *The Woman in the Little House* (1922), a study of working women's lives in Peckham, South London, and their unrelenting struggle with ill-adapted, inconvenient HOUSING, and lack of money and privacy. A work of social investigation, it was based on her own experience as 'one who had lived in that home and known its misery', after she was abandoned by her alcoholic husband, A. W. Eyles, and left to support three young children. By 1932 her circumstances had changed and she was happily married to David Murray (editor of *The Times Literary Supplement*, 1938–44), with a country house in Sussex.

The 'woman question' and an impassioned plea for improved conditions for women as mothers, wives, daughters, and workers remained, nevertheless, at the heart of her work.

Publications include: *Captivity* (1922), *Hidden Lives* (1922), *Women's Problems To*-day (1926), *Eat Well in Wartime* (1940), *Unmarried but Happy* (1947), *Commonsense About Sex* (1956), and an autobiography, *The Ram Escapes: The Story of a Victorian Childhood* (1953).

Suggested Reading

Beauman, Nicola. *A Very Great Profession, The Woman's Novel, 1914–1939* (London: Virago, 1983).

Joannou, Maroula. *'Ladies Please Don't Smash These Windows': Women's Writing, Feminist Consciousness and Social Change, 1918–38* (Oxford: Berg, 1995).

Fiona Hackney

F

Fabians

The Fabian Society took its name from the Roman dictator Fabius, whose military successes were the result of his preference for piecemeal skirmishes. Founded in 1884 by a group of predominantly middle-class intellectuals, the Society aimed to further 'the reconstruction of Society in accordance with the highest moral principles', which for the Fabians meant SOCIALISM. This was to be achieved through democratic and gradual, non-revolutionary means. The Fabians therefore sought to influence government and affect policy through the permeation of institutions by social reformist ideas, rather than by direct power. Fabians criticized the existing system as inefficient and wasteful, and argued that a bureaucratic elite should administer a centrally planned economy to remove the inefficiencies inherent in society, with the aim of combating unemployment and poverty. Their 'inevitability of gradualness' was the philosophy of missionary educators wedded to reform through collectivist solutions, which they felt could be urged upon reforming governments. This call for social justice and a belief in the progressive improvement of society attracted a membership of politicians, intellectuals, artists, and writers, ranging from Keir Hardie, Ramsay Macdonald, and Emmeline PANKHURST to H. G. Wells, Edith NESBIT and Rebecca WEST. This membership carried Fabian influence into local and central government, literature, academia, and the colonies.

With George Bernard Shaw and Sidney and Beatrice WEBB as leaders, the Society gained widespread recognition and helped found the Labour Representation Committee in 1900, which in 1906 became the Labour Party, whilst the New Fabian Research Bureau contributed to the intellectual credibility of the Party. The Fabian idea that the state had a responsibility to create a minimal provision of social WELFARE to enable individuals to reach their uppermost potential also had a marked influence on the welfare reforms introduced by the Edwardian Liberal Party. Fabian Society pamphlets presented a programme for reform; for example, in 1906 it called for the introduction of a minimum wage and in 1911 proposed the creation of a National Health Service. Fabian summer schools, like the Clarion cycling clubs, which became a feature of Fabianism, sought to improve leisure activities, combining lectures on the great issues of the day with exercise. At another level, the Fabian Women's Group became involved in the SUFFRAGE campaign and promoted the need to expand the WOMEN'S MOVEMENT beyond political demands to include issues of economic reform. It also pressed for state-financed family allowances to compensate for the unpaid labour of mothers and guarantee the HEALTH and welfare of their children. However, the Fabians' record of success in promoting socialism was more limited than the attention they attracted, or the influence they were able to exert on the ideas of politicians, intellectuals, artists, and writers.

Suggested Reading

Britain, Ian. *Fabianism and Culture: A Study in British Socialism and the Arts, 1884–1918* (Cambridge: Cambridge University Press, 1982).

MacKenzie, Norman and Jeanne MacKenzie. *The First Fabians* (London: Weidenfeld & Nicolson, 1977).

Terrins, Deirdre and Phillip Whitehead. *100 Years of Fabian Socialism, 1884–1984* (London: Fabian Society, 1984).

Keir Waddington

Farjeon, Eleanor 1881–1965

Novelist, autobiographer, and children's writer, best remembered for her poem 'Morning Has Broken'. While Farjeon wrote 12 novels for adults and two autobiographies, she is generally known as a writer for children. Her religious poems for children were particularly popular, and her work is characterized by enthusiasm for life and faith in the decency of humankind.

Born in London into a literary family, Farjeon enjoyed a childhood surrounded by books – as she later said: 'It would have been more natural to live without clothes than without books.' Indeed, Farjeon's father Benjamin was a novelist and later Eleanor established close friendships with two poets, Robert Frost and Edward Thomas. Though it seems that she fell into unrequited love with Edward Thomas, it was not until she was in her forties that she began a serious romantic relationship: she eloped with a schoolmaster, George Earle, in 1920, and they lived together until his death in 1949.

Farjeon's first autobiography, *A Nursery in the Nineties* (1935), evokes vivid images of life in Victorian and Edwardian England. Her earliest literary success was *Nursery Rhymes of London Town* (1916), a compilation of verses from her time at *Punch*, concerning London street and district names. She made several contributions to *Punch* between 1916 and 1933, with a final entry being a poem entitled 'Come, Commander, Come!' printed in 1942. Her story collection *Martin Pippin in the Apple Orchard* (1921) reflects her love of Sussex and was considered an adult's book until C. E. Brock illustrated it in 1925, after which it was generally categorized as CHILDREN'S LITERATURE. It was followed by *Martin Pippin in the Daisy Field* (1937), and these books are typical of Farjeon's collections, which tend to be intrinsically linked by an emphasis on good overcoming evil.

Farjeon's most famous volume of short fiction, *The Little Bookroom* (1955), was highly regarded in its time and won her both the Carnegie Medal and the Hans Christian Anderson International Medal. Many of these stories have a playful, fairy-tale like content and they tend to promote clear morals. 'The

Seventh Princess', for example, warns of the perils of vanity: it concerns six princesses who 'lived for the sake of their hair alone', competing for the prince's hand in marriage, which was to go to the princess with the longest hair. The seventh princess, however, has short hair and goes out to experience the world: she 'tied on her red handkerchief and ran out of the palace to the hills and the river and the meadows and the markets'.

It seems fitting that Morag Styles says that Farjeon had 'a sweet lyrical, voice and a child-centred vision of the world', and compares some of her work to Christina Rossetti's. Farjeon published several collections of poetry for children, including *Silver-Sand and Snow* (1951) and *The Children's Bells* (1957), the latter being a selection of her personal favourites, but her verse is now most often encountered in anthologies of children's poetry. While her work is no longer widely read or published, her contribution to children's literature is still recognized by the Children's Book Circle, who offer an Eleanor Farjeon Award each year for 'distinguished service to children's books'.

Suggested Reading

Farjeon, Annabel. *Morning Has Broken: A Biography of Eleanor Farjeon* (London: Julia MacRae Books, 1986).

Harvey, Anne. 'Elsie Piddock: Then and Now', *Signal*, 99 (2002) 156–76.

Styles, Morag. *From the Garden to the Street: An Introduction to Three Hundred Years of Poetry for Children* (London: Cassel, 1998).

Ann Alston

Fascism

A political ideology of the earlier decades of the twentieth century, fascism arose in opposition to communism, and was founded on the belief that the individual should be subjugated to the needs of the state, which should have a strong leader embodying the nation's will. A major British branch was founded by Sir Oswald Mosley in 1931 and first known as the New Party, but was renamed as the British Union of Fascists (BUF) in 1932. The party integrated the British Fascisti, the oldest UK fascist organization which was founded by Miss Rotha Lintorn-Orman in 1923. Opposing the union of the two groups, she meant the BF to encourage independence and self-reliance in women, to combat SOCIALIST Sunday schools and to establish BF children's clubs. The BF split in 1925 with the formation of the National Fascists, a group of about 100 that broke away on the grounds that the BF were not sufficiently anti-Semitic nor fascist. The BF split again in 1931 when the party accepted Mosley's merger terms, which were opposed by the women on the committee. A number of smaller groups also resisted integration into the BUF, including the Fascist League, the British Empire and Fascists, and Arnold Spenser Leese's Imperial Fascist League (IFL). The principal difference between the racial nationalism of Leese's tiny IFL, the militant conservatism of the British Fascists, and the racial planning of the BUF was the role anti-Semitism initially played in their respective movements.

Oswald Mosley sacrificed his career in the Labour Party because of what he perceived as the fundamental failure of the Labour, Liberal Democrat, and Conservative Parties to stem the growing economic DEPRESSION and the rise of mass unemployment, numbered at two million in mid-1930. Convinced of his own political destiny, Mosley broke away from friends and supporters to model his movement closely upon the fascist developments that he had witnessed in Germany and Italy. His movement's elaborate symbolism involved ceremonials and a distinct dress code, including black blouses with matching skirts and berets for the women recruited by Mosley's mother, Lady Maud Mosley, who had become director of organization of the Women's Section. In 1932, Oswald Mosley stated his belief that women's sphere was that of motherhood and domestic responsibilities. However, a 1935 pamphlet published by a leading BUF activist, Anne Brock Griggs, aimed at the women's vote by emphasizing women's career choices. She defended women's right to work and their electoral representation by a domestic corporation should they wish to stay at home. BUF Women activists such as Commandant Mary Allen, head of the Women's Auxiliary Service, Norah Elam, and Mary Richardson, later expelled for a personal attack on Mosley's leadership, had either a suffragette background or compared their political activities in the BUF with the SUFFRAGE movement. Mosely's systematic propaganda trained women to speak in public, study ju-jitsu, and set up Propaganda Patrol Squads.

Following the death of his first wife, Mosley was married again in 1936 to Diana Freeman-Mitford, sister of the novelist Nancy MITFORD. Contrary to their other sisters, Diana and Unity Mitford, both personally acquainted with Hitler, had joined the BUF in its early days.

Overall, the BUF generally failed to attract a mass membership from the millions of unemployed that it sought to support. Membership reached 50,000 at its peak in 1934, collapsing to approximately 5000 in 1935 and rising back to 20,000 in 1939. Membership fees were supplemented by Mosley's personal donations and Mussolini's presumed financial support; membership figures also improved with a public campaign by the press magnate Lord Rothermere. Rothermere's retreat from the BUF in 1934, following the Olympia meeting hastened its demise. This failure was partly due to a temporary improvement in the British economy, but the increasingly violent public image of the party was a more significant factor. The extremely large Olympia meeting on 7 June 1934 turned public opinion against the BUF: the violent systematic removal of female and male interrupters during Mosley's speech reinforced the fascists' reputation for brutality, hitherto seen mainly in Germany. The public discussion following the event marked a steep decline in BUF's support and membership. Yet, even with the BUF turning increasingly to political anti-Semitism and attacks on Jewish property, the party was not quashed following the outbreak of war in Europe. Mosley and others were interned in 1940 by the Security Service only when evidence emerged of their potentially treasonable behaviour.

Suggested Reading

Cross, Colin. *The Fascists in Britain* (London: Barrie & Rockliff, 1961).
Durham, Martin. *Women and Fascism* (London: Routledge, 1998).
Thurlow, Richard. *Fascism in Britain: A History, 1918–1985* (Oxford: Basil Blackwell, 1987).

Jana Nittel

Fashion and Youth Culture

Early twentieth-century fashion and youth culture in Britain were heavily influenced by America, particularly during the period described by F. Scott Fitzgerald as the 'Jazz Age'. In Britain, a group known as the Bright Young Things (BYTs) emerged. These were a fashionable younger generation renowned for their extravagant and outrageous behaviour. An article in the *Morning Post* dated 15 July 1914 describes 'a section of the community... whose life seems to consist of cocktail and sherry parties, cabaret and midnight revelries... There are decadent "bright young things".' The heyday of the BYT is considered to have been the years between 1926 and 1929. Their largely high-society London lives were characterized by endless drinking, smoking, dancing, and cavorting. Women's fashions amongst BYTs indicate a radical departure from conventional dress codes, and as early as 1925 a more 'manly' or gamine look had become *de rigeur*. Garments included 'shirt skirts' and baggy trousers, often measuring up to 32 inches at the bottom and known as 'Oxford bags' (from their origins around the University), as well as Fair Isle pullovers, felt hats, and severe bobbed hairstyles. Such boyish fashions, often worn by wealthy society women and popular actresses, were influenced by Parisian *haute couture*, and in particular Coco Chanel's chic and androgynous designs. The BYTs were made famous in novels such as Evelyn Waugh's satirical *Vile Bodies* (1930), set in Mayfair. They also featured in works as late as Waugh's close friend Nancy MITFORD's *The Pursuit of Love* (1945), and Winifred WATSON's *Miss Pettigrew Lives for a Day* (1938).

The concept of 'the flapper' is also integral to the period, and particularly the twenties. The 'flapper' generally describes a young woman approaching maturity, who displays unconventional or flighty opinions, wears risqué skirts, and is frequently marked by a lack of decorum or by silliness. In America the flapper is, to some extent, a descendant of the 'Gibson girl', a term attributable to the magazine illustrations of Charles Dana Gibson. In the early 1900s, Gibson portrayed the 'ideal' American woman as glamorous, with a distinctly aristocratic sense of independence and an improbably narrow waist; Gibson girls wore good clothes, were self-assured, and at one stage even had bizarre, vertically inclined hair. With the rise in the twenties of the less lofty-sounding 'flapper', popular images of fashionable young women become less dignified. 'Flapper', a term which describes the flapping about of ungainly ducks, gave rise to derivatives such as 'flapperdom' or 'flapperhood', and seems to have its origins in the image of 'flapping' clothes and hair. Unlike the Gibson girl, flappers were caricatured as giddy good-time girls, with skinny and angular, frequently boyish or asexual physiques, who seemed all 'freckles and pigtails'. They were further distinguished by a certain pre-nubile, money-hungry pluck, but also a very modern sense of leisureliness. Various images, in particular those associated with the 1920s American cartoonist John Held (the man largely responsible for mythologizing the era as that of the flapper), depict the flappers as audacious, reckless, immoral, but attractive flirts. Largely because of this, their image became very successful in promoting fashionable and desirable items like cigarettes, clothing, handbags, and accessories. Held's illustrations abound with flappers reeling about in rolled stockings and short skirts, with cropped or bobbed hair, lolling over men at noisy jazz parties.

Definitive American accounts of the flapper include Anita Loos's witty *Gentlemen Prefer Blondes* (1925) and the numerous excursions into flapperdom by F. Scott Fitzgerald. Fitzgerald described his first book, *This Side of Paradise* (1920), as 'a novel about flappers written by philosophers', and his second was called *Flappers and Philosophers* (1920). But the flapper found various other manifestations in British and American popular culture and entertainment. Early appearances can be found in Jesse Greer's 1926 piano novelty, *Flapperette*, and there was a series of musicals in the 1920s featuring flappers. These include *Running Wild* (1923), which is widely believed to have introduced the Charleston dance, and Vincent Youmans's smash hit, *No, No, Nanette* (1925), in which a group of young girls appeared on stage just before the finale, singing: 'Flappers are we...most flippant flappers are we.' Flappers were quickly condemned as decadent by churchmen and moralists, and films such as 'The Flapper' (1920) and 'Exalted Flapper' (1929) were heavily criticized. The derogatory term, 'flapper vote', became media currency in Britain during the parliamentary debate surrounding universal female suffrage, which was eventually granted to women of 21 and over in 1928. The term alludes to a certain anxiety, on the part of men, towards women gaining a disproportionate amount of political influence. A related concept in British culture, the 'it' girl, is another Jazz Age term denoting fashionable and youthful sex appeal, one attributed to British novelist Elinor GLYN. Glyn, along with other writers such as Rebecca WEST and Iris BARRY, travelled between Britain and America, and consequently became directly involved in jazz culture.

Suggested Reading

Breward, Christopher. *The Culture of Fashion* (Manchester: Manchester University Press, 1995).

Kitch, Caroline. *The Girl on the Magazine Cover: The Origins of Visual Stereotypes in American Mass Media* (London and Chapel Hill, NC: University of North Carolina Press, 2001).

Melman, Billie. *Women and the Popular Imagination in the 1920s: Flappers and Nymphs* (London: Macmillan, 1988).

Montgomery, John. *The Twenties* (London: George Allen & Unwin, 1957).

Shaw, Arnold. *The Jazz Age: Popular Music in the 1920s* (Oxford: Oxford University Press, 1987).

Sean Purchase

Ferguson, Rachel 1893–1957

Suffragette, actress, journalist, and novelist, best known for her popular 'Rachel' column in *Punch* and her novel *The Brontës Went to Woolworths* (1931). Ferguson, daughter of a Treasury official, was educated privately in Kensington and Italy, and joined the WOMEN'S MOVEMENT, co-founding the juvenile branch of the Women's Social and Political Union (WSPU) and writing a play for the militants. In 1913 she graduated from the Academy of Dramatic Art, but her acting career was cut short by the war, in which she served in the Women's Volunteer Reserve.

She began writing a drama column in the *Sunday Chronicle*; published her first novel, *False Goddesses*, in 1923, and two years later moved to *Punch*. Her reputation was established with *The Brontës Went to Woolworths*, an eccentric and witty novel about a family of three daughters who dramatize their lives through their literary imaginations: 'Katrine was so depressed that she strode like Mrs Crummles, and I was so rasped with life that I hit Goldsmith's tomb with my umbrella.' They are fascinated with the lives of other social classes: Lord Justice Toddington is the key character in their fantasy saga, but they also visit cheap music-halls: 'we both love the twice-a-night atmosphere, and the sequins that are missing from the tabs, and the hurried overture with the band wiping the beer from its lips.'

Ferguson published nine further novels, mainly social comedies, and two volumes of satirical memoirs, *Passionate Kensington* (1939) and *Royal Borough* (1950).

Suggested Reading

Byatt, A. S. Introduction to *The Brontës Went to Woolworths* by Rachel Ferguson (London: Virago, 1987) iii–xiii.

Humble, Nicola. *The Feminine Middlebrow Novel, 1920s to 1950s: Class, Domesticity, and Bohemianism* (Oxford: Oxford University Press, 2001).

Faye Hammill

Frankau, Pamela 1908–1967

Offspring of an Anglo-Jewish literary family, Pamela Frankau published her first novel, *The Marriage of Harlequin* (1927) (written while commuting from her divorced mother's home in Windsor to work in London), at 19 and her first memoir, *I Find Four People* (1935), before she was 30. As well as nearly 30 novels (the last, *Colonel Blessington* (1968), edited by her cousin and published posthumously), she produced short stories, *belles-lettres*, and *Pen to Paper: A Novelist's Notebook* (1961). Her works include incisive comment on society and personal relationships, and reflect her experiences in advertising and journalism. She also tackled paranormal and speculative themes – *A Democrat Dies* (1939) is a political fantasy, and Thomas's clairvoyant and healing abilities play a significant role in the trilogy *Clothes of a King's Son* (1963–7) – and produced a revisionist account of the Biblical 'harlot queen' Jezebel (1937).

From 1931, she had an extra-marital relationship with the poet Humbert Wolfe (d. 1940). During the Second World War she served in the ATS, rising from private to major, and in 1942 converted from Anglicanism to Roman Catholicism. Her 1945 marriage to Marshall Dill, Jr, was dissolved, and her only child died in infancy. She also had relationships with women, a theme obliquely addressed in her novels. Her best known work is probably the novella, 'The Duchess and the Smugs', incorporated into her novel *A Wreath for the Enemy* (1954), reprinted along with *The Willow Cabin* (1949) and *The Winged Horse* (1953) by VIRAGO in the 1980s.

Suggested Reading

Barker, Raffaella. Introduction to *Wreath for the Enemy* by Pamela Frankau (London: Virago, 1988) i–xv.

York, Susannah. Introduction to *The Willow Cabin* by Pamela Frankau (London: Virago, 1988) x–xiii.

Lesley A. Hall

G

General Strike

As a result of an economic crisis in the mining industry in 1925, miners' wages were to be reduced. Stanley Baldwin's government declared a nine-month subsidy of miners' wages as the Royal Commission on the Coal Industry – headed by Sir Herbert Samuel – examined the problems of the mining industry. The Royal Commission's report was published in March 1926 and recommended that the subsidy be withdrawn and wages reduced in order to save the industry. The mine owners then published new terms of employment which included an extension of the seven-hour working day and a reduction in wages. The Trade Union Congress met on this date to announce that a General Strike 'in defence of miners' wages and hours' would begin on the third of the month and last for nine days. The TUC called the strike on the understanding that they would take over negotiations from the Miners' Federation. Concerned that a widespread strike could lead to revolution, the TUC only called out three million men from key industries (such as railway workers, iron and steel workers, dockers, printers). During the previous nine months, the Government had prepared for a labour dispute so that, during the strike, armed forces and volunteer workers maintained basic services. Anti-strike feelings were aroused through emphasizing the revolutionary nature of the strikers.

On 7 May the TUC – without the knowledge of the Miners' Federation – met with Sir Herbert Samuel to negotiate an end to the dispute. The proposals included a minimum wage for colliery workers, alternative employment for miners displaced by pit closures and a National Wages Board. The Miners' Federation rejected the proposals. On the 11th the TUC accepted the terms and called off the strike. Although the TUC had requested that the government ensure that there were no reprisals against the miners, this was refused. Miners continued to strike without widespread support for the next six months. Economic hardship forced most of them back into the pits by the end of November 1926. Some miners were victimized for their strike actions and those who did return to the pits had to accept longer hours and lower wages. In 1927 the Government passed the Trade Disputes and Trade Union Act, making all sympathetic strikes and mass picketing illegal and forbidding the Civil Service unions from affiliating with the TUC.

Suggested Reading
Laybourn, Keith. *The General Strike of 1926* (Manchester: Manchester University Press, 1993).

Stacy Gillis

Georgian Poetry

The use and abuse of the term 'Georgian' slides between periodization (all poetry written during the reign of George V, between 1910 and 1936); Edward Marsh's five *Georgian Poetry* anthologies published between 1912 and 1922; a list of variable names such as Rupert Brooke, John Masefield, Walter De La Mare, and D. H. Lawrence; and a set of characteristics which include a rural setting, colloquial diction, and regular rhyme and form. In becoming polarized to 'BLOOMSBURY', 'Georgian' was caricatured by its weakest aspects and pejoratively associated with escapism, sentimentality, and archaism. Paradoxically, Marsh's intention was to be 'modern' in discarding the abstractions and high diction of Edwardian verse. The Georgian focus on landscape was meant to be a stand against the ravages of urban development, largely for postwar HOUSING. The contemporary idiom made poetry more widely accessible and the recorded sales of Marsh's first four volumes were between 15,000 and 19,000.

Fredegond Shove was chosen as the first, arguably token, woman for *Georgian Poetry, 1918–1919*. Other candidates were Rose MACAULAY, Edith SITWELL and Charlotte MEW. The following and final volume (1920–2) was dedicated to Alice MEYNELL and included seven poems by Vita SACKVILLE-WEST. Women's poetry which qualifies chronologically or technically in its directness, psychological realism or rural environments include the earlier work of Sackville-West, Sylvia LYND, Frances BELLERBY and Dorothy WELLESLEY.

Suggested Reading

Walter, George. 'Loose Women and Lonely Lambs: The Rise and Fall of Georgian Poetry', in Gary Day and Brian Docherty (eds), *British Poetry, 1900–50: Aspects of Tradition* (Basingstoke: Macmillan – now Palgrave Macmillan, 1995) 14–36.

Jane Dowson

Gibbons, Stella 1902–1989

Novelist, short-story writer, poet, and journalist, best known for her immensely successful parodic novel *Cold Comfort Farm* (1932). Gibbons's work earned admiration from many respected writers and intellectuals, and she was elected a Fellow of the Royal Society of Literature in 1950. Nonetheless, her reputation remains firmly middlebrow, a standing she deliberately cultivates in her foreword to *Cold Comfort Farm*: 'I found, after spending ten years as a journalist, learning to say exactly what I meant in short sentences, that I must learn, if I was to achieve literature and favourable reviews, to write as though I were not quite sure what I meant but was jolly well going to say something all the same in sentences as long as possible.'

Gibbons's parody is directed at the fashionable excesses of various literary genres. She described her first published poem, 'The Marshes of My Soul' (1921), as a parody of 'the latest School of Decoratively-Melancholy

Introspectives'. Other early poems mocked MODERNIST experimentation, *vers libre*, and sentimental verse. Her first novel, *Cold Comfort Farm*, targets the popular REGIONAL fiction of Mary WEBB, Constance HOLME and Sheila KAYE-SMITH, as well as canonical rural novels by Emily Brontë, Thomas Hardy, and D. H. Lawrence. The book was awarded the prestigious PRIX FEMINA-VIE HEUREUSE, but was banned by the Irish Free State for its endorsement of CONTRACEPTION.

Stella Gibbons lived for her whole life in Hampstead, North London. Her melodramatic, violent family were not dissimilar to the Starkadders in *Cold Comfort Farm*, and she sought refuge from them in literature, particularly in Romantic poetry and popular late-Victorian novelists – especially Ouida, whose work eventually inspired Gibbons's fantasy novel *Ticky* (1943). Gibbons trained as a journalist at London University in the early 1920s, and began her career at the British United Press. She lost her post in 1926 after miscalculating a currency exchange rate and causing a stock market crash, and went on to work at the London *Evening Standard* and *The Lady*.

During this period, she contributed serious poems to the *London Mercury*, *Queen*, *Country Life*, the *Saturday Review*, and the *New Adelphi*. A particular success was 'The Giraffes' published in T. S. Eliot's *Criterion* in 1927, and admired by Elizabeth BOWEN and Virginia WOOLF. In 1933, Gibbons married Allan Webb, an opera singer, and their daughter was born in 1935. In the 1950s, she became a regular contributor to *Punch*. By 1970, when her last book appeared, she had published 23 novels, three collections of poetry, three volumes of short stories, and a children's book. Most of her novels achieved reasonable sales and favourable reviews, particularly *Nightingale Wood* (1938) and *Starlight* (1967). She was profoundly affected by the war, during which she wrote two of her most accomplished books, *The Bachelor* (1944) and *Westwood* (1946).

Despite this prolific output, she was – to her disappointment – known almost exclusively as the author of one famous novel. Since her death, *Cold Comfort Farm* has attracted very little attention from academic critics, but has remained extremely popular and has been adapted for the stage, radio, CINEMA, and television.

Suggested Reading

English Studies Group, Centre for Contemporary Cultural Studies, University of Birmingham. 'Thinking the Thirties', in Francis Barker et al. (eds), *1936: The Sociology of Literature*, vol. 2 (Colchester: University of Essex, 1979) 1–20.

Hammill, Faye. '*Cold Comfort Farm*, D. H. Lawrence, and Literary Culture Between the Wars', *Modern Fiction Studies*, 47.3 (Fall 2001) 831–54.

Oliver, Reggie. *Out of the Woodshed: The Life of Stella Gibbons* (London: Bloomsbury, 1998).

Faye Hammill

Glyn, Elinor 1864–1943

British novelist, and inventor of 'It', that Jazz Age euphemism for sex appeal. Of Scottish-Canadian parentage, Glyn was born Elinor Sutherland in Jersey. At 28, she married Clayton Glyn; they had two daughters, but the marriage was unhappy, partly due to his infidelity. Bored by marriage, motherhood, and high society, Glyn began to write for pleasure, and in 1900 her epistolary novel, *The Visits of Elizabeth*, was published. With its humorous observations of marriage, morals, clothes, and country houses, the novel was an immediate success, and has been cited as an influence on Anita Loos's *Gentlemen Prefer Blondes*. (A friend was unconvinced that Glyn was the author, protesting, 'But Nellie darling, it can't possibly be you! A really clever person must have written those letters.') *The Reflections of Ambrosine* (1902) and *The Vicissitudes of Evangeline* (1905) cemented her reputation as a light, but satirical novelist of modern manners.

Glyn's most famous novel was *Three Weeks* (1907), which scandalized Edwardian society with its tale of the erotic affair between a mysterious older woman and a young Englishman, and sold over two million copies worldwide. The active role of the Lady in the seduction particularly horrified her contemporaries: 'She purred as a tiger might have done, while she undulated like a snake. She touched him with her fingertips, she kissed his throat, his wrists, the palms of his hands, his eyelids, his hair. Strange, subtle kisses, unlike the kisses of women.' The seduction of the young man on a tiger-skin became legendary, and inspired the famous (but anonymous) lines: 'Would you like to sin/With Elinor Glyn/On a tiger-skin? / Or would you prefer/To err/With her/On some other fur?' The book's success enabled Glyn to tour America in 1908, an experience which inspired *Elizabeth Visits America* (1909), the sequel to *The Visits of Elizabeth*. She continued to write bestselling romances, such as *His Hour* (1911), set in pre-Revolutionary Russia. Her most well received book was *The Career of Katherine Bush* (1917), which, like her earliest novels, told of a young girl's attempts to find her way into society, complete with cynical observations on middle-class manners.

During the Great War, Glyn was a war correspondent in France; in 1919, she was one of only two female journalists present at the signing of the Peace Treaty at Versailles. In 1920, she was invited to Hollywood by Famous Players-Lasky who were filming her novel *The Great Moment*, and 'Madame Glyn', as she styled herself, soon became a member of the Hollywood in-crowd. She wrote the screenplays for *Three Weeks, His Hour* (both 1924) and *Beyond the Rocks* (1922), and numbered Valentino, Chaplin, and Swanson amongst her friends. Her place in film and cultural history was assured when she declared that actress Clara Bow was the only Hollywood star to have 'It'. Paramount, to whom Bow was contracted, commissioned a novella of the same name from Glyn; published in 1927, *It* was then filmed with Bow as the star. Tax problems forced Glyn to return to England in 1929, where she directed two films, *Knowing Men* and *The*

Price of Things (both 1930). Her autobiography, *Romantic Adventure*, was published in 1936, and her last novel, *The Third Eye* in 1940.

Suggested Reading

Beauman, Sally. Introduction to *Three Weeks* by Elinor Glyn (London: Virago, 1996) v–xii.

Etherington-Smith, Meredith and Jeremy Pilcher. *The 'It' Girls: Lucy, Lady Duff Gordon, the Couturiere 'Lucile', and Elinor Glyn, Romantic Novelist* (London: Hamish Hamilton, 1986).

Hardwick, Joan. *Addicted to Romance: The Life and Adventures of Elinor Glyn* (London: Andre Deutsch, 1994).

Louise Harrington

Godden, Rumer 1907–1998

British author of over 60 books, including novels, poetry, plays, and non-fiction. One of four daughters, Margaret Rumer Godden was born in Sussex, but brought up in India from the age of nine months. Her childhood was relived both in her acclaimed novel *The River* (1948) and her memoir *Two Under the Indian Sun* (1966), the latter co-written with her sister Jon. At 20, Godden returned to England to train as a dance teacher, and upon returning to India established a multi-racial dance school in Calcutta. Novels such as *Thursday's Children* (1984) and *A Candle for St. Jude* (1947) reflect her lifelong interest in ballet.

In 1934 Godden married Laurence Sinclair Foster, the father of her two daughters, but the marriage was not happy. In 1936 her first novel, *Chinese Puzzle*, was published and well received. Her first big critical and commercial success, however, was *Black Narcissus* (1939), compared by Arthur Koestler to *A Passage to India*, and later made into a critically acclaimed film. It tells the story of five nuns who settle in a disused palace at the foot of the Himalayas. As they encounter the complexity of local tradition, their Christian rituals seem small and ineffectual, and they realize they are up against spiritual forces they do not understand: 'She had a sudden sense of dismay that came from the house and not from Mr Dean, a sense that she was an interloper in it and the convent life no more than a cobweb that would be brushed away. The house had its own people, strange bare-footed people who had never had a Christmas, not a star, nor a Christ.' Eventually the nuns are forced to leave, and as they do so the rains come and wipe away all remaining traces of them. On the surface a simple tale, it is concerned, like Godden's later novels *The River* and *Kingfishers Catch Fire* (1953), with the loss of innocence and EMPIRE, and with the fragile, complex relationship between Britain and India.

In 1949 Godden married James Haynes-Dixon and settled in Britain. While much of her writing is concerned with India, Roman Catholicism was also central to several of her novels. As well as *Black Narcissus*, both *Five For Sorrow,*

Ten For Joy (1979) and *In This House of Brede* (1969) are set in convents, detailing both challenges to faith and the daily lives of nuns. The latter, Godden's most acclaimed book, is a sequence of interlocking stories of how and why women from different cultural backgrounds enter the enclosed contemplative order of the Benedictines.

Godden also wrote poetry and non-fiction, including *Bengal Journey* (1945), an account of women's WAR WORK in Bengal, and an autobiography, *A Time to Dance, No Time to Weep* (1987). Her last novel was *Cromartie vs. the God Shiva* (1997), praised by Philip Hensher as 'affecting the reader with strange currents of feeling and troubling moments of deep thought'. She was awarded the OBE in 1993.

Suggested Reading

Bloom, Harold (ed.). *British Women Fiction Writers, 1900–1960: Volume One* (Philadelphia: Chelsea House Publishers, 1997).
Chisholm, Anne. *Rumer Godden: A Storyteller's Life* (London: Pan, 1999).

Louise Harrington

Gore-Booth, Eva 1870–1926

Author of two verse dramas, five books of prose, several NEWSPAPER articles and ten books of poems. Born in County Sligo, Ireland, Gore-Booth moved in 1897 to Manchester, where she supported movements for economic and political democracy, including the enfranchisement of women. Her sister Constance (1868–1927) became the Countess Markievicz, the first woman MP in Britain. With the social reformer Esther Roper and 'Miss Reddish', Eva Gore-Booth organized the union of Women Textile Workers; she was a member of the Manchester Education Committee and secretary to the Women's Trade Union Council. She produced pamphlets on issues such as a woman's right to work, edited *Woman's Labour News* and published her writings in various journals.

In 1913, illness forced her to London where she worked ceaselessly in the Women's Peace Crusade. From 1916 she also championed Irish independence, and from 1918 fought against capital punishment. The posthumous *Selected Poems* (1933) has a useful 'Biographical Note' by Esther Roper, who recorded Gore-Booth's 'passionate sympathy for suffering and injustice and a strange feeling of responsibility for life's inequalities'. Although a vociferous SUFFRAGIST, Gore-Booth tends to avoid gender distinctions in her poems. There are occasional references to the IRISH QUESTION and WORLD WAR ONE, but as an *oeuvre* they veer towards a mystical lyricism.

Suggested Reading

Gore-Booth, Constance Georgina, afterwards Countess Markievicz. *Prison Letters of Countess-Markievicz-Constance Gore-Booth. Also Poems and Articles Relating to Easter Week by Eva Gore-Booth and a Biographical Sketch by Esther Roper* (London: Longmans, 1934).

Lewis, Gifford. *Eva Gore-Booth and Esther Roper: A Biography* (London: Pandora, 1988).

Jane Dowson

Goudge, Elizabeth 1900–1984

Novelist and short-story writer; author of both contemporary and HISTORICAL FICTION. Born in Wells, later moving to Ely and Oxford as her father's clerical and academic career progressed, she studied art at Reading College and taught art and design. After her mother's death she moved to Peppard Common, near Henley-on-Thames, living for many years with a friend, Jessie Monroe. Goudge's writing is characterized by a shrewd though compassionate insight into human motivation. Her style ranges from realism to fairytale but in all her writing there is a sense of the past permeating the present. Typically described as 'romances', her novels are not conventional love stories and her characters are far from innately heroic. For example, Rachell in *Island Magic* (1934) is, outwardly, the perfect wife but the reader is privy to her feelings of frustration and resentment towards her kind and gentle, though incompetent and impecunious husband. Likewise, Nadine in *Herb of Grace* (1948) suffers – though not silently – when she gives up her actor-lover to return to her staid husband and boisterous children in the aftermath of the Second World War.

Noteworthy in some novels is the 'twinning' of two characters, one of whom is absent or dead and thus only accessed through her or his writing. For example, in *A City of Bells* (1936), the poet Gabriel Ferranti is primarily known through the great poetic drama he has left behind him. Past and present stories run in parallel as Jocelyn Irvin edits Ferranti's work for publication and gradually comes to realize that it is largely autobiographical. Similarly, in Goudge's final novel, *The Scent of Water* (1963), Mary Lindsay inherits diaries detailing the mental illness from which her cousin and namesake has suffered throughout her adult life. By reading the diaries, Mary learns as much about herself as about her dead cousin.

Goudge is perhaps best known for her historical novel *Green Dolphin Country* (1944), a nineteenth-century drama set in the Channel Islands and New Zealand. However, *Towers in the Mist* (1938) and *The Dean's Watch* (1960) are broader in scope and evoke a greater sense of the past. The former is set in Oxford, and presents a beautifully wrought panorama of everyday life in the Elizabethan era, the narrator even recounting the history that the Elizabethans knew. The latter is a charming Christian fable, set in a cathedral city, and told by a narrator who exhibits a continual awareness of the cathedral's monastic origins.

Goudge's writing for children reinscribes middle-class values and traditional gender roles. However, it contains strong elements of humour and fantasy and focuses less on social mores than on adventures featuring child heroes of both sexes. Thus, *Henrietta's House* (1942) and *The Little White Horse* (1946) both have girl heroes; Maria in the latter confronting a band of robbers in their lair whilst a young male protagonist looks on in horror. Goudge's short stories fill four volumes, the last being a collection entitled *Lost, One Angel* (1971), which gives a representative sample of her characterization and style.

Suggested Reading
Goudge, Elizabeth. *The Joy of the Snow: An Autobiography* (London: Hodder & Stoughton, 1974).

Isaac, Megan Lynn. 'Misplaced: The Fantasies and Fortunes of Elizabeth Goudge', *Lion and the Unicorn: A Critical Journal of Children's Literature*, 21.1 (January 1997) 86–111.

Elaine Hartnell

Grand, Sarah 1854–1943
Pseudonym of Frances Elizabeth Bellenden (Clarke) McFall, novelist, short-story writer, essayist and polemicist, credited with coining the phrase 'the New Woman'. Grand was born in County Down, Ireland. After her father's death the family moved to England, and at the age of 16 Grand married the 39-year-old widower David Chambers McFall. Grand left McFall in 1890.

In common with many other Victorian women writers, Grand chose to write under a pseudonym, but she broke with tradition and asserted herself as a 'New Woman' by choosing an obviously female name. The sensational *The Heavenly Twins* (1893), considered to be one of the first 'New Woman' novels, was one of the most popular of the 1890s. Initially rejected by publishers because of its polemic nature and daring use of syphilitic characters, *The Heavenly Twins* was the first novel to openly attack the sexual double standard.

At the beginning of the twentieth century, Grand took on senior positions in several women's SUFFRAGE organizations, while continuing to publish books, notably the short-story collection *Emotional Moments* (1908) and the first two parts of an intended trilogy, *Adnam's Orchard* (1912) and *The Winged Victory* (1916). In the 1920s, Grand served for six years as Mayoress of Bath.

Suggested Reading
Mangum, Teresa. *Married, Middlebrow, and Militant: Sarah Grand and the New Woman Novel* (Ann Arbor, MI: University of Michigan Press, 1998).

Richardson, Angelique and Chris Willis (eds). *The New Woman in Fiction and in Fact: Fin-de-Siècle Feminisms* (Basingstoke: Palgrave Macmillan, 2001).

Erica Brown

Gregory, Lady Augusta 1852–1932
Anglo-Irish dramatist, theatre manager, translator, and folklorist who played a significant role in the promotion of Irish cultural nationalism through the foundation of the Abbey Theatre, Dublin. Tensions have been identified between her nationalist concerns and her place in the Anglo-Irish Ascendancy,

summed up by Yeats in 'Dramatis Personae': 'Lady Gregory, in her life much artifice, in her nature much pride, was born to see the glory of the world in a peasant mirror.' Born Isabella Augusta Persse, she married Sir William Gregory, who was 35 years her senior, in 1880 and had one child, Robert, in 1881. The Gregorys travelled widely in Europe and Asia, living in Egypt for a time, where Lady Gregory became a supporter of the Egyptian nationalist movement.

In December 1882, she began an eight-month affair with Wilfred Scalwen Blunt, a relationship which inspired 'A Woman's Sonnets', published in 1892. After her husband's death, also in 1892, Lady Gregory moved to his estate, Coole Park, where she began to collect local Galway folktales and legends and became interested in the Irish language. This interest was to become a major influence on her later dramatic works, and led to *Visions and Beliefs in the West of Ireland* (1920). Coole Park became a meeting place for the key figures of the Irish cultural movement, in particular W. B. Yeats, who was a regular guest.

Gregory's translations of Gaelic epics, *Cuchulain of Muirthemne* (1902) and *Gods and Fighting Men* (1904), provided Yeats with material for his plays, and she collaborated on the writing of his controversial play, *Cathleen ni Houlihan* (1902), although she is rarely credited for her contributions to this work. Gregory's career as a dramatist was prolific and wide-ranging in genre. She wrote one-act comedies such as *The Jackdaw* (1902) and *Hyacinth Halvey* (1906) and tragicomedies including *The Caravans* (1906) and *The Deliverer* (1911). She also wrote miracle plays, *The Travelling Man* (1909) and *Dave* (1927); plays for children, *The Jester* (1918) and *The Dragon* (1919); and a ghost play, *Shanwalla* (1915). Her translations included works by Molière, Sudermann, and Goldoni. Her son was killed in Italy in WORLD WAR ONE, and she sold Coole Park to the government in 1927, although she continued to live there as a tenant until she died.

Suggested Reading

Fogarty, Anne. ' "A Woman of the House": Gender and Nationalism in the Writings of Augusta Gregory', in Katherine Kirkpatrick (ed.), *Border Crossings: Irish Women Writers and National Identities* (Tuscaloosa, AL, and London: University of Alabama Press, 2000) 100–22.
MacDonoh, Caroline. 'Augusta Gregory: A Portrait of a Lady', in Jacqueline Genet (ed.), *Rural Ireland, Real Ireland?* (Gerrards Cross: Colin Smythe, 1996) 109–20.

Esme Miskimmin

H

Hall, Radclyffe 1880–1943

Poet and novelist, author of *The Well of Loneliness* (1928), one of the earliest and most important LESBIAN novels in English. Marguerite Antonia Radclyffe-Hall was born in Bournemouth in 1880 (not 1886, as numerous sources state). Her American mother, Mary Jane Sager, and her wealthy socialite father, Radclyffe Radclyffe-Hall, separated shortly after the birth of their unwanted daughter, with custody awarded to the mother. She received a patchy education in London, and began writing poetry as a young girl. Considering herself a 'congenital' homosexual, she adopted a mannish style and became known as 'John'.

Coming of age, she inherited her grandfather's large fortune, and in 1906 paid for the publication of her volume of love lyrics, '*Twixt Earth and Stars*, under the name 'Marguerite Radclyffe-Hall'. It was well reviewed. The following year, she fell in love with Mabel Batten ('Ladye'), a beautiful singer, aged 50. They made their home together in 1911, and under her lover's influence, Hall converted to Catholicism. She continued to publish poetry: *A Sheaf of Verses* (1908), which obliquely refers to lesbianism; *Poems of the Past and Present* (1910), her tribute to Ladye; *Songs of Three Counties, and Other Poems* (1913), marking the peak of her career as a poet; and *The Forgotten Island* (1915), a poem sequence in blank verse. In 1915, Hall began a relationship with Una Troubridge, a married woman seven years her junior. This lasted until Hall's death, despite Hall's affair with a Russian woman, Evguenia Souline.

Hall published two novels in 1924: *The Forge*, a social comedy, and *The Unlit Lamp*, about a woman who refuses to marry. These were followed by *A Saturday Life* (1925), another comic story exploring artistic experience, spirituality, and social obligation, and *Adam's Breed* (1926), a symbolically loaded novel about the life of a waiter who develops a revulsion for food, which won the PRIX FEMINA-VIE HEUREUSE. *The Well of Loneliness*, her only book with an explicitly lesbian theme, pleads for tolerance of homosexuality. The protagonist, Stephen Gordon, named for the son her parents longed for, is alienated and frustrated: 'All her life she must drag this body of hers like a monstrous fetter imposed on her spirit. This strangely ardent yet sterile body that must worship yet never be worshipped in return by the creature of its adoration.'

Stephen does enter a lesbian relationship, but eventually feels she must induce her lover, Mary, to marry so that Mary will not be crushed by society. Hall does not describe their physical relations; famously, the most explicit sentence in the book concludes: 'and that night they were not divided...'. Nevertheless, both the British and American publishers were prosecuted for obscenity (successfully in the British case), and the resulting publicity made the novel a bestseller. Hall published two further novels, *The Master of the House* (1932) and *The Sixth Beatitude* (1936), together with short stories including the much-anthologized 'Miss Oglivy Finds Herself' (1934). In recent decades, her work has generated a large amount of critical commentary, most of it situating her in the context of lesbian history and literature.

Suggested Reading

Baker, Michael. *Our Three Selves: A Life Of Radclyffe Hall* (London: Hamilton, 1985).
Brittain, Vera. *Radclyffe Hall: A Case of Obscenity?* (New York: A. S. Barnes, 1969).
Doan, Laura. *Fashioning Sapphism: The Origins of a Modern English Lesbian Culture* (New York: Columbia University Press, 2000).

Faye Hammill

Hamilton, Cicely 1872–1952

Actress, novelist, playwright, journalist, and suffragist, well known during her lifetime for the commercially successful play *Diana of Dobson's* (1908), the polemical essay *Marriage as a Trade* (1909), and the novel *William: An Englishman* (1919), but largely forgotten today.

Born Cicely Hammill in London, she was brought up by foster parents from the age of ten because her mother had disappeared. She attended a boarding school in Malvern, and later became a pupil-teacher. Critically overlooked, Hamilton's work nevertheless forms an important part of SUFFRAGE history, and *Marriage as a Trade* anticipates ideas later articulated by Virginia WOOLF. Dissatisfied with the activities of the militant suffragists, Hamilton founded the Women Writers' Suffrage League and the Actresses' Franchise League in 1908, and following the success of *Diana of Dobson's*, she became a speaker on the suffrage circuit. Hamilton was a suffragist because the movement challenged conventional perceptions of womanhood and not because she believed simply in the importance of enfranchisement.

Before becoming a writer, she worked as an actress to support herself, her sister, and her two spinster aunts, taking the stage name Hamilton out of consideration for her family. In April 1911, she received critical acclaim in George Bernard Shaw's *Fanny's First Play*, and she continued to appear on stage sporadically until the end of World War One. Hamilton served as an administrator in the Scottish Women's Hospital in France from 1914–16, and then joined Concerts at the Front, performing throughout France and Germany until 1919.

William: An Englishman begins as a satire of militant Left politics and transforms into a novel about the horror of the First World War. William and Griselda, his wife, travel to Belgium in 1914, unaware of the outbreak of war and with no knowledge of French. They 'had talked so long and so often in terms of war; that they had come to look on the strife of nations as a glorified scuffle on the lines of a Pankhurst demonstration. Thus Griselda, taught by *The Suffragette*, used the one word "battle" for a small street row and the fire and slaughter of Eylau.' As the quotation demonstrates, Hamilton was skilled at pushing ideas to their logical extreme in order to highlight their folly, success-fully using humour to soften the didactic nature of her fictional and dramatic work. *William: An Englishman* was awarded the PRIX FEMINA-VIE HEUREUSE.

Hamilton wrote regularly for *Time and Tide* from its inception, and served on its board of directors. Ellen Terry, Edy Craig, Christopher St John, Vera BRITTAIN, Winifred HOLTBY, Elizabeth ROBINS, George Bernard Shaw and H. G. Wells were among Hamilton's close circle of friends. Only two of her books remain in print, *Marriage as a Trade*, and *William: An Englishman*.

Suggested Reading

Thomas, Sue. 'Cicely Hamilton (1872–1952)', in William Demastes and Katherine E. Kelly (eds), *British Playwrights, 1860–1956: A Research and Production Sourcebook* (Westport, CT: Greenwood, 1996) 189–99.

Whitelaw, Lis. *The Life and Rebellious Times of Cicely Hamilton* (London: The Women's Press, 1990).

Lisa Shariari

Hamilton, Helen (dates not available)

Writer of verse and prose, who made her name from the 100-page poetry pamphlet *The Compleat Schoolmarm: A Story of Promise and Fulfilment* (1917). Reprinted several times, it is an extraordinary exposure of the emotionally crippling nature of female EDUCATION. It was dedicated: 'To those women who, striving to make education more human than it at present is, nobly, and despite its drawbacks, remain in the teaching profession.' Hamilton takes a 'heroine' through school, training college, and then a teaching career, which means a life sentence of spinsterhood. The potent undertow of loneliness and exhaustion parallels the narrative of events which the public see as glorious opportunities.

Hamilton's aggressively advertised *Napoo!: A Book of War Bêtes Noires* (1918) consists of satiric dramatic monologues which topple heroic ideals and indicate the popular appetite for anti-war sentiments. 'The Writer of Patriotic "Ad" ', for example, subverts the platitudes and pomposity of poster campaigns. 'The Romancing Poet' and 'Jingo-Woman', similarly dismissive of patriotism, are reprinted in Catherine Reilly's VIRAGO *Book of War Poetry by Women*. Hamilton's later books of lyrics, such as *Hope and Other Poems* (1924), are oddly self-concealing, archaistic, and consoling. Her fiction is notable for *My Husband Still: A Working Woman's Story* (1914), based on a working-class wife's report of a miserable marriage. She has received no attention from critics.

Jane Dowson

Hamilton, Mary Agnes 1884–1962

Novelist, biographer, historian, translator, and SOCIALIST politician. Mary Agnes Adamson was born in Manchester and educated in Scotland and at Newnham, Cambridge, where her awareness of social inequalities and her determination to fight them developed. She married C. J. Hamilton in 1905, but the marriage did not last. Hamilton made her living by undertaking an ambitious publishing schedule, and she was influential in, and influenced by, Labour politics. Some of her biographies were of key figures in the Labour movement – Ramsay Macdonald (1923), Margaret Bondfield (1924), Mary Macarthur (1925), and Arthur Henderson (1938) – and she was a Labour MP herself (1921–31). Her early novels, such as *Dead Yesterday* (1916), *Follow My Leader* (1922) and *Special Providence* (1930), debate gender, politics, and individualism, often in a socialist or PACIFIST setting. Her interest in women's increasing opportunities is reflected in *Newnham: An Informal Biography* (1936), celebrating women's entry into university EDUCATION, and *Women at Work* (1941), about women and trades unionism. She wrote two volumes of memoirs: *Remembering My Good Friends* (1944) and *Up-Hill All the Way* (1953), both of which provide valuable commentary on her circle and her own political development.

Suggested Reading

Klaus, H. Gustav. 'Silhouettes of Revolution: Some Neglected Novels of the Early 1920s', in Gustav (ed.), *The Socialist Novel in Britain: Towards the Recovery of a Tradition* (New York: St Martin's, 1982) 89–109.

Sharon Ouditt

Health and Medicine

Traditionally the period 1900 to 1950 has been seen as one of progress in the history of medicine, culminating in the mass-production of penicillin in the 1940s and the establishment of the NHS. Rising real wages ensured that more people were able to pay for medical care, and the 1911 National Insurance Act created a system of health insurance that underpinned state services. Medicine received considerable publicity through the radio and an active campaign of health EDUCATION. Demand for medical services grew, reflecting the rising authority of medicine and patients' increased willingness to seek care. State medical provision was extended under the new Ministry of Health (established 1919) and various public health programmes were established. A school medical service was set up, whilst infant and child WELFARE services focused local action and encouraged a hospitalization of childbirth. Campaigns were launched to tackle venereal disease and tuberculosis, and new specialist services followed. Government funding for medical research also rose and therapeutic innovation was encouraged by the Medical Research Council. In 1948, the NHS appeared to launch a new era of healthcare for all.

However, a more nuanced picture is possible. Medicine remained male dominated. The period saw a general national anxiety over health that had an impact on wider social debates about poverty, nutrition, and education. Deaths from communicable infectious disease fell, but were replaced as the main cause of death by chronic and degenerative disorders like heart disease, as life expectancy increased. Evidence that levels of health were rising in the interwar period masked pockets of illness in economically underprivileged areas, particularly during the DEPRESSION. The NHS revealed the poor state of many hospitals and the extent of ill health.

Until 1939, healthcare retained its private, voluntary, and public mix, and self-medication remained important. State services were often rudimentary, and the Ministry of Health was traditional in its assessment of health priorities. Voluntary provision expanded, but co-ordination between public and voluntary medical services was limited. Access to care and medical services depended on locality, class, and gender, with the focus in state services essentially male. Although maternal and infant welfare services benefited women, the great majority fell outside the provisions of National Insurance and hence did not gain as much from the expansion of medical services.

A similarly mixed picture can be seen in the medical treatments available. Radium treatment for cancer offered a greater chance of cure, and advances in pathology made cancer diagnosis more accurate. The emergence of reliable blood transfusions in the 1920s increased the scope of surgery. New operations such as tracheotomy were devised; other operations such as hysterectomies and tonsillectomies became fashionable. War saw new methods of handling compound fractures and wound management, and encouragement was given to new specialities like plastic surgery. Only slowly, however, did surgery shift from a preoccupation with removal to a subtler concern with restoration. If the surgeon could do more by the 1940s, daily life continued to revolve around dressings and draining abscesses.

In medicine, considerable faith was placed in the value of antitoxins and chemotherapy. The identification of viral diseases saw the introduction of new vaccines. Drugs such as Salvarsan for the treatment of syphilis and insulin for diabetes came on to the market. Drug production became industrialized, with the emergence of companies like Burroughs-Wellcome. Sulphonamides (for streptococci infections such as puerperal fever) were effective and prescribed in vast quantities, but doctors had few other effective therapies against most infections and were often reluctant to adopt new methods. Penicillin, which proved highly effective, was therefore quickly heralded as a major breakthrough.

New diagnostic technologies, many of them rooted in the laboratory, were developed including the Wassermann test for syphilis. By the interwar period, a growing number of doctors made use of hospital laboratories, sending samples for testing or patients for confirmation of a diagnosis. General Practitioners' manuals in the 1930s recommended that a surgery should contain a microscope and equipment for analysing blood, but in reality, most practices were not so well equipped. By the 1950s, the work of the average practitioner was still seen as '70 per cent art and 30 per cent science'. Developments in medical science offered real improvements, but the period also saw tensions between modernization and the limitations of medical care.

Suggested Reading

Hardy, Anne. *Health and Medicine in Britain Since 1860* (Basingstoke: Palgrave Macmillan, 2001).

Jones, Helen. *Health and Society in Twentieth-Century Britain* (London: Longmans, 1994).

Keir Waddington

Heyer, Georgette 1902–1974

Author of HISTORICAL FICTION and detective thrillers, best known as the originator of the much-imitated Regency romance. Although Heyer's historical novels were consistent bestsellers during her lifetime, she was rarely seriously reviewed and her meticulous historical research, skilful craftsmanship and gift for comedy did not attract the critical acclaim they deserved. Perhaps as a result, Heyer's own attitude to her work became increasingly dismissive: 'I'm a scribbler of trivial romances', she once remarked.

Her early novels were in the swashbuckler tradition of Baroness Orczy and Jeffrey Farnol, featuring male protagonists. The first, *The Black Moth* (1921), about a gentleman highwayman, was written to amuse her brother when he was ill and published when Heyer was 19. In 1925 she married George Ronald Rougier, a mining engineer, and accompanied him to Tanganyika and Macedonia. It was *These Old Shades* (1926), perhaps because it provided light relief from the GENERAL STRIKE, which made her a bestseller. In 1930 Heyer and her husband settled in England, where he trained as a barrister and then became a QC.

The early romances show a fascination with costume, disguise, and masquerade, most noticeable in *The Masqueraders* (1928), which features a cross-dressing brother and sister. Initially Heyer experimented with different periods and biographically based books, including the Elizabethan adventure *Beauvallet* (1929) and *The Conqueror* (1931), about the Norman Conquest. She also wrote four novels with contemporary settings, which reveal a concern with class. They also illuminate her reasons for turning to historical settings for ROMANTIC FICTION. The heroine of *Pastel* (1929) remarks, 'You can't be romantic in these times', citing the dampening effects of psychological studies of sex and of Marie STOPES's marriage manuals.

After *Devil's Cub* (1932), Heyer's romances become increasingly Austenesque comedies of manners in Regency settings, delighting in lively verbal interchanges between hero and heroine. Much of the pleasure of these texts comes from the historically accurate detail of clothes, manners, and social customs, and, perhaps above all, from Heyer's richly inventive dialogue, with its use of 'period' slang, particularly lower-class phraseology or 'thieves cant'. Her 'nattily attired' young bloods are 'Tulips of Fashion' who drive 'neck-or-nothing', visit 'boozing-kens', 'lay out their blunt' on fashionable fripperies, and, finally, get 'leg-shackled' to the heroine. In two of her best novels, *An Infamous Army* (1937) and *The Spanish Bride* (1940), the romance plot is set against meticulous accounts of the battle of Waterloo and the Peninsular War respectively. The former was reputedly used for teaching at Sandhurst.

In the 1930s and 1940s, Heyer wrote several detective thrillers with plots supplied by her husband, often featuring Superintendent Hannasyde and Inspector Hemingway, but these have dated somewhat. In the late 1940s Heyer began the research for a 'serious' historical novel about John, Duke of Bedford, and the first volume was published after her death as *My Lord John* (1975). Heyer's work has been admired by Carmen Callil and A. S. Byatt, and the publication of a critical retrospective suggests that her work is currently being reassessed.

Suggested Reading

Bell, Kathleen. 'Cross-Dressing in Wartime: Georgette Heyer's *The Corinthian* in its 1940 Context', in Pat Kirkham and David Thomas (eds), *War Culture: Social Change and Changing Experience in World War Two* (London: Lawrence & Wishart, 1995) 151–9.

Fahnestock-Thomas, Mary (ed.). *Georgette Heyer: A Critical Retrospective* (Saraland, AL: Prinny World Press, 2001).

Hodge, Jane Aiken. *The Private World of Georgette Heyer* (London: Bodley Head, 1984).

Diana Wallace

Historical Fiction

At the beginning of the twentieth century, historical fiction was in the doldrums, tarnished by association with the popular swashbucklers of Baroness Orczy, Jeffrey Farnol, and Rafael Sabatini. In fact, Orczy's phenomenally successful *The Scarlet Pimpernel* (1905) combined the cloak-and-dagger adventure of the male-orientated swashbuckler with a satisfying romance plot and made the genre appealing to women writers. Her heroic Sir Percy Blakeney, with his pose of dandified foppery, proved an influential model for subsequent heroes. The other bestseller in the Edwardian period was Marjorie Bowen's *The Viper of Milan* (1906). About a fourteenth-century despot and his headlong career of murder and bloodshed, it admirably illustrates the way in which the historical novel freed women writers from the constraints of the romance plot and the domestic, enabling them to write about the wider world.

After 1918, the emergence of the academically trained woman novelist, often with a degree in history, combined with women's new consciousness of themselves as enfranchised citizens within history, produced a flowering of women's historical fiction. Already a hybrid form, in women's hands the historical novel cross-fertilized with the romance, Gothic, fantasy, and myth. Georgette HEYER's *The Black Moth* (1921) and Naomi MITCHISON's *The Conquered* (1923) signalled two important new directions for the genre. Heyer's novels inaugurated the Regency romance as a much-imitated sub-genre and made the historical romance a female form. Mitchison radicalized the historical novel by using it to explore political issues, signalling contemporary parallels through epigraphs and later, in *The Bull Calves* (1947), footnotes. She pioneered the use of contemporary idiom and subverted traditional historical narratives by retelling them from the point of view of those conquered, victimized, or marginalized by the dominant powers. Other notable 1920s historical novelists included D. K. Broster and Hilda Reid, while Virginia WOOLF's *Orlando* (1928) blends history with fantasy to create a hero/ine who lives for over 400 years and changes sex midway through the book.

By the 1930s historical fiction was firmly associated with women writers and readers, and its critical reputation probably suffered because of this. This may explain the neglect of several accomplished individual novels, notably Rose MACAULAY's seventeenth-century *They Were Defeated* (1932), Helen WADDELL's *Peter Abelard* (1933), and Phyllis BENTLEY's novel about Julius Caesar, *Freedom, Farewell!* (1936). The most sophisticated and unaccountably neglected historical novelist of these years was Sylvia Townsend WARNER, whose socialist-feminist novels, *Summer Will Show* (1936), *After the Death of Don Juan* (1938), and *The Corner That Held Them* (1948), were both politically radical and formally innovative.

During and after the Second World War, the demand for escapist fiction opened the way for the 'costume novel', as written by Eleanor Smith and by Magdalen KING-HALL, best known for her highwaywoman-protagonist in *Life and Death of the Wicked Lady Skelton* (1944). This book was, like many costume novels, made into a film. Daphne DU MAURIER's *Frenchman's Creek* (1941) and *The King's General* (1946) have much in common with the costume novel but are more self-reflexive in their deployment of romance and Gothic forms. Also increasingly popular were biographical historical novels, usually focusing on royal women. Successful authors in this mode included Margaret Irwin, best known for her *Young Bess* trilogy (1944, 1948, 1953) about Elizabeth I, Doris Leslie, and Eleanor Burford Hibbert writing as 'Jean PLAIDY'.

In *The Great Tradition* (1948) F. R. Leavis damned the entire genre from Sir Walter Scott on as 'a bad tradition'. The subsequent critical neglect of the historical novel may explain why feminist critics have been slow to engage with it in comparison to other genres. More recent work suggests that this is about to change.

Suggested Reading
Hughes, Helen. *The Historical Romance* (London: Routledge, 1993).
Light, Alison. ' "Young Bess": Historical Novels and Growing Up', *Feminist Review*, 33 (1989) 57–71.
Wallace, Diana. *The Woman's Historical Novel: British Women Writers, 1900–2000* (Basingstoke: Palgrave Macmillan, 2004).

Diana Wallace

Holden, Inez ?1904–1974

Known in the twenties as a bohemian adventuress, in the thirties as a satirist of high society, and in the forties as a SOCIALIST writer of documentary novels of home-front life. Memoirists celebrated her more for her extraordinary personality than her writing, but her literature is important because it extends the radical literary and political goals of the thirties into serious fiction of the forties.

Although Holden was born into a gentry family, she identified herself with the working classes and the non-communist left. Rejected by her parents, who did not even register her birth, she went at age 15 to Paris and then London, living on her wits and good looks. Her first two novels, *Sweet Charlatan* (1929) and *Born Old, Died Young* (1932), are satires of bohemian and high society. Virginia Jenkinson, the adventuress heroine of the second, has been interpreted as Holden's alter ego. Certainly Virginia's observation that 'some of her married friends wore marriage like a becoming fancy dress, they succeeded in draping their own personalities with their husbands' characters and circumstances', displays the unconventional perspective and satirical wit for which Holden was famous.

During the thirties Holden published only one novel, but dozens of stories in mass-circulation dailies and glamour magazines. She was adept at placing scathing satires of the values of the upper classes in publications whose sales depended upon those very values. She translated several of her glamour stories into Basic English, an experimental language designed by C. K. Ogden, and published them as *Death in High Society* (1934).

Holden met George Orwell during the early war years, when she was living in a flat belonging to H. G. Wells. She became a close friend of both men and wrote her most famous and successful novel, *Night Shift* (1941), under their unofficial patronage. Based on her experiences working in an aircraft factory, *Night Shift* is regarded as one of the best documentary fictions to come out of the war, and she turned it into the script for a a film, *Danger Area* (1944). Holden went on to publish a war diary, *It Was Different at the Time* (1943), another wartime industrial novel, *There's No Story There* (1944), and *To the Boating* (1945), a collection of stories about England's internal outsiders – the insane, the ill, the criminal, the abandoned. Her novels of the fifties, *The Owner* (1952) and *The Adults* (1956), brought her admiring reviews but few sales.

Holden, a granddaughter of a Master of Foxhounds who worked as both factory hand and intellectual, offers students of gender, work, and war an unusual subject for investigation. An intelligent, attractive, and uneducated woman with no assured means of support and no instinct for marriage, Holden composed a life and literature out of the colourful materials others overlooked, creating always comic, often serious stories of rich and poor that wittily expose the absurdities, tragedies, and modest beauties of interwar and wartime English life.

Suggested Reading

Bluemel, Kristin. *George Orwell and the Radical Eccentrics: Intermodernism in Literary London* (New York: Palgrave Macmillan, 2004).

Goodman, Celia. 'Inez Holden: A Memoir', *London Magazine*, 33.9/10 (December 1993–January 1994) 29–38.

Hartley, Jenny. *Millions Like Us: British Women's Fiction of the Second World War* (London: Virago, 1997).

Kristin Bluemel

Holdsworth, Ethel Carnie 1886–1962

Poet, novelist, children's author, and editor, who also published as Ethel Carnie and Ethel Holdsworth. Much of Holdsworth's work was politically radical, springing from a working-class, feminist perspective. Born in Lancashire, she began work at the cotton mill aged 11 as a part-timer, and was employed full-time at 13. In an article for *The Woman Worker* (which she edited for six months) published on March 31, 1909, she described the factory worker as 'practically a beggar and a slave', declaring all workers 'dependent on the whims of a master class'. Two weeks later, she wrote of the grind of domestic work, often combined with factory labour, urging women to 'go out and play' and be 'something more than a dish washer'.

Holdsworth's first publications (as Ethel Carnie) were poems, collected in *Rhymes from the Factory* in 1907. Two further volumes followed: *Songs of a Factory Girl* (1911) and *Voices of Womanhood* (1914). Two poems from her second volume were set in a song sequence by Ethel SMYTH (*Three Songs*, 1913) and performed in London; the settings were dedicated to Emmeline and Christabel PANKHURST. Her novel *Helen of Four Gates* (1917) was filmed in 1920. She also began writing CHILDREN's stories and novels, the best of which were influenced by Oscar Wilde. 'The Blind Prince' in *The Lamp Girl and Other Stories* (1913) is a disturbing tale of extreme oppression, concluding with the establishment of a republic and a rather disappointing romance.

Holdsworth's political involvement led her to campaign against conscription during the First World War, to edit (with her husband) an anti-fascist journal, *The Clear Light*, and to publish a series of sonnets in the Anarchist paper *Freedom*, taking up the cause of Anarchists imprisoned in Soviet jails. In a letter accompanying her first sonnet (October 1924), she asserted that she belonged to no political group. Instead, she declared: 'I belong to the folk – from the most undeveloped and illiterate, so confused that they are the bedrock of even reaction, to Whitman and Morris, and Marx, Kropotkin, and Bakunin.'

In her 1909 poem 'Love and Poverty', Holdsworth suggests that love could be achieved only 'When Poverty is not a crime'; the tension between love and poverty operates as political criticism in many of her works. While her best known novel, *This Slavery* (1925), combines romance and melodrama with a tale of industrial conflict, it also indicates the necessity of political action to secure change. Her last novel, *All On Her Own* (1929), written for a series of women's ROMANTIC FICTIONS, combines comments on inequality and land-ownership with arguments about women's need for responsibility and respect.

She drew on a range of styles and genres without a clear sense of hierarchies in literature, and believed in natural genius. Her work may be uneven, but it offers the perspective of a highly politicized working-class woman.

Suggested Reading

Alves, Susan. ' "Whilst working at my frame": The Poetic Production of Ethel Carnie', *Victorian Poetry*, 38.1 (Spring 2000) 77–93.

Fox, Pamela. *Class Fictions* (Durham, NC: Duke University Press, 1994).

Frow, Ruth and Edmund Frow. 'Ethel Carnie: Writer, Feminist and Socialist', in H. Gustav Klaus (ed.), *The Rise of Socialist Fiction, 1880–1914* (Brighton: Harvester, 1987) 251–66.

Kathleen Bell

Holme, Constance 1880–1955

Novelist whose chronicles of Westmoreland life were an important part of the vogue for REGIONAL WRITING between the wars. Holme wrote seven widely admired novels. *The Splendid Fairing* (1919) won the PRIX FEMINA-VIE HEUREUSE, while the enthusiasm of Sir Humphrey Milford, Chairman of Oxford University Press, ensured that Holme was the only contemporary novelist to have all her fiction appear in the World's Classics series. Although she was, apart from Mary WEBB, the best known of the rural writers, her novels do not entirely conform to the model outlined by Stella GIBBONS in *Cold Comfort Farm* (1932). Catastrophe arises from flood, eviction, or poverty rather than family vendetta or sexual transgression. Melodramatic devices are distinctly quirky, as in *The Old Roads From Spain* (1915), in which the hero is haunted by a flock of fey sheep. Work and working practices are central and described in minute detail. The novels are strictly contemporary, with cars, telephones, and gramophones prominent.

Holme was the youngest of 14 children of a Westmoreland land agent, and the family had been land agents for generations. 'Few writers can have had a greater number of fore-elders packed into a few square miles', she noted in the preface to *The Old Roads From Spain*. She married another land agent, Frederick Punchard, in 1916, and lived in Westmoreland throughout her life. Intense familial and professional knowledge informed the novels, which she claimed were 'the natural outcome of over 80 years of land agency'. She also wrote short stories, and several one-act dialect plays, including *The House of Vision* (1932), which was acted by Edy Craig's company.

The three earlier novels are social panoramas. Most notable is *The Lonely Plough* (1914) in which tenant farmers, 'like trustful women sleeping in a tiger's cage', work land reclaimed from the sea by an over-extending landowner and protected by poorly maintained dikes. Round this bleak fable of EMPIRE, Holme evokes a still-dynamic community through horse fairs, hockey matches, choral societies, local elections (where the narrative treats a woman councillor's success ambivalently), and the struggle against the climactic flood. After the war, Holme radically revised her narrative method in response to modernist fiction. The four postwar novels each treat one day in the consciousness of an elderly working person. A tired charwoman returns to work in *Trumpet in the Dust* (1921); a retired couple consider and reject emigration to Canada in *The Things That Belong* (1925), accepting that 'places and houses could hold you against your will'.

In these later novels what Holme called 'the great slide' in rural life has happened. Her move from panorama to single consciousness, from dynamic community to a few tired old people, records this slide. The novels, despite frequent stylistic excesses, are an oddly moving testimony to how rural Westmoreland responded to social change and literary MODERNISM. Long out of critical and popular favour, they are still widely available in secondhand bookshops.

Suggested Reading

Cavaliero, Glen. *The Rural Tradition in the English Novel* (London: Macmillan, 1977).

Trodd, Anthea. *Women's Writing in English: Britain 1900–1945* (London: Longmans, 1998) 103–10.

Anthea Trodd

Holtby, Winifred 1898–1935

Novelist, feminist, SOCIALIST, and social reformer, best known for *South Riding* (1936) and her friendship with Vera BRITTAIN, which is the subject of Brittain's *Testament of Friendship* (1940). Holtby was born in Rudstone, Yorkshire, in 1898. Her mother, Alice, was the first alderwoman on the East Riding County Council and the model for Alderman Mrs Beddowes in *South Riding*. This novel's heroine, the campaigning, independent school teacher, Sarah Burton, is based on the Labour MP, Ellen WILKINSON.

Holtby read history at Somerville College, Oxford, but interrupted her degree in 1918 to join the Women's Auxiliary Army Corps and served briefly in

France. On her return to Somerville, she met Brittain, with whom she afterwards shared a flat in London. Holtby later lived in Brittain's household, helping to bring up her two children. Both thought of themselves as 'old feminists', interested primarily in legislation to produce equality with men, as opposed to 'new feminists' who were more interested in the politics of difference. They threw themselves into progressive and PACIFIST political causes, and supported the Six Point Group, whose motto was 'equality first'. Holtby was torn between her interests in writing and social reform. She lectured for the League of Nations and supported herself as a professional journalist; closely associated with Lady RHONDDA's feminist periodical, *Time and Tide*, she was made a director in 1926. That year, at the invitation of her friend Jean McWilliam, Holtby visited South Africa, where she supported the unionization of black workers. *Women in a Changing Civilisation* was published in 1934, and she wrote a perceptive critical study, *Virginia Woolf*, in 1932.

Holtby's first novel, *Anderby Wold*, was published in 1923 and set in her native Yorkshire. It was followed by *The Crowded Street* (1924), whose heroine attempts to escape the restrictions of provincial life; *The Land of Green Ginger: A Romance* (1927); and *Poor Caroline* (1931). The heroines of all these novels, like Holtby herself, are hard working, practical, idealistic, and tendentially liberal in outlook. *Mandoa, Mandoa! A Comedy of Irrelevance* (1933) satirizes the African infatuation with Western fads and fashions. Both England and the fictional African state of Mandoa are corrupt, the Europeans' exploitation of the Africans matched by the Mandoans' involvement in their own slave trade.

Holtby published a collection of short fiction, *Truth is not Sober and Other Stories*, in 1934. This included 'Why Herbert Killed his Mother', a satire on advertising and maternal possessiveness. A play, about a FASCIST dictator, *Take Back Your Freedom*, was revised and completed after her death by Norman Ginsbery and performed in 1940. Holtby developed Bright's Disease from which she died tragically young. *South Riding* was published posthumously and also made into a film, directed by Victor Saville.

Suggested Reading
Brittain, Vera. *Testament of Friendship* (London: Macmillan, 1940).
Kennard, Jean. *Vera Britain and Winifred Holtby: A Working Partnership* (Hanover, NH: The University Press of New England, 1989).
Shaw, Marion. *The Clear Stream: A Life of Winifred Holtby* (London: Virago, 1999).

Maroula Joannou

Homosexuality (male)

It was only, perhaps, by the end of the twentieth century, when the rights of homosexuals entered the agenda of mainstream political parties, that it became clear that the controversy was one of the most enduring of the century. The invention of the term, and, in Foucault's pervasive view, even the origin of the homosexual as 'species', can be traced to the last decades of the nineteenth century which, in Britain, saw not only the 1885 Criminal Law Amendment Act and the Wilde trial, but also attempts by writers such as Edward Carpenter and Havelock Ellis to promote tolerance. The long controversy has always had deep symbolic overtones, involving sexuality in general, the role of the law in regulating private behaviour, access to knowledge, and the rights of excluded categories. Some feminists, for example, have made common cause with homosexuals whom they have seen as fellow victims of a dominant patriarchy. Protagonists have been divided not only on the ethical questions but on the nature of homosexuality; whether it is social, psychological, or biological in origin and – a more recent addition – whether it is a constructed or an essential category. Literature of every sort, from scientific monographs to novels and memoirs, has formed a major battleground and women authors have been well represented.

Novelists who have raised the issue have attracted more than literary criticism. Women authors recently taken to task for creating unattractive homosexual characters include Sylvia Townsend WARNER for *Mr Fortune's Maggott* (1927), Katherine MANSFIELD for her short story 'Je ne parle pas français', Rebecca WEST for *Black Lamb and Grey Falcon* (1941), and Winifred HOLTBY for *South Riding* (1936). Such criticisms raise two key questions: whether it is meaningful to criticize older texts for not reproducing the sensibilities of the present, and why such depictions should be regarded a slight on all homosexuals. Clearly, literature can be used for purposes of stigmatization, but few novels deserve to be treated as pure propaganda. The problem becomes more acute with Radclyffe HALL, prominent LESBIAN author of *The Well of Loneliness* (1928), who certainly saw herself – and was seen by many others – as a pioneer for tolerance, but is now criticized for depicting the lives of her male and female 'inverts' as tortured. Virginia WOOLF created male homosexuals in greater depth than any other female British novelist and displayed an acute understanding of the prejudices which clouded their lives. In *The Years* (1937), a character feels 'a sharp shiver of repugnance' but quickly recovers; in *Between the Acts* (1941), a man who cannot cope comfortably with another's homosexuality is presented as petty and diminished. Significant homosexual figures also appear in *Mrs Dalloway* (1925) and *The Waves* (1931). Nonetheless Woolf has been criticized for presenting love between men as a private affair, devoid of political content, and without awareness of illegality. The novels of Ivy COMPTON-BURNETT dealt fearlessly with male homosexual characters, but without Woolf's depth of insight. Naomi MITCHISON, in novels with classical settings such as *The Corn King and the Spring Queen* (1931) and *The Blood of the Martyrs* (1939), offered a view of male love which was not only sympathetic but distinctly erotic. Rose Laure Allatini (pseud. A. T. Fitzroy), in *Despised and Rejected* (1918), examined homosexual men sympathetically in the context of the commonality of interest between various rejected despised groups, and a similar approach was taken by June Westbrook in *Strange Brother* (1932).

Suggested Reading

Light, Alison. *Forever England: Femininity, Literature and Conservatism Between the Wars* (London: Routledge, 1991).

Meyer, Michael J. (ed.). *Literature and Homosexuality* (Amsterdam and Atlanta, GA: Rodopi, 2000).

Woods, Gregory. *A History of Gay Literature: The Male Tradition* (New Haven, CT, and London: Yale University Press, 1998).

Chris Nottingham

Housing

The period 1900 to 1950 witnessed an unprecedented expansion in house-building, combining speculative building by private companies and local authority subsidized housing schemes. Most of the building occurred around the perimeters of city centres: suburban areas, constituting privately and publicly financed housing, grew up along the arterial roads and on the outskirts of all major cities. The suburban ideal of homes distanced from the dirt, noise, and crime of the industrial city had been articulated by the middle classes in the later nineteenth century, but extended to working-class families in the twentieth century.

In 1918 the wartime coalition government focused peacetime reconstruction on the planning of a postwar housing policy, encapsulated in the phrase 'Homes Fit For Heroes', and demanded by the perceived housing shortage. From the 1930s onwards this was extended to slum clearance schemes that moved families to new local authority estates. State responsibility for housing established a set of national standards, which were influenced by Ebenezer Howard's Garden City movement and recommended lower housing density, minimum sizes for rooms, separate sculleries, and back and front gardens. This ensured more light, space, and ventilation as narrow, tunnel-back Victorian houses gave way to the horizontal design of all houses built after 1919. The new suburban estates provided a pleasanter environment, with tree-planting, wide road verges, and cul-de-sacs, than the city centres in which many families had previously lived. The growth of suburbia also reshaped the landscape of industrialized countries in Europe, North America, and Australia in the early twentieth century.

Suburbia also produced new forms of family life: the semi-detached house, for example, was designed to house a smaller family with no SERVANTS, making housework easier by means of new DOMESTIC TECHNOLOGIES such as piped water and electricity. Equally importantly, suburbia provided a semi-rural environment in which people could escape the dangers and tensions of city life. The ready availability of mortgages, the active encouragement of home-ownership, and government aid with building costs all combined to produce a buoyant market for house builders and favourable conditions for aspiring purchasers.

By 1939 it was estimated that approximately one-third of the working-class population was housed in new, sanitary accommodation, one-third remained in older houses that, whilst adequate, lacked modern amenities such as water and electricity, and a final third continued to inhabit substandard housing that was dangerous to HEALTH. The outbreak of the Second World War put an end, for the time being, to solving housing problems, but with the establishment of a WELFARE STATE in the postwar period, housing once again became central to government plans for peacetime reconstruction. This focus on housing by successive governments throughout the first half of the twentieth century made it possible for many women to dream of a home of their own away from the pollution and hazards of the city. By the late 1950s middle-class women were running smaller, suburban, servantless homes, often paid for by a mortgage. Working-class women were increasingly enabled to buy or rent a whole house rather than the rooms that had been the norm at the start of the century. Despite the dislike of suburbia by some commentators, such housing offered women safe, comfortable spaces in which to care for children and loved ones.

Suggested Reading
Burnett, John. *A Social History of Housing, 1815–1985* (London: Methuen 1986).
Silverstone, Roger (ed.). *Visions of Suburbia* (London: Routledge, 1991).
Webster, Roger. *Expanding Suburbia: Reviewing Suburban Narratives* (Oxford: Berghahn, 2000).

Judy Giles

Hughes, Mary Vivian 1866–1956
Pioneering educationalist, founder member of Hughes Hall, Cambridge, and trainer of women teachers in the 1890s at Bedford College, London. Also a writer of school textbooks, Hughes is best remembered for her four-volume autobiography (published between 1934 and 1947). It chronicles the life of her family from the 1870s to the outbreak of the Second World War. Although punctuated by the tragedies of sudden deaths (among them her father, her husband, and her infant daughter), the narrative is recounted without sentimentality or self-pity. Instead, Hughes celebrates the lives of the deceased through vivid anecdote. Beginning with *A London Child of the 1870s*, each volume contains the word 'London' but the wealth of anecdote covers not only seven decades but accounts of travels to different part of Britain and as far afield as Canada and the United States. The *joie de vivre* and humour in her accounts of everyday

life challenge the perception that Victorian women's lives were always stifled by convention. She also celebrates the lives of two ordinary but impressive women, her mother and her 'golden aunt', 'Tony', in *Vivians* (1935), the story of her Cornish family. She has received no attention from critics.

Sue Zlosnik

Hull, E. M. (dates unavailable)

Pseudonym of Edith Maud Winstanley, author of *The Sheik* (1919), which was filmed in 1921 with Rudolf Valentino in the title role, and went on to outsell all other novels of the 1920s put together. *The Sheik* is the erotic and sado-masochistic story of the abduction and repeated rape of Diana Mayo, a boyish and free-spirited English aristocrat, by the cruel but charismatic Sheik Ahmed Ben Hassan. The novel dwells continually on the sexual responses of the heroine:

> She writhed in his arms as he crushed her to him . . . the close union with his warm, strong body robbed her of all strength, of all power of resistance . . . 'Oh, you brute! You brute!' she wailed, until his kisses silenced her.

The Sheik was derided by literary critics, and was memorably described by Q. D. LEAVIS in *Fiction and the Reading Public* (1932) as 'a typist's day dream'. It was condemned in the press as lurid pornography, the reason for the outrage (as well as the source of the novel's interest for feminists today) being that *The Sheik* is a rare instance of pornography written for women, by a woman.

Today, both the anti-feminist narrative and racist stereotypes make the novel problematic, to say the least. The regressive sexual ideology at work in *The Sheik* is interpreted by David Ayers as a reaction to the unbalancing of traditional gender roles in the interwar period. The reinstatement of the masterful patriarch and the humiliation of the independent woman are accomplished in Diana's final submission to the Sheik: 'He was a brute but she loved him for his very brutality and superb animal strength.' The novel also squares up the then socially unacceptable idea of interracial sex by revealing in the last chapter that Ahmed is in fact the son of an English lord and is therefore, as Nicola Beauman puts it, a 'decent English chap' after all.

E. M. Hull's follow-up to *The Sheik* was *The Shadow of the East* (1921), in which Barry Craven, the brooding hero, strives to conceal from his young wife his unintentional crime of incest committed many years ago, and exercises a sexual restraint that is in direct contrast to the priapic Sheik. In 1925, Hull returned to the desert romance genre with the sequel *Sons of the Sheik*, also filmed as *Son of the Sheik* (1926). *Camping in the Sahara*, a travel book, appeared in 1926, and is based on her tour of Morocco taken in the company of a female friend.

In all, Hull wrote eight novels, ending with *Jungle Captive* (1939), after which she fell silent. Almost nothing is known about her, apart from the fact that she was married to a Derbyshire gentleman pig-farmer, and even the dates of her birth and death are uncertain. Unlike 'superstars' of twenties popular fiction such as Elinor GLYN, Hull never became a public figure, and no photograph of her survives. It is assumed that she wrote under a pseudonym to avoid bringing shame on her family.

Suggested Reading

Ayers, David. *English Literature of the 1920s* (Edinburgh: Edinburgh University Press, 1999).

Beauman, Nicola. *A Very Great Profession: The Woman's Novel, 1914–1939* (London: Virago, 1983).

Melman, Billie. *Women and the Popular Imagination in the Twenties: Flappers and Nymphs* (Basingstoke: Macmillan, 1988).

Kathy Hopewell

Hunt, Violet 1866–1942

Novelist, short-story writer and biographer. Eldest daughter of the novelist Margaret Hunt (née Raine) and the painter Alfred William Hunt, Isobel Violet Hunt was born in Durham, and brought up in a Kensington household that formed a centre for literary and artistic circles, including the Rossettis, John Ruskin, and Oscar Wilde. Several of her works featured this semi-bohemian milieu and included identifiable figures of the day.

A somewhat underrated New Woman novelist, who has not yet received the recent critical attention accorded to some other members of this group, Hunt led a life which itself reads like a New Woman novel. First studying at the South Kensington Art School, she then turned to literary journalism. Following inconclusive courtship by Oscar Wilde, and his subsequent marriage, Violet pursued an affair with the painter George Boughton, who was over twice her age. This ended on his marriage, but was briefly resumed in the aftermath of her infatuation with an Etonian schoolboy and the attentions of several family-approved suitors. She then had a prolonged affair with Oswald Crawfurd, another older, married, man, a notorious womanizer who gave her syphilis, although she did not realize this until some years after the liaison ended.

In 1900 she and her ageing mother moved to South Lodge, Kensington, where she established herself as a literary hostess, noted for her wit and her encouragement of younger writers, in particular other women. She was an ardent supporter of the SUFFRAGE movement. In 1908 she was introduced to Ford Madox Hueffer (later Ford), 11 years her junior and editor of *The English Review*. She assisted him in this enterprise, and in the following year they became lovers, Hueffer having been unhappily married for some while. The stratagems Hueffer followed in order to marry Hunt (since his wife refused divorce) led to his eventual imprisonment for bigamy, and to open scandal surrounding both of them. This, and issues over their mother's declining health, led to serious difficulties between Hunt and her sisters. The relationship with Hueffer became increasingly stormy, until it ended in 1917.

Hunt's novels were remarkably frank and daring. Even her most sympathetic female characters are neither straightforward heroines nor simple victims, often cynical and calculating rather than passionate, endeavouring to negotiate their survival in a hostile world, and finding that accepted conventions do not fit them comfortably. In *A Hard Woman* (1895) and *Tiger-Skin* (1924, first published in her 1911 volume *Tales of the Uneasy*), a painful yet psychologically intricate study of child abuse, she produced memorably nasty – though complex – villainesses. Her short stories often explored occult and uncanny themes with great success. Her writing can be biting and witty, but she was inclined to take too little trouble with the overall plot and structure of her novels. Her biography of Elizabeth Siddal, *The Wife of Rossetti* (1932), based on her own knowledge of the individuals concerned, aroused controversy, as did her personal memoir *The Flurried Years* (1926). Her later years, suffering from the ravages of advanced syphilis, were spent in seclusion in her beloved South Lodge.

Suggested Reading

Belford, Barbara. *Violet: The Story of the Irrepressible Violet Hunt and Her Circle of Lovers and Friends* (New York: Simon & Schuster, 1990).

Goldring, Douglas. *South Lodge: Reminiscences of Violet Hunt, Ford Madox Ford, and the 'English Review' Circle* (London: Constable, 1943).

Hardwick, Joan. *An Immodest Violet: The Life of Violet Hunt* (London: Andre Deutsch, 1990).

Lesley A. Hall

Huxley, Elspeth 1907–97

Novelist, travel writer, memoirist, biographer, conservationist, political analyst, whose African writing over a period of 50 years is indispensable to our understanding of British colonial relations in East Africa, the ending of the EMPIRE, and its aftermath. Yet Huxley remains neglected, except by those critics who accuse her of usurping an African identity which no colonial subject can rightfully claim. To read Huxley's writing according to her own design reveals a sustained critique of the romantic dreams through which British colonial settlement justified itself, and a continual consciousness of the effects of British colonialism in Africa, and the effects of British ignorance on the peoples of Kenya and on themselves.

A key work dramatizing these effects is her 1939 novel, *Red Strangers*, which investigates the condition of the Kikuyu people before, during, and after colonial settlement. A foreword confesses to Huxley's lack of ethnographic training and reliance on imagination, but she also drew on extensive interviews with

Kikuyu, including the elders working at the farm of Jos and Nellie Grant, Huxley's minor aristocrat parents, who came to Kenya in 1911. In the foreword to *Red Strangers*, she disclaims 'any intention of speaking for the Kikuyu people', stating: 'I am well aware that no person of one race and culture can truly interpret events from the angle of individuals belonging to a totally different race and culture.' Huxley pondered this cultural and hermeneutical problem for the rest of her career, as is evident in her five murder thrillers, including *Murder on Safari* (1938) and *African Poison Murders* (1939), which raise further questions about whether a white woman writer can represent African peoples on their own terms, rather than as pawns of colonial fantasies.

The possibility that fantasy would rule colonial life is taken up by Huxley in her best known work, *The Flame Trees of Thika* (1959), a fictionalized account of the early years of the Grants's residence in Kenya. Its construction of a child's consciousness questions the adult narrator's retrospective wisdom, and the well-intentioned plans of the Grants are constantly undercut by Huxley's interpellation of various colonial voices. The hybrid critical consciousness recounts the emergence of a writing self that is formed by colonial history but that also demands a role in shaping it and searching for its often contradictory meanings.

Although Huxley left Kenya at 18, never to live there again, she returned frequently enough to continue to explore this vexed colonial and then postcolonial relationship as a thwarted adventure of discovery. Two more volumes of memoir recount the colonial experience through WORLD WAR ONE, *The Mottled Lizard* (1962), and *Out in the Midday Sun* (1987). Huxley included WORLD WAR TWO as a shaping force in her 1948 novel, *The Walled City*, and the Mau Mau uprisings in *A Thing to Love* (1954). In the postwar period, she was invited to advise African administrators on land use, resulting in the books *Four Guineas: A Journey Through West Africa* (1954) and *The Challenge of Africa* (1971). Nearly 60 years after her parents took her on their great adventure, Huxley published her last novel, *A Man From Nowhere* (1987), as an act of mourning for an impossible dream. It is a testament to Huxley's great integrity as a late colonial writer that she inscribes this from the start.

Suggested Reading

Achebe, Chinua. *Home and Exile* (New York: Anchor Books, 2001).

Lassner, Phyllis. *Colonial Strangers: Women Writing the End of Empire* (New Brunswick, NJ: Rutgers University Press, 2004).

Webster, Wendy. 'Elspeth Huxley: Gender, Empire, and Narratives of Nation, 1935–1964', *Women's History Review*, 8.3 (1999) 527–45.

Phyllis Lassner

I

Influenza Pandemic

The 1918/19 pandemic was the worst influenza outbreak ever experienced, killing over 25 million in six months. In Britain, approximately 225,000 died. Although outbreaks of influenza were not uncommon during the war, the strain responsible for the pandemic was highly virulent. It first appeared in US army camps in March 1918, spreading through troop movements to Asia, Africa, and Europe. By November, the pandemic was worldwide; by April 1919, it had passed. The privations of war damaged the HEALTH of civilian populations, making them more susceptible to influenza; while postwar dislocation meant that some European states were unable to cope. Although most influenza victims did recover, death could be rapid, with sufferers drowning as their lungs filled with liquid. Young adults were particularly vulnerable and women were hit harder than men.

The psychological and physical impact of the pandemic was considerable. Funeral services were overwhelmed and other public services such as the police were disrupted. Although considerable effort was invested in discovering the aetiology of the outbreak and in devising treatments, no cure was found. Existing medical services were greatly overstretched and preventive policies in Britain were ineffectual. Despite the nature of the influenza outbreak, its long-term impact was small: communities already struggling with the physical and mental effects of war learned few lessons from the pandemic.

Suggested Reading

Johnson, Niall and Juergen Mueller. 'Updating the Accounts: Global Mortality of the 1918–1920 "Spanish" Influenza Pandemic', *Bulletin of the History of Medicine*, 76.1 (Spring 2001) 105–15.

Tomkins, Sandra. 'The Failure of Expertise: Public Health Policy in Britain During the 1918–19 Influenza Epidemic', *Social History of Medicine*, 5 (2001) 435–54.

Keir Waddington

Irish Question

The Irish Question in British politics refers to the controversy surrounding the 1912 Home Rule Bill which ultimately led to the partition of Ireland between North and South. Under the terms of the 1800 Act of Union, the kingdoms of Britain and Ireland were united with direct rule from Westminster. Throughout the nineteenth century numerous attempts, some constitutional and some revolutionary, were made to undermine this Union and win political independence for Ireland, paralleling movements towards independence in other parts of the British EMPIRE. Home Rule referred to plans for a federal system of government for Ireland, with a parliament in Dublin overseeing domestic affairs and the Westminster parliament retaining control over imperial issues. Under such a proposal, Ireland would achieve some independence whilst remaining part of the United Kingdom.

In 1874 the Home Rule Party was formed at Westminster and succeeded in drawing attention to the Irish Question through the effective policy of obstructing parliamentary debate. Under the leadership of Charles Stuart Parnell, the Home Rule Party supported the Liberal Prime Minister William Gladstone's promise of a Home Rule Bill for Ireland, thereby ensuring that the Liberal party was returned to power in January 1886. The Bill was defeated in parliament, resulting in a split within the Liberal party over the Irish Question. This defeat also highlighted the strong opposition to Home Rule amongst Unionist MPs, who represented the Protestant majority in Northern Ireland and who wished to maintain the full political union between Britain and Ireland.

A second Home Rule Bill proposed in 1893, with a new clause allowing for continued Irish representation at Westminster, was passed in Parliament but defeated in the Lords by Conservative and Unionist peers. The third Home Rule Bill, introduced to the House of Commons in April 1912, was to prove more successful. When the 1911 Parliament Act deprived the Lords of the right to veto House of Commons' legislation, and with the Liberals in power once again but relying on Irish support, the Bill was passed. Its implementation was, however, delayed for two years following its defeat in the Lords. The Bill allowed for a parliament in Dublin with limited powers over domestic affairs whilst Westminster retained control over foreign affairs and defence. Ireland was also entitled to send 42 MPs to Westminster.

The reaction to the 1912 Home Rule Bill in Ireland was dramatic. In Northern Ireland, where the majority of the population were Protestant and loyal to the British Crown, the proposal to undermine the Union was met with immediate defiance. Following a mass demonstration in Belfast in September 1912, the Ulster Solemn League and Covenant was drawn up, declaring that Unionists would pledge to use whatever force necessary to prevent the introduction of Home Rule for Ireland. Hundreds of thousands of people signed the covenant, and in 1913 the Ulster Volunteer Force was established to defend the Union. The UVF began to train and guns were illegally imported from Germany in 1914 to arm the force. In the South of Ireland, where the majority of the population was Catholic and nationalist, the idea of greater independence from Britain was widely supported. The call to arms by the Unionists in the North was met with alarm. In response, the Irish Volunteer Force was established to defend Home Rule and Irish freedom, and it too engaged in drilling and gun-running. The threat of civil war in Ireland was now very real, and war was only averted by the decision in Westminster to suspend the Home Rule Bill for the duration of the First World War.

The situation deteriorated following the 1916 Easter Rising, a failed attempt to establish an independent Republic of Ireland. Although supported by only a minority of revolutionary republicans, the swift execution of the leaders of the Rising by the British resulted in a major shift in public support in the South away from Home Rule and in favour of total independence from Britain. As a result the popularity of Sinn Fein, a political party advocating a republic and nothing less, grew whilst support for Home Rule dwindled. Following the 1918 general election, an independent parliament dominated by Sinn Fein was set up in Dublin in January 1921, and a war of independence against the British became inevitable. As the war waged on, with atrocities committed on both sides, the 1920 Government of Ireland Act was passed, introducing Home Rule for the six counties of Northern Ireland. The partition of Ireland between North and South was now complete. In July 1921 a truce was agreed between the British and the Irish Republican Army in the South, and five months later the Anglo-Irish Treaty was signed. This agreement further cemented the partition of North and South with the establishment of a 26-county independent Irish Free State. The new six-county Northern Ireland remained part of the United Kingdom. As a result of this settlement the Irish Question faded into the background of British politics until its re-emergence in the late 1960s with the outbreak of 'the troubles'.

Suggested Reading

Boyce, D. G. *The Irish Question and British Politics, 1868–1996* (Basingstoke: Macmillan – now Palgrave Macmillan, 1996).

Foster, R. F. *Modern Ireland, 1600–1972* (Harmondsworth: Penguin, 1988).

Lee, Joseph J. *Ireland, 1912–1985: Politics and Society* (Cambridge: Cambridge University Press, 1989).

Townshend, Charles. *Ireland: The Twentieth Century* (London: Arnold, 1998).

Caitriona Beaumont

J

Jameson, Storm 1891–1986

Novelist, short-story writer, playwright, critic, poet, and journalist, who reflected on much of the thinking and many of the events of her times. Margaret Storm Jameson, daughter of a Yorkshire sea captain, attended Leeds University and completed her MA in London in 1920. In her early work, she experimented with form and content, ranging from novels of ideas, as in *The Pot Boils* (1919), to a passionate portrayal of jealousy in *The Pitiful Wife* (1923). At the same time she wrote articles on drama, literature, and economics for journals on both sides of the Atlantic. By the mid-twenties her style was lucid and precise; she excelled at painting rural and urban landscapes in words, and her ear for dialogue reflected her love of theatre (a number of her novels are written in draft as plays). In her Mirror of Darkness trilogy: *Company Parade* (1934), *Love in Winter* (1935), and *None Turn Back* (1936), set between the end of WORLD WAR ONE and the GENERAL STRIKE of 1926, she explored the social scene through the eyes of a passionate young writer (Jameson was at the time compared to D. H. Lawrence, but she also has much in common with Orwell).

Jameson's PACIFIST stance was clear during the interwar years, but by the end of the thirties she reluctantly accepted it was inadequate as a response to Hitler's brand of FASCISM. Her position reflected her experiences in her work with refugees and her journeys to Europe for PEN; she was president of the English section from 1938 to 1944. Her writing now showed her looking beyond English society to Europe, and her fiction reflects this, both in its content and in the approach, which includes techniques drawn from her favourite French novelists, such as Stendhal. Many of her finest novels were written over these years. *Europe to Let* (1940), admired by Rosamond LEHMANN, challenges readerly complacency about the realities of life in a darkening Europe. *Cousin Honore*, published in the same year, mirrors the issues and characters dominating European public life, setting them in a small-town situation, a method she also adopts in *Cloudless May* (1943), so that conflicts of personalities and loyalties are given a disturbing intimacy. She also began to write futuristic texts with affinities to SCIENCE FICTION, including *The World Ends* (1937), published under the pseudonym William Lamb, and *Then We Shall Hear Singing* (1942).

Her commitment to her work with refugees (often rewriting works to give them a chance of publication; providing money when PEN's funds ran low) had seriously damaged her health by the end of the war. Despite this, she agreed to visit Poland in 1945, writing up vivid details as in the simple comment that the British Ambassador tells how 'as a curiosity he was shown in a hospital one Jewish child'. Jameson never insults the reader's intelligence by careful explanations. She was a feminist without feeling the need to take to the barricades: in 1928, in an *Evening News* article, she says: 'If a feminist is a person who believes that women are mentally fitted to succeed in any career, then I am a feminist.' But first and foremost, she believed in social justice; her development as a novelist and her choice of style and approach reflect this.

Suggested Reading
Hartley, Jenny. *Millions Like Us: British Women's Fiction of the Second World War* (London: Virago, 1997).

Lassner, Phyllis. *British Women Writers of World War Two: Battlegrounds of Their Own* (Basingstoke: Macmillan – now Palgrave Macmillan, 1998).

Maslen, Elizabeth. *Political and Social Issues in British Women's Fiction, 1928–1968* (Basingstoke: Palgrave Macmillan, 2001).

Elizabeth Maslen

Jarrow March
Proletarian protest of the interwar period included many hunger marches and marches for jobs, often organized by the National Unemployed Workers' Movement. However, the orderly march of 200 men from Jarrow to London (October to November 1936), led by their Labour MP Ellen WILKINSON, achieved greater publicity, drawing attention to Jarrow's unemployment rate of more than 70 per cent after the closure of shipyard and steelworks.

The march, organized by the Town Council and blessed by Jarrow's Bishop, drew support from all local political parties, churches, and chapels. Although the Bishop of Durham condemned the march as 'revolutionary mob pressure', and the national Labour Party and Trades Union Congress expressed disapproval, numerous acts of sympathy greeted the marchers; food, sleeping space, baths, medical care, and boot repairs were provided. Marchers had been medically vetted but the effects of malnutrition were clear.

Ellen Wilkinson's *The Town That Was Murdered* (1939) treats Jarrow as an illustration of the evils of capitalism under which: 'Men are regarded as mere instruments of production, their labour a commodity to be bought and sold.' While Jarrow's situation had improved by 1939, thanks to public sympathy and rearmament, she saw no change in the underlying problem.

Suggested Reading
Wilkinson, Ellen. *The Town That Was Murdered: The Life-Story of Jarrow* (London: Gollancz/Left Book Club, 1939).

Kathleen Bell

Jesse, F[ryniwyd] Tennyson 1888–1958

Novelist, journalist, crime historian, and dramatist, whose major achievement was the novel *A Pin To See The Peepshow* (1934). This book drew on her feminist interests in its well-researched fictional recreation of the case of Edith Thompson, hanged in 1922 for her younger lover's killing of her husband in a public brawl. Jesse's heroine, Julia, hankers after the world of FASHION and celebrity. Round her, Jesse constructs early twentieth-century London in lavish detail: work in a West End dress-shop, marriage in a Chiswick maisonette, a brief encounter with a young seaman. When Julia becomes herself the peepshow, the novel changes into a powerful indictment of the moral panic and social and sexual prejudices which condemn her to hang: 'Two things were hanging Julia Starling – her birth certificate and her place in the social scale.'

Jesse, a vicar's daughter, and great-niece of Alfred Tennyson, explored a wide range of possibilities. She studied painting at the Newlyn School, and was one of the few women war correspondents in WORLD WAR ONE, collecting her reporting in *The Sword of Deborah* (1919). In 1918 she married the dramatist Harold Marsh Harwood, and wrote several social conscience plays successful in West End productions, including, with Harwood, *The Pelican* (1926), about a single mother's self-sacrifice, and, solo, *Anyhouse* (1925), about upstairs-downstairs tensions in a middle-class house. She wrote several historical novels, including *Moonraker* (1927), about a female pirate. Most important of these is *A Lacquer Lady* (1929); Jesse visited Burma to interview people who remembered the British annexation in 1886, and her novel recreates the last days of the Glass Palace in Mandalay. Her Eurasian heroine, Fanny, a palace maid who eventually repudiates her Burmese side, is, like Julia Starling, a fantasist out of her depth. Presenting great events through her deracinated, politically naïve eyes allows Jesse to foreground the psychological and sexual tensions in imperialism.

Jesse's crime writing included the theoretical discussion *Murder and its Motives* (1924), and several volumes in the series *Notable British Trials*, including those on Madeleine Smith (1927) and Alma Rattenbury (1935), two more fantasists in deep trouble. Her most enduring dramatic contribution came when she provided the story for *San Demetrio, London* (1943), one of the best British wartime films. In this recreation of a real case, some sailors without officers reclaim their shelled, abandoned but still just seaworthy oil tanker and bring it safely home. The democratic emphasis is characteristic of wartime films, but also of Jesse's interest in history from below. Jesse became a member of the Royal Society of Literature in 1947, but has received little critical attention. Much of her writing is topically urgent journey work, but her feminist, crime, and documentary interests coalesced very successfully in her finest novel.

Suggested Reading

Colenbrander, Joanna. *A Portrait of Fryn: A Biography of F. Tennyson Jesse* (London: Deutsch, 1984).

Morgan, Elaine. Afterword to *A Pin To See The Peepshow* by F. Tennyson Jesse (London: Virago, 1979) 404–8.

Anthea Trodd

Johnson, Pamela Hansford 1912–1981

Chiefly known as a novelist and critic, but a prolific writer in many genres, including poetry, drama, and radio broadcast. Despite this, there are few recent studies of her life and work. Following the death of her father in 1923, Johnson and her mother lived in comparatively impoverished circumstances. She attended Clapham County Secondary School and went to secretarial college at 16. She worked as a stenographer until 1934, when she gained literary recognition, winning the *Sunday Referee* prize for poetry, which led to the publication of her first volume of poems, *Symphony for Full Orchestra*. In this year she also met, and was briefly engaged to, Dylan Thomas.

The 'shabby genteel' existence of Johnson and her mother formed the basis for much of her early writing, such as her first novel *This Bed Thy Centre* (1935) and also *Here Today* (1937), which she described on the title page as 'a story of the small life'. This 'small life' of suburban existence is represented as seedy and depressing, and both novels employ parallel narratives, focusing both on an individual protagonist and on the wider community. *This Bed Thy Centre*, which details in part the sexual awakening of the strictly moral Elsie Cotton and the infidelities of her fiancé, Roly, provoked a shocked response due to its frank treatment of sex.

Johnson was committed to her social and political ideals; she was a member of the Chelsea Labour party and the Left BOOK CLUB, and the editor of a leftist weekly, the *Chelsea Democrat*. She also took part in demonstrations supporting the loyalists in the SPANISH CIVIL WAR. In 1936, she married an Australian journalist and historian, Gordon Neil Stewart, with whom she collaborated on two murder mysteries, *Tidy Death* (1940) and *Murder's a Swine* (1943), under the pseudonym Nap Lombard. They had two children, but the marriage ended in 1948, due to their prolonged estrangement during WORLD WAR TWO. During the 1940s, Johnson continued to write straight novels under her own name, and developed her career in BROADCASTING, beginning mainly as a book reviewer for the BBC, and progressing to her *Six Proust Reconstructions*, broadcast between 1948 and 1956.

In 1950 she married the novelist C. P. Snow, with whom she had another child. Johnson and Snow collaborated on a series of six plays in 1951, including *The Supper Dance* and *Her Best Foot Forward*, which Johnson later dismissed as 'written very frivolously . . . while on our honeymoon . . . they're of little value'. Johnson continued to write to critical acclaim, branching into comedy with her novel *The Unspeakable Skipton* (1959) and satire in *Night and Silence, Who is Here?* (1963), demonstrating her sustained versatility as a writer.

Suggested Reading

Lindblad, Ishrat. *Pamela Hansford Johnson* (Boston, MA: Twayne, 1982).

Rendell, Ruth. Introduction to *The Unspeakable Skipton* by Pamela Hansford Johnson (London: Prior, 2002) vii–xi.

Esme Miskimmin

K

Kavan, Anna 1901–1968

Novelist, short-story writer and painter, best known for her semi-autobiographical fiction and the Kafkaesque quality of her later work. Born Helen Woods in Cannes, France, Kavan travelled widely as a child and was educated in Europe and California. Twice married and divorced, she began writing while living in Burma with her first husband, Donald Ferguson, and published six novels under her married name, Helen Ferguson. Kavan's experiences in Burma provide the backdrop to *Let Me Alone* (1930). This early novel explores the allures and terrors of isolation and solitude in its portrayal of Anna's negotiation of her marriage to the violent bully, Matthew Kavan: 'She wanted to go through life alone, in her own independent detached fashion. The idea of being bound up with another person in such a relationship was hateful to her.' It is in *Let Me Alone*, and the later novel, *A Stranger Still* (1935), that the character of Anna Kavan, whose name she would legally adopt, appears.

A heroin-user from her mid-twenties, Kavan was plagued by addiction and depression for most of her life, attempting suicide on several occasions and spending periods undergoing treatment for mental illness in England and Switzerland. The spectres of addiction and mental breakdown haunt much of her later writing. The highly acclaimed *Asylum Piece* (1940), the first work published under her new writerly – and personal – identity, is a collection of short stories exploring the multiple faces of insanity and, marking a departure from her earlier novels, establishes the experimental and surrealistic style of her later works. It is here that the 'nocturnal writer' much admired by Anaïs Nin – who praised *Asylum Piece* as 'a classic equal to the work of Kafka' – emerges in full force. These sketches of insanity and despair were followed by the novel *Change the Name* (1941) and *I Am Lazarus* (1945), another series of forays into the nightmarish depths of psychological disturbance and breakdown.

Kavan's sophisticated surrealist experimentation also shapes what she described as the 'night-time language' of *Sleep Has His House* (1948), also published as *The House of Sleep* (1947), and her exploration of the slipperiness of identity and reality in *Who Are You?* (1963). Published in 1967, *Ice*, Kavan's SCIENCE FICTION masterpiece, is perhaps the best known of her fictions, and depicts a man's pursuit of an elusive woman across an icy wasteland. *Julia and the Bazooka* (1970) and *My Soul in China* (1975) were published posthumously, as was *Mercury* (1994), described by Doris Lessing as a 'glittering hallucinogenic novel' which takes the reader into 'a realm of the marvellous, like a latter-day Ancient Mariner compelled to follow the tale, hypnotized by this story-teller who is at last getting the attention she deserves'. Nevertheless, the fact that she destroyed much of her personal correspondence and diaries, combined with her reclusive lifestyle, means that Kavan remains a peculiarly enigmatic writer – reflecting her own aspiration 'to become the world's best-kept secret; one that would never be told'.

Suggested Reading

Callard, David. *The Case of Anna Kavan: A Biography* (London: Peter Owen, 1992).
Garrity, Jane. 'Nocturnal Transgressions in *The House of Sleep*: Anna Kavan's Maternal Registers', *Modern Fiction Studies*, 40.2 (Summer 1994) 253–77.

Rebecca Munford

Kaye-Smith, Sheila 1887–1956

Rural novelist, known for her depictions of the landscape and idiom of her native Sussex. Kaye-Smith was born in St-Leonard's-on-Sea, and started writing early in life. In 1924, she married Theodore Penrose Fry, and they lived in London and subsequently on a farm in Northian, East Sussex. She converted from Methodism to Anglo-Catholicism, and then to Roman Catholicism, and built a chapel on the farm dedicated to St Thérèse de Lisieux, one of the female saints she wrote about in her book *Quartet in Heaven* (1952).

Kaye-Smith's early novel Sussex Gorse (1916) was one of her most successful, and among her many later fictions, *Joanna Godden* (1921) and *The History of Susan Spray, the Female Preacher* (1931) are the best known. Their strong, defiant female protagonists were admired by feminists, and in the 1980s both were republished in the VIRAGO Modern Classics series. Kaye-Smith associated with and supported numerous other women writers, and was a member of the adjudicating committee for the PRIX FEMINA-VIE HEUREUSE. She was not, however, affiliated with the WOMEN'S MOVEMENT. She wrote in *Three Ways Home: An Experiment in Autobiography* (1937): 'I was not opposed to Women's Suffrage – just not interested (I should think better of myself now if then I had at least done a little to help win that nothing which should have been so much).' In 1913, she was accused of burning down Levetleigh, the Borough Member's house, which stood opposite hers, and was probably destroyed by suffragists. She notes: 'I believe that there are still people who think that I burned down Levetleigh. It is just the sort of thing a novelist would do.'

Kaye-Smith participated in the early twentieth-century vogue for REGIONAL WRITING, which came to be known as the Loam and Lovechild school, and which was parodied by Stella GIBBONS in *Cold Comfort Farm* (1932). The original for Gibbons's character Reuben, who is obsessed with his ownership of farmland, can be found in *Sussex Gorse*; while the imaginary Calvinist sect in *Cold Comfort Farm*, the Quivering Brethren, refers to the Colgate Brethren in *Susan Spray*, and more generally to the presence in many rural novels of Old

Testament theology and belief in a vengeful God. Gibbons also parodies Kaye-Smith's purple passages, and the separation of dialect from educated speech in her fiction. Kaye-Smith's attempt to represent regional idiom contrasts sharply with the lyric landscape descriptions in the educated voice of the narrator. This inevitably constructs the characters as far less cultured and articulate than the author, an attitude that some found patronizing. It may, equally, have been a deliberate strategy, designed to explore the discrepancy between the perspective of the rural population and the urban visitor's reading of the English countryside as picturesque and quaint.

Among Kaye-Smith's non-fictional works are two very engaging books on Jane Austen, jointly authored with G. B. STERN, and a book on Anglo-Catholicism. During her lifetime, her novels were extremely popular, and *Joanna Godden* was made into a film in 1947. Today, however, her work attracts few readers and virtually no critical attention.

Suggested Reading

Anderson, Rachel. Introduction to *Joanna Godden* by Sheila Kaye-Smith (London: Virago, 1983) i–xviii.

Montefiore, Janet. Introduction to *The History of Susan Spray, the Female Preacher* by Sheila Kaye-Smith (London: Virago, 1983) i–xiii.

Trodd, Anthea. *Women's Writing in English: Britain, 1900–1950* (Harlow: Addison, 1998).

Faye Hammill

Keane, Molly 1904–1996

Novelist and dramatist, who also published as M. J. Farrell. Keane chronicled, with increasingly black comedy, the Big House life of the Anglo-Irish Ascendancy in the first decades of the twentieth century, exposing their assumed imperviousness to the political and economic realities that would eventually wrench them from their lives of privileged and self-absorbed leisure. As M. J. Farrell, she published 11 novels and six plays between 1926 and 1961, enjoying considerable popularity. A 20-year silence was broken by her masterpiece *Good Behaviour* (1981), the first novel published under her own name.

Born Mary Nesta Skrine in County Kildare to Anglo-Irish gentry, Keane and her four siblings grew up neglected by parents who preferred their own pursuits. Keane readily adopted her father's passion for horses and hunting. Her mother, the poet Moira O'Neill, took refuge in writing and gardening. After an indifferent education by a succession of governesses and at a boarding school, Keane escaped for long periods to Woodruff, the Perry home. There she came into contact with sympathetic people and was taught 'what to read and to go to the theatre'. She and John Perry later collaborated on some of Keane's plays. At Woodruff she also met her husband, Bobby Keane, with whom she had two daughters.

Directly informed by her childhood, Keane's fiction powerfully evokes the texture of life in the Irish big houses, registering the unreflective absorption of childhood, whose 'days slipped past like bright ships, sailing out far beyond remembrance' as well as the 'sadness and propriety' of houses whose walls wait to unleash the accumulated force of ancient family quarrels and unsatisfied passions. The hunting romance *Young Entry* (1928) was followed by two novels directly addressing the IRISH QUESTION: *Mad Puppetstown* (1931) and *Two Days in Aragon* (1941).

As early as *Taking Chances* (1929), Keane began a serious critique of the Anglo-Irish, focusing on the female victims of its mores. Her novels are peopled with remote, manipulative or despotic mothers and with unmarried women: governesses and maiden aunts who pathetically cling to the fringes of family life, and unmarried daughters whose education has been sidestepped. While in *Mad Puppetstown, Devoted Ladies* (1934), and *The Rising Tide* (1937), gardening spinsters turn their initial revolt against the domestic code into a deep and private feeling for place, Keane became less optimistic in later novels about the ability of these oppressed women to create healthy identities. The overweight, obtuse and self-absorbed unreliable narrator of *Good Behaviour* is a direct product of the abuse she has suffered as an unloved daughter and of her training in 'good behaviour'. Shortlisted for the Booker prize, *Good Behaviour* was followed by *Time After Time* (1983) and *Loving and Giving* (1988). With the publication of these three novels, Keane's early work has enjoyed revived interest; many of these novels have been reprinted by VIRAGO. In recent years feminist, postcolonial, and Irish literary scholars have placed Keane's work in literary canons alongside that of Maria Edgeworth, Elizabeth BOWEN, Evelyn Waugh and W. B. Yeats.

Suggested Reading

Backus, Margot Gayle. *The Gothic Family Romance: Heterosexuality, Child Sacrifice, and the Anglo-Irish Colonial Order* (Durham, NC, and London: Duke University Press, 1999).

Lynch, Rachel Jane. 'The Crumbling Fortress: Molly Keane's Comedies of Anglo-Irish Manners', in Theresa O'Connor (ed.), *The Comic Tradition in Irish Women Writers* (Gainesville, FL: University Press of Florida, 1996) 73–97.

Weekes, Ann Owens. *Irish Women Writers: An Uncharted Tradition* (Lexington: University Press of Kentucky, 1990) 155–73.

Stella Deen

Kennedy, Margaret 1896–1967

Novelist and playwright whose intellectual rigour did not prevent her from winning popular success. Born in London, Kennedy, daughter of an eminent lawyer, was educated at Cheltenham Ladies College and Somerville College,

Oxford. Her first two books, *A Century of Revolution, 1789–1920* (1922) and a novel, *The Ladies of Lyndon* (1923), were well received, but no-one predicted the runaway success of her 1924 novel *The Constant Nymph*. It revolves around a bohemian group (apparently based on Augustus John's family), and Kennedy's style is epitomized by the opening lines: 'At the time of his death the name of Albert Sanger was barely known to the musical public of Great Britain. Among the very few who had heard of him there were even some who called him Sanje, in the French manner, being disinclined to suppose that great men are occasionally born in Hammersmith.' The novel spawned a long-running play, four films, and a sequel, *The Fool of the Family* (1930).

Kennedy then wrote further novels, including *Red Sky at Morning* (1927), *Return I Dare Not* (1932), and *A Long Time Ago* (1932), together with plays, including *The Long Weekend* (1927), *Jordan* (1928), and *Come With Me* (1928, with Basil Dean), before achieving a big theatrical hit with *Escape Me Never* (1933). It starred Elisabeth Bergner as an unwed mother who marries a man who does not love her. For her role in the film, Bergner received an Oscar nomination. Despite (or perhaps because of) this triumph in popular culture, from 1938 Kennedy wrote little for 12 years, aside from one play, *Happy with Either* (1948). As she said, she 'had twelve years in which to stroll about and look at things, without being obliged to rush off and turn the *chose vue* into the *chose imaginée* in a sort of pressure cooker'. She spent the war years in the country with her three children, regularly travelling up to town to visit her husband, David Davies, a judge, until their London home was destroyed in the Blitz. Her account of the first year of the war, based on diary entries, appeared as *Where Stands a Winged Sentry* in 1941.

She returned to writing in 1950 with a biography of Jane Austen, and her Austenesque novel *Troy Chimneys* (1953) won the James Tait Black Prize. In 1957 she produced *The Outlaw on Parnassus*, an intellectually austere study of twentieth century fiction and its degeneration in public esteem, and a novel, *The Heroes of Clone*. Other late novels include *A Night in Cold Harbour* (1960), *The Forgotten Smile* (1961), and *Not in the Calendar* (1964).

Margaret Kennedy was considered one of the brilliant intellectual women novelists of the twentieth century, her work distinguished by hardness, gaiety, and moral stamina. The *New York Herald Tribune* conjectured that 'because she has written relatively few books she seems to have had time to savour the persons and circumstances of which she writes, to observe and understand and enjoy small eccentricities, which are not small in their relation to an individual life, to enjoy the contrasts in thought and feeling and action among people whom many would dismiss as merely odd or even ordinary'.

Suggested Reading
Melman, Billie. *Women and the Popular Imagination in the 1920s: Flappers and Nymphs* (London: Macmillan, 1988).

Morgan, Fidelis (ed.). *The Years Between: Plays by Women on the London Stage, 1900–1950.* Preface by Susannah York (London: Virago, 1995).

Powell, Violet. *The Constant Novelist: A Study of Margaret Kennedy, 1986–1967* (London: Heinemann, 1983).

Fidelis Morgan

King-Hall, Magdalen 1904–1971

Historical novelist, journalist, and historian, author of the sensational hoax *The Diary of a Young Lady of Fashion in the Year 1764–1765* (1925) and the twice-filmed *The Wicked Lady* (1946). The daughter of an admiral, King-Hall was born in London in 1904, and as a child often visited her mother's family home, Quintin Castle, County Down. Her first book, the *Diary*, published under the pseudonym Cleone Knox, recounts the adventures of an Irish heiress touring Europe. The heroine is rebellious ('A few weeks of Coz. Charlotte's company, and I shall be ready to open my window to the next young gentleman who has an inclination to enter') and her tone is witty and collo-quial. Experts were convinced the diary was genuine, and the resulting publicity made it a bestseller. In 1926, the *Daily Express* declared the hoax on its front page.

After her marriage in 1929, King-Hall (now Magdalen Perceval-Maxwell), lived in Ireland and the Sudan. Her many other novels include *I Think I Remember* (1927), a burlesque; *Maid of Honour* (1936), an Irish HISTORICAL FICTION; and *Sturdy Rogue* (1941), set in the Elizabethan period. Her last book, *The Noble Savages*, appeared in 1962.

Suggested Reading

Frank Delaney, Introduction to *The Diary of a Young Lady of Fashion in the Year 1764–1765* by Cleone Knox [Magdalen King-Hall] (London: Chatto & Windus, 1984) vii–xxvi.

Faye Hammill

Kingsley, Mary St Leger 1852–1931

Novelist who published under the pseudonym of Lucas Malet. The eldest daughter of Charles Kingsley, she was educated at University College London. She married William Harrison in 1876 and settled in Devon but, upon his death in 1897, she spent much time travelling abroad. The author of 17 novels and numerous short stories, she is best known for *The Wages of Sin* (1891) and *The History of Sir Richard Calmady* (1901), both of which were chosen as Book of the Year. *The Wages of Sin* has a similar plot to Thomas Hardy's *Jude the Obscure* in that it describes an independent woman romantically affiliated with an intel-lectual who has fathered a child with another woman. Unlike in *Jude*, however, Kingsley's protagonist, while losing her fiancé, ends up travelling and enjoying her freedom. *The History of Sir Richard Calmady* describes the psychological development and sexual adventures of a disabled man.

Compared by her contemporaries to George Eliot, Henry James, and William Thackeray, Kingsley challenged gender roles and sexual behaviour. Regarding women writers as 'Amazons, sailing ships into uncharted waters', her sexually explicit and formally experimental work has links with MODERNISM. Although she achieved critical and commercial success, she died in penury.

Suggested Reading

Lundberg, Patricia Lorimer. *'An Inward Necessity': The Writer's Life of Lucas Malet* (New York: Peter Lang, 2003).

Schaffer, Talia. 'Malet the Obscure: Thomas Hardy, "Lucas Malet" and the Literary Politics of Early Modernism', *Women's Writing*, 3.3 (1996) 261–85.

Stacy Gillis

L

Laski, Marghanita 1915–1988

Novelist, journalist, and radio and television personality, famous for her liberal humanist beliefs. In *Ecstasy* (1961) and *Everyday Ecstasy* (1980), Laski enquired into transcendental experiences and their personal and social effects. She wrote five novels. *The Victorian Chaise Longue* (1953) is a chilling example of female Gothic, while *Little Boy Lost* (1949) – adapted for the screen in 1953 – and *The Village* (1953) both deal poignantly with the aftermath of the Second World War. *Love on the Supertax* (1944) and *Tory Heaven, or Thunder on the Right* (1948) satirize the British class system. She also ventured into CHILDREN'S LITERATURE with *Ferry the Jerusalem Cat* (1983) and into drama with *The Offshore Island* (1954), about a group of survivors after a nuclear war. Her interest in nineteenth-century women writers finds expression in lavishly illustrated biographies of Jane Austen and George Eliot and in an edited critical collection on Charlotte Yonge. She was an astute reviewer and provided the first serious critical engagement with Daphne DU MAURIER's work in an anonymous review in *The Times Literary Supplement*. She also submitted some 250,000 illustrative quotations to the Oxford English Dictionary. She has received no attention from critics.

Sue Zlosnik

Lawrence, Frieda 1879–1956

German-English literary personality and memoirist, whose second husband was D. H. Lawrence. Frieda von Richthofen, daughter of Prussian Baron Friedrich von Richthofen, and cousin of Manfred von Richthofen, the Red Baron, grew up in Metz and attended a convent school. At 20, she married Ernest Weekley, an English academic, and they settled in Nottingham and had three children. Between 1902 and 1912 she had a series of affairs, including one with the psychoanalyst Otto Gross. In 1912 she met Lawrence, a student of her husband, and they fell in love, eloping to Europe and marrying in 1914, immediately after Frieda's divorce was finalized. Some of Lawrence's biographers and critics view Frieda as an inspiration to him, through her personality and the continental thought to which she introduced him; others consider her influence disastrous. Keith Sagar, for example, described her as 'amoral, disorderly, wasteful, utterly helpless around the house, lying in bed late, lounging about all day with a cigarette dangling from her mouth'. The couple travelled almost constantly in Europe and America. After D. H. Lawrence's death in 1930, Frieda settled in Taos, New Mexico, with the Italian artist Angelo Ravagli, whom she married in 1950.

In 1934 her memoir of her marriage to Lawrence, *Not I, but the Wind*, appeared, and her later autobiographical writing was published as *Frieda Lawrence: The Memoirs and Correspondence* in 1964.

Suggested Reading

Byrne, Janet. *A Genius for Living: The Life of Frieda Lawrence* (New York: HarperCollins, 1995).

Sagar, Keith M. *D. H. Lawrence: Life Into Art* (London: Viking, 1985).

Faye Hammill

Leavis, Q. D. 1906–1981

Scholar and critic; co-founder, with her husband, F.R. Leavis, of the influential magazine *Scrutiny* 1932–53, though never on its editorial board and never given a tenured post at a university. Queenie Dorothy Roth, daughter of a Jewish hosier in East London, gained first-class honours in 1928 from Girton College, Cambridge. Her marriage in 1929 to the non-Jewish Leavis, caused a permanent rift with her family. Her ground-breaking Ph.D. thesis, supervised by I. A. Richards, became *Fiction and the Reading Public* (1932), still a reference point in discussions of minority and mass culture. Influenced by the anthropologist A. C. Haddon and by Helen and Robert Lynd's *Middletown: A Study in American Culture* (1929), Leavis aimed to account for the perceived decline of literary taste by making an 'anthropological' survey of the attitudes of popular authors, analysing how popular literature was marketed and contrasting a contemporary culture of specialized genres, segregated by high-, middle- or lowbrow status, with the pre-industrialized 'unitary' cultures of the sixteenth and seventeenth centuries. Both method and subject matter were characteristically bold choices since classics rather than anthropology was the discipline against which the newly established English Faculty was self-consciously measuring its academic rigour; to consider texts of low cultural status, even to deplore them, was to risk taint by association.

Leavis's many, often adversarial, articles for *Scrutiny*, challenge positions perceived as modish or the product of class-based coteries. Her 'theory' of Jane Austen's writing, written against the 'Janeites', dispelled notions of Austen as 'inspired amateur'. Her appreciative accounts of how Leslie Stephen, Henry Sidgwick, and H. M. Chadwick shaped the 'Discipline of English Letters' are rooted in structural analysis of the academy and admiration for honest plain-speaking. She also admired Richard Jefferies, the 'peculiarly English' genius whose 'vitality and genuineness' she felt anticipated D. H. Lawrence. Her concern to identify authors' national characteristics later led her to make more dubious assertions about Italian and French literature.

Her postwar readings of nineteenth-century novels (by Austen, the Brontës, and Eliot) combine awareness of their social context and of 'the lessons for life' they offer. Her exposition of the complexities of *Silas Marner*, in particular, epitomizes her concept of 'the novel as dramatic poem'. With her husband, she sought to define 'the great tradition' of the English novel. The drama of both Leavis's stormy relationship with Dickens culminated in their joint endorsement of him in 1970. Q. D. Leavis revived the work of Margaret Oliphant, arguing that *Miss Marjoribanks* (1866) be regarded as the missing link between *Emma* (1816) and *Middlemarch* (1871–2). But she discredits the religiosity of Charlotte Yonge: 'a day-dreamer with a writing itch that compensated her for a peculiarly starved life'. A similar 'ad feminam' attack characterized her resistance to Virginia WOOLF's polemic, *Three Guineas* (1938). She rejects Woolf's 'sex hostility' and reveals her own complicated attitude to gender. Leavis's identification with 'the best kind of masculine mind' was combined with a pride in woman's domestic role. Unlike Woolf, she did write reviews 'while actually stirring the pot'.

Suggested Reading

Lyons, Donald. 'Q. D. L.', *The New Criterion*, 9.7 (March 1991) 22–32.
Mulhern, Francis. *The Moment of 'Scrutiny'* (London: New Left Books, 1979).
Travis, Molly Abel. *Virginia Woolf and Fascism: Resisting the Dictators' Seduction* (Basingstoke: Palgrave Macmillan, 2001).

Mary Grover

Lee, Vernon 1856–1935

Author of over 40 volumes across a remarkable range of genres, and best known for her work on aesthetics. Born Violet Paget near Boulogne, she was educated by her mother, half-brother Eugene Lee-Hamilton, and governesses. After early travels in Europe she spent most of her life in Italy, settling at the Villa 'Il Palmerino' in Florence in 1889, and becoming known as Vernon Lee in both her personal and professional lives.

Lee's first major work, written at 24, was the pioneering *Studies of the Eighteenth Century in Italy* (1880), which was much admired by Edith Wharton. This study of music, drama, and culture gave written form to what Lee described as her 'explorations through that wonder-world of things moth eaten and dust engrained, but sometimes beautiful and pathetic in themselves, and always transfigured by my youthful fancy'. It was followed by the publication, to high critical acclaim, of *Belcaro* (1881), a collection of essays on art, and *Euphorion* (1884), essays on the Renaissance. The imaginative and eloquent scholarship of the latter was praised by Walter Pater as evidence of 'a very great variety and richness of intellectual stock, apprehensions, sympathies and personal observations of all kinds such as make the criticism of art and poetry a real part of the criticism of life'. Her first novel, the three-volume *Miss Brown* (1884), a satire on aestheticism, was received less kindly, and described by its dedicatee Henry James as 'a deplorable mistake', which took 'the aesthetic business too seriously'. James's disgruntled response was worsened with the publication of Lee's novella, *Lady Tal* (1892), which explores gender indeterminacy and the relationship between life and art through the characterization of the novelist Jervase Marion, ' a kind of Henry James, of a lesser magnitude'.

Her visits to Natalie Barney's Rue Jacob Salon in Paris introduced Lee to other expatriate women writers, and her work on psychological aesthetics brought her into contact with prominent figures in the aesthetic movement. Her essay 'Beauty and Ugliness' (1897), written with Clementina (Kit) Anstruther-Thomson, whose friendship provided her with a 'new love and new life' for several years, has been credited with introducing the term 'empathy' into English aesthetic discourse. However, Lee's exploration of the power of feeling can be traced back to her first book. In her travel writings, notably *Genius Loci: Notes on Places* (1899) and *The Sentimental Traveller* (1908), Lee sketched what she called 'the spirit of places', while her supernatural fiction, of which the collection *Hauntings* (1890) is the best known, portrays destructive and desirous encounters with art and landscape. An influential figure in European debates about aesthetics, history, and gender, Lee was also a fervent PACIFIST, as reflected in her dramatic trilogy *Satan the Waster* (1920), an exposition of the devastating psychological effects of the First World War.

Suggested Reading

Colby, Vineta. *Vernon Lee: A Literary Biography* (Charlottesville, VA: University of Virginia Press, 2003).

Robbins, Ruth. 'Apparitions Can Be Deceptive: Vernon Lee's Androgynous Spectres', in Ruth Robbins and Julian Wolfreys (eds), *Victorian Gothic: Literary and Cultural Manifestations in the Nineteenth Century* (Basingstoke: Palgrave Macmillan, 2000) 182–200.

Zorn, Christa. *Vernon Lee: Aesthetics, History, and the Victorian Female Intellectual* (Athens, OH: Ohio University Press, 2003).

Rebecca Munford

Lees, Edith Oldham 1861–1916

Published under married name, Mrs. Havelock Ellis, novels, critical studies, plays, and short stories, directed towards the moral and spiritual regeneration of society. Lees was a well known and tireless lecturer in progressive causes including feminism, marriage reform, sexual freedom, artistic interior decoration and the 'simple life'. She enjoyed close friendships with Olive Schreiner, Eleanor Marx, and Edward Carpenter.

In *Attainment* (1909), she drew on her work as secretary of the Fellowship of the New Life (1889–92) and her experiences in Fellowship House, an experiment in communal living. She was predominantly, if not exclusively, LESBIAN and she and Ellis sought to demonstrate that marriage should be 'companionate'.

She recorded the early years of her marriage in *Seaweed: A Cornish Idyll* (1898), reflected on her troubled early life in *Love Acre* (1914), and on her periods of depression in *The Imperishable Wing* (1921). She also published lighter studies, *My Cornish Neighbours* (1906) and *The Subjection of Kezia* (1908). Her most abstract work was *Three Modern Seers* (1910), in which she celebrated Nietzsche, Carpenter, and progressive prophet of free love James Hinton. She toured the United States as a lecturer, and her essays and lectures were post-humously collected in *The New Horizon of Love and Life* (1921) and *Stories and Essays* (1924).

Suggested Reading

Brandon, Ruth. *The New Women and the Old Men* (London: Secker & Warburg, 1990).

Nottingham, Chris. *The Pursuit of Serenity: Havelock Ellis and the New Politics* (Amsterdam: University Press, Amsterdam, 1999).

Chris Nottingham

Lehmann, Rosamond 1901–1990

Novelist, held in considerable repute in the 1930s and 1940s, but subsequently marginalized. The daughter of Liberal MP and *Punch* contributor Rudolph Lehmann, and the sister of actress Beatrix Lehmann and poet John Lehmann, she studied modern languages at Girton College, Cambridge. Her first novel, *Dusty Answer* (1927), was an instant bestseller, garnering Lehmann extraordinary reviews and literary fame. Among her best novels are *Invitation to the Waltz* (1932), its powerful sequel *The Weather in the Streets* (1936), and *The Ballad and the Source* (1944). She moved in the BLOOMSBURY circle, and was intimate with Lytton Strachey, Carrington, and Virginia WOOLF. Twice married, first to Leslie Runciman and then Wogan Philipps, she also had a long relationship with the poet Cecil Day Lewis, reflected in her penultimate novel *The Echoing Grove* (1953). Both Lehmann's literary output and reputation declined rapidly in the postwar years, but she enjoyed a revival in the 1980s when her books were reissued by VIRAGO Press. She was awarded the CBE in 1982.

Lehmann's loss of literary reputation can in part be attributed to the great tragedy of her life, when her 24-year-old daughter Sally died of poliomyelitis in 1958. Lehmann's grief led her to become passionately involved in spiritualism and psychic research, an interest reflected in her autobiography *The Swan in the Evening* (1967) and in her last novel *A Sea-Grape Tree* (1976). These beliefs were both personally and professionally detrimental to Lehmann, exposing her to ridicule. Also, Lehmann's fictional concentration on the emotional lives of upper-middle-class women has pigeonholed her as a women's writer, concerned only with love affairs and domesticity, but as Gillian Tindall observes: 'She seems at times to be offering the reader a view into her own heart when in fact she is offering something subtly alternative, transformed by art and consciousness; and the texture of her work is richer and more sophisticated than it may appear.'

Lehmann's novels also examine thorny subjects: *Dusty Answer* concerns a lesbian relationship, *Invitation to the Waltz* is a subtle analysis of the British class system, and *The Weather in the Streets* portrays unmarried pregnancy and illegal ABORTION. Despite this, critics have complained of the lack of political or social commentary in her work. However, more recent studies have emphasized Lehmann's concentration on women's conflicted relationship with male economic and social power, and on the struggle to construct and maintain a feminine identity. Her writing is also notable for her powerful use of modernist techniques such as interior monologue, shifting narrative perspectives, and free indirect discourse.

Suggested Reading
Hastings, Selina. *Rosamond Lehmann* (London: Chatto & Windus, 2002).
Tindall, Gillian. *Rosamond Lehmann: An Appreciation* (London: Chatto & Windus, 1985).
Wallace, Diana. *Sisters and Rivals In British Women's Fiction, 1914–39* (Basingstoke: Palgrave Macmillan, 2000).

Louise Harrington

Lesbianism
The first half of the twentieth century was a crucial period in the history of love between women: it saw the emergence of the *idea* of lesbianism in British culture, and the gradual widening of opportunities for women to pursue same-sex relationships. Late nineteenth-century sexual science, which categorized and pathologized female homosexuality, exerted a growing influence on medical literature and legal discourses, and on the development of lesbian identity between the wars. Havelock Ellis's 'female invert' with her masculine behaviour and gender identity was translated into culture in 1928 through the widely reported prosecution of Radclyffe HALL's novel *The Well of Loneliness*, both author and heroine personifying a 'butch' mannish style. However, a variety of other images of the lesbian appeared in literature, journalism, and the middle-class imagination. The Maud Allan lesbian libel case of 1918 evoked the decadent femme fatale, the sexually powerful seducer who was a feminine parallel to Oscar Wilde. A text which is often overlooked but was immensely influential in constructing the idea of the lesbian was Clemence DANE's best-selling novel *Regiment of Women* (1917), which depicts the malign corrupting influence of a schoolmistress who emotionally manipulates (but does not physically seduce) both pupils and a younger colleague. Frequently cited in anxious British middlebrow and professional writing on sexuality between the wars, this lesbian figure was invested with considerable power to disrupt society

and heterosexual marriage in a period of women's growing independence. It is likely that this range of fears and images increasingly appeared in popular culture, though historians have yet to research this extensively. By the late 1940s the popular press, for example, began to associate love between women with female masculinity and criminality, and name it as 'perversion' or 'unnatural passion'.

Evidence for the ways in which women who had primary relationships with other women saw their sexual identity and organized their lives is patchy. Sex between women was not illegal, so there are fewer formal records than for gay men. Most women in the first half of the twentieth century were constrained by low wages and family expectations from creating households with female partners. Among elite and bohemian social circles there are some rich clues to lesbian couples and networks, although with the growing profile of lesbianism from the 1920s and the declining acceptability of romantic friendship, many women were circumspect about leaving evidence of their love in letters and diaries. Sylvia Townsend WARNER and her lover Valentine ACKLAND, were important exceptions, leaving an intimate record of the joys and vicissitudes of their lengthy relationship. It is much more difficult to piece together a sense of how working-class and lower-middle-class women lived lesbian lives. Some, such as school teachers and office workers, were able to live respectably as couples because of the continuing presumption of women's asexuality. Occasional discoveries of 'female husbands' throughout this period indicate that a few predominantly working-class women found cross-dressing a solution. Still socially stigmatized, lesbians could rarely acknowledge their identity in public in the 1940s and 1950s, although in the years after WORLD WAR TWO some lesbian meeting places such as the Gateways Club in Chelsea, began to appear.

Suggested Reading

Doan, Laura. *Fashioning Sapphism: The Origins of a Modern English Lesbian Culture* (New York: Columbia University Press, 2001).

Oram, Alison and Annmarie Turnbull. *The Lesbian History Sourcebook: Love and Sex Between Women in Britain from 1780 to 1970* (London, Routledge, 2001).

Alison Oram

Libraries

In the twentieth century, libraries underwent a substantial shift in usage and patron demographic because of the shift from subscription libraries to large, free public libraries. The term subscription library refers to two types of library. The first is a collection run with funds raised from its members, by subscription. The second is the commercial lending library, also known as the circulating library, deriving its income from charging a small annual fee and/or a subscription for each volume borrowed. It was the latter which rose to prominence between the wars.

Subscription libraries initially appeared in the eighteenth century in response to public concern that circulating libraries contained unsuitable reading matter. Subscription libraries were thus, in part, a form of civic duty, with books selected for self-help and mutual improvement. Part public and part private, they were set up by learned societies for the benefit of intellectuals and colleges but were also open to the public. In the nineteenth century, popular fiction colonized many subscription libraries, for example, Mudie's Circulating Library, established in London in 1842. Libraries such as Mudie's could account for up to 75 per cent of a popular novel's edition. Although the subscription library did not survive the twentieth century, commercial lending libraries such as Boot's and W. H. Smith's successfully employed the subscription format in their stores well past WORLD WAR TWO.

Established in 1898, the Boot's Book Lending service was the brainchild of Florence Boot, wife of the head of the company. The daughter of a bookseller and stationer, she saw the potential in including a book-lending service in those shops with a stationery department. Initially small-scale, by 1903 nearly half of Britain's 300 Boot's stores had a Booklovers' Library. Members either paid an annual membership or a returnable deposit on the books, in addition to a weekly fee. In 1925, Boot's libraries exchanged over 25 million volumes; by 1938 this figure was 35 million books. W. H. Smith's established a similar system, linking the leisure practice of reading with CONSUMER culture. Boot's and W. H. Smith's gained considerable influence in the publishing world because of the number of volumes they purchased. The interwar years were the heyday of these libraries, the last of which closed its doors in 1966.

Although one reason for the demise of the subscription library was the growing investment in public libraries throughout the twentieth century, it was the decreasing cost of paperbacks that dealt them a deathblow. More cost-effective paper production and the linotype allowed PUBLISHERS to compete directly with libraries by issuing inexpensive editions of popular novels and using advertising rhetoric to convince readers to buy rather than borrow. In 1935 Penguin introduced the sixpenny book, branding each genre a different colour. This made books, for the first time, a mass medium as Harold Raymond noted in a lecture on publishing in October of 1938: 'Penguins are an even greater portent than Twopenny Libraries or Book Clubs, and are already exerting a far more revolutionary effect on the book trade . . . they are far better produced; their average standard of literary quality is higher; they consist of more recent publication, and indeed some of their titles appear in Penguins for the first time.' Other publishers, such as Hutchinson's, soon followed suit. This publishing boom – coupled with the growth of CINEMA, the success of BOOK CLUBS, and the growing investment in large free public libraries – substantially diminished the attractions of the subscription libraries.

Suggested Reading

Manley, K. A. and Dennis Keeling. 'Sunshine in the Gloom: The Study of British Library History', *Libraries and Culture: A Journal of Library History*, 25.1 (Winter 1990) 80–5.

Manley, K. A. and William Munford. *Careering Along with the Books: Studies in the History of British Public Libraries and Librarianship* (London: Library Association, 1996).

Stacy Gillis

Little Magazines

No period has been more marked by its literary, art, and avant-garde magazines than the modernist. The immense growth of the reading public and the influence of advertising radically changed magazine publication between the nineteenth and twentieth centuries. At the same time, following the fall of the Victorian 'Great Review', magazines shifted from the cultural centre to its margin, so that most magazines which emerged during 1900–50 were considered 'little'. While they document trends in literature and art, they also register the social and political upheavals of the period.

Though disagreement remains as to what qualifies as a 'little' magazine, there is broad consensus about how they fostered modern literature and other artistic movements by providing alternative routes of publication. Whereas the sensational and uncritical 'bigs' and 'slicks' began to feature advertising, games, contests, and crossword puzzles to increase circulation, little magazines sought to reflect a cultural situation, illustrate a tendency, or advance critical values. As public forums for debate, these magazines were often adversarial; they had a much smaller audience than mainstream magazines and NEWSPAPERS; they were produced inexpensively but defined by individuality and innovation; and they were often short-lived, sharing a disregard for economic profit and a voluntary marginality. Awareness of women's involvement in and editorship of these magazines is crucial to our understanding of MODERNISM.

Early modernist periodicals include *The English Review* (1908–37) and *The New Age* (1894–1938), which were at their most influential under the editorship of Ford Madox Ford (1908–10) and A. R. Orage (1907–22), respectively. Though it only made two appearances in 1914 and 1915, Wyndham Lewis's avant-garde *Blast* was energetically modern in its art, prose, poetry, and bold typography. Important, too, was the *Egoist* (1914–19), which first appeared as the *Freewoman* (1911–13) led by Dora Marsden and focusing chiefly on the concerns of the WOMEN'S MOVEMENT and SUFFRAGISM, then briefly as the *New Freewoman* (1913–14) sponsored by Harriet Shaw Weaver, when it began to publish more poetry and fiction. The magazine exercised greatest influence as the *Egoist*, offering an Imagist number in 1915 and featuring editors such as Richard Aldington, H. D., and T. S. Eliot.

The 1920s witnessed the emergence of several critical organs alongside more experimental and eclectic magazines. Eliot's *The Criterion* (1922–39) was dynamic and creative, publishing a wide range of literature and criticism that marked modernism's coming of age. It was complemented by the *Adelphi* (1923–55) and *The Calendar of Modern Letters* (1925–7). Though published in Paris, *transition* (1927–38) deserves mention for its enthusiastic promotion of avant-garde work by James Joyce and the Surrealists. *Close Up* (1927–33), a collaboration among BRYHER, Kenneth Macpherson and H. D., established a critical discourse on CINEMA and photography and featured work by Dorothy RICHARDSON and Gertrude Stein. But *Time and Tide* (1920–79) remains the most important journal to emerge in this period, both for its dedication to women's issues and for its ambition to change a 'nation's habit of mind'. Under the guidance of Lady RHONDDA until her death in 1958, the weekly maintained its critical independence and was among the most influential political and literary periodicals in Britain.

In the 1930s, *Scrutiny* (1932–53) launched an Arnoldian project to shore up the standards of culture against the levelling processes of modern civilization. Led by F. R. Leavis, who co-founded the magazine with Q. D. LEAVIS, it had a significant impact on the way English literature was taught. *New Verse* (1933–9) is still regarded as one of the best poetry magazines of its time, and *Poetry* (1939–51) continued where *New Verse* left off, becoming the foremost poetry periodical in the 1940s. *Left Review* (1934–8) narrowed the gap between art and propaganda, fostering working-class writing, reportage, and British Marxism. *Our Time* (1941–9) represents one of the more populist and 'glossy' magazines of the 1940s, while Cyril Connolly's *Horizon* (1940–50) and John Lehmann's several *New Writing* magazines indicate the shift from the political tendencies of the 1930s magazines to the eclectic concerns of the 1940s. Along with the monthly *London Mercury* (1919–39), other notable weekly magazines include *The New English Weekly* (1932–49), *New Statesman* (1913–31), and *New Statesman and Nation* (1931–57).

Since many British writers published in American magazines, some names should be mentioned. Two of the most influential were edited by women. The *Little Review* (1914–29), edited by Margaret C. Anderson and Jane Heap, was fiercely individualist, enduring a lawsuit for serializing Joyce's *Ulysses*. *Poetry*, founded in 1912 and edited until 1935 by Harriet Monroe, assisted by Alice Corbin Henderson, helped establish 'modern poetry' and continues to publish today. Other important American magazines include Emma Goldman's anarchist *Mother Earth* (1906–18), *The Dial* (1920–9), edited by Scofield Thayer and Marianne Moore, *The Hound and Horn* (1927–34), *The Masses* (1911–17), *The New Masses* (1926–48), and *Partisan Review* (1934–2003).

Suggested Reading
Marek, Jayne E. *Women Editing Modernism: 'Little' Magazines and Literary History* (Lexington, KY: University Press of Kentucky, 1995).

Morrison, Mark S. *The Public Face of Modernism: Little Magazines, Audiences, and Reception, 1905–1920* (Madison, WI: University of Wisconsin Press, 2001).

Ohmann, Richard M. *Selling Culture: Magazines, Markets, and Class at the Turn of the Century* (New York: Verso, 1996).

Sullivan, Alvin (ed.). *British Literary Magazines, Volume 4: The Modern Age, 1914–1984* (Westport, CT: Greenwood Press, 1983).

Robin Edward Feenstra

Lowndes, Marie Belloc 1868–1947

Novelist and journalist. Marie Adelaide Belloc was the daughter of Louis Belloc, a French lawyer, and the prominent British writer and women's rights campaigner, Bessie Rayner Parkes. The Catholic writer Hilaire Belloc was her brother. Louis Belloc died in 1872, and subsequently a bad investment reduced the family to poverty. Moving between Sussex and her father's family's home near Paris, Marie developed an intimate knowledge of French and English literature. A committed Catholic, she once declared: 'My heart is all French.' Unlike Hilaire, Marie had virtually no formal education, but wrote from the age of 16. She began her career as a journalist, covering the Paris Exhibition of 1889 for the *Pall Mall Gazette*. She developed a specialism in sketches of literary figures and articles on French literature. Discussing journalism as a profession for women in *Leisure Hour* in 1903, she warned 'so-called literary young ladies' about the difficulties of undertaking work for the London press. Remarking tartly that 'leisurely scholarly' work, 'a pretty literary style and the power of graphic description' were not sufficient equipment for the would-be woman journalist, she advocated a pragmatic professionalism that combined business acuity with wide-ranging knowledge of the arts and current affairs.

Marrying *Times* journalist Frederick Sawray Lowndes in 1896 (they had two sons and a daughter), she continued to write and published over 60 books, 40 of which were novels. Her early publications included royal biographies, HISTORICAL novels, and short stories of sensation, romance, and mystery. Her reputation was established, however, as a writer of crime fiction, and a number of her novels were based on the murder cases that fascinated Victorian and Edwardian society. These included *The Chink in the Armour* (1912), based on the Gould murder at Monte Carlo, and *Letty Lynton* (1931), a fictionalized account of the Madeleine Smith murder case of 1857. *The Lodger* (1913), which initially appeared as a short story in *McClure's Magazine* (January 1911), was the first, and arguably the best, fictional account of the Jack the Ripper murders of 1888. It has remained in print and has been made into a play, an opera, and several films, including Alfred Hitchcock's *The Lodger* (1926), starring Ivor Novello. Belloc Lowndes was interested in legal procedure, often incorporating courtroom scenes, and in the psychological motivations of criminals, particularly women.

She was a well-known figure in literary circles, and her social life and close friendships with Henry James, George Moore, Prime Minister Asquith, and many others are recorded in a series of autobiographical works including *The Merry Wives of Westminster* (1946) and *A Passing World* (1948).

Suggested Reading

Lowndes, S. (ed.). *Diaries and Letters of Marie Belloc-Lowndes, 1911–1947* (London: Chatto & Windus, 1971).

Fiona Hackney

Loy, Mina 1882–1966

Poet, painter, feminist, and actress, best known for her experimental free verse, which was admired by William Carlos Williams and Ezra Pound. Born Mina Gertrude Lowy in London, to a Hungarian Jewish father and English Protestant mother, Loy was stunningly beautiful and lively minded. She studied art in Munich and London, and then married Stephen Haweis in 1903. They lived in Paris, and had three chidren. Loy successfully combined motherhood with painting and drawing, and was introduced to Stein, Appollinaire, Picasso, and Rousseau. Moving to Florence in 1905, she continued to paint and also began to write. She met and had affairs with Futurists Filipo Marinetti and Giovanni Papini, who influenced her poetry, and she also became a convert to Christian Science.

Loy began to publish in LITTLE MAGAZINES. Her 'Aphorisms on Futurism', a long poem in the form of a manifesto, appeared in Alfred Stieglitz's *Camera Work* in 1914. One of the aphorisms runs: 'LOVE the hideous in order to find the sublime core of it.' She later rejected the Futurist movement when it became allied with Fascism. In 1915, a group of New York poets founded the magazine *Others*, and Loy's 'Love Songs' formed the centrepiece of the first issue.

In 1916 she moved to New York, became part of the bohemian community, and began to act with the Provincetown Players. The following year she met Arthur Cravan, a poet, boxer, and draft dodger. He had to flee to Mexico a few months after meeting Loy, and she went there to join him. They married, and travelled in Mexico for six months, but then Cravan mysteriously disappeared, leaving Loy pregnant and distraught. She returned temporarily to New York, and appeared in court defending the *Little Review's* publication of *Ulysses*. In 1923, her first book, *Lunar Baedecker*, appeared, and she settled in Paris and earned a living partly through painting lampshades. Her social circle there included Djuna Barnes, who based the character 'Patience Scalpel' in her *Ladies Almanack* on Loy.

Oscillating between Paris and New York, Loy wrote little in the 1930s, but became fascinated by Bowery Bums, collecting images as they collected detritus, and in 1951 a New York gallery exhibited her Bowery constructions. At the age of 71, she moved to Colorado where her two daughters lived. In 1950, she published the long poem *Hot Cross Bums* in *New Directions* 12, which distinctly anticipates Beat poetry.

She never got over Cravan's disappearance, and her last poem, 'Letters of the Unliving', was about him. Mina Loy's magazine contributions appeared in volume form as *Lunar Baedeker and Time-Tables* (1958), while *The Last Lunar Baedecker* (1982) collects most of her verse, and was completed by *The Lost Lunar Baedeker* (1991).

Suggested Reading

Burke, Carolyn. *Becoming Modern: The Life of Mina Loy* (New York: Farrar, Straus & Giroux, 1996).

Hanscombe, Gillian and Virginia Smyers. *Writing for their Lives: The Modernist Women, 1910–1940* (London: The Women's Press, 1987).

Shreiber, Maeera and Keith Tuma. *Mina Loy: Woman and Poet* (Orono, ME: The National Poetry Foundation, 1998).

Gina Wisker

Lynd, Sylvia 1888–1952

Primarily a poet, Sylvia (née Dryhurst) Lynd also wrote essays, fiction, and critical reviews. She attended the Slade School of Art and the Academy of Dramatic Art, and in 1909 married Robert Lynd, a writer and editor. She was an editor for the radical liberal *News Chronicle*, a reviewer for *Time and Tide*, and editor of the *Augustan Books of English Poetry*. Between 1916 and 1945 she produced six volumes of poetry, including a *Selected* (1928) and *Collected Poems* (1945). Her universalizing celebrations of the English countryside maintain the regularity of GEORGIAN metrics but had widespread and enduring appeal. More contemporary, 'The Solitary' evokes the isolation of the period's many unmarried women.

'Beauty and the Beast', published in *Best Poetry* for 1931, similarly unsettles social codes and assumptions about male–female relations. Lynd's novels, *The Chorus: A Tale of Love and Folly* (1915) and *The Swallow Dive* (1921), are less conventional and more obviously woman-centred than the majority of her poems. Her short stories were collected in 1920, and she also edited anthologies of CHILDREN'S LITERATURE and produced a study of English children.

Suggested Reading

Dowson, Jane. *Women's Poetry of the 1930s: A Critical Anthology* (London: Routledge, 1996).

Jane Dowson

Lyon, Lilian Bowes 1895–1949

Primarily a poet, she published one novel, *The Buried Stream* (1929). Born into an aristocratic family, a cousin to the Queen Mother, the contrast between the two worlds she inhabited – the peaceful countryside in Northumberland and the urban congestion of London – heightened her sense of privilege and led to considerable social action. During the 1930s and 1940s, her six collections were in steady demand; individual poems were printed in several journals, particularly *The Listener*, and often anthologized. She draws upon the Northumbrian landscapes of her youth for natural symbols, but 'Pastoral', chosen for *The Year's Poetry* in 1936, is a response to war, not an eulogy of England.

For several years, she headed the Women's Voluntary Services, and in 1942 moved to a flat in the East End of London, from where she could care for the war wounded. Even when severely injured during the Blitz, she continued providing aid to refugees and children and carried on writing. *Uncollected Poems* (1981) contains searing responses to suffering after she lost both legs and the use of both hands. Other victims of social evils and inequalities are dramatized in 'The Blind Tramp' and 'A Refugee', in which untidy rhythms accentuate the interconnectedness of physical and mental pain, while 'A Woman Knitting' explores the cost of women's selfless lives.

Suggested Reading
Dowson, Jane. *Women's Poetry of the 1930s: A Critical Anthology* (London: Routledge, 1996).

Jane Dowson

M

Macaulay, Rose 1881–1958

First World War poet, essayist and critic, travel writer, and historian, but best known as a novelist. Macaulay had a lifelong attachment to the Anglican faith, but her work is marked by religious crisis since she left the Church for many years while in an intense relationship with a married man. Her best loved novel is her last, *The Towers of Trebizond* (1956). In it, her themes of exile, failure, the corrupting power of the media (including the art of the novelist), sin and remorse, the glory and despair of sexual love, and the salvation represented by the Church, reach their greatest expression. The novel famously opens: ' "Take my camel, dear," said my aunt Dot, as she climbed down from this animal on her return from High Mass', demonstrating Macaulay's comic treatment of the perils of the modern world. In part a narrative of history and travel, based on Macaulay's own visit to Turkish Trabzon, the book concludes with narrator Laurie's evocation of the city as an unreachable spiritual home: 'Still the towers of Trebizond, the fabled city, shimmer on the far horizon, gated and walled and held in a luminous enchantment.' For Laurie, unlike her creator, there is no return to the Anglican Church after the end of an adulterous relationship.

Laurie is the last in Macaulay's series of ambiguously gendered leading characters. Believing in a commonality of experience between men and women, Macaulay makes a point in her early fiction of showing boyish heroines evading marriage, together with anti-heroic males with feminine names such as 'Mr Jayne' in *Told by An Idiot* (1923). Some of her heroines foolishly drift into marriage, such as Denham Dobie in *Crewe Train* (1926), who feels entrapped in stultifying suburban life but also dislikes the literary London parties she attends with her writer husband; this novel is one of Macaulay's early satires on her profession. Known for disavowing her own literary achievements, Macaulay's reticence was allied to her profound sense of the potential of art to corrupt the truth. In her satire of the popular press in *Potterism: A Tragical-Farcical Tract* (1920), loosely based on the Northcliffe and Beaverbrook empires, 'tabloid' journalism is shown to pervert both national life and intimate relationships. *Dangerous Ages* (1921), a satire of PSYCHOANALYSIS, won the PRIX FEMINA-VIE HEUREUSE.

One of Macaulay's last publications was the non-fictional *Pleasure of Ruins* (1953), which celebrates the ruined buildings which elsewhere in her work represent the decline of Western civilization. Eliot's *The Wasteland*, published in the aftermath of one war, haunts Macaulay's treatment of another in *The World My Wilderness* (1950). Set in France and London in 1946, the novel superbly realizes Macaulay's ambivalence about belonging to a landscape where more than buildings are in ruins. Heroine Barbary, a young girl who has grown up amoral due to the anarchy and lawlessness of occupied France, all too obviously signifies the wilderness growing over the bombed London through which she wanders. Her fate is polarized between mother-love and father-law. For Barbary, love wins, but her brother makes his way across ruins to St Paul's church.

Suggested Reading

Crawford, Alice. *Paradise Pursued: The Novels of Rose Macaulay* (London: Associated University Presses, 1995).

Emery, Jane. *Rose Macaulay: A Writer's Life* (London: John Murray, 1991).

LeFanu, Sarah. *Rose Macaulay* (London: Virago Press, 2003).

Susan Rowland

Mannin, Ethel 1900–1984

Novelist, travel writer, polemicist, author of educational children's books, and left-wing activist, characterized by H. W. Nevinson as a member of 'The Stage Army of the Good'. Mannin professed herself a 'Tolstoyan anarchist averse to the State in any form, Capitalist, Communist, Fascist'. Initially inspired by the socialist convictions of her father, an Irish postal worker in London, she was further radicalized while editing a theatrical magazine, *The Pelican* (1917–19). In 1933 she joined the International Labour Party. Though initially pro-Soviet, her experience of bureaucracy on her second visit to the USSR, documented in *South to Samarkand* (1936), reinforced her libertarianism. She sent her only child, of her first, brief marriage, to Summerhill School, celebrating A. S. Neill's educational philosophy in two guides to child rearing and in the novel, *Linda Shawn* (1932). Influenced by the Quaker Reginald Reynolds, whom she married in 1939, she became an advocate of Palestinian autonomy and Indian independence. She encouraged working-class writers such as Walter Greenwood, and campaigned against the banning of *Ulysses* and *The Well of Loneliness*.

All Mannin's works reflect stages in her ideological journey. Explicitly polemical, *Bread and Roses* (1944) is a utopian 'blueprint'; *Women and the Revolution* (1938) argues that women's freedom depends upon the abolition of class; the novel *Late Have I Loved Thee* (1948) dramatizes a heroic Augustinianism. *Comrade O Comrade* (1947) expresses her disillusion with political cant and her repudiation of art as propaganda. This novel, like her *Connemara Journal* (1947), reflects attempts, later abandoned, to root her identity in her Irishness.

Mannin's regular volumes of memoirs chart her engagement with left-wing ideologies and personalities. Her earliest memoir, *Confessions and Impressions* (1930), was, as she ruefully acknowledged, a *succès de scandale*, ensuring a market for regular journalism and romantic novels. Extensive correspondence with W. B. Yeats, a lover who enjoyed her 'salty' conversation, and the American anarchist, Emma Goldman, whom she succeeded as chair of the Solidaridad Internacional Antifascista, are evidence of a gift for friendship. Mannin fictionalized Goldman's life in *The Red Rose* (1941).

Her style and productivity (over 90 books) made Mannin vulnerable to accusations of superficiality. However, her morally charged prose, combined with high-toned gossip and an unabashed use of cliché and romance forms, communicated radical ideas to a middlebrow audience. Romantic novels, such as *Children of the Earth* (1930), *Cactus* (1935) and *The Dark Forest* (1946), have a utopian force, despite their grim determinism worked out over successive generations. Mannin's works were so widely read that, in *Privileged Spectator* (1939), she identifies with the bestseller writer, deploring the value placed on the avant-garde. Mannin declares that, unlike modernist authors, she does not want 'a language that burns black the tongue of the one who speaks it and scars the one who listens' but 'a language that will make meaning clear'.

Suggested Reading

Croft, Andy. 'Ethel Mannin: The Red Rose of Love and the Red Flower of Liberty', in Angela Ingram and Daphne Patai (eds), *Rediscovering Forgotten Radicals: British Women Writers, 1989–1939* (Chapel Hill, NC: University of North Carolina Press, 1993) 205–25.

O'Rourke, Rebecca. 'Were There No Women? British Working-Class Writing in the Interwar Period', *Literature and History*, 14.1 (Spring 1988) 48–63.

Mary Grover

Manning, Olivia ?1908–1980

Novelist, short-story writer, and journalist, most widely known for her WORLD WAR TWO epics, the Balkan and Levant trilogies. Manning's great achievement was to complicate the relationship between the forms of modern fiction and the twentieth century's most devastating onslaught. Her Balkan trilogy comprises *The Great Fortune* (1960), *The Spoilt City* (1962), and *Friends and Heroes* (1965); while *The Danger Tree* (1977), *The Battle Lost and Won* (1978), and *The Sum of Things* (1980) make up the Levant trilogy. These books transform her experiences on the run from the Nazis into a chronicle of historical crisis and personal loss. The trilogies unsettle the boundaries between realist and MODERNIST fiction. Despite this accomplishment, and that of her travel books, short fiction, and reportage, published in *Horizon* and the

Spectator, together with comic pieces in *Punch,* Manning's reputation is still to be made.

Manning's life parallels the century's witness to exile and loss of stability. She was born in Portsmouth of an Anglo-Irish mother and naval commander father, and suffered economic and emotional privations as a girl. After grammar school and an abortive attempt to study art, she moved to London, working as a typist and a script reader. Her first publications were short fiction in *New Stories* and a novel, *The Wind Changes* (1937), about the Irish Troubles. Their exploration of political turbulence thwarting the establishment of a stable sense of self and of national identity antici-pates her major fiction. In 1939, she married Reginald Donald Smith, and they immediately left for Bucharest where he served as British Council lecturer.

As Nazi Germany began its assaults, Manning and Smith escaped eastwards to Greece, and then to Cairo and Jerusalem. Though Manning's fictions of this period were written later, each conveys the immediacy of wartime crisis. Set in 1943 Jerusalem and written from the perspective of an exiled and orphaned English boy, her novel *School for Love* (1951) dramatizes unresolved tensions between Jewish refugees and the lethally impotent colonial British. In her Second World War trilogies, as her heroine, Harriet Pringle, endures a distracted and myopic husband, domestic drama resonates with the perils of the historic moment and individual moral and political engagement with Hitler's victims and the role of the British EMPIRE. As Manning told Kay Dick, 'I have no fantasy. I don't think anything I've experienced has ever been wasted.'

Manning confronted the political consciousness of the writer in her 1949 novel *Artist Among the Missing;* in her journalism; and in short fiction such as 'The Journey' in *Growing Up* (1948) and 'The Last Civilian Ship' in *The Wind-mill* (1945). She dissected the grim implications of what was celebrated as the 'Swinging Sixties' in her 1969 novel *The Play Room* and transformed the end of Empire into absurdist comedy in *The Rain Forest* (1974). Official recognition was awarded in the form of a CBE in 1976, while her writing continues to redefine our questions about relations between political crisis and individual consciousness.

Suggested Reading

Lassner, Phyllis. *British Women Writers of World War II: Battlegrounds of Their Own* (Basingstoke: Palgrave Macmillan, 1998).

Lassner, Phyllis. 'The Game is Up: British Women's Comic Novels of the End of Empire', in Graeme Harper (ed.), *Comedy, Fantasy and Colonialism* (London: Continuum, 2002) 39–58.

Mooney, Harry J., Jr. 'Olivia Manning: Witness to History', in Thomas F. Staley (ed.), *Twentieth-Century Women Novelists* (Basingstoke: Macmillan, 1982) 39–58.

Phyllis Lassner

Mansfield, Katherine 1888–1923

New Zealand's most famous writer and poet, who excelled in the writing of short stories and was influenced by, and often compared to, Anton Chekhov. Mansfield writes about ordinary people, sex, marriage, social division, loneliness, and love. As she recalls: 'Looking back, I imagine I was always writing. Twaddle it was too. But better far write twaddle or anything, anything, than nothing at all.' She writes with a warm humanity, a subtle sense of humour and a sharp eye for detail that often turns the most simple everyday objects into significant symbols. In the *Journal of Katherine Mansfield* she claims: 'The mind I love must have wild places, a tangled orchard where dark demons drop in the heavy grass... a pool that nobody's fathomed the depth of.'

Katherine Mansfield Beauchamp was born in Wellington into a wealthy family, and in 1908 went to London for musical training. After a short-lived marriage to George Brown, she fell in love with Garnet Trowell and toured with his opera company. After giving birth to a stillborn child, she separated from Trowell. Whilst in Germany she completed a collection of satirical stories entitled *In a German Pension*, which appeared in 1911. That was also the year she met the literary critic John Middleton Murry, who became her husband. In 1918, following the death of her beloved brother Leslie in the war, Mansfield began writing short stories about New Zealand and about her own childhood, adolescence, and family life. 'Prelude', the first and longest of these fictions, appeared later that year, and was then included in her collection *Bliss and Other Stories* (1920), which secured Mansfield's place as a major MODERNIST writer. Some of her most critically acclaimed stories, such as 'The Daughters of the Late Colonel' and 'The Garden Party', were collected in *The Garden Party and Other Stories* (1922).

Mansfield's five-year-battle with tuberculosis began in 1918, and from this period she divided her time between London, the Riviera, and Switzerland. She and Murry exchanged letters, which Murry edited and published in 1928. They attracted the same critical attention as her literary work, since they sincerely and bravely deal with love, writing, infidelity, war, disease, and her coming death. Her three last stories, 'Poison', 'The Fly', and 'The Canary', were published posthumously in *The Dove's Nest and Other Stories* (1923).

Although Mansfield now qualifies as a national literary icon, it was only in 1959, with the establishment of the Katherine Mansfield Memorial Awards, that she started to receive the recognition she deserved. Today her work is widely taught and attracts substantial critical attention. In New Zealand her stories have been adapted for film, television, workshop theatre, ballet, opera-drama, and radio.

Suggested Reading

Fullbrook, Kate. *Katherine Mansfield* (Hemel Hempstead: Harvester, 1986).

Smith, Angela. *Katherine Mansfield: A Literary Life* (Basingstoke: Palgrave Macmillan, 2000).

Tomalin, Claire. *Katherine Mansfield: A Secret Life* (London: Viking, 1987).

Kiriaki Massoura

Marsh, Ngaio 1899–1982

The true architect of the country house 'whodunnit', author of DETECTIVE FICTION in which well-bred policeman Roderick Alleyn superbly negotiates the British class system. Alleyn marries artist Agatha Troy, who provides a 'feminine' perspective in works such as *Artists in Crime* (1938).

Born in New Zealand of English descent, Marsh had a dual career as a theatrical producer in her birth country and writer of 'cosy' crime fiction in Britain. Her writing is suffused with anxieties about class, and with a sense of its theatricality. Consequently her work is characteristically 'camp'; the country house functions as a stage for the construction of class identity, as in *Death and the Dancing Footman* (1941). Her explicitly anti-racist plots play with English xenophobia, while the moral corruption is always to be found within English identity. However, Marsh is more fearful of sexuality, particularly in women, and often portrays as deviant women who refuse passivity or marginalization. *False Scent* (1960), horrifically, has an ageing actress who has become a 'nuisance' eliminated by a pesticide. She is told: 'You're a cannibal, Mary, and it's high time somebody had the guts to tell you so.'

Suggested Reading

Lewis, Margaret. *Ngaio Marsh: A Life* (London: Chatto & Windus, 1991).

Rowland, Susan. *From Agatha Christie to Ruth Rendell: British Women Writers in Detective and Crime Fiction* (Basingstoke: Palgrave Macmillan, 2001).

Susan Rowland

Mass-Observation

An independent research organization founded in 1937 by a group of young left-wing friends. Their aim was to apply ethnographic methods to the study of the British, and create what they called an 'anthropology at home'. Although the key figures associated with the founding of Mass-Observation are male (Tom Harrisson, adventurer and self-taught anthropologist; Charles Madge, poet and journalist; and Humphrey Jennings, DOCUMENTARY FILMmaker), it is clear that women were enormously influential members of the group. They included Kathleen RAINE (then Madge's wife), Gay Taylor, Kathleen Box, Naomi MITCHISON, Zita Baker (later

Crossman), and many other women whose energies and creativity were key to the success of Mass-Observation.

When war was declared in 1939, Mass-Observation argued that it was ideally suited to the task of recording wartime morale. For about a year, its research services were used by the Home Intelligence department (Ministry of Information), then directed by the redoubtable Mary Adams, former Head of Talks at the British BROADCASTING Corporation, and a close friend of Harrisson. During wartime, the Mass-Observers documented every aspect of civilian life from the impact of air raids to the emergence of the WELFARE STATE, from sleeping habits to hemlines. Most of the field-workers were women, notably Celia Fremlin, Mollie Tarrant, and Nina Hibben. Their reports and surveys are complemented by contributions from volunteer writers. Mass-Observation also invited people all over the country to record their everyday lives in a daily diary. Over half of the 500 people who responded to this invitation were women.

One of the most prolific was Nella Last, a middle-aged housewife from Barrow-in-Furness, whose account is a wonderful mixture of amusing self-importance and searing self-criticism. Her younger son is conscripted into the army and her diary is a poignant reflection on wartime life. Another Mass-Observation diary which, like Nella Last's, has been edited for publication is that of Naomi Mitchison, who spent the war years at her farm in Scotland. Extracts from other diaries have been published and at the time of writing, a number of new anthologies and edited diaries are going to press. It total, over 25 books have been produced based on the studies of wartime Mass-Observers, and although much material remains unpublished, it is available in the Mass-Observation Archive at the University of Sussex.

The special value of the archive is that it not only contains enormous amounts of information *about* women's lives between 1937 and the mid-1950s but that most of this writing is *by women themselves*, mostly women whose writing would not otherwise have survived. This is a unique treasure trove for the history of women and women's writing of the period. Mass-Observation continued as a market research organization well after the 1950s, and its early achievements have inspired many more recent projects including, since 1981, a revival based at the Archive to which over 3000 'ordinary' people make regular autobiographical contributions. The great majority of these are women.

Suggested Reading

Broad, Richard and Suzie Fleming (eds). *Nella Last's War* (Bristol: Falling Wall Press, 1981).

Sheridan, Dorothy (ed.). *Wartime Women: An Anthology of Women's Wartime Writing For Mass-Observation, 1937–45* (London: Heinemann, 1990).

Sheridan, Dorothy. 'Using the Mass-Observation Archive as a Source for Women's Studies', *Women's History Review*, 3.1 (Spring 1994) 101–13.

Dorothy Sheridan

Mayor, F. M. 1872–1932

Novelist, whose masterpiece was *The Rector's Daughter* (1924), and who was, in the words of her biographer Sybil Oldfield, 'a significant link between Mrs Gaskell and Virginia WOOLF'. Flora Macdonald Mayor was born in Kingston, Surrey, to intellectual parents: her father was professor of classics at King's College, London, and her mother was a musician and linguist. At Newnham College, Cambridge, Mayor read History, but was so delighted by the bicycling, talking, dancing, and acting that she nearly failed her final exams. She then retreated to Surrey doing good works and teaching at Sunday School, and also travelled – in a Forsterian spirit – to Italy. While trying to be an actress, in 1901 she published a collection of stories for children under her stage name Mary Strafford. In 1903 Ernest Shepherd, her fiancé, died in India; this was the great tragedy of her life. She became ill and, with worsening asthma, was in poor health for the rest of her life. In 1913 she published *The Third Miss Symons*, the story of an unmarried woman who longs for love; and in 1914 *Miss Browne's Friend – a Story of Two Women*, which describes the relationship between a respectable suburban woman and a prostitute, ran as a serial in the *Free Church Suffrage Times*.

The Rector's Daughter, published ten years later by The Hogarth Press, is about Mary Jocelyn, who lives a muted life at Dedmayne Rectory but finds happiness through love, even though it is unfulfilled. As Oldfield writes, 'it is the story of an unconsummated, lifelong passion between a man and a woman...Most of the novel's action takes place in one dull East Anglian household...but by the end of the book that dark, quiet rectory has witnessed ecstasy and despair.' E. M. Forster, one of her contemporaries at Cambridge, told Flora (in reply to her letter praising his own *A Passage to India* of the same year) that 'it interested and moved me much...Mary begins as ridiculous and ends as dignified: this seemed to me a very great achievement.' John Masefield wrote to her that it was, 'a remarkable book and confirms you in your remarkable rank'. And Sylvia LYND asserted in *Time and Tide* that it 'belongs to the finest English tradition of novel writing. It is like a bitter *Cranford*. The rector's daughter is one of those sad figures of whom it is said that nothing has ever happened to them. Mrs Mayor reveals the meaninglessness of that phrase.' More recently the writer Susan Hill has described Mayor's book as 'a flawless English novel...a true work of the creative imagination...most beautifully written, with economy, plain elegance, perspicacity, grace'. Another novel, *The Squire's Daughter*, came out in 1929 and a collection of short stories, *The Room Opposite*, appeared posthumously in 1935.

Suggested Reading
Hill, Susan. Introduction to *The Rector's Daughter* by F. M . Mayor (Harmonds-
worth: Penguin, 1992) 1–4.
Oldfield, Sybil. *Spinsters of This Parish: The Life and Times of F. M. Mayor and
Mary Sheepshanks* (London: Virago, 1984).

Nicola Beauman

Mew, Charlotte 1869–1928

Poet and short-story writer, who published her first story in *The Yellow Book*
in 1894, and her principal poetry collection, *The Farmer's Bride*, in 1916.
The eldest daughter of an architect, Charlotte Mew was born in
BLOOMSBURY, and was educated at the Lucy Harrison School for Girls, later
attending lectures at University College. Her family life was shadowed by
physical and mental illness: her elder brother and youngest sister were both
diagnosed as schizophrenic and placed in asylums. Herself emotionally
sensitive and fearing hereditary insanity, Mew consequently vowed a determined celibacy; her own sexuality was in any case highly ambiguous.
Perhaps the most significant relationship of her life was her friendship with
May SINCLAIR, which lasted for only three years from 1913 to 1916, but
dramatically influenced the development and publication of Mew's writing.
Up until this point Mew had published little beyond a run of poems, prose,
and essays in *Temple Bar* between 1899 and 1904. Sinclair, a respected and
well-connected novelist and literary critic, read much of Mew's work, and
promoted it to London's most influential literary editors, including Edward
Garnett at the *Nation*, Austin Harrison at *The English Review* and Ezra Pound
at *The Egoist*. After the publication of *The Farmer's Bride* by The Poetry Bookshop, however, Sinclair discontinued the association, reportedly due to
LESBIAN advances by Mew.

Mew's writings do not fit neatly into period categories. Both her life and
her work were transitional, moving from the moral values and aesthetic
conventions of one century to the expectations and anxieties of the next.
She has been described as 'one of the last Victorians', and as something of
an anachronism within the prewar London scene of burgeoning MODERNISM.
Yet the themes of women's sexual temptation, exploitation, oppression,
and frustration in her poetry, along with the imaginative, gothic scenarios
of her short stories, align her with the 'new woman' fiction of the late nineteenth century, as she attacks and rewrites male-orientated Victorian narratives of womanhood and sexual identity. Moreover, her experimentation
with poetic form and genre, her rejection of prescriptive morality, and her
focus on subjective experience anticipate the concerns of early modernism.
It is perhaps a combination of erotic intensity, fatalism, and the macabre

that most typifies Mew's work, characteristics that she shared with Thomas Hardy, the writer who held her in highest esteem.

After Mew's suicide, her impassioned poetic voice was largely forgotten. Feminist literary criticism, however, has recently afforded her modest recognition as an important poet of the early modernist period.

Suggested Reading

Leighton, Angela. *Victorian Women Poets: Writing Against the Heart* (Hemel Hempstead: Harvester, 1992).

Walsh, Jessica. ' "The Strangest Pain to Bear": Corporeality and Fear of Insanity in Charlotte Mew's Poetry', *Victorian Poetry*, 40.3 (Fall 2002) 217–40.

Deborah Parsons

Meynell, Alice 1847–1922

Essayist, poet, and journalist, who earned wide admiration from her contemporaries for her work. Alice Meynell led an unconventional childhood of travelling, and lived partly on Italy's Ligurian Coast, where she was strictly educated by her father. Her essay 'The Child of Tumult' recounts this painful experience. In 1868, on a journey to Malvern with her mother, she became a Catholic. She married Wilfred Meynell in 1877, and bore eight children, one dying in infancy. Her daughter, Viola, later became a writer herself.

Her first book of poems, *Preludes* (1875), was enthusiastically received, and was followed by *Poems* (1892), *Other Poems* (1896), and *Later Poems* (1901). Much of her poetry, particularly that written towards the end of her life, is concerned with the religious and spiritual. Despite the good reviews, Alice suffered the torment of self-doubt, noting in her diary: 'But whatever I write will be melancholy and self-conscious as are all women poets.' Her own cure was constant hard work. Financial imperatives caused a 13-year lull in her poetry, and instead she focused on journalism and essays. With her husband she edited the Catholic periodical *The Weekly Register*, and also *Merry England*, and the short-lived *The Pen*. Meynell published several collections of essays, the first being *The Rhythm of Life* (1892). In 1893 she started writing a weekly contribution for the *Pall Mall Gazette* called 'The Wares of Autolycus', later collected in *The Colour of Life* (1896). She wrote regularly for NEWSPAPERS and magazines including the *Spectator*, the *Saturday Review*, the *World*, the *Scots Observer*, *The Tablet*, *The Magazine of Art* and *The Art Journal*.

In 1892 Meynell cultivated a friendship with the eminent poet Coventry Patmore, which was to last many years until his obsessive jealousy was cause to end it. Her poem 'Why Wilt Thou Chide?' in *Other Poems* was aimed at Patmore. She was also a friend of the poet Francis Thompson, who greatly admired her work and said of her: 'The head in most portraits drooped as with the weight of thought.' In 1897 Meynell became President of the SOCIETY OF WOMEN WRITERS AND JOURNALISTS; the following year she published a book on the life of John Ruskin; and in 1901 she embarked on a very successful lecture tour to America. She published articles about her American experiences in the *Pall Mall Gazette*. Meynell was an advocate of non-militant SUFFRAGISM, and marched in demonstrations from 1910 to 1912.

Her book *Mary, the Mother of Jesus* (1912) is a celebration of motherhood, but also explores its limitations. Despite, by her own admission, being a bad mother, her books on motherhood and children were well received, and included *The Children* (1897) and *Childhood* (1913). Her poem for the tercentenary, 'To Shakespeare' (1916), she called 'My one, *one* masterpiece'. She continued writing until her death, and *Last Poems* was published posthumously in 1923.

Suggested Reading

Armstrong, Isobel. *Poetry, Poetics and Politics.* (London: Routledge, 1993).

Badeni, June. *The Slender Tree: A Life of Alice Meynell* (Padstow: Tabb House, 1981).

Leighton, Angela. *Victorian Women Poets: Writing Against the Heart* (Hemel Hempstead: Harvester Wheatsheaf, 1992).

Laura Christie

Meynell, Viola 1886–1956

Novelist, short-story writer and poet, Viola Meynell is perhaps best known for her poignant memoirs of her mother, the poet and essayist Alice MEYNELL (1929), and her father, Wilfred Meynell (1952). Viola Meynell grew up in a close and affectionate Catholic family. Her work was published at a young age, and her mother commented in a letter: 'Yes, Viola looks young but she is curiously wise, wiser than her books seem to represent her, written as they are in that now prevalent impartial mood that commits the writer to nothing.'

Her first books were *Martha Vine: A Love Story of a Simple Life* (1910) and *Cross-in-Hand Farm* (1911), follwed by *Lot Barrow* (1913), which received pleasing reviews. She married John Dallyn, a neighbour from Greatham, in 1922, and they had one son.

Altogether, Meynell produced around 20 volumes of prose and verse, and also edited anthologies and collections of letters. Her novels are mostly after the style of Hardy, stories of love and longing, with rural settings, while her poetry is usually haunting and sorrowful. Just before her death she published a collection of her stories, spanning the years 1925–56.

Suggested Reading

Badeni, June. *The Slender Tree: A Life of Alice Meynell* (Padstow: Tabb House, 1981).

Laura Christie

Miller, Betty 1910–1965

Novelist and biographer. Miller established her literary reputation with a biography of Robert Browning (1952), but it is her fiction of English domestic life, with its sensitive explorations of the complexities of marriage and parenthood, that now attracts admiring readers. Her most highly acclaimed novel, *On the Side of the Angels* (1945), is based on her observations of her husband, the psychiatrist Emanuel Miller, during his wartime service in a military hospital. Its subtle, powerful indictment of militarism emerges out of the intimate details of family life: the way husbands, housewives, teachers, and children participate in the psychology of war.

Miller was born in Cork to a Jewish family. Her mother had grown up in Sweden with Polish parents and her father, a prosperous businessman, had emigrated to Ireland from Lithuania. In 1920 the Troubles made it necessary for the family to leave Ireland, and Miller spent two years in Sweden with her mother and siblings before settling in London. She graduated with a degree in journalism from University College in 1930. Three years later, the precocious 22-year-old had published her first novel, *The Mere Living* (1933) with Victor Gollancz. Delighted with his new protegée, Gollancz promptly published her next two novels, *Sunday* (1934) and *Portrait of the Bride* (1935). However, when presented in 1935 with her fourth (tentatively titled *Next Year in Jerusalem*), Gollancz rejected the book, traumatizing its young author who retreated into journalism for the next six years.

Before Gollancz's rejection, Miller had confidently told a friend that she was soon to be the author of 'one of the best novels Victor Gollancz Ltd have ever published'. Her understanding of the book's qualities was keener than Gollancz's, although she was naïve to expect that readers would admire her aim of 'tackling the social and psychological conflicts of a Jew in the modern world'. The novel tells the story of Alec Berman, a Jewish boy from working-class Brighton who becomes a successful London film producer, but who struggles throughout his life with the effects of anti-Semitism within himself and within the English culture that he idealizes. The novel finally appeared in 1941 as *Farewell Leicester Square*. Its publisher, Robert Hale, also brought out Miller's last three novels, *A Room in Regent's Park* (1942), *On the Side of the Angels* (1945), and *The Death of the Nightingale* (1948).

In the early fifties Miller decided she was through with fiction. Energized by the success of her Browning biography, which earned her a place in the Royal Society of Literature, she completed an edition of the letters of Elizabeth Barrett to Mary Russell Mitford, and several chapters of a biography of Kipling. This work came to a sudden and tragic end when, in 1959, she was diagnosed with Alzheimer's disease.

Suggested Reading

Hartley, Jenny. 'Warriors and Healers, Impostors and Mothers: Betty Miller's *On the Side of the Angels*', in Aranzazu Usandizaga and Andrew Monnickendam (eds), *Dressing Up for War: Transformations of Gender and Genre in the Discourse and Literature of War* (Amsterdam and Atlanta, GA: Rodopi, 2001) 173–88.

Miller, Jane. Introduction to *Farewell Leicester Square* by Betty Miller (London: Persephone Books, 2000) vii–xix.

Miller, Sarah. Introduction to *On the Side of the Angels* by Betty Miller (London: Virago, 1985) vii–xviii.

Kristin Bluemel

Mitchison, Naomi (1897–1999)

Scottish novelist, playwright, poet, memoirist, and journalist. In later life, Naomi Mitchison published three memoirs: *Small Talk: Memories of an Edwardian Childhood* (1973), *All Change Here: Girlhood and Marriage* (1975), and *Among You Taking Notes: Wartime Diary 1939–45* (1985). The books revealed a writer whose early privileges, as a daughter of the aristocratic Haldane family, did not preclude the development of her active, Leftist feminism. Critics of Mitchison's interwar fictions question the motives of her upper-class female protagonists who controversially use sex as a point of contact with the proletariat. Although novels including *We Have Been Warned* (1935) eroticize working-class characters, they also express an earnest longing to share with the other that is at once sexual and political. These aspirations also informed Mitchison's SOCIALISM, feminism (she practised open marriage and challenged the traditional notion of ownership of, and by, one's spouse), and acknowledgement of the material sacrifices her class should make in order to create a classless Britain.

In the interwar period, Mitchison was celebrated for her HISTORICAL FICTION, and cleverly used distant settings as comfortable backgrounds for radical plots. She was lauded for *The Corn King and the Spring Queen* (1931), her epic fiction of Marob, a kingdom transformed after contact with more civilized cultures. Sparta and Egypt compare negatively with relatively barbaric Marob; influenced by Frazer's *The Golden Bough*, Mitchison subverted the hierarchy of civility and barbarism by criticizing great empires for their lack of such community love as informed Marob's earthy religion. Recent feminist scholars praise Mitchison's use of a questing bisexual heroine, Erif Der, who struggles between her roles as witch, wife, mother, and queen, sympathetically reflecting the complexity of modern women's identities. Auden described *The Corn King* as 'hotter than anything I've ever read'; sharp criticism resulted for Mitchison's equally erotic contemporary novel *We Have Been Warned*. She learned that overt sex was 'apparently...all right when people wear wolf skins and togas'. Her reputation never quite recovered from the later novel's failure.

Mitchison's children's books used ancient settings for similar political ends. These neglected works challenged official histories by imagining the lives of children, women, and slaves. Mitchison's pedagogical socialism is apparent in her collection *An End and a Beginning and Other Plays* (1937) in which she described Christ as a proto-communist: 'He was a rebel with all sorts of queer ideas about brotherhood and poor men being as good as rich men.' Some of her CHILDREN'S LITERATURE echoed the socialist Christianity presented to adults in *The Blood of the Martyrs* (1939).

During WORLD WAR TWO, Mitchison was devoted to life on her estate, Carradale, where she housed evacuated children and endeavoured a communal life. She composed one novel, *The Bull Calves* (1947), and kept a Mass-Observation diary. She also attempted group writings and staged unpublished plays with her workers. In later years, Mitchison served on the Argyll County Council and, following her African travels, was made an honorary 'Mother' of the Bakgatla tribe in Botswana. She turned to feminist SCIENCE FICTION with *Memoirs of a Space Woman* (1962) and *Solution Three* (1975), novels as frankly sexual as any of her 1930s texts. Mitchison's death, aged 101, ended a life that had observed and participated in the transformations of an entire century.

Suggested Reading

Benton, Jill. *Naomi Mitchison: A Biography* (London: Pandora Press, 1990).

Calder, Jenni. 'More Than Merely Ourselves: Naomi Mitchison', in Douglas Gifford and Dorothy McMillan (eds), *A History of Scottish Women's Writing* (Edinburgh: Edinburgh University Press, 1997) 444–55.

Maslen, Elizabeth. 'Naomi Mitchison's Historical Fiction', in Maroula Joannou (ed.), *British Women Writers of the 1930s: Gender, Politics and History* (Edinburgh: Edinburgh University Press, 1996) 138–50.

Ashlie Sponenberg

Mitford, Nancy 1904–1973

Novelist, essayist, biographer, best known for her ideas about 'u' (upper-class) and non-'u' (non-upper-class) linguistic usage, and for her light-hearted bestselling novels, *The Pursuit of Love* (1945) and its sequel, *Love in a Cold Climate* (1949). Mitford was born in 1904 in London, the eldest of the six Mitford sisters. One sister, Diana, married Oswald Mosley. Another, Unity, became infatuated with Hitler. The left-wing Jessica lived in America.

In her essay 'The English Aristocracy' published by Stephen Spender in *Encounter* in 1954, Nancy Mitford provided a glossary of 'u' and non-u vocabulary thereby initiating a national debate about English class-consciousness and snobbery. The essay was reprinted in book form as *Noblesse Oblige: An Inquiry into the Identifiable Characteristics of the English Aristocracy* in 1956.

Mitford's eight novels portray with wit and hyperbole the mannered, extravagant and arcane behaviour of the English aristocracy and exhibit her love of an elaborate 'tease'. Her first novel, *Highland Fling* (1931), brings together Bright Young Things and middle-aged grouse-shooters in a Scottish castle. Her second, *Christmas Pudding* (1932), depicts dyed-in-the-wool ageing conservatives and the fashionable young, while *Wigs on the Green* (1934) offers a thinly veiled portrait of Unity Mitford as an heiress with FASCIST sympathies. *Pigeon Pie* (1939) is a comedy of manners which ends with the capture of German spies in Britain.

The Pursuit of Love is a fictionalized account of Nancy Mitford's own bizarre upbringing with her father, Lord Resedale, recognizable in the irascible Uncle Matthew. It is a romantic novel, but its comic tone differentiates it from many works of ROMANTIC FICTION. It was an immediate success, selling 200,000 copies in its first year, and has never been out of print. Mitford's ill-starred love affair with Gaston Palwski, a confidante of General de Gaulle, provided her with the template for the relationship between Linda and Fabrice in *Love in a Cold Climate* (1949). Her last novel, *Don't Tell Alfred* (1960), is based on the British Embassy in France and uses characters from her earlier work.

Much of Mitford's work reflects her love of France, particularly *The Blessing* (1950), a romantic comedy about an English woman reunited with her philandering French husband by their son. Mitford published two books of family letters about her cousins, the Stanleys: *The Ladies of Alderley* (1938) and *The Stanleys of Alderley* (1939). She also wrote several historical biographies: *Madame de Pompadour* (1954), *Voltaire in Love* (1957), *The Sun King* (1966), and *Frederick the Great* (1970). Her work fell out of fashion following her death, but interest has revived since a BBC adaptation of *Love in a Cold Climate* in 2001.

Suggested Reading

Acton, Harold. *Nancy Mitford: A Memoir* (London: Hamish Hamilton, 1975).
Hastings, Selena. *Nancy Mitford* (London: Hamish Hamilton, 1985).
Joannou, Maroula. 'Nancy Mitford and *The Pursuit of Love*', in Jane Dowson (ed.), *Women's Writing, 1945–1960: After the Deluge* (Basingstoke: Palgrave Macmillan, 2003) 117–30.

Maroula Joannou

Modernism

Late nineteenth- and early twentieth-century phenomenon in the arts that challenged the dominance of realism. Modernism is broadly typified by a break from the hitherto conventional understanding of consciousness and representation, towards greater aesthetic self-reflexivity and abstraction, and an emphasis on new stylistic and formal strategies for the rendering of modern life. The term 'modernism' was first used in relation to the literature of the 1910s and 1920s in Robert Graves and Laura Riding's *A Survey of Modernist*

Poetry in 1927, and did not become literary currency until its institutionalized configuration as a singular and highly selective critical category in the 1940s and 1950s. As a cultural moment, however, the term subsumes a range of distinct avant-garde movements, including Futurism, Imagism, Vorticism, Dadaism, Surrealism, and Expressionism, as well as the diverse and divergent aesthetic and ideological outlooks of individual writers and artists. Transnational and largely urban in location, these were the product of, and offered varying responses to, the conditions and energies of their time; an age of rapid commercial, scientific, and technological development, but also of social and political upheaval, conflict and crisis.

The focal point of prewar cultural and aesthetic innovation was Paris, where Picasso, Appollinaire, Stravinsky, and Diaghilev led the revolt of a 'modern' art against the conservative critical establishment, rejecting the enervating effect of bourgeois tradition for the immediacy of the modern. The scandalized yet fascinated response of Parisian society to the perspectivism of Cubist art, to Stravinsky's tribal rhythms, to the exoticism and vigour of the Ballet Russes, or to the aggressive oratory of Marinetti's 'Futurist Manifesto', consolidated the status of the French capital as a nexus of creative rebellion and transformation, its artistic coteries forming a highly influential melting-pot of European cultural energies. London experienced its own moment of dynamic and cosmopolitan cultural avant-gardism immediately prior to WORLD WAR ONE. 'On or about December 1910', Virginia WOOLF declared in retrospect in 1924, 'human character changed.' Generally understood as a reference to the opening of Roger Fry's *Manet and the Post-Impressionists* exhibition at the Sackville Gallery, which introduced the work of artists such as Cézanne, Gaugin, and Van Gogh to the British public for the first time, the date coincides more broadly with a period of significant social, cultural, and political attack on the national *status quo*. While post-impressionism was particularly influential upon BLOOMSBURY aesthetics, another significant arrival for English literary modernism was the American poet and critic Ezra Pound, with his doctrine of 'make it new'. Pound's promotion of a poetry of unsentimental, 'hard' images through his development of Imagism, and his collaboration with T. E. Hulme, Wyndham Lewis, and Henri Gaudier-Brzeska in the kinetic and geometric art of Vorticism, brought the London avant-garde broad public recognition.

The trajectory of 'English' modernism was profoundly shaped by the crisis of 1914, and the main proponents of postwar aesthetics would be non-combatants, notably Pound and T. S. Eliot. It was during the war years that the latter's literary and critical sway over the formation of literary modernism developed, beginning with his editorship of modernism's critical mouthpiece, the LITTLE MAGAZINE the *Egoist*, in 1917, and consolidated by the publication of *The Waste Land*, described by Pound as 'the justification of the 'movement', of our modern experiment', in 1922. The poem both expressed the social and cultural tone of the postwar age, and articulated a conceptual and formal ideology for postwar modernism. With the past torn away by the fissures of war, rebellious iconoclasm had given way to a profound sense of social failure and psychological dislocation. The emergent cultural identity and imagination of this era, struggling with its rejection of the past and nostalgia for a lost stability, was characterized by an evasion rather than embrace of the anarchic forces of modernity. Moreover, the war experience impacted on literary style and authorial perspective: its fracturing of conventional temporal linearity, narrative logic, and the stability of subjective consciousness required new writerly forms and strategies.

Here two, arguably opposing, literary trends came into tension. Equally central to Anglo-American modernist aesthetics as the objectivist focus of Imagism, Vorticism, and Eliotian 'high' modernism is a subjectivist focus concerned with the fragmentation and flux of modern consciousness, as manifest in the interior realism and associated stylistic techniques of writers such as Woolf, Dorothy RICHARDSON and James Joyce. That Eliot's doctrine of impersonality would prevail and be legitimized as the theoretical basis of institutional accounts of modernism in the 1950s and 1960s, while Woolf's aesthetic was sidelined as domestic, enclosed, and insubstantial, and Richardson all but forgotten, was in part the result of Eliot's appropriation of Joyce. The formalism of modern art, Eliot argued in an idiosyncratic reading of *Ulysses* that has perhaps become the archetypal statement of Anglo-American modernist dogma, provided, 'a way of controlling, of ordering, of giving a shape and a significance to the immense panorama of futility and anarchy which is contemporary history'. Modernism in this sense, as Astradur Eysteinsson states, 'is viewed as a kind of aesthetic heroism, which in the face of the chaos of the modern world . . . sees art as the only dependable reality and as an ordering principle of a quasi-religious kind. The unity of art is supposedly a salvation from the shattered order of modern reality'. Postwar literary modernism, faced with the void of history between a lost past of accepted values and beliefs, and a new world of disillusionment and loss, put its faith in the power of aesthetic reconstruction.

Anglo-American literary historiography has traditionally differentiated itself from the insurgent and often nationalist aesthetic energies of the European avant-garde, downplaying the complex cross-currents with Futurism, Expressionism, or Surrealism for example, and identifying at the core of modernist thought the principles of objective impersonality and classicism delineated by Eliot's critical writings and his interpretations of the work of Hulme and Joyce. Opposition to the authority of the formalist readings of the 1950s and 1960s came with the revisionism of feminist literary and art criticism, which challenged the ways in which the literary institution had constructed modernism in terms of masculinist canons and formalist conventions, and disputed its silencing of women writers. Drawing attention to the active role and varied aesthetic and ideological allegiances of women as writers, critics, publishers, and patrons within the modernist period, feminist critics constructed an alternative female canon in which H. D., Dorothy RICHARDSON, Gertrude Stein, Natalie Barney, Mina LOY, Djuna Barnes, and Jean RHYS, among others, were reinstated as key literary figures alongside the acknowledged but marginalized figures of Woolf and Katherine MANSFIELD. Furthermore, in highlighting women writers' embrace of the social and professional possibilities of modernity as well as the challenge to traditional notions of gender they posed in their works and their own lives, and in arguing for a commonality between modernist and feminist aesthetics, feminist critics exposed literary history's hitherto selective formulation of 'modernism'.

The impossibility of setting out a clear definition of modernism that is not qualified by recognition of its complexities is by now a critical given. The theoretical trends and cross-disciplinary initiatives of the past decade have led to a significant rethinking and remapping of the multiple parameters of modernism; its relationship to bourgeois and middlebrow culture, to the mass and the marketplace, to technology and the new sciences, to its nineteenth-century past. Contemporary modernist studies is a revitalized and dynamic discursive field; exploring the broad social, political, cultural, and intellectual contexts, as well as the international and interdisciplinary reach of the aesthetic innovations within the turbulent period of modernity and modernization.

Suggested Reading

Eliot, T. S. '*Ulysses*, Order, and Myth' (1923), repr. in William Van O'Connor (ed.), *Forms of Modern Fiction: Essays Collected in Honor of Joseph Warren Beach* (Minneapolis, MN: University of Minnesota Press, 1948) 120–4.

Elliott, Bridget and Jo-Ann Wallace. *Women Artists and Writers: Modernist (im)positionings* (London: Routledge, 1994).

Eysteinsson, Astradur. *The Concept of Modernism* (Ithaca, NY: Cornell University Press, 1992).

Levenson, Michael (ed.). *A Genealogy of Modernism* (Cambridge: Cambridge University Press, 1984).

Miller, Tyrus. *Late Modernism: Politics, Fiction, and the Arts between the World Wars* (Berkeley: University of California Press, 1999).

Scott, Bonnie Kime. *The Gender of Modernism* (Bloomington: Indiana University Press, 1990).

Deborah Parsons

Moore, Olive *c.*1905–*c.*1970

Scandalously under-read English MODERNIST, journalist, and poet whose real name was Constance Vaughan. Between 1929 and 1934, Moore published four brilliant books that earned her the reputation as an *enfant terrible* of British literature. She then disappeared from public view, and is virtually unknown to readers and literary historians today. In an autobiographical sketch initially published in *Authors Today and Yesterday* (1933), Moore writes: 'I am by nature solitary and contemplative, very happy, very morose. I loathe books and never read them.' Aside from those provided in this provocative essay, few details of her personal life are available, and she never even disclosed her birth date. Moore did not marry, and made her living as a reporter for the London *Daily Sketch*; she was a part of Charles Lahr's Red Lion Street Circle, a literary group that gravitated toward radical literature; she was acquainted with the Scottish poet Hugh MacDiarmid; and the sculptor Savas Botzaris produced a striking bust of her.

Moore's four experimental texts earned her accolades from respected authors and constitute a remarkable modernist achievement. Three of her books are novels: *Celestial Seraglio* (1929), an account of a British girl's coming of age in a Belgian convent; *Spleen* (1930) – arguably her masterpiece – about an English-woman who goes into self-imposed exile in Italy after giving birth to a deformed son; and *Fugue* (1932), the story of a young female journalist who, unmarried and pregnant, lives amidst the English literati in an Alsatian village. The fourth book is *The Apple is Bitten Again* (1934), a dazzling, caustic, and bracing collection of aphorisms on modern culture, art, nationality, religion, and the inequality between the sexes. In this volume, Moore critiques Virginia WOOLF's literary ascendancy and her condemnation of interlopers like herself: 'Example of how a verdict is obtained in the English Literary Courts. Mrs. Woolf in a literary weekly reviews the books of newcomers, and finds neither interest nor distinction.' *The Apple is Bitten Again* also includes 'Further Reflections on the Death of a Porcupine (Final Word on D. H. Lawrence)', originally published in 1932 as a limited edition pamphlet.

Moore's witty and lyrical style has been described as a cross between Woolf and Djuna Barnes. Her novels break chronological sequence, use shifting and multiple points of view, contain impressionistic snatches of fractured dialogue, and avoid chapter breaks. Like her contemporary, Mary BUTTS, Moore employs the lower case when using nationalities as adjectives (for example, 'english person'), a practice which suggests her vexed relationship to the category of nationality. Her obsessive subject was female consciousness, despite the fact that she often comes across as a misogynist. While Moore self-consciously rejected an essentialist understanding of feminine inscription – writing in 1934, she dismisses 'that warm menstrous flow of womanly prose' – her work contains one of the most sophisticated and penetrating critiques of gender in modern literature.

Moore is said to have chosen her pseudonym because Olive represented an 'acquired taste, dry and sophisticated', and the author believed that once the taste had been experienced, her readers would 'want more'. Indeed, Moore's concise, provocative, and deliciously biting prose proves addictive. The whereabouts of her manuscripts are unknown, and no obituary has been found.

Suggested Reading

Garrity, Jane. *Step-Daughters of England: British Women Modernists and the National Imaginary* (Manchester: Manchester University Press, 2003).

Jane Garrity

Morrell, Lady Ottoline 1873–1938

Literary patron and memoirist, renowned hostess of some of the most celebrated salon parties of the early twentieth century, given at her London home in Bedford Square and later at her country residence, Garsington Manor, near Oxford. Born Lady Ottoline Violet Anne Cavendish-Bentinck, she was the half-sister of the sixth Duke of Portland, and from an early age her unconventional behaviour and appearance gave concern to her family. After travelling around Europe from 1896 to 1897 and making two unsuccessful attempts at a university education (at St Andrews and Somerville, Oxford), she married the Liberal candidate for South Oxfordshire, Philip Morrell, in 1902.

In 1906, Philip was elected MP and Ottoline gave birth to twins: a son, Hugh, who died at three days old, and a daughter, Julian. The family moved to Bedford Square, Bloomsbury, and by 1908 Ottoline had begun her Thursday evening 'at homes', famous for their eclectic mix of political, artistic and literary figures, including Asquith, Ramsay MacDonald, Augustus John, Henry Lamb, Max Beerbohm, and W. B. Yeats, and which were described by the painter William Rothenstein as 'the most delightful salon in London'. She became acquainted, although never intimate, with the members of the BLOOMSBURY group, a relationship strengthened by the Morrells's support of conscientious objectors in WORLD WAR ONE. In 1913, the Morrells bought Garsington, and Ottoline continued to entertain prominent figures including Virginia WOOLF, Lytton Strachey, Dora Carrington, and Katherine MANSFIELD. In 1914, she met D. H. Lawrence, and became for a while his patron and benefactor.

Although the Morrells seem to have been a mutually caring and supportive couple, Ottoline embarked on innumerable affairs, including a relationship with Bertrand Russell, begun in 1911, which generated more than 3000 letters between them. Throughout her career, Morrell cultivated a unique and exotic persona, playing on her unconventional looks and exhibiting a forceful and often inconsistent personality. This inconsistency was often reflected in others' attitudes towards her, and she became the subject of several parodies; 'Lady Omega Muddle', as Strachey referred to her, was the basis for Lawrence's character

Hermione Roddice in *Women in Love* (1920), and the way of life at Garsington was satirized in Huxley's *Crome Yellow* (1921). Both books wounded Morrell considerably. Despite her erratic and often overbearing personality, Ottoline Morrell was an enthusiastic and generous patron of the arts. Her memoirs, kept from 1873 to 1915 and published posthumously in two volumes, are a fascinating and insightful record, not only of her own personal life, but of the world she inhabited and the people she interacted with.

Suggested Reading

Darroch, Sandra Jobson. *Ottoline: The Life of Lady Ottoline Morrell* (London: Chatto & Windus, 1976).

Seymour, Miranda. *Ottoline Morrell: Life on a Grand Scale* (London: Hodder & Stoughton, 1992).

Esme Miskimmin

Muir, Willa 1890–1970

Humanist novelist, memoirist, poet, essayist, best known as a translator of European novels. Born Willa Anderson in Scotland, she was educated at Montrose Academy and graduated with a First in Classics from St Andrews University. She married the writer Edwin Muir in 1918; they travelled Eastern Europe together, Willa mastering new languages along the way.

The Muirs were the first to translate Kafka's novels into English, beginning with *The Castle* in 1930, and several of their Kafka translations are still in print. The pair also translated Gerhart Hauptmann, Leon Feuchtwanger, and Hermann Broch, amongst others. Willa also translated independently, under the pseudonym Agnes N. Scott. She was rarely recognized as the more skilled linguist, and often put her own writing aside in order to encourage his and to take the greater share of familial duties. Her 1968 memoir, *Belonging*, however, depicted their marriage as a loving partnership.

Muir's 1925 essay *Women: An Inquiry* argued that feminine logic was different from, and complementary to, that of men. She also published *Laconics, Jingles and Other Verses* (1969), and fiction including *Mrs Grundy in Scotland* (1936), which satirizes the English class system: 'The mob from below and Mr Goschen from above were grinding [Mrs Grundy] between the upper millstone of taxation and financial debt and the lower millstone of Socialism.' She has received no attention from critics.

Ashlie Sponenberg

N

Nesbit, E. 1858–1924

Poet and novelist, best known for her children's books, particularly *The Railway Children* (1906). London born, she spent her childhood in France and later at Hallshead Hall, Kent, the eventual location for *The Railway Children*. She published her first poems at 17 in *The Sunday Magazine*, following them with short stories and novels for children. In 1880, Nesbit married journalist and philanderer Hubert Bland, both becoming founder members of the FABIAN SOCIETY. She subsequently published some of her work as E. Bland, and she and her husband used the joint pseudonym Fabian Bland for their eight adult novels, including *The Prophet's Mantle* (1885) inspired by the anarchist Peter Kropotkin's stay in London. The couple's three children shared the family home with Hubert's illegitimate children and one of his mistresses. Nesbit mixed with the Rossettis, Swinburne, and William Morris, friends of her sister Mary.

Nesbit really wanted to be a poet, and published her Pre-Raphaelite influenced verse in *New Age* in 1907–8, and a volume, *Ballads and Lyrics of Socialism* in 1908. But she had much greater success with her children's fiction. *The Railway Children* features Bobbie, a young girl poised on the edge of adulthood, sheltered from truths of her father's imprisonment and encouraged to run wild. It concludes with a sentimental, Victorian reunion with the father. Nesbit also wrote three novels about the Bastable family: *The Story of the Treasure Seekers* (1898), *The Wouldbegoods* (1901), and *The New Treasure Seekers* (1904). Her *Five Children and It* (1902), *The Phoenix and the Carpet* (1904), and *The Enchanted Castle* (1907) mix a magical, innocent, escapist world with the everyday, bottom-of-the-garden lives of children.

Nesbit published 40 children's novels or story collections in her own right, and nearly as many in collaboration with others. Julia Briggs, her biographer, credits her with inventing the children's adventure story and developing children's books which, unlike their Victorian predecessors, were entertaining, without being didactic. Nesbit helped reverse the great tradition of CHILDREN'S LITERATURE, inaugurated by Carroll, MacDonald, and Kenneth Grahame, turning away from the 'secondary world' to tough truths won from encounters with things-as-they-are, previously the province of adult novels.

Nesbit also produced adult ghost stories. The protagonist of 'Hurst of Hurstcote', in her 1910 collection *Fear*, mesmerized his lovely wife in courtship, and cannot imagine her dying. His bond is that her soul should not leave her body after death until he joins her. The story suggests that eternal love is terrifying, and also critiques ROMANTIC FICTIONS, although Nesbit herself wrote romantic novels. She also published reviews and articles on politics and daily life. When Bland's brush manufacturing business collapsed, Nesbit sold her work to Fleet Street and took to making greeting cards. After Bland died in 1913, Nesbit married kindly ship's engineer Thomas Tucker. Her work continues to be widely read. *The Railway Children* was filmed in 1970 and 2000, and *Five Children and It* in 2004.

Suggested Reading
Bell, Anthea. *E. Nesbit* (London: The Bodley Head, 1968).
Briggs, Julia. *A Woman of Passion: The Life of E. Nesbit, 1858–1924* (London: Hutchinson, 1987).

Gina Wisker

Net Book Agreement
Following a century of booksellers' shared efforts to wrestle arrangements with publishers that would protect their trade, the Net Book Agreement was finalized in 1900. The Agreement gave PUBLISHERS the right to set net prices which must be honoured by booksellers in exchange for a significant trade discount. According to its provisions, any bookseller found in breach of net pricing would not be supplied by member publishers. This policy was tested in 1906, when the net publishers boycotted the Times Book Club, which had been slashing new title prices, and the *Times* attacked the publishing trade as a monopoly. The 'Book War' ended in 1908, when the *Times* finally signed the Agreement.

Ashlie Sponenberg

Newspapers and Periodical Journals
The period 1900 to 1950, was a time of fluctuating fortunes for newspapers and periodicals. New publications constantly sprang up, and often died quickly, but this was not necessarily a reflection of their quality. The DEPRESSION brought many casualties, as did the onset of both wars, but as some publications folded, new ones would emerge, often in response to the very causes that destroyed others. So the widespread anti-war feeling of the twenties and early thirties ensured the success of a number of PACIFIST journals such as *Peace News*, while unemployment in the thirties inspired such publications as *The Highway and the Plebs*. During the Second World War, the thirst for reading matter ensured the success of such periodicals as *Penguin New Writing* and *Selected Writing*.

Most periodicals and newspapers had women writing for them throughout this period. During the First World War, Margaret COLE, for example, was contributing to publications on both sides of the Atlantic, while Storm JAMESON wrote for LITTLE MAGAZINES such as *The New Age* and the *Egoist*. However, the number of women contributors steadily increased from the 1920s onwards. Among others, Winifred HOLTBY and Vera BRITTAIN wrote feature articles on a range of issues, from feminism to politics, in, for example, the *Yorkshire Post*, the *Manchester Guardian*, the *News Chronicle*, the *Daily Chronicle*, the *Daily Herald*, the *Evening News*, the *Evening Standard*, *Time and Tide*, *John O' London's Weekly*, and *Good Housekeeping*, while Naomi MITCHISON wrote regularly for *Time and Tide* and the *New Statesman and Nation*, and on occasion for the *Manchester Guardian*, the *Observer*, the *Scotsman* and the *Glasgow Herald*.

British women also appeared increasingly in American newspapers. Rebecca WEST, as well as writing for many British publications, wrote feature articles or columns in, for example, the *New York Times*, the *New Yorker*, and the *New York American*, and Sylvia Townsend WARNER likewise wrote for the *New Yorker*. Women also contributed to journals elsewhere: Naomi Mitchison, for instance, to journals in Africa and Storm Jameson to the *New Delhi Aryan Path*, while Sylvia PANKHURST started a newspaper in Ethiopia. Apart from feature articles, women very often undertook reviewing. To give a few examples, Rebecca West for the *New York Herald Tribune* and the *Bookman*, Rosamond LEHMANN for the *Spectator*, Storm Jameson for the *New English Weekly* and Phyllis BENTLEY for the *Yorkshire Post*.

While journals and newspapers did not, for the most part, make overt distinctions between men and women writers, there was sometimes an attempt to prescribe suitable topics for women writers. They were often in demand to write fairly lightweight articles on specifically women's issues. Rose MACAULAY, in an essay on 'What the Public Wants' (1925), maintains that such contributions were very well paid so as to tempt women to write on frivolous topics. In the late twenties, Storm Jameson succumbed for a few years to writing articles for the *Evening News* and the *Evening Standard* on such topics as 'Can Women Stand This "Freedom"?', and she commented in a letter to Valentine Dobree: 'Why in the name of God have I no self respect?.' However, along with, for example, Dorothy RICHARDSON and Ethel SMYTH, Jameson was also writing feature articles for these papers. In these, she championed an anti-war stance or a more humane approach to divorce – such articles usually earned a few words from the editor, introducing them as 'controversial'.

Short stories and serialized fiction were common in a number of newspapers and periodicals on both sides of the Atlantic. The Sunday papers in Britain carried serials by, for example, Ethel MANNIN, and some papers paid highly for serials of novel length. WOMEN'S MAGAZINES, like *Good Housekeeping*, and a wide range of literary periodicals such as *Horizon*, *Transformation*, the *Atlantic Monthly*, and *The Cornhill* published and commissioned short stories from both men and women.

Women, too, ran some journals. In 1920, Lady RHONDDA founded *Time and Tide*, an independent feminist weekly which published many women writers, such as Stella BENSON, E. M. DELAFIELD, Elizabeth ROBINS, Cicely HAMILTON, and Helena SWANWICK. Meanwhile, in the thirties, Lady Houston became editor of the *Saturday Review*, printing articles by Hitler and Mussolini, and eventually championing the idea of dictatorship for Britain. The success and final demise of this periodical marks changing public perceptions of events in Europe.

It is fascinating to explore changes in journal editorial policies during these 50 years, as they sought to challenge or bolster public perceptions of events. One key issue which is crucial for an understanding of the period is the widespread interest in theosophy and spiritualism after the First World War, which is reflected in a large number of newspapers and journals in Britain until the 1950s, many of them carrying regular columns devoted to these subjects. Several writers, not simply a few unrepresentative individuals who do not accept institutionalized religion, are drawn to these areas as a response to the traumas of the times.

Suggested Reading

Chielens, Edward E. (ed.). *American Literary Magazines: The Twentieth Century* (Westport, CT, and London: Greenwood Press, 1992).

Drost, Henry (ed.). *The World's News Media: A Comprehensive Reference Guide* (Harlow: Longman Current Affairs, 1991).

Linton, David (ed.). *The Twentieth-Century Newspaper Press in Britain: An Annotated Bibliography* (London: Mansell, 1994).

Stewart, James D., with Muriel E. Hammond and Erwin Saenger (eds). *British Union Catalogue of Periodicals: A Record of the Periodicals of the World, from the Seventeenth Century to the Present Day, in British Libraries*, 4 vols, with supplements (London: Butterworths, 1968–70).

Sullivan, Alvin (ed.). *British Literary Magazines: The Modern Age, 1914–1984* (Westport, CT, and London: Greenwood Press, 1986).

Elizabeth Maslen

O

O'Brien, Kate 1897–1974

Irish novelist, travel writer, and journalist. Born in Limerick, O'Brien became a convent boarder at the age of five, following her mother's death. She won a scholarship to University College, Dublin, in 1916, studying English and French for her BA. Moving to England, she worked initially as a translator for the *Manchester Guardian* and later as a teacher and a book reviewer for the *Spectator*. She was married (for less than a year) to a Dutch journalist, Gustaaf Renier; afterwards it appears that she was exclusively LESBIAN.

Although she wrote a well-received play, *Distinguished Villa* (1926), and was a prolific critic, it is as a novelist that O'Brien is most renowned. Her first novel, *Without My Cloak* (1931), which won the Hawthornden Prize and the James Tait Black Prize, chronicles a family of Catholic shopkeepers in a small Irish town, spanning three generations from 1789 to 1877. The novel, like O'Brien's later works *Mary Lavelle* (1936), *As Music and Splendour* (1958), and her most successful novel *That Lady* (1946), details the desire and the struggle, particularly for women, to obtain love and liberty when confronted with the demands of family, society, and religion.

O'Brien was increasingly in conflict with the ideals of her native Ireland, with both *Pray for the Wanderer* (1938) and *The Last of Summer* (1943) criticizing the smug puritanism that flourished under Eamonn de Valera's rule. *The Land of Spices* (1941) depicts a European convent community in Mellick (a fictionalized Limerick) headed by an English Mother Superior whose relationship with the Irish priests and nuns is strained, due to their insularity, parochialism, and bourgeois snobbery: 'The Irish liked themselves, and throve on their own psychological chaos...They were an ancient martyred race, and of great importance to themselves – that meagre handful of conceptions made a history, made a problem – and made them at once unconquerable and a little silly.' *The Land of Spices* is a subtle attack on all things the Irish constitution considered natural: the state, the family, the position of women, and marriage. Both it and *Mary Lavelle* were banned for many years in the Irish Free State on grounds of obscenity. As a result of her travelogue *Farewell Spain* (1937), which openly criticized Franco, she was banned from entering Spain until 1957.

After living in England for many years, she returned to Ireland in 1950, settling in County Galway. As well as her final two novels, *The Flower of May* (1953) and *As Music and Splendour*, she wrote a biography of St Teresa of Avila (1951) and the autobiographical *Presentation Parlour* (1963). She spent the last years of her life in England. Although critically neglected at the time of her death,

O'Brien has since attracted interest due to her charting of the relationship between Catholicism and nationalism, and its effect on the social mores and emotional and sexual dilemmas of the Irish middle class.

Suggested Reading

Walshe, Eibhear (ed.). *Ordinary People Dancing: Essays on Kate O'Brien* (Cork: Cork University Press, 1993).

Weekes, Ann Owens. *Irish Women Writers: An Uncharted Tradition* (Lexington, KY: The University Press of Kentucky, 1990).

Louise Harrington

P

Pacifism

The religious, political, or humanitarian belief that war can never be justified. *Pacificism*, related but distinct, allows that war is sometimes necessary. Combining integrity of belief with political credibility is problematic for pacifists. During the First World War, the introduction of conscription in 1916 politicized pacifism. Absolutists faced prison, but most conscientious objectors accepted alternative service. Few unconditional exemptions were granted, and Quakers, respected for their beliefs and aware of their rights, were awarded the majority of these.

During the 1920s, many pacifists espoused *pacificism* through international co-operation, hoping that the League of Nations (founded 1919) could effect disarmament and control recalcitrant nations. But the rise of FASCISM in the early 1930s caused many intellectuals to embrace pacifism, fearing a yet more devastating war. In 1936, Abyssinia's subjugation, the Rhineland's remilitarization, and the SPANISH CIVIL WAR emphasized Britain's vulnerability, but most pacifists hoped that APPEASEMENT would prevent war. The Peace Pledge Union (founded 1936) condemned war and sought a negotiated settlement.

When the Second World War began, most conscientious objectors co-operated with the war effort: the unacceptable alternative was to pursue peace on any terms. At the end of the war, pacifism, lacking political but not spiritual credibility, was repositioned as a personal creed rather than a political stance.

Suggested Reading
Ceadel, Martin. *Pacifism in Britain, 1914–1945: The Defining of a Faith* (Oxford: Clarendon, 1980).

Marie Askham

Pankhurst, Emmeline 1858–1928

Suffragette and founder of the Women's Franchise League and the Women's Social and Political Union (WSPU). In 1879, Emmeline married Richard Marsden Pankhurst, a Manchester barrister, who had been the author of the first women's SUFFRAGE bill in Britain and of the Married Women's Property Acts of 1870 and 1882. She founded the WSPU with her daughter Christabel in 1903, the 'permanent motto' of which was 'Deeds, not words', marking a departure from the more peaceable lobbying strategies of the National Union of Women's Suffrage Societies (NUWSS) led by Millicent Fawcett. Moving to London in 1906, Pankhurst continued to direct the increasingly militant activities of the WSPU. She was imprisoned on many occasions only to be repeatedly released and reincarcerated, following hunger strikes, under the 'Cat and Mouse Act'.

With the outbreak of war in 1914 the government released all suffragette prisoners and the Pankhursts suspended the suffrage campaign. 1914 was also the year in which Emmeline Pankhurst published her autobiography, *My Own Story*. In 1926, following several years of lecturing in North America, she joined the Conservative Party and was a prospective Parliamentary candidate for an East London constituency. In 1928, the year of Pankhurst's death, women were given equal franchise.

Suggested Reading
Phillips, Melanie. *The Ascent of Woman: A History of the Suffragette Movement and the Ideas Behind It* (London: Little, Brown, 2003).

Rebecca Munford

Pankhurst, Sylvia 1882–1960

SUFFRAGETTE, SOCIALIST and COMMUNIST, who saw her art and her writings as integral to her political activism. In the prewar years, (Estelle) Sylvia Pankhurst used her journalism to highlight women's employment conditions. She was a militant member of the Women's Social and Political Union, led by her mother Emmeline PANKHURST and sister Christabel, but her socialist commitment caused a rift with them. In 1913 Sylvia established the East London Federation of Suffragettes, and then threw herself into anti-war agitation. She edited her own newspaper, *The Women's Dreadnought*, and was a founder member of the Communist Party in 1921. She also carried out social welfare work amongst East End women, as described in her book *The Home Front* (1932).

At the age of 45, Sylvia gave birth to a son, Richard, whose father was the Italian socialist exile Silvio Corio. Although active in the fight against FASCISM, Sylvia concentrated on her writing during the interwar years. Her most influential text was *The Suffragette Movement* (1931), and she also wrote *The Life of Emmeline Pankhurst* (1935), as well as a commentary on events in India, *India and the Earthly Paradise* (1926), and an argument for better maternity care, *Save the Mothers* (1930). In 1935–6 she took up the cause of Ethiopian independence and began a journal, *New Times and Ethiopian News*, which she edited for 20 years. After the death of Corio in 1954 she moved to Ethiopia.

Suggested Reading
Dodd, Kathryn (ed.). *A Sylvia Pankhurst Reader* (Manchester: Manchester University Press, 1992).
Romero, Patricia. *E. Sylvia Pankhurst: A Portrait of a Radical* (New Haven, CT: Yale University Press, 1986).

Winslow, Barbara. *Sylvia Pankhurst: Sexual Politics and Political Activism* (London: University College London Press, 1996).

June Hannam

Panter-Downes, Mollie 1906–1997

Novelist, journalist, and short-story writer, who contributed to the *New Yorker* magazine for nearly 50 years, publishing an extraordinary 852 pieces between 1938 and 1984. Panter-Downes was born in London and later lived in Sussex and Surrey. In 1939 she married Clare Robinson, and the couple had two daughters. Her first novel, *The Shoreless Sea* (1923), was written when she was 16: it was a bestseller, which was a great help to her mother, a war widow. Three more novels followed – *The Chase* (1925), *Storm Bird* (1929), and *My Husband Simon* (1931) – together with various magazine stories, all of which Panter-Downes later disowned, preferring to imply that her career only started when she began writing for the *New Yorker* in 1938. They first published a poem she submitted, then a short story, and in September 1939 asked her to contribute a regular 'Letter from London', which she did all through the war with consistent wit and incisiveness. Some of the Letters appeared as *Letters from England* in 1940 and again as *London War Notes* in 1972. Her funny and perceptive short stories for the *New Yorker* were unknown to English readers until they were reprinted as *Good Evening, Mrs Craven* (1999) and *Minnie's Room* (2002).

Just after the war Panter-Downes wrote one of the great novels of the last century, *One Fine Day* (1947), which is set in the summer of 1946 and shows a middle-class couple struggling to adapt to the realities of postwar life. It is an English classic, beautifully written, and deeply evocative of the struggles of ordinary people to adjust to a changed society; it is also razor-sharp about middle-class failure to change:

> 'Now, darling', said Mrs Heriot, 'the servants will be coming back, they will be glad to get out of those awful uniforms, out of those appalling huts into a decent house with hot baths and a nice bed. And when they did not, she simply could not understand it....So the mahogany continued to reflect the silver polo cups pleasantly, the Heriot world held together for a little longer in its deadness of glacial chintz strewn with violets and side tables strewn with the drooping moustached faces of yesteryear.

Panter-Downes also published a book based on a visit to India, *Ooty Preserved: A Victorian Hill Station in India* (1967), and a biographical study, *At The Pines: Swinburne and Watts-Dunton in Putney* in 1971. She remains very little known in Britain because she was seen as a mere journalist rather than the consistently excellent writer that she in fact was.

Suggested Reading
Beauman, Nicola. Introduction to *One Fine Day* by Mollie Panter-Downes (London: Virago, 1985) vii–xvi.

Nicola Beauman

Pargeter, Edith 1913–1955

English novelist who published under the pseudonyms of Ellis Peters, John Redfern, and Jolyon Carr. She is best known for the Inspector Felse series (1951–78), the medieval Brother Cadfael detective novels (1977–94; also a successful television series) and the Heaven Tree trilogy (1961–3), set in the Welsh borders of the twelfth century. Born in Shropshire, where she spent most of her life, Edith Mary Pargeter worked as a chemist's assistant on leaving school. During the Second World War she was a teleprinter operator for the Women's Royal Navy Service in Liverpool, for which she received the British Empire Medal. Her wartime experiences form the basis of *She Goes to War* (1942). The author of 65 novels, Pargeter was also nationally recognized for her translations of Czech poetry and prose. Amongst her awards are the British Crime Writers Association's Silver Dagger, the Cartier Diamond Dagger, an Edgar from the Mystery Writers of America, and an OBE (1994). Keenly interested in embedding historical detail in her fiction, much of her work from her first novel *Hortensius, Friend of Nero* (1936) onwards is set outside the twentieth century.

Suggested Reading
Lewis, Margart. *Edith Pargeter: Ellis Peters* (1994; rev. edn Bridgen: Seren, 2003).

Stacy Gillis

Party Politics

The period 1900 to 1950 was characterized by splits and divisions, and saw the appearance of the Labour Party as a new political force and the decline of the Liberal Party. The former emerged from the Labour Representation Committee, which had been established in 1900 from a federation of socialist societies and trade unions. Initially it had only two MPs, but in 1906, partly as the result of an electoral pact with the Liberals, it gained 30 seats and became the Labour Party under the leadership of Keir Hardie. Its main aims were a national minimum wage, democratic control of industry, and a revolution in national finance. The party offered its support to the new Liberal government. With the Conservative Party at odds over free trade, Liberal hegemony lasted until 1915. During this period, the Liberal government largely completed the unfinished agenda of Victorian radicalism, introducing Irish Home Rule, disestablishing the Church of England in Wales, and restricting the powers of the Lords, which deprived the British establishment of a bastion of political influence. It also implemented a programme of social reform that included the introduction of old age pensions (1908) and National Insurance (1911). The IRISH QUESTION, however, caused bitter political conflict. The Liberal Party, having lost its majority in 1910, was relying on the Labour Party and Irish nationalists to remain in office, and a division between the two was only prevented by the outbreak of war in 1914.

War nevertheless split both the Liberal and the Labour Parties. A coalition government under Asquith was formed in 1915, but the Liberals remained divided, initially over whether or not to fight, and more decisively in 1916 over conscription, which many Liberal supporters considered undemocratic. Discontent with Asquith's leadership led to the creation of a new coalition under Lloyd George, which pursued the war with renewed vigour and efficiency. Asquith went into opposition, while the Conservatives and a section of the Liberals followed Lloyd George. At the general election in 1918, Lloyd George and his Liberals allied with the Conservatives against Asquith's independent Liberals and Labour. The result was a victory for Lloyd George but a disaster for the Liberals, whose beliefs were increasingly ill suited to the interwar economic climate.

Lloyd George, however, was perceived to be failing on his election promise to build the 'land fit for heroes'. In 1922, the Conservatives broke with Lloyd George and formed a purely Conservative government, attracting support from previously staunch Liberal sections of the population. Whereas the Victorian Conservative Party had been identified with the defence of the constitution and the interests associated with it, from around the First World War these traditional causes were largely superseded by socio-economic issues and it became more a party of business and middle-class interests. Under Baldwin, it dominated British politics in the interwar period. Between Labour and the Conservatives, the Liberal Party had effectively become ideologically redundant.

Labour emerged from the war less badly damaged, mainly as the result of the collapse of the Liberal vote and the influx of newly enfranchised working-class voters into the electorate following the 1918 Representation of the People Act. The declining fortunes of the Liberal Party, despite the adoption of a new political programme inspired by Keynes, saw Labour become the official opposition and a major force in municipal politics. During the interwar years, Labour adopted a distinctive socialist political stance. It formed its first governments under Ramsey MacDonald in 1924 and 1929–31. Although its efforts at reform were frustrated by the absence of parliamentary majority, it demonstrated that it was a responsible party of government.

The financial crisis of 1931 split the Labour Party. In defiance of his party, MacDonald formed a National Government with the aid of Liberals and the Conservative Party. Intended as a temporary measure to meet the severe economic crisis and a run on the pound, the coalition stayed in office until 1939, but divided both the Liberal and the Labour Parties. Labour's representation in parliament dwindled in the 1931 elections and the Conservative Party dominated the new government. MacDonald and his supporters were seen as traitors to SOCIALISM and the National Government as a Tory sham. By 1935, the government had become Conservative in all but name. It increased taxes, reduced benefits, abandoned the Gold Standard, and introduced protectionist measures. In foreign policy, it advocated a policy of APPEASEMENT under Neville Chamberlain, tarnishing the party's image. In contrast, the Labour Party advocated increasingly doctrinaire socialist policies and it was only towards the late 1930s that it began to regain its electoral appeal. The Liberal Party failed to recover, and by the mid-1930s it had been reduced to 19 MPs.

The Second World War undermined the dominant position of the Conservative Party. The party rebelled against Chamberlain following a British naval disaster in Norway, and he was replaced by Winston Churchill, who headed a coalition and brought Labour into government and into the management of the 'home front'. Although Churchill remained popular, the Labour Party's support of the Beveridge Report (1942), which called for a full-scale reform of HEALTH and social services and universal social insurance, convinced many that, while the Conservatives were winning the war, Labour would win the peace. Many Conservatives were nevertheless surprised that they were defeated by Labour at the polls in 1945. Buttressed by a landslide election victory, Labour implemented a programme of nationalization, whilst developing the many WELFARE reforms begun during the war. The party's main achievement was Bevan's establishment of the National Health Service in 1948. Exhausted by its reforms, it lost office in 1951 to the Conservatives. They had adapted to the new circumstances by accepting the nationalization of some state-run services (such as the railways) and social welfare institutions, and won the election on opportunistic proposals to end rationing and to build more public HOUSING.

Suggested Reading

Clarke, Peter. *Hope and Glory: Britain, 1900–90* (Harmondsworth: Penguin, 1996).
Wrigley, Chris. *A Companion to Early Twentieth-Century Britain* (London: Blackwell, 2004).

Keir Waddington

Persephone Books

A small independent publishing house, set up in 1999 by the critic and biographer Nicola Beauman to reprint books by (mostly) women writers; it revives books overlooked by the feminist publishing houses of the 1980s and 1990s because of their domestic slant. The titles include novels, short stories, cookery books, diaries, and poetry. Two are published each quarter, and by the summer of 2004, 50 were in print. Persephone does not in general sell through bookshops, but by mail order via a quarterly magazine; in a very small way it tries to emulate organizations such as the Book-of-the-Month Club and the Book Society.

Nicola Beauman

Pitter, Ruth 1897–1992

Poet, widely admired for her original and unsentimental examination of the fabric and traditions of English rural life. Hilaire Belloc was an early supporter; W. B. Yeats, George Orwell, C. S. Lewis, Kathleen RAINE, Elizabeth Jennings, and Thom Gunn were other influential enthusiasts.

Pitter's career spanned most of the century. Early works, some of which appeared in *New Age* and *New English Weekly*, were collected as *First Poems* in 1920; the last of the 14 volumes which followed (*A Heaven to Find*) was published in 1987. Among a lifetime of honours, she was the first woman to be awarded the Queen's Medal for Poetry in 1955, became a Companion of Literature in 1974, and a CBE in 1979. Pitter was born in Ilford to school-teacher parents whose altruism, ideals, and interests, particularly their love of the countryside, much influenced their sensitive daughter. She refused to expect to make a living from writing. In the thirties, her work painting traditional furniture for a Suffolk firm led to the founding of an independent craft and furniture business, in partnership with her lifelong companion Kathleen O'Hara. The success of the venture enabled this energetic promoter of poetry to remain proudly independent of publishers's agendas and avoid hack work.

Formally accomplished but heavy with late-Victorian archaisms, Pitter's early work is her least distinctive; a more effective simplicity emerges in *A Trophy of Arms* (1936), awarded the Hawthornden Prize in 1937. While this collection rarely engages explicitly with the approaching menace of war, the pared-down idiom of poems like 'Buried Treasure' is frank about the artist's difficulties. The recognition of truth's elusiveness persists amid the optimism with which, for example, 'Stormcock in Elder' answers Hardy's 'The Darkling Thrush'. The securing of Pitter's discreetly troubled religious faith (she became an Anglican in middle-age) in the natural world is replayed in a poetry which knowingly distances itself from both MODERNISM and Romanticism but eschews neither. In common with many poets of her generation, she tends to skirt gender issues: few of her poems are explicitly woman-centred ('The Primordial Cell' is a notable exception), or adopt a discernibly female voice. She nevertheless negotiated confidently with poetic tradition. Charting the self's effort to make spiritual sense of the prospect of war, *The Spirit Watches* (1939) summons William Blake ('The Bird in the Tree') and W. B. Yeats ('The Fishers'). The exquisite portraiture of flora and fauna and wry, affectionate, often humorous sketches of English rurality collected in *The Bridge* (1945) compares interestingly with 'nature poets' like John Clare and Edward Thomas as well as Hardy. Robert Frost is perhaps the most suggestive echo in her finest collection, the Heinemann Award-winning *The Ermine* (1953), especially its superb title poem. However, Pitter's work also resonates constructively with that of other leading female contemporaries like Raine, Jennings, Anne RIDLER and E. J. SCOVELL, all of whom in their different ways scrutinize the complex relationship between spirit, self and nature.

Suggested Reading
Russell, Arthur (ed.). *Homage to a Poet* (London: Rapp & Whiting, 1969).

Alice Entwistle

Plaidy, Jean 1906–1993

Pseudonym of Eleanor Alice Burford, English historical and romance novelist. Other pseudonyms were Philippa Carr, Elbur Ford, Victoria Holt, Kathleen Kellow, and Ellalice Tate. Born in London, Burford worked as a typist and a jeweller's assistant during her teens. At this time she met George Percival Hibbert, who left his wife and family to live with her. Little else is known about Burford, as she guarded her private life carefully.

She began by submitting short stories regularly to the *Daily Mail* and the *Evening News*. Recommended to write romance fiction for commercial reasons, she went on to publish more than 200 novels, and was the most popular British historical novelist of the twentieth century. Her first novels were *Daughter of Anna* and *Passionate Witness*, both published in 1941; her last was *The Black Opal*, published posthumously in 1994.

Burford used pseudonyms in order to distinguish between the different genres in which she wrote – including ROMANTIC FICTION, HISTORICAL FICTION, DETECTIVE FICTION and Gothic suspense. She is best known for the books published under the pseudonyms of Philippa Carr, Victoria Holt, and Jean Plaidy. As Carr she published the *Daughters of England* series and as Holt she published Gothic romances and suspense novels, including the bestselling *Mistress of Mellyn* (1960), which were set, for the most part, in the nineteenth century. The Plaidy novels are historical fictions, including series on the Medicis, the Stuarts, the Plantaganets, the Queens of England, the Borgias, and the Tudors. Novels by Plaidy, Holt, and Carr are repeatedly in the top 100 most requested authors from LIBRARIES. At the time of her death the Plaidy novels alone had sold more than 14 million copies worldwide. Each of these pseudonyms has inspired fierce loyalty in their readers, few suspecting that Carr, Holt, and Plaidy are the same author.

Burford has received little critical attention and has been largely dismissed as writing escapist trash. The conflation of gender and genre – and the fact that, as a woman, she was encouraged to write romance fiction – cannot be ignored. Her fiction contains many powerful female characters and her historical novels were well researched and full of useful detail. Bringing historical events and figures to a wider readership, she was well aware of the commercial exigencies of the genres in which she was writing, pointing out that one had to 'keep on giving them books, so they don't forget your name'. Burford's work should form part of any study of the historical novel, and also Gothic romance, in the twentieth century.

Suggested Reading
Bayer-Berenbaum, Linda. *The Gothic Imagination: Expansion in Gothic Literature and Art* (Rutherford: Fairleigh Dickinson University Press, 1982).

Stacy Gillis

Poetry Anthologies
Anthologies were often the first outlet for women poets, and many women were involved in their production. The ground-breaking imagist anthologies, which ran from 1914 to 1917, are best perceived as an Anglo-American initiative for the promotion of free verse. After Ezra Pound withdrew, the annual *Some Imagist Poets* was edited by Amy Lowell. Other women whom the volumes promoted or inspired were H. D. and May SINCLAIR. Edith SITWELL's controversial *Wheels* annuals (1916–21) stimulated considerable debate about the boundaries and morality of poetry. The eponymous poem was by Nancy CUNARD who, along with Iris TREE and Helen Rootham, provided Sitwell with a female team of writers and editors. Their intellectual and urban practices of imagism and MODERNISM represented a move away from rural verse, but this was countered by the popularity of Edward Marsh's five male-dominated GEORGIAN *Poetry* anthologies which came out between 1912 and 1922. Thomas Moult's annual *Best Poetry* collections brought poetry by American and British men and women to both literary and general readers. Additionally, several anthologies emerged from the 'provinces', such as Merseyside and Birmingham.

Women's reputations were enhanced by inclusion in the most influential collections: *The Faber Book of Modern Verse* (1936), edited by Michael Roberts; W. B. Yeats's *The Oxford Book of English Verse* (1936); and *Recent Poetry 1923–1933*, edited by Alida and Harold Monro (1933). Significantly, women's political poems were not selected, and overtly political writers such as Valentine ACKLAND, Sylvia Townsend WARNER, Naomi MITCHISON, Nancy CUNARD, Winifred HOLTBY and Stevie SMITH, were only included in liberal and left-wing publications and not always in these. This period is book-ended by two important gender-segregated selections, Lady Margaret Sackville's *A Book of Verse by Living Women* (1910) and *The Distaff Muse: An Anthology of Poetry written by Women*, edited by Clifford and Meum Stewart Bax (1949).

In 1941, the new edition of T. S. Eliot's *The Little Book of Modern Verse* (1934) was edited by Anne RIDLER who also produced the supplement to the revised edition of *The Faber Book of Modern Verse* in 1951, while Gwendolen Murphy edited and introduced *The Modern Poet: An Anthology* (1938). In the 1930s and 1940s, the radio provided opportunities for production and performance. Janet Adam Smith was instrumental in its poetry programmes and edited the anthology of BROADCAST poems, *Poems of Tomorrow*, in 1935.

Suggested Reading

Dowson, Jane. '"Humming an entirely different tune"? A Case Study of Anthologies: *Women's Poetry of the 1930s', The Value of Literature*, Working Papers on the Web, vol. 2 (Electronic Journal, Sheffield Hallam University, November 2000).

Thacker, Andrew. 'Amy Lowell and H. D.: The Other Imagists', *Women: A Cultural Review*, 4.1. (Spring 1993) 49–59.

Jane Dowson

Pope, Jessie d.1941

Jessie Pope has an extensive list of publications; her poems, humorous fiction, and articles appeared in *Punch* and other popular magazines and newspapers. She produced illustrated books for children and edited *The Ragged Trousered Philanthropists* (1914). She is best known for her nationalistic war poetry – *Jessie Pope's War Poems* (1915), *More War Poems* (1915), and *Simple Rhymes for Stirring Times* (1916) – which was widely circulated and approved of by conservative papers. Pope is understood to be the target of Wilfred Owen's denouncement of 'a certain poetess' for her apparently uninformed articulation of war experience. Her uncritical parroting of patriotic propaganda continues to jar with contemporary, particularly feminist, readers. However, among the compliant clichés and facile rhythms it is possible to hear a subtle denial of chivalric platitudes, for example, in poems such as 'No' from *War Poems*. In 'War Girls', Pope offers a more palpable hint that women's prescribed support for recruiting rhetoric was fuelled by their enjoyment of the unprecedented opportunities which life without men provided. She produced a fourth book, *Hits and Misses*, in 1920.

Suggested Reading

Dowson, Jane. *Women, Modernism and British Poetry 1910–39: Resisting Femininity* (Aldershot: Ashgate, 2002).

Jane Dowson

Potter, Beatrix 1866–1943

Children's author, illustrator, conservationist, and farmer. Helen Beatrix Potter was brought up in London, and spent the summer holidays in Scotland and the Lake District. Her father was a keen photographer, whose subjects included his friends John Everett Millais and William Gaskell. She had no formal schooling but a series of governesses encouraged her interest in drawing and natural history. She and her brother had many pets, which formed the subject of her drawings. Potter had a keen eye for nature: her notebooks contain thousands of detailed pictures of flora and fauna, and a paper she authored on spores was presented to the Linnean Society in 1897.

In 1890 Potter began submitting her illustrations to publishers, but met with little success. She paid for *The Tale of Peter Rabbit and Mr McGregor's Garden* to be privately printed in 1901. It was republished by Frederick Warne in 1902, and the company published all her subsequent work. The picaresque hero Peter Rabbit met with immediate and enormous success, and related merchandise quickly followed. Potter had a global fan base, corresponding with children around the world despite her claim that 'I have never cared tuppence either for popularity or for the modern child; they are pampered and spoilt with too many toys and books.' She wrote 23 small format books, including *The Tale of Squirrel Nutkin* (1903), *The Tailor of Gloucester* (1903), *The Tale of Tom Kitten* (1907), and *The Tale of Pigling Bland* (1913). Her literary output slowed considerably in the 1920s, as a result of the deterioration of her eyesight and her growing interest in farming and land conservation.

On a trip to the Lake District in 1882 she met Hardwicke Rawnsley, who helped found the National Trust in 1895. His determination to preserve the area from the incursions of industry and tourism was an inspiration to Potter. With the proceeds from her books she began to buy land in the Lake District in 1904, and it remained her home for the rest of her life. In 1913, she married a local solicitor, William Heelis. She acquired an important role in the farming and sheep-breeding community and her animals regularly won prizes. Thousands of acres were left to the National Trust in her will.

The anthropomorphized animals in Potter's drawings are endearing but they also reflect the realities of animal and farm life. Graham Greene, in 'Beatrix Potter: A Critical Estimate' (1933), compared her with Henry James, and also noted that: 'The obvious characteristic of Beatrix Potter's style is selective realism, which takes emotion for granted and puts aside love and death with a gentle detachment reminiscent of E. M. Forster.' Although the cheery Peter Rabbit and Tom Kitten are perhaps her best known characters there is a dark edge to her narratives, exemplified by the Falstaffian Samuel Whiskers in *The Roly-Poly Pudding* (1908).

Suggested Reading

Hobbs, Anne Stevenson. *Beatrix Potter's Art, Paintings and Drawings* (London: Warne, 1989).

Mackey, Margaret. *The Case of Peter Rabbit: Changing Conditions of Literature for Children* (New York: Garland, 1998).

Taylor, Judy. *Beatrix Potter: Artist, Storyteller and Countrywoman* (Harmondsworth: Penguin, 1986).

Stacy Gillis

Prix Femina-Vie Heureuse

Prestigious literary prize that has been awarded annually since 1904. It was founded by female journalists working on the French magazines *Femina* and *Vie Heureuse* as an alternative to the *Prix Goncourt*, which was considered unlikely to be awarded to a woman. With a jury made up exclusively of women of letters, the prize currently consists of two categories, one for the best work of imagination published by a French author each year, and the other (the *Prix Étranger*) for a fictional work translated into French from another language. During the years from 1920 to 1939, Femina-Vie Heureuse prizes were also awarded to English-language books. These were selected by the French jury from among three nominations made annually by a committee of British women. Committee members included Rebecca WEST, May SINCLAIR, Margaret KENNEDY, Violet HUNT, and many other eminent writers. The winning novels included *Dangerous Ages* (1921) by Rose MACAULAY, *Precious Bane* (1922) by Mary WEBB, *Adam's Breed* (1926) by Radclyffe HALL, *To the Lighthouse* (1927) by Virginia WOOLF, and *Cold Comfort Farm* (1932) by Stella GIBBONS. Although many of the winners are female, the prizes are nevertheless open to both sexes, with, for example, E. M. Forster's *A Passage to India* winning in 1924.

Louise Harrington

Prostitution

Prostitution impacted on women's writing in the first half of the twentieth century in different ways: panic about white slavery and the social purity movement; arguments about women's access to EDUCATION and employment, including employment as writers; and the notion of the amateur prostitute. Awareness of white slavery, the sale of English girls into prostitution in foreign countries (particularly South America), was raised by Josephine Butler's work in the nineteenth century to end the prostitution of children. Butler also campaigned for the repeal of the Contagious Diseases Acts that enabled the police to arrest women suspected of prostitution and forcibly examine them for venereal disease. Section 40D of the Defence of the Realm Act in 1915 was widely perceived by feminist groups as a reinstatement of the Contagious Diseases Acts (repealed in 1886), since it penalized women and not men for the spread of venereal disease.

Writers who addressed prostitution include Cicely HAMILTON, who emphasized that without the opportunity for women to earn their income, marriage was tantamount to prostitution; Virginia WOOLF, who used the metaphor of 'whoring' to describe her more commercial writing; and Jean RHYS, who explored the notion of the amateur prostitute, a woman who occasionally sleeps with men for money.

Suggested Reading
Parsons, Deborah L. *Streetwalking the Metropolis* (Oxford: Oxford University Press, 1999).

Lisa Shariari

Psychoanalysis

The body of ideas, techniques and treatments which defines human subjectivity as split between conscious and unconscious parts, and which attempts to work upon the neuroses which arise out of unresolved desires located in the unconscious impinging upon conscious life. Psychoanalysis was invented by Sigmund Freud in the 1890s. Beginning his career as a neurologist, Freud became convinced of the psychological origins of certain apparently organic neurological conditions. In 1895 Freud and Joseph Breuer published *Studies in Hysteria*, which details the analyses of five female 'hysterics'. In each case, the treatment of these women by 'talking cure' (the phrase coined by Breuer's most famous patient 'Anna O', the feminist Bertha Pappenheim), revealed the complex relationship between early childhood experiences and adult psychic and bodily distress. Patients were encouraged to 'free associate' with the analyst, so that the unconscious might be accessed, and problematically repressed material worked through, via the analyst's interpretation. Building on clinical evidence, Freud's conceptualization of the psyche argues that infantile sexuality remains a structuring presence in adult life and identity; his theorizations, and the revisions these have undergone by later generations, have bequeathed Western culture key concepts and terms, including the unconscious, the Oedipus complex, transference and infantile sexuality.

Psychoanalysis has grown in a multitude of ways since its initial definition and revisions by Freud. In the early years, splits occurred between Freud and his colleagues, most notably Alfred Adler and C. G. Jung, both of whom went on to develop their own conceptualizations of the psyche and culture. One of the most important shifts in psychoanalytic theory occurs in the work of Melanie Klein who, in her analyses of children, shifts the analytic focus from the Oedipus complex to the pre-Oedipal life of the infant and its relationship with the maternal body. Klein's theorization of the importance of external objects to the psyche was taken up by some of her own training analysands, such as D. W. Winnicott and W. R. D. Fairbairn. Another crucial development was Jacques Lacan's revision of Freud, which included the transformative notion that the unconscious is structured like a language. This marrying of the psychoanalytic with the linguistic, coupled with a poststructuralist account of culture, allowed psychoanalytic thinking to address itself fully to social and cultural analysis.

For much of the twentieth century, feminism has conducted an often conflicted relationship with psychoanalysis. This is due, in large part, to Freud's complicated relationship with female sexuality and femininity. Nevertheless, in the past 40 years, feminist theorists committed to fathoming the processes of acculturation and socialization by which human beings are gendered have located, in psychoanalysis, a set of enabling and explanatory discourses. Psychoanalytic FEMINISM has contributed vastly to the development of psychoanalysis, both in terms of the theorization of the psyche and the practice of psychoanalytic treatment.

In the early twentieth century, many women writers were influenced by psychoanalysis and its mapping of the internal world of the psyche. May SINCLAIR drew on Freud and Jung, Lettice COOPER had a lifelong interest in Freudian psychoanalysis, and Virginia WOOLF describes herself in her diary as 'gulping up Freud'. The attitude of this early generation of authors writing in the contemporary context of Freud stands in stark contrast to the vehement critique levelled at psychoanalysis by later feminists. Simone de Beauvoir's *The Second Sex* (1948) takes issue with Freud's inability to interrogate his own valorization of maleness and masculinity, particularly his notion of 'penis-envy'. Second-Wave feminism, in its early incarnations in the late 1960s, particularly singled out Freudian psychoanalysis for attack. In *Sexual Politics* (1969), Kate Millett constructs Freudian theory as one of the most influential patriarchal discourses, which provides both sanction and vocabulary for misogynistic representations of women.

This decimation of psychoanalysis was rebutted by one of the most important recuperative works of feminist theory, Juliet Mitchell's *Psychoanalysis and Feminism* (1974). Rather than talking about an essentialist feminine identity, Mitchell argues, Freud's radical discussion actually focuses on the ways in which the culturally constructed category of 'femininity' is lived within the psyche, thus enabling exposure of the seemingly naturalized processes by which women are made into 'woman'. An important phase in feminist psychoanalytic thought was inaugurated by the emergence of New French Feminism, the psychoanalytically based work of Julia Kristeva, Luce Irigaray, and Hélène Cixous, who, following Lacan, turn to language to theorize identity and gender relations. Both 'mainstream' and feminist literary criticism and theory, as well as women's creative writing, have utilized psychoanalysis in two ways: as critical and conceptual vocabulary and as methodology.

Suggested Reading
Minsky, Rosalind. *Psychoanalysis and Gender: An Introductory Reader* (London: Routledge, 1996).

Parkin-Gounelas, Ruth. *Literature and Psychoanalysis: Intertextual Readings* (Basingstoke: Palgrave Macmillan, 2001).

Rose, Jacqueline. *On Not Being Able to Sleep: Psychoanalysis and the Modern World* (London: Verso, 2004).

Wright, Elizabeth (ed.). *Feminism and Psychoanalysis: A Critical Dictionary* (Oxford: Blackwell, 1992).

Joanne Winning

Publishers

The methods and attitudes of the Victorian period persisted, for the most part, in the early twentieth century publishing industry, with the first major change resulting from the creation of the mass-market paperback in the mid-1930s. In the 1890s, many new firms (including Heinemann, Fisher Unwin, Grant Richards, and John Lane/Bodley Head) established themselves and published more avant-garde titles; yet despite these new influences, the years between 1900 and 1914 saw established firms, such as Macmillan and Chapman and Hall, still publishing staple titles from the previous century. This period saw an increase in the number of volumes produced per year, but most of these were reprints. A few publishers, including Ward Lock, recognized the need for expanded middlebrow catalogues; J. M. Dent's Everyman's Library was established in 1906, and Oxford's World's Classics imprint began two years later, both producing reprints of classic literature meant to appeal to educated, middle-class tastes.

Between the wars, the lists of most British publishing houses remained conservative, despite increased competition from radio and sound CINEMA. John Feather asserts that the effects of new technologies on the book trade were not all damaging: better home lighting (combined, of course, with more widespread adult literacy) increased the size of the reading audience, and in 1922 the Society of Authors negotiated a standard sale-of-rights agreement for books adapted for BROADCAST by the BBC. Larger British publishers also enjoyed the benefits of the Commonwealth market; Longmans, Macmillan, and Oxford all published educational books for the colonies, but this branch of the trade was reduced after 1945. The NET BOOK AGREEMENT also ensured a relatively safe market, despite the economic DEPRESSION that affected other industries.

Important new firms were also established during the interwar period, notably Jonathan Cape in 1921 and Victor Gollancz in 1928. Several houses began to cater for multiple markets: for example, Allen and Unwin, associated with 'serious' writers such as Bertrand Russell, also published popular women writers including Ethel M. DELL. Gollancz likewise specialized in both DETECTIVE FICTION (including Dorothy L. SAYERS) and leftist political works. Allen Lane's publication of the first mass-market paperbacks, Penguins, in 1935, had an enormous impact on the industry. Lane's first Penguin printings included Cape reprints and such middlebrow authors as Sayers and Mary WEBB; by 1937, the Penguin list included E. H. YOUNG, E. Arnot ROBERTSON, Vita SACKVILLE-WEST, and Rose MACAULAY, among other women writers.

The years of the Second World War brought many difficulties for the industry. Paper rationing was instituted in 1940, and the import of foreign paper was banned. The Publishers' Association somewhat counteracted the effects of rationing with their Book Production War Economy Agreement (1941), which restricted paper quality and font size. The Blitz also had disastrous effects: more than 20 London houses lost their entire stocks. The destruction in 1940 of Stationers Hall and the country's sole book wholesaler, Simpkin and Marshall, increased the industry's losses. Yet despite supply problems, the war years saw an increase in public demand for books.

Paper rationing continued until 1949, and special provision had to be made for the replacement of depleted education texts. New title production steadily grew into the early 1950s, with consumer demand still reasonable even after the BBC resumed television transmission in 1946. However, Feather argues that since the end of the war, an ever-increasing output from British publishers seems to be attracting its audience from the educated classes, while television and other leisure activities draw the attention of a large section of the public that claims not to read for pleasure at all. Today, most of the early twentieth-century publishers still in existence are imprints of larger conglomerates. While the archives of many of these companies are available for consultation, the papers of many smaller firms have been lost, making it now difficult to produce a full picture of British publishing activities in the years 1900 to 1950.

Suggested Reading

Feather, John. *A History of British Publishing* (London: Routledge, 1988).
McDonald, Peter D. *British Literary Culture and Publishing Practice, 1880–1914* (Cambridge: Cambridge University Press, 1997).

Ashlie Sponenberg

R

Raine, Allen 1836–1908

Author of Cardiganshire romances, ranked as one of the four bestselling British novelists of her day, but now largely forgotten. Born Anne Adaliza Evans in Newcastle Emlyn, she was educated in Cheltenham and London under the care of the Reverend Henry Solly who was linked to a literary set that included Dickens and George Eliot. She married Beynon Puddicombe in 1872. Raine returned in 1900 to her beloved Cardiganshire, where she wrote the majority of her work, adopting the pen name 'Allen Raine' that appeared to her in a dream.

Her first novel, *A Welsh Singer* (1897), sold over 316,000 copies by 1908 and was followed by ten other novels, including *Torn Sails* (1898), *Garthowen* (1900), and *A Welsh Witch* (1902). Her greatest literary achievement was *Queen of the Rushes* (1906), a romance set during the Welsh religious revival of 1904 in which the trappings of the genre are blended in a sophisticated manner with sociocultural issues and rich portraits of the local landscape and community. Largely dismissed by academics as romantic gush, it was undoubtedly her work and its popularity that established Wales as a setting for fiction. Raine highlighted specifically Welsh issues and the WELSH LANGUAGE at a time when others shied away from such subjects. The twentieth-century flowering of Welsh fiction in English has been a conspicuously male affair; none of it would be possible, however, without the work of Allen Raine.

Suggested Reading

Gramich, Katie. Introduction to *Queen of the Rushes* by Allen Raine (Dinas Powys: Honno, 1998) 1–21.

Jones, Sally. *Allen Raine* (Cardiff: University of Wales Press, 1979).

Lucy Thomas

Raine, Kathleen 1908–2003

Poet, scholar, literary critic, co-founder of the periodical *Temenos* (1981) and the Temenos Academy of Integral Studies (1990), she remains one of the best known of the women poets to begin writing between the wars. Born in Ilford, East London, to a Methodist schoolmaster from Durham and a Scottish mother, Raine was an only child. Having spent some of her childhood in Northumberland, she always considered herself a northerner. A scholarship to study natural sciences at Girton College, Cambridge (where she heard Virginia WOOLF lecture) brought her into contact with William Empson and his circle. Renowned for her beauty, the lower middle-class Raine – having inherited her mother's romantic imagination – felt ill at ease in a still upper-class Cambridge where the scientific materialism of I. A. Richards' New Criticism held sway.

The thirties brought critical attention to her work but were turbulent: her first marriage, to Hugh Sykes-Davies, ended when she eloped with another poet, Charles Madge. They married in 1932, and both became involved with MASS-OBSERVATION, but Raine left Madge after six years, settling with their two children in the Lake District. Although happy there, she returned to London in the early forties, leaving the children with a friend, to publish her first collection, *Stone and Flower*, in 1943. The stringently simple, often balladic manner of her early work confirms the technical virtuosity of her idiom. This became increasingly visionary, even though she converted to Catholicism in the forties. The anti-materialist temper of her poetic imagination converged – despite the scientific precision of her observation – with a scholarly interest in Neo-Platonic philosophy and symbolism. The vision of the world conjured in 'Word Made Flesh' (*The Pythoness*, 1948) animates the pantheistic outlook of her mature idiom, represented by poems like 'Message from Home' in *The Year One* (1951). Her fourth collection, this appeared in the same year as her first critical study, of William Blake.

A distinguished scholarly career took off with a research fellowship at Girton (1954–9), which coincided with the end of her ill-starred relationship with the man she regarded as her soul-mate, homosexual author Gavin Maxwell. One of her poems supplied the title for his book, *Ring of Bright Water*. Their passionate but troubled friendship stands behind the more reflective poems collected in *The Hollow Hill* (1964), perhaps her most well-received work. Apart from several critical works on Blake, including the two-volume standard *Blake and Tradition* (1968), she also produced studies of Coleridge (1953), Yeats (1972), Hopkins (1972), and David Jones (1974). Although she never forgot being passed over (in favour of Roy Fuller) for the Oxford Chair of Poetry in 1968, Raine went on to win many distinctions including various honorary degrees and the Queen's Gold Medal for poetry in 1992. *Autobiographies* appeared in 1991, and she was given a CBE in 2000, the year in which the third, definitive version of her *Collected Poems* was published.

Suggested Reading

Bradbrook, Muriel. ' "The Lyf so Short, the Craft so Long to Learn": Poetry and other works of Kathleen Raine', in *Women and Literature, 1779–1982: The Collected Papers of Muriel Bradbrook*, vol. 2 (Sussex: Harvester Press, 1982) 132–51.
Lindop, Grevel (ed.). 'Kathleen Raine: The Tenth Decade', *PN Review*, 27.2 (November/December 2000) 36–50.

Alice Entwistle

Rathbone, Eleanor 1872–1946

Feminist social reformer and writer on social and political issues. Eleanor Rathbone came from an eminent Liverpool family of radical nonconformists. After studying Philosophy at Somerville College, Oxford, she embarked on a career of public service which situated the radical tradition inherited from six William Rathbones in a twentieth-century feminist context. She served as a City Councillor in Liverpool, as a Justice of the Peace, and as MP for the Combined Universities. Her writings display her pragmatic and dogma-free approach, as well as a refreshing awareness of the realities of life. Her best known work, *The Disinherited Family* (1924), set out the case for Family Allowances and was influential in achieving this reform. Her method of objective analysis and evaluation of possible solutions may be observed in detailed reports on topics such as casual labour at the Liverpool docks, the payment of seamen's wives, and the Poor Law relief of widows. Her interests and publications were extensive and she applied the same objective analytical approach to a defence of the League of Nations and the ideal of collective security, *War Can Be Averted* (1938), as well as to the plight of child brides in India in *Child Marriage: The Indian Minotaur* (1934).

Suggested Reading

Alberti, Johanna. *Eleanor Rathbone* (London: Sage, 1996).
Pederson, Susan. *Eleanor Rathbone and the Politics of Conscience* (New Haven, CT, and London: Yale University Press, 2004).

Terry Phillips

Rathbone, Irene 1892–1980

Poet; writer of feminist and anti-war fiction. An actress before the First World War, Rathbone served during the war as a volunteer at two French YMCA camps and as a VAD nurse in London hospitals. Her experiences provided material for her best known novel, *We That Were Young* (1932), whose protagonist, Joan, loses her lover and brother in the war, undertakes vengeful service in a munitions factory, and finally converts to PACIFISM. Similarly to BRITTAIN's *Testament of Youth*, Rathbone's novel celebrates a war generation ('We were the youth of the world, we were on the crest of life, and we were the war. No one above us counted, and no one below'), but also graphically depicts the harsh conditions of the lives of female munitions workers: 'She had leant a fraction too far forward, and the wind from the flapping belt had blown her hair onto the wheel of the drilling machine...The wheel continued to revolve; but it had now grown a wiry black beard which at each revolution flicked up into sight.' The text is now considered a neglected classic of war literature, and has been kept in print by VIRAGO and the Feminist Press. Rathbone's other works include the novels *Susan Goes East* (1929), *The Gold Rim* (1933), and *Seeds of Time* (1952), and the poem *Was There a Summer?* (1943).

Suggested Reading

Brassard, Genevieve. 'From Private Story to Public History: Irene Rathbone Revises the War in the Thirties', *NWSA: National Women's Studies Association Journal*, 15.3 (Fall 2003) 43–63.

Ashlie Sponenberg

Regional Writing

In the early decades of the twentieth century, regional writing was both a popular and a respected literary mode in Britain. Many of the most successful regional authors were women: among them, Winifred HOLTBY, Mary WEBB, Sheila KAYE-SMITH, Constance HOLME, Lettice COOPER, Daphne DU MAURIER, Vita SACKVILLE-WEST, Flora THOMPSON, and Alison UTTLEY. These writers, along with their male peers, including D. H. Lawrence, T. F. Powys, J. C. Powys, Eden Philpotts, and Francis Brett-Young, engaged with the impact of industrialization and sociopolitical change on the nature of British rural and provincial life. Almost all these authors exhibit a degree of nostalgia for lost or disappearing ways of life. Some were influenced by primitivist thinking, which led them to lament the estrangement between man and nature, and which connects them with the GEORGIAN POETS. Others use rurality as a way of working out some of the issues of modernity, including gender relations, urbanization and increased mobility

'Regional writing' and 'rural writing' are often used synonymously, but while both refer to literature which is distanced from, or resistant to, the style and ideals of the metropolitan centre, regional writing is a larger category. It encompasses novels set in provincial towns and cities, such as Cooper's *We Have Come to a Country* (1935), which takes place in Leeds and bears affinities to Gaskell's *North and South* (1855), or Holtby's *South Riding* (1926), an evocation of Yorkshire life modelled on Eliot's *Middlemarch* (1871–2). Cooper and Holtby were among the pre-eminent political writers of their generation, and their writing was firmly in the classic realist mode, but the regional novel was also espoused by popular authors who favoured romance conventions and drew on a rather different set of nineteenth-century regional texts. Du Maurier's Cornish novels are explicitly indebted to the Brontës, and she, like Kaye-Smith and Webb, often relied on melodramatic plots inherited from Victorian sensation fiction, concerning family feuds and gloomy mysteries, unfolding in isolated settings. Old Testament theology and belief in a vengeful God or Fate are manifested in many of these novels. The plots, language, and ideology of popular rural fiction – particularly Kaye-Smith's Sussex fictions and Webb's novels set in Shropshire – were successfully parodied in Stella GIBBONS's *Cold Comfort Farm* (1932), which has proved more enduring than many of its target texts.

In contrast to the melodrama of their peers, Constance Holme and Flora Thompson concentrated their attention on work practices and the texture of daily life in small, hard-pressed agricultural communities. These authors are, however, rarely mentioned in studies of interwar writing about working-class experience, and neither are the numerous WELSH women writers who depicted the lives of poor rural communities.

Although Wales, Scotland, and Northern Ireland produced some important regional writing during the period, English writers enjoyed a special prestige as they were assimilated to the rhetoric of Englishness which prevailed following the First World War. As Anthea Trodd points out: 'The classic status enjoyed by rural writing in this period derived from the insistently diffused belief that the real England was rural England... in which continuity with the past was still clearly visible.' A shared love of the countryside was perceived as one basis for national unity, and the literary establishment endorsed rural writing whole-heartedly: Vita Sackville-West's long poem *The Land* (1926) won the Hawthornden Prize; all of Holme's Westmoreland novels were published in the World's Classics Series in the 1930s; and Holme, Webb, and Gibbons all won the prestigious PRIX FEMINA-VIE HEUREUSE.

Suggested Reading

Keith, W. J. *Regions of the Imagination: The Development of British Rural Fiction* (Toronto: University of Toronto Press, 1988).

Snell, K. D. M. (ed.). *The Regional Novel in Britain and Ireland, 1800–1990* (Cambridge: Cambridge University Press, 1998).

Trodd, Anthea. *Women's Writing in English: Britain, 1900–1945* (London: Longmans, 1998).

Williams, Raymond. *The Country and the City* (London: Chatto & Windus, 1973).

Faye Hammill

Renault, Mary 1905–1983

Pseudonym of Eileen Mary Challans, novelist best known for work set in Ancient and Classical Greece. Renault studied English at Oxford, then trained as a nurse at the Radcliffe Infirmary, where she met her lifelong partner, Julie Mullins; they moved to South Africa in 1948. Renault's first novel, *Purposes of Love* (1939), had a hospital setting and doctor-nurse romance; however, it was remarkably confident in including gay and bisexual characters who mostly took their sexuality for granted. As one character writes: 'We are people first, and belong to our sexes rather incidentally.' This confidence with sexual themes runs throughout Renault's novels with contemporary settings, but it was not until *The Charioteer* (1953) that she wrote of an unambiguously gay protagonist. *The Last of the Wine* (1956) marked Renault's transition into Greek topics and a setting where homosexual love was taken for granted.

Whatever their setting, Renault's novels draw consciously on Plato, considering the ethics of sexual love and its relation to politics and society. Renault can be read as denying liberty to her female characters, but Caroline Zilboorg praises 'Renault's sophisticated feminist sensibility' which sees sexuality as a continuum.

Suggested Reading
Sweetman, David. *Mary Renault: A Biography* (London: Chatto & Windus, 1993).
Zilboorg, Caroline. *The Masks of Mary Renault* (Columbia and London: University of Missouri Press, 2001).

Kathleen Bell

Revue

A rapid parade of songs, monologues, parodies, and pastiche, Revue dominated the West End stage during the 1930s and 1940s. Often biting, sometimes sentimental, and frequently erudite, Revue demanded great personality and virtuosity from writers and actors. The most celebrated among them, Hermione Gingold, wrote and performed in the *Sweet and Low* shows, *Rise Above It*, and *The Gate Revues*. One of her monologues, *Sky High*, explains how to make your own bicycle:

> Now remove some wheels off an old pram, or it will save you trouble if you remove some wheels off an old bike. And why not remove the handles at the same time? You will be silly if you don't.
>
> Perhaps some of you young ladies have a boyfriend. Don't be too shy to ask him to come round some night and help you adjust your mudguard. And perhaps he will put a spoke in your wheel at the same time.

Nina Warner Hook's sketches include *Amazons*, in which two elderly women plan a bloodbath for any Germans who might happen to arrive at their nice Surrey home, and *Front Door Steps*, a monologue for an old woman who sits and chats on a flight of steps, all that remains of her blitzed home.

Diana Morgan, a contract screenwriter at Ealing Studios, wrote *The Guardsman* (banned by the Lord Chamberlain), in which olden and modern times are compared. In the first vignette a man is surprised *in flagrante* by his lover Evelyn, a pretty young woman. The second, similar, scene ends with the entrance of Evelyn, a dashing guardsman. Revue was effectively killed off in the 1960s by *Beyond the Fringe*, the show by Jonathan Miller, Alan Bennett, Peter Cook, and Dudley Moore, which ushered in the new theatrical sensation – satire.

Suggested Reading
Barker, Clive and Maggie B. Gale (eds). *British Theatre Between the Wars, 1918–1939* (Cambridge: Cambridge University Press, 2000).
Morgan, Fidelis (ed.). *The Years Between: Plays by Women on the London Stage, 1900–1950*. Preface by Susannah York (London: Virago, 1995).

Fidelis Morgan

Rhondda, Lady 1883–1958

Lady Rhondda (Margaret Haig Thomas) was the founder, financier, and long-term editor of the weekly review *Time and Tide* (first issue 14 May 1920). She had been an enthusiastic if undistinguished member of the Women's Social and Political Union (WSPU) from 1908 and had a leading role organizing women's national service in the latter part of the First World War. She was convinced of the need to articulate a distinctive political voice for women as part of postwar reconstruction as well as social justice. Hence also the campaigning Six Point Group, which she founded in 1920 to work for equal opportunities and rights for men and women, including unmarried mothers.

As an only child, it was her 'fantastic luck' to inherit the money and experience that made these ventures possible. Her father, D. A. Thomas, a South Wales coal magnate, had been frustrated in his political ambitions but had made a fortune in business. A highly effective recruit to wartime government, he had been rewarded with both a Viscountcy and a special remainder to enable his title to pass to his daughter. In 1922 she mounted a test case to assert her right to sit in the House of Lords – but lost.

Time and Tide started as an all-female publication with Helen Archdale, feminist and international SOCIALIST, as its first editor. Lady Rhondda was then a director of over 30 public companies as diverse as Cambrian Collieries and Sanatogen Tonic Wine. In 1926 she became the first woman president of the Institute of Directors and took over the editorship of her magazine. Business interests took second place and her fortune declined. Much went into *Time and Tide*'s annual subsidy, some into a rich woman's lifestyle (see her caricature as 'Mary Maud' in Ellen Wilkinson's novel *Clash*), and an undisclosed amount into support for her father's second, secret family.

Her first book, published in 1921, was a tribute to his memory. *Leisured Women*, published by Leonard and Virginia WOOLF in 1928, is a glorious polemic aimed at women 'of the protected classes' who believe that the production of two children and their upbringing (with household help and boarding school EDUCATION) is sufficient justification for existence. More measured opinions were expressed in *Notes on the Way* (1937). The book which best repays rereading is *This Was My World* (1933), which describes her Welsh childhood, involvement with the WSPU, and failed marriage to a sporting baronet with a surprisingly gentle humour.

Lady Rhondda moved *Time and Tide* away from overt feminism, included men, and developed her concept of the magazine as a source of intelligent opinionated conversation where people stifled by their class or gender could feel that they were 'coming up for air'. Its best years may have been those up to 1935 when she was working closely with Winifred HOLTBY. Holtby's premature death was both a professional and a personal blow. Lady Rhondda spent the rest of her life with Theodora BOSANQUET who offered quasi-spiritual solace as well as practical help on the paper. The majority of women featured in this encyclopedia either contributed to, or were reviewed by, *Time and Tide*.

Suggested Reading

Eoff, Shirley. *Viscountess Rhondda: Equalitarian Feminist* (Columbus, OH: Ohio State University Press, 1991).

Spender, Dale. *Time and Tide Wait For No Man* (London: Pandora, 1984).

Julia Jones

Rhys, Jean 1890–1979

Dominican novelist and short-story writer, best known for her novel *Wide Sargasso Sea* (1966). Born Ella Gwendoline Rees Williams to a Welsh doctor father and a white-Creole mother, Rhys came to England in 1907 to study at the Perse School in Cambridge. She trained briefly at the Academy of Dramatic Art in London, and became a touring chorus girl. Her first husband, Jean Lenglet, with whom she had a daughter, Maryvonne, was imprisoned for fraud, during which time she had a relationship with Ford Madox Ford. Rhys based her first novel, *Quartet* (1928, initially published as *Postures*), on her experiences living with Ford and his wife, Stella Bowen, in Paris. Ford recognized Rhys's talent, published a section of an early novel, 'Triple Sec', in his *transatlantic review*, and wrote an introduction to her first volume of short stories, *The Left Bank* (1927).

Rhys's novels of the 1930s (*After Leaving Mr Mackenzie*, 1930; *Voyage in the Dark*, 1934; *Good Morning Midnight*, 1939) confirm her status as one of the most important women writers of the MODERNIST period. Loosely autobiographical, they are powerful evocations of the alienation of women in the modern city. Rhys's urban geography (Paris and London) is marked by instability; her heroines move relentlessly from bedsit to hotel, sometimes forced into PROSTITUTION. In *Voyage in the Dark*, Rhys investigates the position of the colonial subject in the 'heart of empire' through her Creole protagonist, Anna Morgan: 'This is England...I had read about England ever since I could read – smaller meaner everything is never mind – this is London – hundreds thousands of white people white people rushing along and the dark houses all alike frowning down one after the other all alike all stuck together.' Anna's 'Africanization' in the metropolis, her desire to counter British racism and ignorance about her homeland, together with her empathy for Afro-Caribbeans, make this a powerful anti-imperialist novel.

Rhys married twice more (Leslie Tilden Smith and Max Hamer) and during the 1940s and 1950s led a reclusive life in London, Kent, Cornwall, and Devon. In 1957 Selma Vaz Dias successfully traced Rhys to obtain permission for a BBC radio play of *Good Morning Midnight*. After this famous 'rediscovery', Rhys returned to *Wide Sargasso Sea*, which she had begun in the 1930s. Eventually published in 1966, it brought her the critical acclaim she had always deserved. Set in Jamaica in the 1830s, the novel gives voice to Edward Rochester's West Indian wife, Bertha Mason, in *Jane Eyre*. As in much of Rhys's work, imperial and patriarchal power are inextricably linked in Rochester's destructive relationship with the Creole heiress whom he is sent out to marry.

The focus of critical work on Rhys has changed markedly over the last two decades. Initially, her work was read in autobiographical terms but, ironically, the most important aspect of her autobiography – her Caribbean identity – was overlooked. More recently, however, critics have foregrounded the sociopolitical, postcolonial, and modernist contexts of her work. This has meant that the vulnerability and dependencies of her protagonists are read not as simply a result of their gender, but part of Rhys's depiction of social injustice, an injustice all to do with Englishness, EMPIRE and economics.

Suggested Reading

Carr, Helen. *Jean Rhys* (Plymouth: Northcote House, 1996).

Gregg, Veronica Marie. *Jean Rhys's Historical Imagination: Reading and Writing the Creole* (Chapel Hill, NC: University of North Carolina Press, 1995).

O'Connor, Teresa. *Jean Rhys: The West Indian Novels* (New York: New York University Press, 1986).

Anna Snaith

Richardson, Dorothy 1873–1957

Novelist and journalist, best known for the 13-volume *Pilgrimage*, her semi-autobiographical life's work. A pioneer of the stream-of-consciousness style, she was credited by Virginia WOOLF with inventing the 'psychological sentence of the feminine gender'. Born into an aspiring middle-class family, at 17 Richardson was forced by deteriorating financial circumstances to earn her own living, working as a teacher in Germany and north London. In 1893 her father was declared bankrupt and her mother committed suicide two years later. Richardson then worked as a dental receptionist in Harley Street, living in cheap lodgings in BLOOMSBURY. Embracing the freedom and self-sufficiency offered by her meagre salary, she revelled in the social, political, and aesthetic bohemia of the city. Close friendships ensued, but Richardson jealously guarded her autonomy and perhaps the only truly passionate relationship of her life was with London itself, 'this mighty lover, always receiving her back without words, engulfing and leaving her untouched, liberated and expanding to the whole range of her being'.

In 1896 Richardson met H. G. Wells, with whom she embarked upon an animated intellectual affair. Their battles about FABIANISM and feminism encouraged Richardson's confidence in expressing her opinions, and in 1906 she began to contribute reviews to the monthly magazine *Crank*. The relationship with Wells became physical, culminating in 1907 in an unwanted pregnancy.

A miscarriage, overwork, and undernourishment resulted in breakdown, and Richardson finally resigned from her Harley Street position to recuperate in a Quaker community. She continued to write, however, mainly literary sketches for the *Saturday Review*. By 1912, she felt ready to begin a much longer piece of writing, its aim 'to produce a feminine equivalent of the current masculine realism'.

'Pointed Roofs', the first volume of *Pilgrimage*, which recalls Richardson's teaching experiences, was published in 1915 to broad, if not popular, acclaim. Two years later she married the artist Alan Odle. *Pilgrimage* is a memoir, through the fictional protagonist Miriam Henderson, of Richardson's life from 1895 until 1917, and one that took her a further two decades to complete. Challenging Victorian norms of representation and gender, it rejects the conventions of plot and character, focusing instead on the receptive conscious-ness of a young woman amidst the everyday life of modernity. Richardson developed a radically experimental psychological realism. As May SINCLAIR stated in an influential review of *Pilgrimage* in 1918, 'Nothing happens. It is just life going on and on. It is Miriam Henderson's stream of consciousness going on and on.' Regularly associated in the 1920s with the work of Joyce, Proust, and Woolf, *Pilgrimage* was yet never a high seller, since most readers were bemused by Miriam's singularly uneventful existence. By the publication of the later volumes, Richardson was all but forgotten, her claims in old age to be a writer ignored by her nurses as a delusion. It was not until the advent of feminist literary criticism in the 1970s that Richardson's reputation began to be reassessed, and her major role within the histories of literary MODERNISM and women's writing again recognized.

Suggested Reading

Kime Scott, Bonnie (ed.). *The Gender of Modernism* (Bloomington: Indiana University Press, 1990).

Woolf, Virginia. 'Romance and the Heart', review of *The Grand Tour* by Romer Wilson and *Revolving Lights* by Dorothy Richardson, *Nation and Athenaeum* (19 May 1923). Repr. in Woolf, *A Woman's Essays: Selected Essays, Volume I*, ed. Rachel Bowlby (Harmondsworth: Penguin, 1992) 50–2.

Deborah Parsons

Ridler, Anne 1912–2001

Poet, verse dramatist, librettist, editor, and translator who has long been respected by critics if not by the public at large. The daughter of a Rugby schoolmaster who lost his eldest son in the First World War, Ridler was educated at Downe House before taking a diploma in journalism at King's College London. Her work as a secretary at Faber and Faber brought her into contact with various literary figures including T. S. Eliot, Lawrence Durrell,

Norman Nicholson, and Charles Williams. Her marriage in 1938 to Vivian Ridler (Printer to University of Oxford from 1958–78 before running Perpetua Press) produced four children.

Ridler's first two collections, *Poems* (1939) and *The Nine Bright Shiners* (1943), reflect wartime anxieties in the unsentimental concentration on themes of love – romantic, familial, and religious – and place. A sense of what the poet calls 'threatened happiness' colours a distinctively Christian occasional poetics. Much of the manner and phrasing of the early work seems overtly Eliotesque while the *Waste Land*-like title poem of *The Golden Bird* (1951), an Arthurian grail quest, transforms its legendary source into a long moral narrative of cultural recovery intended for a postwar world. While endorsing her interest in sixteenth- and seventeenth-century lyric poets like Wyatt and Traherne, Eliot's example must also have encouraged the verse dramas Ridler produced in the forties and fifties: *Cain* (1943), *Henry Bly* (1947), and *The Trial of Thomas Cranmer* (1956), written to mark the 400th anniversary of the martyr's death. Her *oeuvre* is less obviously woman-centred than that of her friend E. J. SCOVELL, nevertheless, some of Ridler's most successful poems are about children and motherhood, experiences seen as part of a kind of communal spiritual process. Early texts like 'For A Child' offer context to those like the title poem of what is perhaps her finest work, *A Matter of Life and Death* (1959), commended by Elizabeth Jennings, among other critics, in *Poetry Today* (1961). This poem, Ridler explains, traces the progression 'from not being to being; and how we lose, say, the brightness of childhood in later life, and yet it's still there in each person'.

Ridler worked extensively as an editor, of Elizabeth Jennings, Traherne, Charles Williams, Walter de la Mare, and James Thomson, as well as of *The Little Book of Modern Verse* in 1941, and a revised *Faber Book of Modern Verse* in 1951. Ridler also wrote a number of plays and several original verse librettos, translating many more. She continued to write poetry into her last years. The eighties saw the appearance of *Dies Natalis: Poems of Birth and Infancy* (1980), *Ten Poems* with Scovell (1984), and a *New and Selected Poems* (1988). Carcanet marked the conclusion of a lengthy poetic career with a *Collected Poems* in 1994.

Suggested Reading

Lindop, Grevel. 'Anne Ridler In Conversation', *PN Review*, 21. 3 (1995) 17–22.
Spanos, William V. *The Christian Tradition in Modern British Verse Drama* (New Brunswick, NJ: Rutgers University Press, 1967).

Alice Entwistle

Roberts, Kate 1891–1985

Short-story writer, novelist, literary journalist, and Welsh nationalist, Kate Roberts was the greatest and most influential WELSH LANGUAGE writer of the twentieth century. Like many Welsh women writers, Roberts benefited from the rapid development of native universities in the late nineteenth and early twentieth centuries. She obtained a First from Bangor and taught in numerous grammar schools throughout South Wales before moving to Denbigh in 1935, where she bought and edited the nationalist newspaper, *Y Faner ac Amsera Cymru* ('The Banner and Times of Wales').

Roberts was the first writer from Wales in either language to purposefully and successfully employ European literary models in order to circumvent English cultural and linguistic influence. Her early short fictions are clearly influenced by her reading of Maupassant, Turgenev, and especially Chekhov – another writer who encapsulated historical and political changes through focusing upon the family sphere in a simple, direct narrative style. Almost all her short stories predominantly centre on the experiences of women within an industrial landscape, and in pieces such as 'Y Condemnedig' ('The Condemned', 1939) and 'Y Golled' ('The Loss', 1929) Roberts vocalizes the stoicism that she believed was at the heart of Welsh female identity.

Her most impressive work is her first novel, *Traed mewn Cyffion* (*Feet in Chains*, 1936). Although concerning the lives of a quarrying family, the novel almost entirely disregards the masculine site of work in order to focus on the Welsh custom of *gwerin* – literally meaning 'folk', but signifying the culture of communality, Nonconformism, and regional self-reliance inherent in rural Welsh-speaking Wales. This compressed epic chronicles the destruction of this culture due to the combined forces of colonialism, poverty, and apathy. It is a breakdown epitomized by the geographical break-up of the family and the death of Twm, the youngest son, killed in the trenches of the First World War – an event his Welsh-speaking parents cannot comprehend from the English telegram they receive.

Roberts claimed that personal and cultural loss drove her to write as a therapeutic necessity. Her later writing concerns the steady erosion of the *gwerin* culture she had known in her youth in a period of financial improvement. Yet it also questions the nostalgic view of her Nonconformist and communal past: 'He had written about people with backbone, and had survived into an age when eels were trying to hold up the world: and yet there was a place for eels in life and literature.' Her language is as spare and as unadorned as the landscape that surrounds her characters. And unlike many other Welsh writers (in either language) who wrote of the decline of their native culture in the face of increased anglicization, Roberts never resorted to crass sentimentality. Wales, for Roberts, was never that caricature of colonial complicity – a land of romance and song.

Several translations of Roberts's work are available in English, including *Feet in Chains*, *Tea in the Heather* (*Ty yn y Grug*, 1959), and *The World of Kate Roberts: Selected Stories, 1925–1981*, translated by Joseph P. Clancy.

Suggested Reading

Knight, Stephen. ' "The Uncertainties and Hesitations That Were the Truth": Welsh Industrial Fictions by Women', in Gustav Klaus and Stephen Knight (eds), *British Industrial Fictions* (Cardiff: University of Wales Press, 2000) 163–80.

Morgan, Derec Lywd. *Kate Roberts* (Cardiff: University of Wales Press, 1974).

Williams, Rhydwen (ed.). *Kate Roberts: Ei meddwl a'I Gwaith* (Llandybie: Christopher Davies, 1983).

Rob Gossedge

Roberts, Lynette 1909–1995

Poet, critic, and short-story writer. Lynette Roberts was the most prominent woman writer of the 'First-Flowering' of Anglo-Welsh poetry – a group that included, among others, Dylan Thomas, Alun Lewis, and David Jones. Along with the latter, Roberts was the most overtly MODERNIST Welsh writer working in English – particularly in her second volume of verse, *Gods with Stained Ears*, which was published in 1951 but mostly written during the Second World War, and contains much-admired depictions of the Blitz. Although critically derided for her 'domestic' politics, her experimental verse was championed by T. S. Eliot and published by Faber and Faber.

Born in Buenos Aires to Australian-Welsh parents and educated mainly in England, her later proclamation of Welsh nationality is disturbed by the fact that her poetry's narrative voice is always that of a cultural outsider. In *Poems* (1944) Roberts explored various forms of social and literary alienation through her deliberately 'primitive' style and her disparate use of form – Horatian odes, Sapphic metres, bardic praise-poems, and intense, obscure and personal lyrics. After her divorce from the influential editor, publisher, and poet Kiedrych Rhys in 1949, Roberts moved to England, where she suffered a nervous breakdown and ceased to write. In 1983, issue 19.2 of *Poetry Wales* was dedicated to her work, and reproduced her correspondence with Robert Graves, including her notes and revisions to his *White Goddess*.

Suggested Reading

Conran, Tony. *Frontiers in Anglo-Welsh Poetry* (Cardiff: University of Wales Press, 1997).

Rob Gossedge

Robertson, E. Arnot 1903–1961

Born in Surrey, the daughter of Dr G. A. Robertson, Eileen Arnot Robertson was educated at Sherborne Girls' School, which she loathed, and on the continent. In 1927 she married Henry E. Turner (later Sir Henry), of the Empire Press

Union, who died by accidental drowning in 1961. A few months later Robertson committed suicide. They had one son.

Her first novel, *Cullum* (1928), is astringent and unsentimental. Its female protagonist anticipates her later central characters: she is tough and competent (though often insecure) but far from feminist, scornful of feminine frivolity and stupidity. The satire *Three Came Unarmed* (1929) soon followed, and then *Four Frightened People* (1931), which was filmed in 1934. *Ordinary People* (1933), probably her most enduringly popular work, about a Suffolk boating family from the point of view of an alienated daughter. These early novels introduced a still-unusual physiological realism about women's lives.

She acted as an adviser on films during the Second World War, and developed a second career as a radio film critic, leading to a libel suit against MGM for excluding her from its screenings in retaliation for unfavourable reviews. These other occupations perhaps accounted for the slower production of her later novels.

Suggested Reading

Devlin, Polly. Introduction to *Four Frightened People* by E. Arnot Robertson (London: Virago, 1982) i–xix.

Devlin, Polly. Introduction to *Ordinary Families: A Novel* by E. Arnot Robertson (London: Virago, 1982) i–xvii.

Lesley A. Hall

Robins, Elizabeth 1862–1952

Author, actress, and radical feminist, who achieved success in many spheres of public and literary life. Robins was born in America but moved permanently to London in 1888, following the suicide of her husband, George Richmond Parks. During her stage career (1881 to 1902), she was one of the most respected actresses of her day, identified in particular with Ibsenite roles. She subsequently became, a SUFFRAGIST, a publicist for the Women's Social and Political Union (WSPU), a founding director of *Time and Tide*, and president of the Women Writers' Enfranchisement League.

Robins's writing includes drama, fiction, journalism, and polemic. Several of her novels and short-story collections of the 1890s appeared under the pseudonym C. E. Raimond; subsequently she used her own name. Her major novels are *The Open Question: A Tale of Two Temperaments* (1898), *Come and Find Me* (1908), *The Mills of the Gods* (1908), and *My Little Sister* (1913, filmed 1919). In 1904, she underwent a rest cure, and her novel about this experience, *A Dark Lantern* (1905), was filmed in 1920. Her feminist polemic *Ancilla's Share* (1924) influenced Woolf's *Three Guineas*, and she is best remembered for her 1907 play *Votes for Women*, which was followed by a novel, *The Convert* (1907), based on the same material.

Suggested Reading
Gates, Joanne E. *Elizabeth Robins, 1862–1952: Actress, Novelist, Feminist* (Tuscaloosa, AL, and London: Alabama University Press, 1994).
John, Angela V. *Elizabeth Robins: Staging a Life* (London: Routledge, 1995).

Faye Hammill

Romantic Fiction

Timelessly popular, romantic fictions offer narratives of fulfilled desire, satisfying what Lacan defines as 'lack', the longing for an unreachable symbolic unity with another which will provide a sense of personal wholeness. Feminist theorists of popular romance Janice Radway and Tania Modleski identify the narrative trajectory of romantic fictions as deriving from fairy-tales. In the 1970s and 1980s, feminists denigrated popular romantic fictions as silly escapism for entrapped housewives. Later they recuperated romance, recognizing both its culturally engaged narrative forms and its subversive potential.

In the early twentieth century, popular pulp fictions gained an audience through circulating LIBRARIES and through magazines including *Peg's Paper* (1919), *Red Star* (1929), *Secrets* (1932), and *Oracle* (1933). The tropes of latent desire, overturned social inequality, fidelity, and eternal love reinforce idealized visions of patriarchally informed heterosexual relationships. E. M. Hull's *The Sheik* (1919) exploits the erotic potential of sexual violence, and became a phenomenal bestseller. Among the other leading romance writers of the early decades of the century were Georgette HEYER, originator of the Regency romance and prolific author of romantic HISTORICAL FICTION, and Ethel M. DELL, whose dramatically plotted romantic adventures of duels and escapes idealize marriage and the EMPIRE and are tinged with the erotic. Q. D. LEAVIS considered Dell's books to be energetic, but characterized by 'bad writing, false sentiment, sheer silliness'. Barbara CARTLAND began publishing novels in 1923, and rapidly became the leading British author of romantic fiction. The hundreds of formulaic tales she produced were dictated, explaining their rather truncated, simplistic style, while their storylines reinforced gendered stereotypes, economic divisions, and the view that women live only for the reward of love and marriage.

Romance publishing has been dominated through most of the twentieth century by Mills and Boon. The company was established in 1908 as a general fiction publisher, but the growing appetite for escapism during the DEPRESSION encouraged them to concentrate on romantic fiction. Mills and Boon developed several imprints, ranging from the more conventional to the rather racy, and provide specific guidelines for their formulaic fictions in which relationships begin in antagonism: at least one partner has been hurt in life, producing an initial response of attack followed by a gradual revelation of deepening desire. Delays and misadventures accompany the maturity and transformation produced by real love, leading to heterosexual coupling in marriage. Pleasure, resolution, and the sense of an ultimately benign universe are key elements. The female protagonist is often positioned as passive, yet possessed of certain forms of power over the hero. Most Mills and Boon imprints reproduce stereotypes of economically superior men who are tall, dark, handsome, and in need of taming by nurturing, sexually passive heroines.

Romantic fictions were, however, both replayed and critiqued from the 1930s onwards by a range of woman writers, notably Daphne DU MAURIER. In *Rebecca* (1938), Maxim de Winter and his nameless wife are disturbed by the persistent haunting of a love match gone sour. The figure of Maxim's first, murdered wife, the wayward yet beautiful Rebecca, shadows their marriage and subsequently becomes a figure haunting any simplistic reading of romance.

Several pre- and post-Second World War writers initially considered to be producing pulp romantic fictions have been recuperated, and their work is now seen to problematize certain beliefs about love, marriage, and women's roles. Among them are Elizabeth TAYLOR, who resists the genre's sentimentality by exploring death and despair; Olivia MANNING, who wrote war trilogies and tales of marital tensions; Elizabeth GOUDGE, whose gentle fictions range from realism to romance and fairy-tale, and evoke a spirit of place; and Nancy MITFORD, who eschewed the happy ending and adopted a humorous approach to love. The morally daring Kate O'BRIEN mixes realism with romance; she confronted and condemned self-righteous judgements on sexuality, and her later works deal with LESBIAN relationships.

Suggested Reading

Baker, Niamh. *Happily Ever After?* (Basingstoke: Macmillan, 1989).

Belsey, Catherine. *Desire: Love Stories in Western Culture* (Oxford: Blackwell, 1994).

Modleski, Tania. *Loving with a Vengeance: Mass Produced Fantasies for Women* (London: Methuen, 1982).

Pearce, Lynne and Jackie Stacey (eds). *Romance Revisited* (London, Lawrence & Wishart, 1995).

Radway, Janice. *Reading the Romance: Women, Patriarchy and Popular Literature* (Chapel Hill, NC: University of North Carolina Press, 1984).

Gina Wisker

Royde-Smith, Naomi 1875–1964

Poet, journalist, novelist, and editor. Royde-Smith was brought up in Yorkshire and wrote about her childhood in *In the Wood* (1928). She began her professional career by writing poetry and book reviews, as well as the problem and competition pages of the Saturday *Westminster Gazette*. In 1912 she became the first woman ever to be a literary editor, commissioning pieces from contemporaries such as Rupert Brooke and D. H. Lawrence. She and her friend Rose MACAULAY gave parties together in her flat in Kensington, and the latter based the gossipy, interfering Aunt Evelyn of *Crewe Train* (1926) on her. In 1926

Royde-Smith married the actor Ernest Milton, 15 years younger than herself and became art reviewer for *Queen* magazine.

In 1925 Royde-Smith's first book, *The Tortoiseshell Cat*, appeared; 40 more novels would follow over the next 35 years, the most successful of which are *The Delicate Situation* (1931), *For Us in the Dark* (1937), and *The Altar-Piece: An Edwardian Mystery* (1939). She also wrote four plays and several biographies. Her novels are little read nowadays but admirers of Walter de la Mare are interested in her work because he was in love with her from about 1911 to 1916 and wrote her 400 letters.

Suggested Reading
LeFanu, Sarah. *Rose Macaulay* (London: Virago, 2003).

Nicola Beauman

Ruck, Berta 1878–1978
Popular romance novelist who, in a career spanning over 60 years, published nearly 80 novels, together with memoirs, articles, and short stories. Amy Roberta Ruck was originally an artist, and her writing career began when she realized that she could improve on many stories that she was illustrating for periodicals. Her success, however, was not instantaneous and she joked that she could wallpaper a room with letters beginning: 'The Editor regrets'. Her first novel was the reworking of a successful serial, *His Official Fiancée* (1914), originally appearing in the WOMEN'S MAGAZINE *Home Chat*. She acknowledged author Oliver Onions, whom she married in 1909, as a continued support in her writing. Although their styles differed they maintained a mutual respect, often exchanging criticism and ideas. After his death in 1961, Ruck edited his final manuscript, *A Shilling to Spend* (1965).

Despite her self-deprecating claim that she wrote to fund her sons' education, her notebooks reveal a conscientious, professional writer. By the 1920s, although recognized by the popular press as a FASHION arbiter because her books catalogued changing fashions, her work often subtly introduces more serious, carefully researched, contemporary issues. In *The Arrant Rover* (1921) she artfully mentions, by way of advertisement, her friend Marie STOPES's controversial book, *Married Love* (1918). *The Clouded Pearl* (1924) questions the effect of modernity on the HEALTH of young women, and she evaluates EUGENICS in *Kneel to the Prettiest* (1925). In *Sweet Stranger* (1921), the strict moral stance of the popular press is challenged when the hero's apology for a kiss without first proposing marriage, is countered by the heroine's: 'Oh, darlin'! then how were you to know whether or not you wanted to marry me at all?'

Her work is always pervaded with an air of common sense, with her heroines often employed in quite ordinary occupations which plot the changing career roles open to women during the first half of the twentieth century. The heroines are variously maids, nurses, secretaries, FASHION models, beauticians, and journalists, before finally settling down with the dependable hero. Ruck makes no apology for being 'A Happy-Ender', and in response to critics of popular fiction, says that she would 'rather be "good Bad" than "bad Good" '. When Virginia WOOLF claimed that she had inadvertently included Ruck's name on a gravestone in *Jacob's Room* (1922), Ruck magnanimously wrote to her 'grave-digger' and mischievously entertained the BLOOMSBURY group with the music-hall song 'Don't Never Let a Sailor an Inch above your Knee'.

During the Second World War, she toured the country lecturing to women's organizations and the armed forces on such diverse subjects as 'What Women Learn from Men and Vice Versa' and 'Dreams and the Supernatural'. She progressed to BROADCASTING on BBC radio and appeared on television's *Yesterday's Witness*: 'Two Victorian Girls' (1970). After the publication of her last novel, *Shopping for a Husband* (1967), she concentrated on family history, which culminated in her final publication *Ancestral Voices* (1972). Her papers are held at the National Library of Wales.

Suggested Reading

Jackson, Elaine. ' "Only a Story: It's more than that!": Race, Eugenics and Birth Control in Popular Romance between the Wars', *Diegesis: Journal of the Association for Research in Popular Fictions*, 6 (Spring 2000) 46–54.

Ruck, Berta. *A Storyteller Tells the Truth* (London: Hutchinson, 1935).

Elaine Jackson

Russell, Dora 1894–1986

Feminist birth control advocate, pacifist, educationalist, and rebel, best known today for *The Tamarisk Tree*, her lively and informative three-volume autobiography (1975, 1980, 1985). Russell began her adult life as a promising academic. Her father, Sir Frederick Black, a distinguished civil servant, was a Liberal with unusually radical views concerning women's EDUCATION. Dora Black was given a first-rate secondary education, and went on from Sutton High School to Girton College, Cambridge, where she earned a First in Modern Languages, although as a woman, she could not receive an actual degree. She became involved in the intense intellectual, political, and social life of the university, notably through her association with C. K. Ogden's Heretics society, a centre for radical thought at Cambridge in the early years of the twentieth century. She lost her conventional Anglican faith, became a self-described feminist, and explored PACIFISM and SOCIALISM.

Returning to Cambridge with a Fellowship at Girton, she met the eminent philosopher Bertrand Russell. Although she had feminist misgivings about marriage, she became his second wife in 1921, viewing the marriage as a brave modern experiment. Bertrand and Dora saw themselves as offering an avant-garde model for sexual liberation, for equality between the sexes, and for parenthood. In the 1920s both became well-known public advocates of a radical restructuring of marriage that would allow each partner to love others, while at the same time ensuring a firm and lasting bond in a relationship that involved children. Each found it impossible to live up to these precepts, and the marriage ended in divorce in 1935. Dora Russell wrote about her radical views concerning marriage and motherhood in *Hypatia: or Woman and Knowledge* (1925), *The Right to be Happy* (1927), and *In Defence of Children* (1932), as well as in numerous newspaper and magazine articles.

One of Dora Russell's most significant achievements was the founding of Beacon Hill School, a libertarian educational experiment launched initially in 1927 as a joint venture with Bertrand, but run as hers alone for much of its 16-year history. Dora Russell wrote about the school in her autobiography, most extensively in the second volume, *The Tamarisk Tree: My School and the Years of War*. In the years after the Second World War, Russell was actively involved in the cause of world peace; for example, organizing and publicizing the Women's Caravan of Peace in 1958. Then, in the final decade of her life, she devoted herself to writing, producing her autobiography, and completing her book *Religion and the Machine Age* (1982).

Suggested Reading

Tait, Katharine. *My Father Bertrand Russell* (New York and London: Harcourt, Brace Jovanovich, 1975).

Ward, Harriet. *A Man of Small Importance: My Father Griffin Barry* (Debenham, Suffolk: Dormouse Books, 2003).

Deborah Gorham

S

Sackville-West, Vita 1892–1962

Novelist, poet, biographer, travel writer, reviewer, radio broadcaster, and creator, with her husband Harold Nicolson, of the famous garden at her home, Sissinghurst Castle. Immortalized by her intimate Virginia WOOLF in *Orlando*, this free-spirited woman of letters published over 40 books in the course of her life. An accomplished but in many ways underrated writer, her reputation as a poet mattered most to her; she described her *Collected Poems* (1933) as 'the only book of mine I shall ever have minded about'. She probably remains best known, however, for her historical novels.

Only child of the third Baron Sackville and his part-Spanish wife, Victoria Sackville-West grew up in the ancestral home of Knole in Kent which, to her lasting resentment, as a woman she could never inherit. In life, as in her art, the conservative was held in tension with the progressive: her outwardly conventional marriage, in 1914, to Nicholson (a bisexual like herself) was long and tranquil, and produced two sons but did not prevent her involvement in a series of society scandals, most notoriously the elopement with Violet TREFUSIS in 1920. Her much-discussed 'Sapphist' relationship with Woolf dominated the latter half of a decade which brought poetic recognition with the widely-admired pastoral *The Land*, awarded the Hawthornden Prize in 1927. This carefully wrought neoclassical study of English rural life, in which the memory of the First World War remains fresh, thrust its author into the limelight; she was soon after nominated as a possible Poet Laureate. Although it brought with it the unfashionable label 'GEORGIAN', a classification which still haunts her work, the poem foregrounds an interest in place which colours much of her *oeuvre*. However, in focusing on the outward conventionalities of her work, commentators have often overlooked the ambivalence with which locality is treated by Sackville-West, a keen chronicler of her own travels. As Jane Dowson observes of 'Sissinghurst', celebrating the part-ruined buildings which the Nicolsons acquired in 1930, 'the mood is one of restlessness as much as of contentment'. The poem closes in typically philosophical, rather than nostalgic, mood.

Several of Sackville-West's biographies focus on women, including *Pepita* (1937), about her grandmother and her mother; *Aphra Behn* (1929); *Joan of Arc* (1936); and an account of St Teresa of Avila and St Therese of Lisieux, *The Eagle and the Dove* (1943). These books prove that she finds historical, social, cultural, and aesthetic 'place' as compelling a subject as locale. This is confirmed by novels like the bestselling *The Edwardians* (1930), and *All Passion*

Spent (1931), which – inflected by *A Room of One's Own* – explores social constraints on female behaviour through the experiences of an elderly widow. The prize-winning *The Garden* (1946), a response to the end of war which received little attention from reviewers, marks the premature silencing of her poetic voice. Although much time in later years was absorbed by Sissinghurst, its development documented in the gardening columns written for the *Observer* from 1946–61, she continued to write novels until just before she died.

Suggested Reading

Glendinning, Victoria. *Vita: The Life of Vita Sackville-West* (London: Weindenfeld & Nicolson, 1983).

Raitt, Suzanne. *Vita and Virginia: The Work and Friendship of Vita Sackville-West and Virginia Woolf* (Oxford: Oxford University Press, 1993).

Alice Entwistle

Sandys, Oliver (Countess Barcynska) 1886–1964

Pseudonym of Marguerite Florence Laura Jervis, popular author of short stories and 135 romance novels. She wanted to 'make a name' for herself rather than do 'nothing at all except have babies like my mother'. She wrote for periodicals to supplement her acting income and was briefly sub-editor for *Sievier's Monthly*. Her first Sandys novel, *Chicane* (1912), began life as a serial therein.

In 1911, as a 'literary collaboration', she married Armiger Barclay/Barcynsky who suggested adding the spurious title 'Countess' as a pseudonym. Later, he unsuccessfully tried to claim her work as his own. Ironically, her first Barcynska novel, *The Honeypot* (1916), highlights the moral dangers of the theatrical world and defends the 'fallen woman' as 'an ebullient girl who loves a man of the world too generously'. Other novels address similar pitfalls in the contemporary film world, particularly *God and Mr Aaronson* (Barcynska, 1937). Several were filmed, most famously Alfred Hitchcock's directing debut, *The Pleasure Garden* (Sandys, 1923).

In 1933 she married writer Caradoc Evans, with whom she undertook theatrical ventures in Kent and Wales, funded by her pen. After his death she wrote his biography and other autobiographical works exploring her belief in spiritualism and the supernatural. She has received no attention from critics.

Suggested Reading

Sandys, Oliver. *Full and Frank: The Private Life of a Woman Novelist* (London: Hurst & Blackett, 1941).

Elaine Jackson

Sayers, Dorothy L. 1893–1957

Theologian, dramatist, novelist, and poet, best known for her DETECTIVE FICTION and her aristocratic sleuth, Lord Peter Wimsey. Dorothy Leigh Sayers was the only child of the Reverend Henry Sayers, headmaster of the Christ Church Choir School, Oxford, and Helen Mary Sayers (née Leigh). In 1897, the family moved to Bluntisham-cum-Earith, Huntingdonshire, where Henry Sayers had been offered the living. Her upbringing instilled a strong faith and theological interest in Sayers at a young age, which was sustained into her adult life, informing all aspects of her writing. Sayers was educated at home until 1909, when she was sent to Godolphin School, Salisbury.

Sayers went up to Somerville College, Oxford, in 1912, and gained a first in modern languages, although like the other women students, she was not awarded her BA and MA until 1920. She had several poems published in *The Oxford Magazine* and wrote two volumes of poetry, *Op 1* (1916) and *Catholic Tales and Christian Songs* (1918). Whilst rarely associated with poetry as a genre, Sayers's technical ability and capacity for lyrical description are evident in her later works, both drama and prose, such as the following description of Oxford in the detective novel *Gaudy Night* (1935):

> There, eastward, within a stone's throw, stood the twin towers of All Soul's, fantastic, unreal as a house of cards, clear-cut in the sunshine, the drenched oval in the quad beneath, brilliant as an emerald in the bezel of a ring...and Queen's with her dome of green copper; and, as the eye turned southward, Magdalen, yellow and slender, the tall lily of towers.

Her poetic capabilities were also fundamental to her work as a copywriter with S. H. Benson, a job she took in 1921 after a brief period of employment with Blackwells and as a teacher in Hull. Sayers remained at Benson's until 1931.

Her first detective novel, *Whose Body?* was published in 1923, and followed by several collections of short fiction and 12 more novels. In 1924, she gave birth to her only, illegitimate, child, John Anthony White (Fleming), who was cared for by her cousin, Ivy Shrimpton, and whose existence remained a secret to even her close friends until after her death. In 1926, she married Oswold Arthur (Mac) Fleming, a journalist. The marriage was not always happy, and Sayers turned increasingly to her writing out of personal and financial necessity.

After the collection of short stories *In the Teeth of the Evidence* (1939), Sayers wrote no more detective fiction, focusing instead on essays and papers, such as *Begin Here* (1939) and *Unpopular Opinions* (1946). She began writing religious dramas for the radio and stage, such as *The Man Born to be King* (1943), a radio play for children on the life of Christ, and *The Just Vengeance* for the 1946 Lichfield festival. In these works, her commitment to presenting both personal and theological arguments in an interesting and accessible way is evident, as is her often unique and occasionally dogmatic approach to life. Sayers's final work was her translation of Dante's *Divine Comedy*, completed after her death by her friend and biographer, Barbara Reynolds.

Suggested Reading

Brunsdale, Mitzi. *Dorothy L. Sayers: Solving the Mystery of Wickedness* (Oxford: Berg, 1990).

Coombes, David. *Dorothy L. Sayers: A Careless Rage for Life* (Oxford: Lion, 1992).

Reynolds, Barbara. *Dorothy L. Sayers: Her Life and Soul* (London: Hodder & Stoughton, 1998).

Esme Miskimmin

Science Fiction and Fantasy

Science Fiction (SF) might seem initially an inappropriate genre for women because of its focus on technology and its tendency to represent women as victims. Ever since Mary Shelley's *Frankenstein* (1818), however, women authors have used SF to critique the blind masculinist worship of science, rationalism, and violence, sometimes substituting alternative, emotionally intelligent matriarchies. Fantasy, of which SF is a branch, frequently uses the uncanny to destabilize and defamiliarize everyday realities and relationships, while fantastic settings, metamorphosis and other disruptions provide alternatives to the *status quo*.

The period 1900–50 produced many intriguing SF and fantasy texts by women. A major example is Sylvia Townsend WARNER's *Lolly Willowes* or *The Loving Huntsman* (1926), which concerns a typically marginalized female figure, Laura, a maiden aunt who resists her relatives' efforts to absorb her life into theirs and requisition her inheritance. She moves to the village of Great Mop, which is filled with male and female witches. She lives happily alone and walks out at night: 'That was the advantage of dealing with witches; they do not mind if you are a little odd.' The novel is a lively, optimistic fantasy of women's independence and creativity.

Some of the most important futuristic texts of the period were produced by Storm JAMESON. *In the Second Year* (1936) projects a fascistic Britain, while *The World Ends* (1937), published under the pseudonym William Lamb, concerns a second Flood that is followed by the emergence of a patriarchy. In *Then We Shall Hear Singing: A Fantasy in C Major* (1942), a victorious German Reich dominates an unnamed country, but is unable to eliminate the resistance of the individual consciousness. *The Moment of Truth* (1949) describes a post-Holocaust UK ruled by communists. Jameson's SF novels derive from her interest in the politics of change, and project extremist political 'solutions' into the near future. Naomi MITCHISON combines fantasy and SF with classical history and myth, and her radical plots frequently unfold in settings removed in space or time. She repeatedly explores the parallel between sex and death, a recurring motif in SF.

While her 1930s novels are set in imagined pre-Christian communities, her later texts, such as *Memoirs of a Spacewoman* (1962) and *Solution Three* (1975), fit more neatly into the genre of feminist SF.

Virginia WOOLF is rarely thought of as a fantasist but several of her fictions conjure supernatural presences. The narrator of 'A Haunted House' (1921) lives in a house which retains mysterious traces of the loving couple who previously inhabited it, while the dead Mrs Ramsay becomes a ghostly presence in the later sections of *To The Lighthouse* (1927). The domineering, imperialistic doctor character in *Mrs Dalloway* (1922) is presented using vampire imagery, while Charlotte MEW's disturbing tale 'A White Night' (1907) likewise indicts imperialism and sexism through the trope of the live burial of a woman in white.

Rose MACAULAY's *What Not: A Prophetic Comedy* (1919) concerns a postwar British autocracy. Cicely HAMILTON's *Lest Ye Die: A Story from the Past or the Future* (1928) bitterly depicts a future war in whose aftermath the people of the UK, driven out of the cities, revert to superstitious barbarism. In Agatha CHRISTIE's *The Big Four* (1927), Hercule Poirot and Captain Hastings hunt an evil organization whose ultimate goal is world domination through chaos. Alison UTTLEY's *A Traveller in Time* (1939) is a poignant historical ghost story.

Other fantasy texts of the period include E. NESBIT's *The Story of the Amulet* (1905), 'The Five Senses' (1909), 'Dormant' (1911), and 'The Pavilion' (1915); Florence L. BARCLAY's *Returned Empty* (1920); Rebecca WEST's *Harriet Hume: A London Fantasy* (1929); and Edith PARGETER's *The City Lies Four-Square: A Novel* (1939).

Suggested Reading

Armitt, Lucie (ed.). *Where No Man Has Gone Before: Women and Science Fiction* (London: Routledge, 1991).

Bleiler, Everett F. *Science-Fiction: The Early Years* (Kent, OH: Kent State University Press, 1990).

Jackson, Rosemary. *Fantasy: The Literature of Subversion* (London: Methuen, 1981).

Lefanu, Sarah. *In the Chinks of the World Machine: Feminism and Science Fiction* (London: The Women's Press, 1988).

Rose, Jacqueline. *States of Fantasy* (Oxford: Clarendon Press, 1996).

Gina Wisker

Scovell, E. J. 1907–1999

Poet whose relatively limited output, though highly regarded in critical circles since the fifties, and despite revived interest in the eighties, has been unjustly neglected. The daughter of a clergyman, Scovell was born in Sheffield, schooled in Cumberland, and read English and Classics at Oxford, where she edited the magazine of the Oxford Women's Colleges, *Fritillary*. After graduating in 1930, she began writing seriously while also working as a secretary in London. For a time she was employed on the feminist review *Time and Tide*. She married Charles Elton, an ecologist, in 1937, occasionally accompanying him on field trips to the tropics; they made their home in Oxford and had two children.

The first two collections, *Shadows of Chrysanthemums* (1944) and *The Midsummer Meadow* (1946), establish the graceful, plain-speaking idiom for which Geoffrey Grigson, anthologizing her in *Poetry of the Present* (1949), declared Scovell 'the purest woman poet of our time'. Her work usually focuses on moments of intimate reflection, beside a fire, in an autumnal garden, or over a sleeping child. However, Scovell's anonymized searching of apparently domestic, woman-centred experience, if it strenuously avoids making large claims for itself, is rarely as self-sufficient as it seems. The evocative 'Poems On Infancy' sequence, included by her friend Anne RIDLER in the revised *The Faber Book of Modern Verse* (1951), goes further than simple portraiture when, repeatedly capturing children in sleep, it gravely explores the dialogue between light and dark, conscious and unconscious, expression and impression by which human endeavour is defined. Typically she discovers in darkness, together with its analogues sleep and death, a mystery which is compelling rather than menacing in its potential. Discerning the human 'soul' in the unconscious, the confessedly agnostic Scovell finds in childhood innocence an instructive spiritual state. The sense of possibility held in reserve underpins her poetic approach: 'I should like the surface to be entirely clear, and the meaning to be entirely implicit.' By extension, 'ground' proves as resonant as 'dark' and 'light'; in 'Heavy as Lead', while parents provide a stable 'ground' from which the child can strike out towards individuality, children themselves become the 'ground' that gives birth to the parents.

The lengthy silence following *The River Steamer* (1956), comprising new and reprinted works, was finally broken by *The Space Between* (1982) and *Listening To Collared Doves* (1986). A *Collected Poems* was published in 1988 (winning a Cholmondeley Award), followed by *Selected Poems* (1991). Scovell's unwaveringly restrained, formally subtle idiom, sometimes gently reminiscent of Emily Dickinson, maps a deepening sense of the inherently transitional nature of experience over the obtruding context of family, friends, house, and garden. Some pieces suggest that poetry offers the agnostic another way of surviving death's finality.

Suggested Reading

Poster, Jem. 'In Love with Space', *PN Review*, 19. 4 (March/April 1988) 24–7.

Rumens, Carol and John Mole. 'A Visionary in Sensible Shoes: The Poetry of E. J. Scovell', *Poetry Review* 6.4 (1986) 37–40.

Scupham, Peter. 'Shelf Lives 9: E. J. Scovell', *PN Review*, 26.3 (January/February 2000) 26–8.

Alice Entwistle

Servants

The decline in residential domestic service was one of the most significant changes in domestic life in the twentieth century. In 1891 there were 1,386,167 domestic servants in England and Wales. This figure represented 34 per cent of all women categorized as 'employed'. By 1951 only 11 per cent of women in the labour market were registered as 'indoor domestic', a drop of over 50 per cent in 60 years. Despite the decline in servant-keeping, few women born before 1950 remained untouched by the system of domestic service. Middle-class women grew up assuming that it was both natural and right that domestic chores, particularly the 'rough' work of scrubbing and cleaning, should be assigned to others. For working-class women, domestic service, which had once been seen as a respectable occupation, became increasingly stigmatized. Wherever there were other employment options, women were reluctant to enter domestic service. Fervent discussions about the 'servant problem', how domestic work could be organized without servants, and how working-class women could be persuaded to enter an occupation that they increasingly detested, took place throughout the early part of the twentieth century. Successive government initiatives attempted to increase the supply of servants, while interventions by women's groups and servants themselves, through the Domestic Workers' Union, focused on the need to improve training, wages, and conditions of service.

Nevertheless, by the late 1950s, the Victorian system of residential domestic service had all but disappeared except in the homes of the very affluent. It was replaced by part-time, non-residential domestic help for those middle-class families that could afford it. One of the reasons given for the demise of the residential system was the growth in labour-saving DOMESTIC TECHNOLOGY. The other reason was the proliferation of jobs in light engineering, clerical work, and retail, as industrialized economies shifted from a reliance on heavy manufacturing to commodity production and the service industries. Working-class women were enabled to choose jobs that did not involve quite the same degree of regimentation, servitude, and deference. However, these jobs often echoed the demands of domestic service: hairdressing, waitressing, cleaning in institutions, working as a shop assistant, and cooking for restaurants and cafés. The anxieties of servant-keeping, and the possibility of managing without servants were frequently fictionalized by women writers in the period 1900 to 1950, testifying to the pervasive cultural significance of domestic service.

Suggested Reading

Dyhouse, Carol. *Feminism and the Family in England, 1880–1939* (Oxford: Blackwell 1989).

Giles, Judy. *The Parlour and the Suburb: Domestic Identities, Class, Femininity and Modernity* (Oxford: Berg. 2004).

Judy Giles

Sexology

In the late nineteenth century, a number of factors led to an increasing tendency to analyse the phenomena of sex in a rational and (relatively) dispassionate way, using the rhetoric, and some of the tools, of science. Among these factors were Darwin's emphasis on sexual selection as a mechanism of evolution, growing public HEALTH concerns over the serious consequences of venereal diseases, an increasing refusal among homosexuals to accept stigmatization, and the observations of anthropologists, which undermined assumptions about universal patterns of marriage and sexual behaviour. What has often been overlooked in this aetiology was the role played, at least in the UK, by protofeminist critiques of existing sexual institutions, both marriage and prostitution, as designed to accommodate men at the expense of women. The best known British pioneers in the field of sexology, Edward Carpenter, Havelock Ellis, Sir Patrick Geddes, and J. Arthur Thomson, were embedded within a milieu of social reform and debate on the relations of the sexes. This debate was strongly influenced by the agitation against the Contagious Diseases Acts of the 1860s, which penalized prostitutes in port and garrison towns (but not their customers), as the statutory embodiment of the sexual double standard.

While these pioneers often manifested some degree of blindness towards the specific problems faced by women, they were well-meaning in their desire to promote the interests of women and to challenge the unthinking conventional morality which divided women into two classes, chaste and fallen. Their work was taken up by feminists, who were challenging accepted assumptions about sexual arrangements increasingly articulately. Women of the period were also themselves engaging in the growing explorations of a previously taboo area. However, because they were publishing their ideas in a range of genres which were not scientific monographs or articles, their contributions have often been overlooked or assumed to be merely popularization of the ideas of male thinkers.

The ideas of sexologists about female sexuality and the desirability of sexual expression pervade fictional works of the early twentieth century, though they were not necessarily treated uncritically. The theories of Ellis and Carpenter on 'sexual inversion', or HOMOSEXUALITY, both male and female, were probably more influential than those of Freud for several decades. Radclyffe HALL sought a preface by Ellis for her controversial novel *The Well of Loneliness*, and similar ideas can be found in other works of the day.

Suggested Reading

Bland, Lucy and Laura Doan (eds). *Sexology and Culture: Labelling Bodies and Desires* (Oxford: Polity Press, 1998).

Hall, Lesley A. 'Heroes or Villains? Reconsidering British Fin-de-Siècle Sexology and Its Impact', in Lynne Segal (ed.), *New Sexual Agendas* (London: Macmillan, 1997) 3–16.

Hall, Lesley A. 'Suffrage, Sex and Science', in Maroula Joannou and June Purvis (eds), *The Women's Suffrage Movement, New Feminist Perspectives* (Manchester: Manchester University Press, 1998) 188–200.

Lesley A. Hall

Sharp, Margery 1905–1991

A comic novelist for adults and entertaining essayist, but best known for her children's series about intrepid mice, the first of which, *The Rescuers* (1959), was animated by Disney in 1977. After a childhood in Malta and Streatham, South London, Sharp studied at Bedford College and Westminster Art School. In 1938 she married Major Geoffrey Castle, an aeronautical engineer.

Sharp raises and thwarts narrative expectations as insouciantly as her heroines transgress boundaries of gender, class, and culture. Though often orphaned, unsophisticated, and impoverished, they satisfy their needs in ways that surprise others. Guiltlessly relinquishing her daughter to the father's family, Julia, in *The Nutmeg Tree* (1937), is free to perform music-hall; in *Martha in Paris* (1962), Martha leaves her illegitimate baby with the father's concierge to pursue her career as a cubist painter. The heroine of *Cluny Brown* (1944) is a clumsy parlourmaid but competent plumber, while *The Eye of Love* (1957) was admired by Q. D. LEAVIS as an authentic portrait of a female artist's development. For Sharp's heroines, sexuality and marriage can threaten creativity and vitality. In *Sophy Cassmajor* (1934), a dark, fable-like novella illustrated as though for children, sexual initiation, initially as satisfying as redcurrant jelly, unleashes destructive events which threaten Sophy's appetite for life itself.

Though categorized as middlebrow, Sharp's writing was culturally sophisticated and admired by Elizabeth BOWEN and Elizabeth Jane Howard. Sharp herself plays ironically with the middlebrow status of her own writing.

Suggested Reading

Newquist, Roy. *Counterpoint: Sixty-Three Interviews With Authors and Columnists and Publishers* (London: George, Allen & Unwin, 1964).

Mary Grover

Sinclair, May 1863–1946

Although an essayist, poet, philosopher, and author of 24 novels and six volumes of short stories, May Sinclair is perhaps best remembered for coining the phrase 'stream of consciousness' in a review of Dorothy RICHARDSON's *Pilgrimage*. Born into a once wealthy family, Sinclair's childhood was characterized by gradual financial decline, continual geographical upheaval, and her father's alcoholism. In 1897 she published her first novel, *Audrey Craven*, in an effort to earn money to support her ailing mother, her only surviving relative. After the subsequent publication of *The Three Sisters* (1914), *Mary Olivier: A Life* (1919), and *The Life and Death of Harriet Frean* (1922), she was considered among the most distinguished novelists in England, enjoying the respect of Ezra Pound, E. M. Forster, and T. S. Eliot.

After an early loss of religious faith, she turned first to German Idealist philosophy and then to the theories of Freud and Jung – which she later incorporated into her work, becoming one of the first successful psychological novelists. She was briefly, and later somewhat ashamedly, involved in the women's SUFFRAGE movement and was outspoken, both in fiction and journalism, about the constraining forces of marriage upon female creativity.

Sinclair keenly participated in the First World War, seeking 'Reality – naked, shining, intense Reality', which she believed could only be experienced in its highest degree by women, due to their natural affinity with the 'Life-force' of procreative impulses ('Influence of the War on Life and Literature'). Of the 25 writers to sign an 'Author's Declaration' in favour of the war in *The Times* on 18 September 1914, she was one of only four women. She worked for a time as an ambulance-nurse in Belgium. This was not a success, though it did provide much material for her later work, particularly *The Tree of Heaven* (1917), *The Romantic* (1920), and *Anne Severn and the Fieldings* (1922), the latter being a somewhat bitter and self-heroizing portrait of the artist at this time. Her journals were one of the first wartime women's diaries to be published in Britain, and initial notices were positive, the North American Review describing them as 'the most genuine and vital piece of writing that has come from the war era'.

Harriet Frean perhaps demonstrates Sinclair's skill more fully than any other work. It chronicles a young woman's desire to please her domineering family and refrain from what is termed morally 'ugly'. Its measured tone and restrained symbolism perfectly reflect the life of sacrifice that Harriet is forced to endure, only for it to be annihilated by the last 300 or so words – a brilliant explosion of MODERNIST prose that exposes the ideals of female subservience which underpin the narrative as fundamentally false and corrupt. Like the eponymous heroine of *Harriet Frean*, Sinclair never formed any lasting relationships, and after the death of her mother she lived alone. For the last 15 years of her life she was incapacitated with Parkinson's disease.

Suggested Reading

Miracky, James J. *Regenerating the Novel: Gender and Genre in Woolf, Forster, Sinclair and Lawrence* (London: Routledge, 2003).

Raitt, Suzanne. *May Sinclair: A Modern Victorian* (Oxford: Oxford University Press, 2000).

Rob Gossedge

Sitwell, Edith 1886–1964

Experimental poet, biographer, critic, and novelist, chiefly known for *Façade* (1922), a poem sequence revelling in wordplay and sound, set to music by William Walton. Daughter of Sir George Sitwell and his wife Ida, whose parents, the Earl and Countess of Londesborough, owned most of Scarborough, precocious Edith was brought up by grandparents at Renishaw Hall, Derbyshire, later commenting: 'I was like one dead, like a small ghost.' From 1919 until 1938, Sitwell lived with her governess, friend, and guide Helen Rootham. She has the reputation of being one of the 'bright young things' of the 1920s, but in fact criticizes rather than celebrates their frivolous worldliness. Edith and her brothers Osbert and Sacheverell were intellectuals, neither uncritically right-wing nor wealthy. Much of her poetry recreates a childlike, surreal world of fantasy, simultaneously pleasant, frightening, and absurd.

Sitwell courted public recognition, associating with major celebrities (notably Marilyn Monroe) and dressing eccentrically all her life: even in her 1960s BBC 'Monitor' appearance, her sharp, intelligent face was offset by a slightly ludicrous turban. She was capable of lofty, amusing dismissals of her contemporaries, but she championed young writers, notably Wilfred Owen, through her editorship of the *Wheels* POETRY ANTHOLOGIES (1916–21). An experimental modernist with a radical edge, hers is poetry of dazzling surfaces, full of artifice and fantasy, drawing attention to sounds, rhymes, rhythms, signifiers.

Sitwell's seemingly nonsensical, sing-song verse tests the possibilities of language. She frequently uses the four-stress accentual metre, and her poems are influenced by music and dance forms. The satirical 'Gold Coast Rhythms' (1929), for example, draws on jazz rhythms, and refers to African Ashanti rituals. She satirizes religion, artifice, pretence, and the superficialities of Bohemian life. In the Gothic, fierce, 'Lo, this is she that was the world's desire', Helen of Troy represents women fooled by valorizing beauty, menaced by 'the appalling lion-claws of age', while Venus has grown old and lost her nose. Other poems deal with historical or mythological incidents, in which women's roles have traditionally been relegated to the margins: 'Anne Boleyn's Song' and 'Eurydice' give women a voice.

Edith Sitwell's political, critical poetry is seriously overlooked. 'Myself in the Merry-Go-Round' uses roundabout images, critiquing the century's excess and disorder. In 'The Ghouls', vampiric images of dancing on floors 'slippery with blood' indict the older generation's monstrous culpability in sending young men to war.

She also wrote several works in prose, including a study of Pope (1930), *English Eccentrics* (1933), *Aspects of Modern Poetry* (1934), a commercially successful biography of Queen Victoria (1936), and a novel about Jonathan Swift, *I Live Under a Black Sun* (1937). Made a Dame in 1954, she was received into the Catholic Church in 1955. Her contributions to both MODERNISM and feminism have yet to be fully realized.

Suggested Reading
Elborn, Geoffrey. *Edith Sitwell: A Biography* (London: Sheldon Press 1981).
Glendinning, Victoria. *Edith Sitwell: A Unicorn Among Lions* (London: Weidenfeld & Nicolson, 1981).
Wisker, Gina and Gary Day. 'Recuperating and Revaluing: Edith Sitwell and Charlotte Mew', in Gary Day and Brian Docherty (eds), *British Poetry: 1900–1950: Aspects of Tradition* (Basingstoke: Macmillan – Palgrave Macmillan, 1995) 65–80.

Gina Wisker

Smith, Dodie 1896–1990

British playwright and novelist. Born Dorothy Gladys Smith in Lancashire in 1896, she grew up in Manchester with her widowed mother. Her childhood, including her stage career as a child actress, is detailed in her memoir *Look Back With Love* (1974). Determined to pursue an acting career, she entered the Academy of Dramatic Art in 1914, but was not a successful professional (she deemed herself 'too short and not attractive enough'), instead becoming a manager in a department store. In 1931, her first play, *Autumn Crocus*, written under the pseudonym C. L. Antony, was produced on the London stage, and was a great triumph. Over the next seven years, Smith wrote five successful plays, including *Call it a Day* (1935) and *Dear Octopus* (1938).

Smith moved to the United States in 1938, since her husband, Alec Beesley, was a PACIFIST opposed to the imminent outbreak of war in Europe. They lived in Hollywood, where Smith became a scriptwriter for Paramount, an occupation she found lucrative but uncompelling. Smith missed England greatly, but she and Beesley did not return after the war's end because they could not bear to put their beloved Dalmatians into quarantine. Her homesickness inspired Smith's first novel, the hugely acclaimed *I Capture the Castle* (1948). From its riveting opening sentence 'I write this sitting in the kitchen sink', the story of the teenage narrator Cassandra, who lives in a dilapidated castle with her eccentric family, has captivated both child and adult readers, and was voted one of the top 100 books of all time in the BBC's The Big Read poll of 2003. Smith's close friend and fellow émigré Christopher Isherwood wrote that it was 'like a really good carving; the more you look at it, the more you see'.

Smith's most famous book is *The One Hundred and One Dalmatians* (1956), inspired by her first Dalmatian, Pongo, the name given to the book's canine hero. It has been adapted for CINEMA in both cartoon and live action versions, and is considered a classic of CHILDREN'S LITERATURE. Smith's later books include *The New Moon with the Old* (1963), *It Ends with Revelations* (1967), and *The Girl From the Candlelit Bath* (1978). She also wrote four volumes of autobiography,

Look Back with Love: A Manchester Childhood, Look Back with Mixed Feelings (1978), *Look Back with Astonishment* (1979), and *Look Back with Gratitude* (1985).

Suggested Reading
Grove, Valerie. *Dear Dodie: The Life of Dodie Smith* (London: Chatto & Windus, 1996).

Louise Harrington

Smith, Helen Zenna 1901–1985

The pseudonym of Australian-born Evadne Price, actress, journalist, playwright, television broadcaster, and writer of ROMANTIC FICTION and children's books. In WORLD WAR ONE, Price served in the British Ambulance Corps in France; from 1943 she was a war correspondent of *The People*, reporting on the liberation of concentration camps. After her retirement to Australia in 1976, she contributed a regular horoscope feature to Australian *Vogue*.

Under the Zenna Smith name, Price wrote a series of novels about an imaginary Helen Smith, beginning with *Not So Quiet... Step-Daughters of the War* (1930) in which Helen is an upper-class volunteer ambulance driver in wartime France. Commissioned as a parody of Remarque's *All Quiet on the Western Front* (1929), the book is a bitter anti-war text, which heaps up horrors unremittingly, offering a simultaneous critique of upper-class England, encapsulated by: 'You were glad some new fiendish torture had been invented by the chemists who are running this war. You were delighted to think some German mother's son was going to have the skin stripped from his poor face.' The sequels, *Women of the Aftermath* (1931), *Shadow Women* (1932), *Luxury Ladies* (1933), and *They Lived with Me* (1934), reflect a bitterness and pessimism about the postwar world, in which 'Nello' fails to find a role for herself. After a series of unsuccessful liaisons, she finds herself homeless on the Embankment, reflecting the discontent of a female 'lost generation'.

Suggested Reading
Marcus, Jane. 'Corpus/corps/corpse: Writing the Body in/at War', in Helen M. Cooper, Adrienne Auslander Munich and Susan Merrill Squier (eds), *Arms and the Woman: War, Gender, and Literary Representation* (Chapel Hill, NC, and London: University of North Carolina Press, 1989) 124–67.

Terry Phillips

Smith, Stevie 1902–1971

Poet and novelist, who continues to attract critical admiration for her deceptively simple, but strikingly original, poems and her three semi-autobiographical novels: *Novel on Yellow Paper* (1936), *Over the Frontier* (1938), and *The Holiday* (1949). Religious doubt, obsession with death, and a sharp but witty eye for the telling, ironic detail characterize her work and belie its apparent simplicity. In what is perhaps her most famous poem, 'Waving Not Drowning', many of her typical themes come together as Smith emphasizes the ways in which the simple gestures of life are so often and so tragically misread.

Born Florence Margaret Smith, she moved with her mother and older sister from Yorkshire to Palmers Green, London, after her father deserted the family when Smith was four. Smith would live the rest of her life with her beloved Aunt Margaret. Unspectacular as a student, Smith attended North London Collegiate School for Girls and a secretarial training college before beginning a 30-year secretarial career with the publishers C. Arthur Pearson (later Newnes, Pearson). In the mid-1920s she began writing poems, but was unsuccessful in publishing them until six were accepted by David Garnett at the *New Statesman* in 1935. After a collection of her poetry had been rejected and the editor told her to 'go and write a novel', she did, drafting it at work on the yellow carbon paper used at Pearson. *Novel on Yellow Paper* was a critical success and established Smith on the London literary scene. Her first book of poetry, *A Good Time Was Had by All*, followed in 1937 and the sequel to *Novel on Yellow Paper, Over the Frontier*, in 1938. The 1940s and 1950s were more uneven times for Smith, although several further collections of poetry and one more novel appeared. She attempted suicide in 1953, and when she could not return to work, was given a pension. She turned to book reviewing to supplement this meagre allowance and continued to try to publish her poetry.

In the early 1920s, Smith gained her nickname 'Stevie' (after the popular jockey Steve Donaghue) after being teased about her horseriding abilities and her physical approximation to a jockey. She relished this playful moniker – which was emphasized by her physical presentation of herself as well as by the illustrations which she insisted accompany her poems – and during the late 1950s and 1960s, with works like *Selected Poems* (1962), she came back into critical and popular favour. Her celebrity led to a host of readings and awards, including the Cholmondeley Award for Poetry in 1966 and the Gold Medal for Poetry, presented to her by Queen Elizabeth II in 1969. In the years since her death, popular attention and critical interest has consistently grown. Hugh Whitmore's 1977 play, *Stevie: A Play from the Life and Work of Stevie Smith*, was turned into a movie, *Stevie*, starring Glenda Jackson the following year, and scholarly studies continue to appear.

Suggested Reading

Civello, Catherine A. *Patterns of Ambivalence: The Fiction and Poetry of Stevie Smith* (Columbia, SC: Camden House, 1997).

Severin, Laura. *Stevie Smith's Resistant Antics* (Madison: University of Wisconsin Press, 1997).

Sternlicht, Sanford (ed.). *In Search of Stevie Smith* (Syracuse, NY: Syracuse University Press, 1991).

Jennifer Holberg

Smyth, Ethel 1858–1944

Composer, SUFFRAGIST, and autobiographer, of equally high repute in music and literature. Dame Ethel (or Ethyl) Smyth's most admired compositions are *Mass in D* (1891) and *The Wreckers* (1902–4). She also wrote the suffragette anthem, *The March of The Women* (1910). During a visit to Holloway, where Smyth was imprisoned for political protest, Sir Thomas Beecham described her 'Bacchic frenzy' as she conducted, with a toothbrush, fellow inmates singing the anthem below her cell window. In her late fifties, while engaged in WAR WORK as a radiographer in Paris, she began her ebullient and informative memoirs. Loss of hearing eventually curtailed musical composition but gave scope to her writing. *Impressions That Remained* (1919), the first of nine books, is the most popular and successful.

Smyth was a wildcat girl who grew into a virago of a woman. One of eight children from a high-ranking military family, she grew up in Frimley, near Aldershot. Her five sisters married, whilst she insisted on a musical training. She chose a single life, travelled widely and loved hunting, mountaineering, bicycling, and golf. After her musical apprenticeship in Leipzig, where she met Brahms, Grieg, and Clara Schumann, she struggled to get her operas performed. The precarious foothold of a female English composer was completely dislodged when war broke out in 1914. In England she had greater success, supported by influential friends and royal patronage, although she lamented the lack of an English operatic tradition and what she called a scarcity of 'mixed bathing in the sea of music'. She was awarded three Honorary Doctorates in music and became a Dame of the British Empire in 1922.

Impressions adeptly summons up characters, events, and ways of life now lost, and bears witness to a lifelong passion for women friends, the 'shining threads in my life'. Later autobiographies, including *As Time Went On* (1936) and *What Happened Next* (1940), candidly acknowledge physical attraction, as well as devotion, to many women and to one man. A mysterious chain of events in *Impressions* is later explained when she admits to the consummation in 1884 of an affair with Henry Brewster (H. B.). He sustained her emotional, intellectual, and creative life for the next 20 years, although she wrote to him 'I wonder why it is so much easier for me to love my own sex passionately, rather than yours?'

Smyth's books are exuberant and detailed, her similes graphic. For instance, she likens her friendship with the ex-Empress Eugénie, as fiery in disposition as herself, to 'a stroll on the upper slopes of Vesuvius'. In 1930 she met Virginia WOOLF, the last of her *grandes passions*. Woolf encouraged Smyth to write more explicitly: 'I should like an analysis of your sex life as Rousseau did his. More introspection. More intimacy.' While praising her books for their 'ripeness', Woolf also expostulates 'Lord! What an inconsistent woman you are!' Testy when criticized, Smyth always worked in sporadic bursts. Her spirit was indomitable and feminist and she leaves behind a rich musical portfolio, unjustly marginalized in its time, and a legacy of memorable writing.

Suggested Reading

Beecham, Thomas. 'Dame Ethel Smyth (1858–1944)', *The Musical Times*, 99 (July 1958) 363–5.

Crichton, Ronald (ed.). *The Memoirs of Ethel Smyth* (New York: Viking, 1987).

St John, Christopher. *Ethel Smyth: A Biography* (London: Longmans, 1959).

Val Scullion

Socialism

Socialists added a different perspective to late nineteenth-century debates over the 'Woman Question' and many of them played an important part in the campaigns of the WOMEN'S MOVEMENT. Socialist groups developed in Britain in the 1880s and 1890s, including the Social Democratic Federation (SDF, 1884), the FABIAN SOCIETY (1884), and the Independent Labour Party (ILP, 1893). In contrast to other political parties, they accepted women as full members and their rhetoric of equality included sex equality. They concentrated on 'making socialists', exploring the interconnections between personal emancipation, sexual politics, and social emancipation. This 'new life' socialism emphasized the importance of prefiguring the relationships of a future society in the everyday lives of individual socialists, and was expressed in cultural forms, including Clarion cycling clubs, rambling groups, literature, and socialist Sunday schools. This project proved attractive to women. Eleanor Marx, Katharine Bruce Glasier, Isabella Ford, Dora Montefiore, Enid Stacy, Margaret McMillan and Carolyn Martyn were among the pioneers who were popular platform speakers and also journalists. They were educated women from middle-class backgrounds, but a few working-class women also came to the fore. These included Ethel Carnie HOLDSWORTH, a former mill worker and prolific writer, and Ada Neild Chew, whose letters to the local newspaper on conditions of employment in the tailoring trade in Crewe in 1894 brought her to the attention of the ILP. She became a trade union organizer and later an organizer for the National Union of Women's Suffrage Societies.

Women activists increasingly found that there was a gap between socialist rhetoric of sex equality and political practice. Despite 'new life' socialism, the mainstream movement focused on economic questions, the class struggle, and the interests of male workers in industry. For many socialists, the 'woman question' was a bourgeois issue and of marginal concern. Some, however, attempted to explore the link between women's emancipation and the struggle for socialism and to theorize the relationship between sex and class. August Bebel's *Woman Under Socialism* (1879) examined the extent to which gender was socially constructed rather than biologically determined, and Frederick Engels's *The Origins of the Family, Private Property and the State* (1884) argued that women's oppression had an economic cause and that the first class oppression was by men over women in the family. Neither author, however, challenged the sexual division of labour.

Women socialists argued that only under socialism would women's emancipation be achieved, but contested the view that women's issues were peripheral to the class struggle. By questioning the emphasis on production rather than consumption and insisting that areas such as marriage, reproduction, and the relationship between men and women were political rather than personal issues, they began to reconfigure the nature of socialism itself. Women found a space to express their views in newspapers such as the *Clarion* and the *Labour Prophet* and also in the women's columns of the official newspapers of socialist groups. Glasier, Ford, McMillan, and many others also used novels or short stories to explore these questions.

Tensions between gender and class were brought into sharp relief by the campaign for women's SUFFRAGE in the decade before the First World War. The demand for a limited franchise, which would have excluded many working-class men and women, and the premise that sex oppression united all women in a common cause, meant that the suffrage campaign was a controversial question for socialists. Nonetheless, socialist and labour women were involved from the start. At the turn of the century, textile workers organized a petition in favour of women's suffrage and pursued the question through their local trade union or socialist group. The Women's Social and Political Union was established by members of the Manchester ILP who drew on their experience of socialist agitation in developing militant methods. Socialist women also took their interest in the economic and social problems faced by working-class women into the suffrage movement. They argued that the suffrage must take priority, since only if they were enfranchised could women work alongside men to achieve the kind of socialist society that would ensure women's emancipation.

After their partial enfranchisement in 1918, many socialist women pursued their feminist goals through the Labour Party, taking up issues such as family allowances, married women's right to work and access to CONTRACEPTION information. However, few gains were made as women faced hostility from a Party dominated by the trade unions and an emphasis on class. By the 1930s, the DEPRESSION, the rise of FASCISM and the threat of war made it even more difficult to give priority to gender inequalities. The Second World War raised women's expectations, but it was not until the late 1960s, a period of general political and social protest, that socialist women came to the fore once more in challenging women's unequal social and economic position. Throughout the twentieth century, therefore, socialist women have had to juggle competing loyalties to sex, class, and party, and their priorities have shifted according to the broader political context.

Suggested Reading

Hannam, June and Karen Hunt. *Socialist Women: Britain, 1880s to 1920s* (London: Routledge, 2001).

Laybourn, Keith. *The Rise of Socialism in Britain* (Stroud: Sutton, 1997).

Rowbotham, Sheila and Jeffery Weeks. *Socialism and the New Life* (London: Pluto, 1977).

June Hannam

Society of Women Writers and Journalists

Originally the Society of Women Journalists, the Society was founded in 1884 by the newspaper proprietor and philanthropist Joseph Snell Wood. It was amended in 1952 to include practitioners from other genres. 'An Association of Women for the benefit of Women and to be managed by Women', the Society aimed to promote and protect the personal and professional interests of its members in the United Kingdom, the Colonies, and abroad. It also intended to improve the status of journalism as a profession for women. While 65 women did belong to the Institute of Journalists, it was felt that this predominantly male organization 'did not engage the confidence of the ladies'.

In the first two months of the Society's life, 200 women, paying a subscription of one guinea, applied for membership. Snell Wood, who was a Director of *The Graphic* and *The Bystander* and Managing Director of *The Gentlewoman*, acted as Honorary Director for the first three years. The first President was Mrs Humphrey WARD, followed by Pearl Craigie (who wrote novels under the name of John Oliver Hobbes). Other Presidents included: Alice MEYNELL; the Duchess of Sutherland; Vera BRITTAIN; Flora Annie STEEL; the romantic novelist and journalist Annie S. Swan who was associated with the popular middle-class magazine *Woman at Home*; and the prominent *Daily Telegraph* journalist, Mary Billington. Writers such as Mrs Belloc LOWNDES, Sarah GRAND, and Lady Troubridge served as Vice-Presidents, while Rebecca WEST, Alice Head (editor of *Good Housekeeping*), and Julia Cairns (editor of *Weldon Publications*), among others, served as Council members. More recently Clemence DANE, Joyce Grenfell, and Nina Bawden have taken the role of President. Claiming not to be a 'politically "feminist" organization', its membership nevertheless included such controversial figures as Marie STOPES and Radclyffe HALL.

Since 1910 the Society's publication, *The Woman Journalist*, has reported on Society events and prizes, and reviewed members' publications. Maintaining strong ties with writers' organizations overseas, the Society is still in existence, with a worldwide membership of 500.

Suggested Reading

Livermore, Joan and Jean Bowden. *Centenary of The Society of Women Writers and Journalists, 1894–1994* (London: Phoenix Press, 1994).

Fiona Hackney

Somerville and Ross

Collaborative pseudonym for cousins Edith O'Enone Somerville (1858–1949) and Violet Florence Martin (1862–1915), writers of travel books, journalism, and novels including *The Real Charlotte* (1894), widely considered as the finest Irish novel of the nineteenth century, and the comic *Irish R. M.* trilogy (1899, 1908, 1915). Their writing sends up the customs of the Anglo-Irish Big House families and rural communities of the late Ascendancy period. From their earliest publications, the pair were noted for their use of idiomatic Anglo-Irish speech, which they described in a 1910 essay as 'a fabric built by Irish architects with English bricks, quite unlike anything of English construction'.

The pair met in 1886, after Edith had trained as an illustrator and Violet had begun publishing occasional journalism. Both were unusual for their period and class as suffragettes, foxhunters, and financially independent, working women. However, domestic responsibilities shaped their writing lives: estate debts required them to write profitable journalism, and frequent familial interruptions disturbed their creative privacy. From 1905, they lived together, and recent biographers emphasize the LESBIAN nature of their partnership, although their private writings do not indicate consummation. Edith continued to publish through the 1930s as Somerville and Ross, asserting that her deceased partner communicated with her through automatic writing.

Suggested Reading

Greene, Nicole Pepinster. 'Dialect and Social Identity in *The Real Charlotte'*, *New Hibernia Review*, 4.1 (Earrach/Spring 2000) 122–37.

Robinson, Hilary. *Somerville and Ross: A Critical Appreciation* (Dublin: Gill & Macmillan, 1980).

Ashlie Sponenberg

Spanish Civil War

A complex, brutal war, lasting from July 1936 to March 1939, fought principally between General Franco's Nationalist forces and the Republican government forces, although there were many factions on both sides. Monarchists, Catholics, and fascists supported Franco, and supporting the Republicans were COMMUNISTS, SOCIALISTS, and anarchists. Municipal elections held on 12 April 1931 revealed diminishing support for the monarchy, and on 14 April, following the abdication of King Alfonso XIII, Spain became a republic. However, many on the political right rejected social reform, and in July 1936, Franco's generals revolted against the legitimately elected Republican government and the war began.

The generals' revolt generated outrage outside Spain, particularly among intellectuals, communists and socialists, and by October 1936 International Brigades (groups of volunteer forces) were arriving in Spain, mainly to support the Republic. Many women went to give humanitarian aid, and some fought with the militia. Most volunteers were there to combat FASCISM, which was seriously threatening European political stability following the coming to power of Hitler in 1933. In August 1936, Europe adopted a policy of non-intervention in the war, to which the French and British governments adhered. However, fascist Germany and Italy, under Hitler and Mussolini, defied the Non-Intervention Agreement and supplied Franco with arms, equipment, and troops.

Massacres, assaults, and battles occurred all over Spain as Republicans and Nationalists tried to seize military advantage and civilians and combatants suffered alike. Key was the bombing of Guernica, the cultural centre of the Basque region in northern Spain, by German planes on 26 April 1937: the first example of the destruction of a town by aerial bombardment. The attack was indicative of terrifying future trends in aerial warfare and was the inspiration behind Picasso's painting *Guernica* (1937).

The Republican government, denied arms by the Western democracies, was no match for the Nationalists, supported by foreign fascist regimes. Franco's forces entered Madrid on 27 March 1939, and by the end of the month, the country was under Nationalist control. The war was over. Over half a million people had died, and more would die later. After the war, it was dangerous for Republicans to remain in Spain and many fled the country. Franco maintained a harsh and dictatorial rule until his death in 1975, with many political reprisals and executions in the years immediately following the war.

Suggested Reading

Preston, Paul. *A Concise History of the Spanish Civil War* (London: Fontana, 1996).

Fyrth, Jim and Sally Alexander (eds). *Women's Voices from the Spanish Civil War* (London: Lawrence & Wishart, 1991).

Marie Askham

Stark, Freya 1893–1993

Explorer, travel writer, photographer, and memoirist, best known for books on the Middle East. Stark began travelling as an infant, since her artist parents were constantly on the move in search of picturesque scenes. Her early years were divided between Italy and Devon, and as a small child she spoke English, Italian, and German. When her parents separated in 1903, she and her mother settled in Dronero, Piedmont. They had very little money, and when Freya was 11, she lost part of her scalp in an accident at a textile mill. In 1912 she began to study English and history at Bedford College, England, and during the war worked as a nurse and a censor. A broken engagement and four years of illness followed.

Stark started learning Arabic in 1921, and later attended the London School of Oriental Studies. In 1927, she made her first trip to the Middle East, visiting Damascus, Jebel, Druze, Transjordan, Palestine, and Egypt; and two years later, she visited Baghdad and worked as a subeditor for *The Baghdad Times*. In 1930–1 she made the solitary journey to eastern Iraq and Persia (Iran) which is described in the first and most famous of her 22 books, *The Valleys of the Assassins and Other Persian Travels* (1934). It recounts her search for the castles of the Assassins, a medieval Shia Muslim sect, and also tells of Luristan in western Persia, a little-known territory which she was the first woman to explore:

> In the wastes of civilisation, Luristan is still an enchanted name. Its streams are dotted blue lines on the map and the position of its hills a matter of taste. It is still a country for the explorer.... I spent a fortnight in that part of the country where one is less frequently murdered, and I saw the Lurs in their own medieval garb.

The Valleys of the Assassins combines detailed description of landscape and local culture with lively, witty accounts of the author's interactions with the Persians. The book was much admired on publication, and has remained in print.

During the Second World War, Stark organized anti-fascist propaganda in the Middle East, and travelled to the United States to rally support for the Arab cause and work against Zionism. In 1947, she married Stewart Perowne, but they divorced in 1952. In the same period, she began writing her memoirs, which cover the years from 1893–1946: *Traveller's Prelude* (1950), *Beyond Euphrates* (1951), *The Coast of Incense* (1953), and *Dust in the Lion's Paw* (1961). Stark continued to explore well into her sixties, and her journey through Asia in the footsteps of Alexander the Great resulted in three of her most widely read books, *Ionia: A Quest* (1954), *The Lycian Shore* (1956), and *Alexander's Path: From Caria to Cilicia* (1958). Stark was made a Dame of the British Empire in 1972, and spent her last years based in Asolo, Italy, often travelling with male companions, and relishing her fame and the media attention she received.

Suggested Reading
Geniesse, Jane Fletcher. *Passionate Nomad: The Life of Freya Stark* (London: Chatto & Windus, 1999).
Izzard, Molly. *Freya Stark: A Biography* (London: Hodder & Stoughton, 1993).
Maitland, Alexander. *A Tower in a Wall* (Edinburgh: Blackwood, 1982).

Faye Hammill

Steel, Flora Annie 1847–1929

Novelist, short-story, and non-fiction writer whose work draws mainly on her experiences in colonial India, where she lived and worked for 22 years. Steel published over 30 books, becoming somewhat of a literary celebrity. Born in Harrow into the cultural milieu of British imperialism, the daughter of Isabella MacCallum and government official George Webster, Flora Steel received little formal education but was renowned in her large family for her energy. Marriage in 1867 to civil servant Henry Steel took her to India where a daughter, Mabel, was born in 1870. Steel refused the role of a typical *memsahib*, but learnt Punjabi and took an active interest in local matters of HEALTH and EDUCATION, eventually becoming inspector of girls' schools in the Punjab region. Although supporting British rule in India, Steel strongly emphasized the moral responsibility it generated.

Her first publication, a book of tales based on Indian folklore, *Wide Awake Stories* (1884), was republished in England as *Tales of the Punjab* (1894), and illustrated by J. L. Kipling. Further collections followed, including *From the Five Rivers* (1893) and *In the Permanent Way* (1897).

Steel returned to Britain in 1889, but much of her best work, including her first novel, *Miss Stuart's Legacy* (1893), revisits and demonstrates the complexities of colonial India. *India through the Ages* (1908) is a non-fictional work aimed at educating the British public, and she wrote four historical novels on the lives of the Mogul Emperors, involving murder, disguise, and victorious campaigns.

Steel's literary reputation was firmly established with her novel about the Indian Mutiny of 1857, *On the Face of the Waters* (1896). This and other works on India reveal, however, a certain inability to transcend contemporary racist ideologies. Whether racist attitudes evident in her novels should be attributed to Steel or to her characters remains a moot point, but *On the Face of the Waters* was certainly written in a spirit of mutual understanding and respect. It is an attempt, as Steel writes, 'to give a photograph – that is a picture in which the differentiation caused by colour is left out – of a time which neither the fair race or the dark race is ever likely to forget or forgive'.

Steel also wrote two dramatic novels set in Britain, *A Sovereign Remedy* (1906) and *The Gifts of the Gods* (1911). A self-published pamphlet demonstrates her ardent support of women's SUFFRAGE, and her belief that sex is at the root of the subjugation of women is evident in her last novel, *The Curse of*

Eve (1929). An autobiography, *The Garden of Fidelity* (1929), was published posthumously.

Rivalling Kipling in her day as a writer of EMPIRE, Steel's work has now virtually disappeared from that canon. *Tales of the Punjab*, however, remains in print, a new edition in 2002 bringing some deserved attention to Steel's life and work.

Suggested Reading

Powell, Violet. *Flora Annie Steel: Novelist of India* (London: Heinemann, 1981).
Richardson, LeeAnne Marie. 'On the Face of the Waters: Flora Annie Steel and the Politics of Feminist Imperialism', in Brenda Ayres (ed.), *Silent Voices: Forgotten Novels by Victorian Women Writers* (London: Praeger, 2003).

Luanda Stannard

Stern, G. B. 1890–1973

Gladys Bertha (later changed to Bronwyn) Stern was born in London to a non-practising Jewish family with cosmopolitan connections, who underwent substantial business losses during her teens. Educated at Notting Hill High School, she travelled in Germany and Switzerland before spending two years at the Academy of Dramatic Art (where she later instituted a named prize for 'potential talent'). She was associated with the South Lodge set of young writers around Violet HUNT and Ford Madox Hueffer.

In 1914 she published the first of her many novels, *Pantomine* (1914). She also wrote plays (some of them adapted from her novels), short stories, and a series of 'ragbag chronicles' of personal reminiscences and observations, which take a non-linear approach to autobiographical narrative. Her passion for Jane Austen led to two volumes of essays on her work, produced in collaboration with Sheila KAYE-SMITH. She also loved R. L. Stevenson, publishing biographical and critical studies of him, and editing collections of his work. She dabbled in many genres: *The Shortest Night* (1931) is a mystery; *Credit Title* (1961), a novel for children, draws on her experiences in Hollywood, including an earthquake; and *Bouquet* (1927) gives an account of a gastronomic and oenophilic tour in France. Her fondness for dogs resulted in several canine-centred fictions, of which *The Ugly Dachshund* (1938) is probably the best known.

Stern married Geoffrey Holdsworth in 1919, and they collaborated on a number of works. The marriage was dissolved some ten years later. She had an extensive network of friends in the literary and theatrical worlds of the time, to whom she was known as 'Peter', from the heroine of her early novel, *Twos and Threes* (1916), who preferred to be known by this abbreviation of the sentimental 'Pepita' bestowed by her father. Stern was a close friend of Rebecca WEST, who called her 'Tynx'. Her devotion to her friends found expression not only throughout her volumes of memoirs but also in *And Did He Stop and Speak To You? Essays on Friends of the Author* (1957). She travelled a good deal, and after the Second World War she converted to Roman Catholicism. Stern appears to have suffered at least two nervous breakdowns.

Her most popular works were undoubtedly the five volumes of the Rakonitz chronicles, which draw on her family background. They begin with *Tents of Israel* (1924), reissued as *The Matriarch*, and conclude with *The Young Matriarch* (1942), which took the saga up to the Second World War. Issues of Jewish identity were also addressed in *Children of No Man's Land* (1919), and more obliquely in *The Augs: An Exaggeration* (1933), surely a response to current events in Germany. Stern's work also engaged with the problems facing women during a period of social changes and new moral codes. Her style is full of vivacity and ebullience, with flashes of satiric astringency. She has received no attention from critics.

Suggested Reading

Neuberger, Julia. Introduction to *A Deputy Was King* by G. B. Stern (London: Virago, 1988) i–xii.

Lesley A. Hall

Stopes, Marie 1880–1958

Scientist and author, but best known as a birth control campaigner and sex guru. Marie Charlotte Carmichael Stopes was a second generation feminist, her mother being the feminist and literary scholar Charlotte (née Carmichael) Stopes. After obtaining a B.Sc. at University College London in 1902, she had a remarkably successful career in paleobotany, the study of fossil plants. Stopes married Canadian botanist Reginald Ruggles Gates in 1911, retaining her own name and continuing her professional career. Concerned at her failure to become pregnant, Stopes studied scientific works on sex in the British Museum, and finally obtained an annulment on grounds of non-consummation in 1916. In 1915 she learned about modern contraceptive methods from American birth control campaigner Margaret Sanger. Via the birth control movement, Stopes met Humphrey Verdon Roe, a wealthy young Royal Flying Corps officer, who put up the £200 required to publish her manuscript on marriage, based on her research and personal experience.

Appearing early in 1918, *Married Love* became a runaway bestseller, generating a huge correspondence, and was followed by *Wise Parenthood* (1918) and numerous other works. In the same year, Stopes married Roe. Early in 1921, they established a birth control clinic in a poor area of North London, and held a mass meeting at the Queen's Hall, breaching existing taboos on discussing CONTRACEPTION publicly. In 1923 Stopes's libel suit against Catholic doctor Halliday Sutherland for writing of a 'Doctor of German Philosophy' giving pernicious advice to working women provided her, and the birth control movement, with enormous publicity, although the verdict was inconclusive. In 1924 Stopes's son Harry was born (following an earlier stillbirth), and she was presented at Court. The rest of her life saw a decline. She became increasingly dogmatic and unable to co-operate with the rest of the birth control movement. None of her later works rivalled the success of *Married Love* and *Wise Parenthood*. She became estranged from her son as a result of her objections to his marriage, and also from her husband, though she enjoyed a number of amorous friendships with younger men.

Her non-fictional work shows Stopes as an excellent writer, capable of striking the tone suitable for her intended audiences, but her more literary efforts – plays, poems, novels, and short stories – largely failed. Her only published novel, *Love's Creation*, published under the pseudonym Marie Carmichael (1928) is not a success, and most of her poetry is deeply embarrassing. Her *Journal from Japan* (1912), however, is an underrated example of women's travel writing, and some of her plays were produced to moderate success.

Her work as a scientist was of some importance, but Stopes's lasting significance derives from her work in promoting birth control, and disseminating sexual advice. She has been criticized for EUGENICIST views, pervasive at the time, but these seem to have impinged little on practice in her clinics or the advice she gave to individuals. What struck contemporaries was her clarion call for the acknowledgement of women's rights to sexual pleasure, and to control over their reproductive systems.

Suggested Reading

Geppert, Alexander C. T. 'Divine Sex, Happy Marriage, Regenerated Nation: Marie Stopes's Marital Manual *Married Love* and the Making of a Best-seller, 1918–1955', *Journal of the History of Sexuality*, 8 (1998) 389–433.

Hall, Lesley A. 'Uniting Science and Sensibility: Marie Stopes and the Narratives of Marriage in the 1920s', in Angela Ingram and Daphne Patai (eds), *Rediscovering Forgotten Radicals: British Women Writers, 1889–1939* (Chapel Hill, NC: University of North Carolina Press, 1993) 118–36.

Lesley A. Hall

Storm, Lesley 1903–1975

Novelist and playwright, of English and Scottish descent. The daughter of a minister, Storm gained an MA at Aberdeen University. She planned to be a journalist, but her marriage prevented this. After several novels, which she claimed she preferred to forget, Storm wrote exclusively theatre and film scripts. Her play *Dark Horizon* (1934) was a prophetic picture of London during the Blitz, while *Tony Draws a Horse* (1939) ran for over a year in the West End, had several postwar London revivals and was filmed twice. *Heart of a City*

(1942) showed the spirit of The Windmill Theatre ('We never closed!') and was later filmed as *Tonight and Every Night*.

Black Chiffon (1949), a psychological study of a woman driven to the edge by her demanding family and diagnosed as being unhealthily attached to her son, ran for 416 West End performances. It was successfully revived, toured, televised, and went on to become a repertory warhorse. *Roar Like A Dove* (1957) was described in one review as: 'A play that talks or thinks about the sexual act for two and a half hours.'

Her film scripts range from the B Movie to the sublime. Among the best known are *The Fallen Idol* (1948), adapted with Graham Greene from his short story; *The Heart of the Matter* (1953), also adapted from Greene; and *The Spanish Gardener* (1956), adapted from A. J. Cronin.

Suggested Reading

Gale, Maggie B. *West End Women: Women and the London Stage, 1918–1962* (London: Routledge, 1996).

Morgan, Fidelis (ed.). *The Years Between: Plays by Women on the London Stage, 1900–1950*. Preface by Susannah York (London: Virago, 1995).

Fidelis Morgan

Strachey, Julia 1901–1979

A niece of Lytton Strachey, who never fulfilled her enormous promise but nevertheless wrote one novella, *Cheerful Weather for the Wedding* (1932), which is a minor classic. Strachey went to Bedales School, where she was a contemporary of Frances Partridge, and the Slade School of Fine Art, after which she worked as a photographer, a publisher's reader, and a model. She was married twice, the second time to the art critic Lawrence Gowing.

Julia Strachey worked obsessively on her two novels (her second, *The Man on the Pier*, came out in 1951). *Cheerful Weather* is a very funny, sardonic, painful book about a girl on her wedding day who realizes her mistake while her mother continues to be inexorably and maddeningly cheerful: '"Half-past twelve already!" said Mrs Thatcham. She stared round the hall with her clear, orange, glassy eyes. "Has Dolly gone up to dress yet?" she asked, with a haggard look at Kitty.' Frances Partridge wrote that: 'The chief stars in Julia Strachey's galaxy were Chekhov, James, Proust and Groucho Marx', while Virginia WOOLF said of *Cheerful Weather* that it was 'a very cute, clever, indeed rather remarkable acidulated story...I think it astonishingly good...It's extraordinarily complete and sharp and individual.'

Suggested Reading

Partridge, Frances. Introduction to *Cheerful Weather for the Wedding* by Julia Strachey (London: Persephone Books, 2002) v–x.

Strachey, Julia and Frances Partridge. *Julia: A Portrait of Julia Strachey by Herself and Frances Partridge* (London: Gollancz, 1983).

Nicola Beauman

Strachey, Ray 1887–1940

Suffragette, PACIFIST, and author of *The Cause: A Short History of the Women's Movement in Great Britain* (1928). Born Rachel Conn Costelloe in London, Strachey experienced much upheaval in her early life. Following her parents' separation, she went to live with her father; when he died, her grandmother was given custody. Strachey's feminist mother believed in women's sexual freedom, but at Newnham College, Cambridge, Strachey developed a different interest in a feminism of public service. In 1909, she established the 'Younger Suffragists' with a friend who introduced her to the Strachey family; eventually she married Oliver, brother of Lytton. This was only one of her links to BLOOMSBURY: an aunt married Bertrand Russell, and her sister married Adrian Stephen, Virginia WOOLF's brother.

An active SUFFRAGIST, Strachey became critical of PANKHURST militancy and devoted herself to the National Union of Women's Suffrage Societies (NUWSS) and its founder, Millicent Garrett Fawcett, of whom she wrote a biography in 1913. Strachey is best remembered for *The Cause*, in which she controversially praised John Stuart Mill above Mary Wollstonecraft, who was much more in vogue with feminists of the time: 'Mill had pondered, as no man had pondered before, over the implications and the results of the subjection of a whole sex . . . It was the removal of the age-long subjection and submission of women from which he hoped so much.' Strachey also wrote *Women's Suffrage and Women's Service* (1927) and *Our Freedom and Its Results* (1936).

Suggested Reading
Caine, Barbara. 'Mothering Feminism/Mothering Feminists: Ray Strachey and *The Cause*', *Women's History Review*, 8.2 (1999) 295–310.

Ashlie Sponenberg

Struther, Jan 1901–1953

British novelist, poet, hymn-writer, and journalist, creator of the famous Mrs Miniver. Born Joyce Anstruther in 1901, she was the daughter of Liberal MP Harry Anstruther and Dame Eva Anstruther. Educated privately in London, she married Anthony Maxtone Graham, a Lloyd's broker, in 1923, and had three children.

During the 1930s, Struther wrote poems and essays for various NEWSPAPERS and journals, including *Punch*, the *New Statesman*, and the *Spectator*. She published *Try Anything Twice: Essays and Sketches* (1938) and two collections of poetry, *Betsinda Dances and Other Poems* (1931) and *Sycamore Squares and Other Verses* (1932); Valerie Grove writes that her poems are 'crisp, succinct, metropolitan lyrics full of memorable and pertinent lines on love and loss, youth and age'. In 1937 editor Peter Fleming asked Struther to liven up the Court Page of *The Times*, which he thought seemed to consist solely of articles about woodpeckers and stoats. He requested the diary of 'an ordinary sort of woman who leads an ordinary sort of life – rather like yourself', and so Mrs Miniver, a middle-class housewife and mother, was created, and her journal entries were published in book form in October 1939.

Unlike the 1942 Hollywood film version, which portrayed the Miniver family as exemplifying the traditional British stiff upper lip during the Blitz, Struther's book is a series of sketches about respectable British life in the 1930s prior to and during the Phoney War. It is a work that is easy to criticize because of its genteel heroine and comfortable middle-class domesticity, but Struther has Mrs Miniver gently poke fun at her acquaintances (of one she writes that 'She would have gone to the guillotine sooner than use the expression "week-end" ') and she also expresses exasperation with the conservative rituals of her social milieu: 'How silly it was, this convention – relaxed a little nowadays but still surprisingly obstinate – that you must not invite one half of a married couple to dinner without the other. Even when both were equally charming, she often wished she could ask them on different days.' Notable not only for its humour, but also for its portrayal of class, and its preoccupation with both Englishness and foreignness, *Mrs Miniver* has often been compared to E. M. DELAFIELD's *The Diary of a Provincial Lady*.

Mrs Miniver was enormously popular, especially in America, where the MGM film starring Greer Garson won six Oscars. President Roosevelt told Struther that *Mrs Miniver* hastened America's entry into the war, while Winston Churchill said it had done more for the Allied cause than a 'flotilla of battleships'. MGM released a sequel, *The Miniver Story*, in 1950; Struther disliked it, and successfully sued the studio for killing off Mrs Miniver.

During the war years, Struther lectured extensively in the United States, and as well as poems and articles, she also wrote hymns, of which the most famous is 'Lord of All Hopefulness, Lord of All Joy'. She and Maxtone Graham divorced in 1947, and shortly afterwards she married Adolf Placzek, a Jewish refugee from Vienna. Jan Struther died of cancer in New York.

Suggested Reading

Grove, Valerie. Introduction to *Mrs Miniver* by Jan Struther (London: Virago, 1989) i–xxi.

Light, Alison. *Forever England: Femininity, Literature and Conservatism Between the Wars* (London: Routledge, 1991).

Maxtone Graham, Ysenda. *The Real Mrs Miniver* (London: John Murray, 2001).

Louise Harrington

Stuart, Muriel 1885–1967

Author of five books of poems published between 1916 and 1927, which were well reviewed in Britain and America, but are now mostly forgotten. One reason for the oversight is the surprising scarcity of her work in anthologies, probably because of its frankness about social injustices. A new, slightly altered, edition of Muriel Stuart's *Selected Poems* (1927), published in 2000, is a useful indication of her range. Her original frontispiece paid tribute to Thomas Hardy, who had called her poetry 'superlatively good'. In 1926, Henry Savage declared, 'there is no English woman poet living today who is Muriel Stuart's peer'.

Christ at Carnival, and Other Poems (1916) includes sharply dramatized protests against war, and was followed in 1922 by *Poems*. Stuart's dramatic monologues, such as 'Mrs Effingham's Swan Song' or 'Mrs Hamilton', are reminiscent of the Victorian poet Augusta Webster's exploration of women's socially constructed roles and values. In 'The Bastard', a jilted woman addresses her unborn child, whom, she feels, will weary of her body even as her lover did, and she will pay the price. Like this poem, several of Stuart's other pieces are cynical anti-sentimental dramatizations of relationships between men and women; for example, 'In the Orchard' or 'The Gay Girl to the Good Girl'.

Suggested Reading

McCulloch, Margery Palmer. 'Forgotten Founder: The Poetry of Muriel Stuart', *PEN International* 45.1 (1995) 29–32.

McCulloch, Margery Palmer. 'Muriel Stuart: A Cuckoo in the Nest of Singing Birds?', *Scottish Literary Journal* 16.1 (1989) 51–8.

Jane Dowson

Suffragism

Women's suffrage was one of the most controversial issues raised by feminists before 1914, since the demand that women should take an active part in politics challenged gender divisions and undermined conventional definitions of 'femininity'. An organized campaign for the vote began as early as the 1860s, but it was the militant tactics adopted in the decade preceding the First World War that captured the imagination of the public and provided the images that are still familiar today. The campaign was spearheaded by new, national organizations: the National Union of Women's Suffrage Societies (NUWSS), formed from provincial groups in 1897 and led by Millicent Fawcett; the Women's Social and Political Union (WSPU), established by Emmeline and Christabel PANKHURST in 1903; and the Women's Freedom League (WFL), set up as a breakaway group from the WSPU in 1907 by Teresa Billington-Greig and Charlotte Despard. The movement drew on a broad basis of support, including textile workers, teachers, clerical workers, and nurses as well as educated women from middle- and upper-middle-class families.

The leaders of the WSPU, who had gained experience in the SOCIALIST movement, began to develop new, direct action tactics. At first they disrupted political meetings by shouting the slogan 'Votes for Women', but later turned to large-scale smashing of windows, setting fire to empty buildings, and destroying paintings. This led to arrests and imprisonment. After 1909, suffrage prisoners went on hunger strike to protest at being denied the status of political prisoners and many were then forcibly fed. The WFL did not agree with the destruction of property but carried out their own forms of militant action, including tax resistance and a boycott of the 1911 census. Militants were described as suffragettes by contemporaries to distinguish them from the 'constitutional' suffragists of the NUWSS who were reluctant to break the law, although they gradually began to take part in large demonstrations and processions.

Women artists and writers produced propaganda for the campaign. Each group had its own newspaper: *The Common Cause* (NUWSS), *Votes for Women* (WSPU) and *The Vote* (WFL). Pamphlets, novels, drama, and poetry were all used to good effect: the two plays, *How the Vote Was Won* (1908) by Cicely HAMILTON and *Votes for Women* (1907) by Elizabeth ROBINS, were performed regularly by local suffrage groups. Members of the Artists' Suffrage League produced striking imagery for posters and banners which, Lisa Tickner suggests, had the power to 'shape thoughts, focus debates and stimulate action'.

The intensity of feeling and the daring of suffragettes encouraged women from a variety of backgrounds to give up everything for the cause, and transformed the lives of those who took part. The campaign for the vote led to debate about the causes of women's oppression and the meaning of women's emancipation. This went beyond the question of political exclusion to explore sexual issues and men's power over women within marriage. Christabel Pankhurst's influential pamphlet *The Great Scourge and How to End It* (1913) claimed that women's economic, political, and sexual subordination to men was responsible for PROSTITUTION and the spread of venereal disease, while Cicely Hamilton's bestselling book, *Marriage as a Trade*, drew a parallel between prostitution and women's economic dependence within marriage. Despite their differences, women who took part in the movement did gain a heightened sense of solidarity with other women and developed a feminist consciousness. This was difficult to sustain in the more hostile climate of the interwar years and had to be discovered anew by the women's liberation movement of the 1960s and 1970s.

Women over 30 who were local government electors or married to such electors were granted the right to vote in 1918. Approximately five million women were still excluded until 1928 when women over 21 were enfranchised, thereby finally ensuring equal voting rights for both sexes.

Suggested Reading
Bartley, Paula. *Votes for Women, 1860–1928* (London: Hodder & Stoughton, 1998).

Holton, Sandra Stanley. *Suffrage Days: Stories from the Women's Suffrage Movement* (London: Routledge, 1996).
Joannou, Maroula and June Purvis (eds). *The Women's Suffrage Movement: New Feminist Perspectives* (Manchester: Manchester University Press, 1998).
Tickner, Lisa. *The Spectacle of Women: Imagery of the Suffrage Campaign, 1907–1914* (London: Chatto & Windus, 1987).

June Hannam

Swanwick , Helena M. 1864–1939

Suffragist, pacifist, writer, and editor, with a high profile in British political life. Born Helena Sickert in Germany, she moved to England with her family when she was four. Both her father Oswald and her brother Walter were artists. She attended Girton College, Cambridge, and in 1888 married Frederick Tertius Swanwick, who died in 1931. She worked as a lecturer and a journalist, and published her first book, *The Small-Town Garden*, in 1907.

In 1909, Swanwick became the first editor of *Common Cause*, the magazine of the NUWSS. Her PACIFIST views made her antagonistic to the WSPU, and eventually to the NUWSS itself, when the leadership refused to condemn Britain's involvement in the First World War. *The Future of the Women's Movement* (1913) set out her views on universal SUFFRAGE, and she went on to publish numerous books and pamphlets on subjects including the Union of Democratic Control, the League of Nations, foreign policy, war, and international security. She was a member of the British government delegation to the League of Nations Assembly in 1924 and 1929, and in 1931 was made a Companion of Honour for her distinguished public work. In her autobiography, *I Have Been Young* (1935), she traces her feminist views back to a childhood realization that 'All my brothers had rights as persons; not I.' In 1939, depressed by failing health and the rise of FASCISM in Europe, she committed suicide.

Suggested Reading
Spender, Dale. *Time and Tide Wait For No Man* (London: Pandora Press, 1984).

Faye Hammill

Syrett, Netta 1865–1943

Novelist, short-story writer, playwright. Her first stories appeared in *The Yellow Book* during the 1890s, and during her long career she published 38 novels, 27 short stories, four plays, and 20 children's books. Her themes and subjects were topical ones: SOCIALISM, the Woman Question, Irish folklore, the Labour Movement, EDUCATIONAL reform and Aestheticism.

Born in London, she trained as a teacher, but she soon turned to writing to make her living. Her earliest stories and novels deal with marriage and the New Woman; these include *The Day's Journey* (1906), *Rose Cottingham* (1915), and

Drender's Daughter (1911). In 1938, her novel *Portrait of a Rebel* (1929) was made into a successful movie, *A Woman Rebels*, starring Katherine Hepburn. She channelled her love for teaching into writing plays, travel books, and fairy-tales for young people, *Tinkelly Winkle* (1923) being her best known. Her later books, including her last novel, *Gemini* (1940), often deal with psychic phenomena. Her works are not widely available, but they provide a valuable insight into the mental, moral, and social climate of her day.

Suggested Reading

Ardis, Ann. 'Toward a Redefinition of "Experimental Writing": Netta Syrett's Realism, 1908–12', in Alison Booth (ed.), *Famous Last Words: Changes in Gender and Narrative Closure* (Charlottesville: University Press of Virginia, 1993), 259–79.

Owens, Jill T. 'Netta Syrett: A Chronological, Annotated Bibliography of Her Works, 1890–1940)', *Bulletin of Bibliography*, 45 (March 1988) 8–14.

Jill Jones

T

Taylor, Elizabeth 1912–1975

Novelist and short-story writer who has been compared to Jane Austen for her restrained, witty, and penetrating prose. In her lifetime, Elizabeth Taylor was popular and highly acclaimed, but her novels fell out of print until they were revived in the 1980s by VIRAGO Press. Born in Reading, she worked as a governess and librarian before marrying John Taylor, a businessman, in 1936. She had two children, and the family lived in Penn, a Buckinghamshire village. Taylor wrote her first novel, *At Mrs Lippincote's* (1945), during the war while her husband was in the RAF. An immediate success, it introduced themes and a tone which would endure throughout her career. The story is deceptively simple and quiet, recounting the difficulties of Julia, the wife of an RAF officer, when she follows him to a wartime posting in the north of England. The novel is driven by the character of Julia and her conflict with those around her, addressed with an economical, sophisticated wit. Taylor's key concern is the awkward inability of people to understand each other.

Taylor wrote in *The New York Herald Tribune*: 'I...very much like reading books in which practically nothing ever happens' (11 October 1953). With her mastery of restraint and understatement, the drama in her work is beneath the surface. Her dissections of human emotions are acute, as this, from her second novel, *Palladian* (1946), demonstrates: 'She smiled gallantly, controlling her trembling lips. It was the worst thing she could have done. Tom could not bear stoicism in those he hurt, could not bear the guilt of forcing them into such courage.' Such style won Taylor many admirers. Rosamund LEHMANN described her as 'sophisticated, sensitive, and brilliantly amusing, with a kind of stripped, piercing feminine wit and a power of creating and maintaining a fine nervous tension'.

Elizabeth Taylor published 12 novels, including *Angel* (1957), which was selected in 1984 by the Book Marketing Council as one of the 'Best Novels of Our Time', and *Mrs Palfrey at the Claremont* (1971), an examination of the loneliness and indignities of old age, which featured in 2003 in a list of 'The Greatest Novels of All Time', in the British newspaper the *Observer*. She also published four highly acclaimed collections of short stories.

Like Austen, Taylor concerned herself with a small section of English life. She wrote 'I should like to feel that the people in my books are essentially English and set down against a truly English background.' Until now Taylor's work appears to have largely escaped academic critical attention, perhaps because of the characterization of her novels as popular, middle class, domestic, and limited in scope. This is now beginning to change as academics turn their attention to the middlebrow female writers of the early and mid-twentieth century.

Suggested Reading

Brown Gillette, Jane. ' "Oh, What a Something Web We Weave": The Novels of Elizabeth Taylor', *Twentieth Century Literature*, 35.1 (Spring 1989) 94–112.

Humble, Nicola. *The Feminine Middlebrow Novel, 1920s to 1950s* (Oxford: Oxford University Press, 2001).

Leclercq, Florence. *Elizabeth Taylor* (Boston: Twayne, 1985).

Erica Brown

Tey, Josephine 1896–1952

The pseudonym of Elizabeth Mackintosh, author of crime fiction challenging most of the established tropes, including the notion of historical 'fact'. She worked as a Physical Education teacher, which provided rich material for the intense training college setting in *Miss Pym Disposes* (1946). Tey was successful as a playwright under the name Gordon Daviot, but is now remembered for her crime fiction.

Her 1929 debut, *The Man in the Queue*, presented the 'great detective' as Alan Grant, a working policeman, whose uncanny intuition proves as fallible as it is insightful. Her spinster sleuth, Lucy Pym, author of a bestselling psychology book, discovers a subversive truth about herself: that she is incapable of sending a killer to the gallows. Tey is probably best known for her late work, *The Daughter of Time* (1951), in which a bedridden Grant rehabilitates Richard the Third by uncovering the bias and poor research of the historical record. In one of her more startling plots about imposture, *Brat Farrar* (1949), the so-called villain, much to his own surprise, turns out to be both detective and key to the mystery.

Tey works through independent single figures of both genders, who learn to live socially engaged lives without leaning on others. Her main characters are preoccupied with faces as the starting point for knowledge. To Grant, Richard III, 'had that incommunicable, that indescribable look that childhood suffering leaves behind it'.

Suggested Reading

Martin, Christina R. 'Josephone Tey: Scottish Detective Novelist', *Studies in Scottish Literature* 29 (1996) 191–204.

Susan Rowland

Thirkell, Angela 1890–1961

Children's author, biographer, and novelist, best known for her 'Barsetshire' series, beginning with *High Rising* (1933) and ending with *Three Score and Ten* (1962). Though Thirkell's locale is borrowed from Trollope, Jane Austen is her model. These novels become increasingly elegiac for an imagined Edwardian social stability in which gentlewomen of the rural Home Counties are, with the assistance of 'Nurse', free to enjoy the sensuous pleasures of mothering babies and the picturesque delights of the mischievous and unfettered young. Thirkell thought herself 'too reticent to describe passion' but the episodic plots of such novels as *Wild Strawberries* (1935), *Before Lunch* (1939), and *Growing Up* (1943) are structured by romance conventions.

Family and community life offers a poignant but absurd spectacle for the ageing mother whose viewpoint often focuses the narrative. Despite their conservatism, which became more overtly political after the Second World War, Thirkell's novels explore the imaginative independence of middle-aged women, some of them writers. Mrs Morland, a single mother, supports her son, Tony, the 'demon' in *The Demon in the House* (1934), by writing bestselling whodunnits with a female dressmaker as detective. Though Mrs Morland may be, as Thirkell acknowledged, an idealization of herself as writer, it is through the figure of Mrs Brandon, the apparently indolent mistress of a large family house, that Thirkell most subtly negotiates her middlebrow cultural status. In *The Brandons* (1939), Mrs Brandon's authority is closely linked to her power to assert control over what is read to her by a sequence of infatuated, aspiring male authors, who need her approval far more than she needs theirs. Her security derives from both her economic and cultural capital and her sexual invulnerability.

Thirkell herself inherited considerable cultural capital but was sexually vulnerable. Her childhood, celebrated in *Three Houses* (1931), introduced her to a range of artists, scholars, and literary figures. She was the daughter of an eminent classicist, J. W. Mackail, granddaughter of Edward Burne-Jones, cousin of Kipling and Stanley Baldwin, and friend of John Buchan. However, two failed marriages left her financially insecure. She had two sons by her first husband, an abusive alcoholic, and a third by her second, an Australian engineer whom she divorced in 1928 after eight years in Australia. Her journey out became the thinly fictionalized account of a journey on a mutinous troop-ship, *Trooper to the Southern Cross* (1934), republished by VIRAGO in 1985. Her success in representing the discourse and attitudes of her narrator, a decent but unsophisticated Australian doctor, reveal a talent for black dead-pan humour unlike the more Wodehousian comedy of the Barsetshire novels.

In the thirties Thirkell's work was very varied. *Ankle Deep* (1933), comparable to Elizabeth BOWEN's novels, verges on tragedy. *Tribute for Harriette* (1936) is a study of the Regency courtesan, Harriette Wilson. Thirkell's cultural eclecticism is reflected in the aspiration of a character in *Summer Half* (1937) to marry 'someone like Hamlet and Richard the Second and Richard Hannay and Browning'.

Whereas Thirkell's son, the novelist Colin McInnes, dismissed his mother's work as 'sterile and life-denying', recent studies recuperate her as a social satirist and stylist.

Suggested Reading

Fritzer, Penelope. *Ethnicity and Gender in the Barsetshire Novels of Angela Thirkell* (Westport, CT: Greenwood, 1999).

Mather, Rachel R. *The Heirs of Jane Austen: Twentieth-Century Writers of the Comedy of Manners* (New York: Peter Lang, 1996).

Strickland, Margot. *Angela Thirkell: Portrait of a Lady Novelist* (London: Duckworth, 1972).

Mary Grover

Thompson, Flora 1876–1947

Fiction-writer, essayist, and poet, best known for her *Lark Rise to Candleford* trilogy, based on her early life in Oxfordshire. The eldest of six children of a stone mason, Flora Timms grew up in poverty. The girls from her village normally went into service, but Flora became a Post Office clerk instead. She began working at 14, and ten years later married another clerk, John Thompson. They moved to Bournemouth, where Flora continued to work but also bore two children and began writing, secretly at first, to avoid the disapproval of her relations. She won a prize for an essay on Austen, and began to contribute love stories and articles about nature and village life to local papers, WOMEN'S MAGAZINES, and later national NEWSPAPERS. From 1920 to 1927 she contributed a monthly column of notes on country life to the *Catholic Fireside*. From 1922 these were titled 'The Peverel Papers', and selections were published in volume form in 1979 and 1986. Her collection of poems, *Bog Myrtle and Peat*, appeared in 1921. Her reputation was established with her subtle evocation of the countryside of her childhood in *Lark Rise* (1939), *Over to Candleford* (1941), and *Candleford Green* (1943), later published together as *Lark Rise to Candleford* (1945).

Thompson's detailed accounts of houses, food, clothes, working habits, and community life suggests the perspective of a social historian, while the tone combines affectionate nostalgia with unsentimental honesty about poverty:

> In nearly all the cottages there was but one room downstairs, and many of these were poor and bare, with only a table and a few chairs and stools for furniture and a superannuated potato-sack thrown down by way of hearthrug. Other rooms were bright and cosy, with dressers of crockery, cushioned chairs, pictures on the walls and brightly coloured hand-made rag rugs on the floor.... In the older cottages there were grandfathers' clocks, gate-legged tables, and rows of pewter, relics of a time when life was easier for country folk.

The layering of temporal perspectives contrasts the time of writing, the present of the narrative, and the past remembered by the older inhabitants of the village. Towards the end, the emphasis shifts to the gradual yet marked changes which take place as Flora (renamed Laura) grows older: 'In the country at the time now recorded, the day of the old skilled master-craftsman, though waning, was not over.'

The *Lark Rise* books were very well received on publication: they appeared at a time when REGIONAL WRITING was still in vogue. Yet Thompson eschews the fine writing and melodrama of the most popular rural writers of the preceding decades. Her work is still read and valued, although the rural, domestic character of her subject matter has led to her classification as a minor writer. Her novel *Still Glides the Stream* (1948) was published posthumously.

Suggested Reading

Bloxham, Christine. *The World of Flora Thompson* (Oxford: Robert Dugdale, 1998).

Lindsay, Gillian. *Flora Thompson: The Story of the 'Lark Rise' Writer* (London: Hale, 1990).

Trodd, Anthea. *Women's Writing in English: Britain, 1900–1945* (London: Longmans, 1998).

Faye Hammill

Thompson, Sylvia 1902–1968

Author of the bestselling novel *The Hounds of Spring* (1926), written at the age of 23, and of many subsequent novels and short stories, none of which repeated her early success. Thompson's fiction concerns young people between the wars, and focuses on women's experiences of grief and their desire for safety and order.

Sylvia Elizabeth Thompson belonged to the Oxford generation that included Margaret KENNEDY and Winifred HOLTBY, which Vera BRITTAIN called 'The Somerville School of Novelists'. Her first novel, *The Rough Crossing* (1921), was followed by *A Lady In Green Gloves* (1924), and then *The Hounds of Spring*, whose heroine thinks her lover is dead and so marries another man, but finds herself in a dilemma when he reappears. Thompson married an American artist, Theodore Lulling, in 1926. Until WORLD WAR TWO they lived in Venice, which she used as the setting for *Third Act in Venice* (1936), about a man torn between two loves, a sacred and a profane. Thompson's daughter, Elizabeth, also became a writer.

In 1928 Thompson published *Battle of the Horizons*, about an American woman who has trouble adapting to the English family she has married into. Her other novels include *Chariot Wheels* (1929), *Winter Comedy* (1931), *Summer's Night* (1932), *Unfinished Symphony* (1933), *Silver Rattle* (1935), *Recapture the Moon* (1937), *The Gulls Fly Inland* (1941), *The People Opposite* (1948), and *The Candle's Glory* (1953). Thompson's novels are now remembered only in reference to the 1920s.

Suggested Reading

Beauman, Nicola. *A Very Great Profession. The Woman's Novel, 1914–39* (London: Virago, 1983).

Ouditt, Sharon. *Fighting Forces, Writing Women. Identity and Ideology in the First World War* (London: Routledge, 1994).

Laura Christie

Titanic

While on its maiden voyage from Southampton to New York, the glamorous and 'virtually unsinkable' RMS *Titanic* hit an iceberg in the North Atlantic, and sank in the early hours of 15 April 1912, with the loss of 1503 passengers and crew. Since the disaster, the name *Titanic* has resounded with images of cowardice and heroism, of class conflict, of nature versus modernity, and of man's overconfidence in technology.

Designed to accommodate 3511 persons, the *Titanic* only provided lifeboat capacity for 1178. Furthermore, many lifeboats left the sinking ship less than half full; the first lifeboat, capable of holding 40, contained only 12 people. Most of those saved were first-class passengers, while many of the drowned were steerage, a statistic heavily emphasized in James Cameron's 1997 film, *Titanic*. Survivors such as Sir Cosmo and Lady Duff Gordon and J. Bruce Ismay, managing director of the White Star Line, were vilified by the American press for saving their own skins. Ismay, however, had helped to load many lifeboats before getting into one himself. Meanwhile, the captain, Edward Smith, was hailed as a hero who went down with his ship, but in actuality it was he who ignored the ice warnings. Whatever the facts, the story of the *Titanic* continues to exert a powerful hold over the public imagination, and has inspired numerous books and films.

Suggested Reading

Bergfelder, Tim and Sarah Street (eds). *The Titanic in Myth and Memory: Representations in Visual and Literary Culture* (London: I. B. Tauris, 2004).

Louise Harrington

Travers, Pamela Lyndon 1899–1996

Author of *Mary Poppins*, one of the best-loved children's books of the twentieth century. Born in Queensland, Australia, she moved to England at 17 to work as an actress and dancer. Initially known as a dramatic critic and poet, it was with the arrival in 1934 of Mary Poppins, 'flying on the East Wind', that her career blossomed. *Mary Poppins* was quickly followed by *Mary Poppins Comes Back* (1935), and a few years afterwards, *Mary Poppins Opens the Door* (1943), and *Mary Poppins in the Park* (1952), later expanded to include *Mary Poppins in the Kitchen* (1975), *Mary Poppins in Cherry Tree Lane* (1982), and *Mary Poppins and the House Next Door* (1988). With Walt Disney's adaptation (1964) of Mary

Poppins's first adventures, she became a phenomenal bestseller. Her stories, full of mysticism, mixing the subversive characteristics of fantasy with the orthodoxy of realism, encapsulate the literary ethos of much CHILDREN'S LITERATURE of the time. Ironic descriptions, throughout the Mary Poppins series, provide deliberately clichéd representations of early twentieth-century British society, with its desire for rigour, but also its need for escapism and enchantment.

Suggested Reading
Demers, Patricia. *P. L. Travers* (Boston, MA: Twayne, 1991).
Hunt, Peter. *Children's Literature: A Guide* (Oxford: Blackwell, 2001).

Sebastien Chapleau

Tree, Iris 1897–1968

Along with Nancy CUNARD and Edith SITWELL, she forged an avant-garde poetry by British women which mediated between the forms of traditional English verse and innovative European art and music. Daughters of aristocrats, their reaction against stifling English propriety was an impulse for literary revolution. Iris Tree attended the Slade School of Art and became a close friend of Dora Carrington, who was one of several to paint her portrait. Centred in London and associated with the Eiffel Tower group, Tree married an American artist, Curtis Moffatt, but was separated by 1924. She then took an apartment in Paris, where she associated with Cunard and other 1920s Left Bank intellectuals. She later married (and divorced) Friedrich Ledebur and lived nomadically between the United States and Europe, maintaining an association with experimental theatre groups.

Tree's poems were circulated through the controversial *Wheels* and other anthologies and magazines. She published four collections (1919, 1920, 1927, 1966), three of which solely or additionally came out in the United States. Apart from some love lyrics, Tree's poems challenge 'crumbling roads of worn-out creeds'. She explores psychological alienation from modernity while pushing to 'make it new'. Tree gradually became more versatile with the differing line lengths and cadences of free verse, and experimented with polyphonic prose.

Suggested Reading
Fielding, Daphne. *The Rainbow Picnic: A Portrait of Iris Tree* (London: Methuen, 1974).
Pearson, John. *Facades: Edith, Osbert and Sacheverell Sitwell* (Basingstoke: Macmillan, 1978).

Jane Dowson

Trefusis, Violet 1894–1972

Novelist, best known for her elegant comedy, *Hunt the Slipper* (1937), and her turbulent affair with Vita SACKVILLE-WEST. Daughter of the charismatic Edwardian hostess Alice Keppel, who became the mistress of Edward VII, Violet

Keppel Trefusis was born into a privileged aristocratic culture, her ambivalence towards which is explored in her writing.

Her consuming three-year love affair with school friend Vita Sackville-West began in 1918. This intense, and public, relationship continued after Violet's marriage to army officer Denys Trefusis in 1919, a union that was much encouraged by her mother. Violet famously wrote in a letter to Vita in March of that year: 'You are my lover and I am your mistress and kingdoms and empires and governments have tottered and succumbed before now to that mighty combination.' However, in the end, their elopement to France was thwarted not by empires and governments, but by the interventions of their husbands and families.

In 1921 Trefusis moved to Paris with Denys, with whom she was reunited publicly, if not privately. She spent the rest of her life in France and Italy – in her home in Saint-Loup-de-Naud and her mother's villa in Florence – only returning to England during the years of the Second World War to escape the German invasion. Her first novel, *Sortie de Secours* (1929), was written in her adopted French, as were *Echo* (1931) and *Les Causes Perdues* (1941). Published in 1937, *Hunt the Slipper* was Trefusis's fifth novel, and the second one written in English. Set in England and Paris, this witty commentary on English manners portrays the tormented relationship between the profligate Nigel and the tenacious but passionate Caroline, and explores the slipperiness of pleasure and the duplicitous allure of place and possession. Trefusis's years as an exile in France inform both the continental perspective and the knowing distance of her writing. In her autobiographical *Don't Look Round* (1952) she writes: 'It is not an exaggeration to say that places have played at least as important a part in my life as people. Indeed it is almost as if the places had generated the people.'

Unfortunately, Trefusis's literary accomplishments have too often been eclipsed by the melodramatic narrative of her affair with Sackville-West, and its subsequent literary dramatization. She appears as the wily lover of his mother in Nigel Nicolson's *Portrait of a Marriage* (1973), and as the anarchic Eve in Sackville-West's *Challenge* (which was withdrawn from her publisher in the 1920s and did not appear in England until 1973). Trefusis's *Broderie Anglaise* (1935), written in French, is a *roman à clef* about Sackville-West's relationship with Virginia WOOLF. Its portrayal of the tumultuous affair between Alexa and the aristocratic John Shorne is in many respects a riposte to Woolf's *Orlando* (1928), in which the characterization of the French-speaking Russian princess Sasha, who 'never shone with the steady beam of an Englishwoman', is based on Trefusis.

Suggested Reading
Jullian, Philippe, and John Phillips. *The Other Woman: A Life of Violet Trefusis* (Boston, MA: Houghton Mifflin, 1976).

Sage, Lorna. *Moments of Truth: Twelve Twentieth-Century Women Writers* (London: Fourth Estate, 2001).

Souhami, Diana. *Mrs Keppel and Her Daughter* (New York: St Martin's Press, 1997).

Rebecca Munford

Tynan, Katherine 1861–1931

Prolific Irish poet, novelist, and journalist, one of the most popular and highly regarded writers of her generation, but now largely overlooked by critics. Born in Dublin to a Roman Catholic family of 11, Tynan was very close to her father Andrew, and attributed to him her introduction to poetry and Irish politics. This double interest formed the basis of her later friendship with W. B. Yeats, who, along with other Irish Literary Revival writers, was a regular guest at the Tynan family home in Clondalkin.

Beginning with her first volume of poems, *Louise de la Vallière* (1885), Tynan's verse focuses on themes of nature, faith, war, and family, drawing on her personal experiences of all of these. She had poor eyesight, describing herself as 'purblind', and as a result her imagery, as Jean Halladay notes, is 'more often auditory than visual'.

In 1893, Tynan moved to England, where she stayed with Wilfred and Alice MEYNELL, and in the same year met and married Henry Albert Hinkson. It was a happy marriage which produced five children, although two died in infancy. Her family life further inspired her poetry, as she explored her personal experiences as wife and mother, but also the vital role of the woman in family life. Much of her war poetry is focused on motherhood since her sons fought in WORLD WAR ONE.

Hinkson's sudden death in 1919 left Tynan virtually destitute, resulting in a proliferation of 'hack' journalism and formula novels, which she herself acknowledged as 'potboilers'. These include *Denys the Dreamer* (1921), *A Mad Marriage* (1922), *Pat, the Adventurer* (1928), and *Philippa's Lover* (1931). This later phase of popular writing tends to overshadow her earlier work, both her critically acclaimed poetry and her work for the Revival movement, such as the four-volume *Cabinet of Irish Literature* that she selected and edited in 1902–3. In addition, Tynan wrote four volumes of memoirs/autobiography, *Twenty-Five Years* (1913), *The Middle Years* (1916), *Years of the Shadow* (1919), and *The Wandering Years* (1922). The manuscripts of these, together with some of her correspondence and articles on literary topics, such as 'The Anglo-Irish' and 'English Women Poets', are to be found in the Morris Library Katherine Tynan Hinkson Collection at the Southern Illinois University, Carbondale.

Suggested Reading

Halladay, Jean R. *Eight Late Victorian Poets: Shaping the Artistic Sensibility of an Age* (Lampeter: Edwin Mellen Press, 1993).

Esme Miskimmin

U

Underhill, Evelyn 1875–1941

Poet, novelist, and one of the most prolific writers on spirituality and mysticism in the twentieth century. As a young woman, Underhill belonged to the Order of the Golden Dawn, but converted to Christianity in 1907, the year of her marriage, and eventually joined the Anglican Church. She wrote, taught, and led religious retreats, and this work brought her international renown.

Underhill's writing shows great variety of form. Her first published work, in 1902, was a collection of poetry, and she wrote three novels dealing with mysticism and the occult, the most successful of which is *The Column of Dust* (1909). The novels were well received, but they are overwritten and lack imagination. In 1911 Underhill published the major work of her early career, *Mysticism*, which went into 13 editions. She produced several more works on the subject, and became a leading voice of the revival of interest in mysticism around the First World War. In 1921 she became the first woman to lecture on theology at Oxford. She was religious editor for the *Spectator* and wrote for *Time and Tide*. Her later writing is almost entirely devotional, climaxing with *Worship* (1936). Her reputation declined following her death, but the 1990s saw a renewed interest in her writing on mysticism.

Suggested Reading

Greene, Dana. *Evelyn Underhill: Artist of the Infinite Life* (London: Darton, Longman & Todd, 1991).
Loades, Anne. *Evelyn Underhill* (London: Fount, 1997).

Leigh Wilson

Uttley, Alison 1884–1976

Prolific author of stories, fairy-tales, novels, and plays for children, as well as a series of nostalgic reminiscences of her childhood on a Derbyshire farm. Uttley is best known for her animal tales, in particular the 'Little Grey Rabbit' series, which began in 1929 with *The Squirrel, The Hare and The Little Grey Rabbit*. These illustrated stories, alongside tales of Sam Pig, Tim Rabbit, Little Brown Mouse, and Little Red Fox, combine convincing details of rural life with fantasy and the lively characterization of hedgerow creatures.

Alison Uttley (born Alice Jane Taylor) graduated with a physics degree from Manchester University (where she was later awarded an honorary Litt.D.) and trained as a science teacher, but she recalls an early urge to write down her more imaginative experiences: 'I began to make up stories when I was a little child, as soon as I could hold a pencil, for all the world of strange objects was filled with life.' She married James Uttley in 1911 and rediscovered her storytelling talent when her son, John, was born three years later. Her writing became a financial, and no doubt emotional, necessity when James committed suicide in 1930.

Uttley's work is often compared to the tales of Beatrix Potter and is sometimes considered derivative, but she herself was intensely proud of the originality of her imaginative output and had a number of confrontations with illustrator Margaret Tempest regarding who had truly created the Little Grey Rabbit characters. When Uttley moved permanently to Buckinghamshire in 1938, she also developed a deep dislike for Enid BLYTON, who was one of her neighbours and commercially very successful. However, Uttley did become friends with Walter de la Mare later in life, and they shared an interest in nature, fantasy, and dreams.

Some of Uttley's most acclaimed works are her fictionalized memoirs and autobiographical essays, variously reviewed as 'charming', 'wholesome', and 'whimsical'. *The Country Child* (1931) was the first book she wrote, though not the first published, and its success prompted a series of country recollections such as *Ambush of Young Days* (1937) and *Country Hoard* (1943), as well as articles on rural traditions and even a cookery book, *Recipes from an Old Farmhouse* (1966). Perhaps her greatest literary accomplishment is the children's novel *A Traveller in Time* (1939), which fuses expert rural knowledge with elements of fantasy in telling the story of the Derbyshire Babingtons and their attempted plot to rescue Mary, Queen of Scots.

Uttley was industrious to the end, producing the last Little Grey Rabbit title, *Hare and the Rainbow*, the year before her death. There is remarkably little critical work on Alison Uttley, possibly because her writing is deemed to be slight and nostalgic, but perhaps also due to the dominance of Potter and Kenneth Graham as writers of fanciful and rustic animal stories.

Suggested Reading

Judd, Denis. *Alison Uttley: Creator of Little Grey Rabbit* (Stroud: Sutton, 2001).

Saintsbury, Elizabeth. *The World of Alison Uttley: A Biography* (London: Howard Baker, 1980).

Alison Waller

V

Vaughan, Hilda 1892–1985

Novelist renowned for her authentic depiction of rural Wales. Vaughan was brought up in Builth Wells, and her work for the Women's Land Army in Breconshire and Radnorshire in the First World War influenced her writing, bringing her into contact with the lives of women on the local farms. Attending a writing course at Bedford College for Women, she met her husband Charles Morgan. Morgan was soon to become a writer of renown and Vaughan's work has been overshadowed by his. Recognizing his wife's superior narrative skill, however, Morgan observed: 'The great thing is that you have a tale to tell and you tell it. It's a gift to rejoice in.'

Vaughan was an adventurous author of ten varied novels. Her first, *The Battle to the Weak*, explores self-sacrifice and rebellion, *The Invader* (1928) is a comedy, *The Soldier and the Gentlewoman* (1932) is an ironic tragedy, and *Iron and Gold* (1948) reworks an old Welsh folk tale. In her finest work, *A Thing of Nought* (1934), the heroine, Megan Lloyd, is closely linked with her natural surroundings. Megan compares her life to the 'shadows as do pass to and fro across the Cwm, and are leavin' no trace of theirselves behind'. Vaughan's work met with favourable reviews from her contemporaries but has been ignored by academic criticism. Such neglect is a loss to modern readers, as few have matched the haunting lyricism of her prose.

Suggested Reading

Aaron, Jane. Introduction to *Iron and Gold* by Hilda Vaughan (Dinas Powys: Honno, 2002) vii–xviii.

Newman, Christopher W. *Hilda Vaughan* (Cardiff: University of Wales Press, 1981).

Lucy Thomas

Virago Press

The brainchild of Carmen Calli in 1972, this publishing firm is today the world's largest women's imprint. Virago's successful series include the Reprint Library, the Travellers Series, and also the Modern Classics Series, the aim of which is, according to the Virago website, 'to demonstrate the existence of a female literary tradition and to broaden the sometimes narrow definition of a classic'. The Modern Classics Series reintroduced many neglected female authors featured in this encyclopedia, including BRITTAIN, JAMESON, KEANE, and LEHMANN. Virago continues to reprint forgotten women novelists, to promote the writing of Black and Asian women, and to publish new titles that have won the Guardian Fiction and Fawcett Society prizes.

Ashlie Sponenberg

Von Arnim, Elizabeth 1866–1941

Pseudonym and, later, adopted name of Mary Annette Beauchamp, renowned wit and author of more than 20 novels and a memoir. May, as she was nicknamed, moved from Australia to England in 1870, eventually becoming a British citizen. She was educated at home and at the Royal College of Music and became an accomplished organist. She married Count Henning von Arnim in 1891, and although successful in German aristocratic circles, she felt frustrated by the patriarchal rules of her husband's class. Experiences from the early years of her marriage influenced her fiction, which often features tyrannical husbands (often German), restrictive marriages, and women who desire an escape from duty.

In 1896, May lived alone at her husband's castle, Nassenheid, and avoided housekeeping by spending days in the garden. She fictionalized her blissful irresponsibility in her first anonymous novel, *Elizabeth and Her German Garden* (1898). It was an instant bestseller, with speculation regarding her identity spurring English sales. In its examination of the conflict between a woman's domestic and private selves, the book was a statement of Elizabeth's – as she was henceforward known – feminism. Its sequel, *The Solitary Summer* (1899), was signed 'By the Author of *Elizabeth and Her German Garden*', an anonymous form later shortened to 'Elizabeth'.

Further novels continued Elizabeth's semi-autobiographical depictions of female flight, and established her reputation in England. A 1901 holiday became the basis for her successful comic novel *The Adventures of Elizabeth in Rügen* (1906), which reiterates her desire for escape: 'It has been a conviction of mine that there is nothing so absolutely bracing for the soul as the frequent turning of one's back on duties.' Her 1917 novel *Christine*, concerning the war, appeared under the name 'Alice Cholmondeley'.

The Enchanted April (1922), her best-remembered novel, was completed after a trip to Portofino. In it, the frumpy Mrs Wilkins and her friend, Mrs Arbuthnot, advertise for two other women to share the expense of an Italian holiday, conceived as an escape from their marriages. After a lifetime of obedience, Mrs Wilkins felt that she 'had taken off all her goodness and left it behind like a heap of rain-sodden clothes, and she only felt joy. She was naked of goodness, and was rejoicing in being naked.'

In other novels, Elizabeth expressed more vehement opposition to marriage. In *The Pastor's Wife* (1914), the English protagonist leaves her German husband and runs away to Italy with an artist. In *Vera* (1921), Elizabeth fictionalized her disastrous second marriage to Earl Russell, whom she later divorced. Her unflattering portrait of an abusive, murderous husband scandalized several of Russell's influential friends, and her popularity within English literary circles began to suffer.

Elizabeth's final novel, *Mr Skeffington* (1940), was the only one in which she represented the current European conflict; its protagonist is reunited with her Jewish husband, a victim of Nazi torture. For this reason she is often overlooked as a political writer; however, by her insistence upon feminist themes, Elizabeth's writing was markedly political throughout. At the start of the Second World War, Elizabeth fled to America, where she died.

Suggested Reading

Hennegan, Alison. 'In a Class of Her Own: Elizabeth von Arnim', in Maroula Joannou (ed.), *Women Writers of the 1930s: Gender, Politics and History* (Edinburgh: Edinburgh University Press, 1999) 100–12.

Usborne, Karen. *'Elizabeth': The Author of Elizabeth and Her German Garden* (London: The Bodley Head, 1986).

Ashlie Sponenberg

W

Waddell, Helen 1889–1965

Scholar, translator, novelist, and cultural historian, very influential in inspiring interest in medieval culture and literature. Her work of cultural history, *The Wandering Scholars* (1927), was an instant surprise success with both popular and academic audiences. It recreated the world of the twelfth-century vagrant scholars, the Vagantes, whose songs sprang from 'the leaf-drift of centuries of forgotten scholarship', and revived pagan sensuality in Christendom. Waddell's glamorous evocation of these ribald, restless scholars, who 'kept the imagination of Europe alive', was enormously influential in literary reconstructions of medieval culture. Her only novel, *Peter Abelard* (1933), achieved comparable success, adapting the doomed romance of Abelard and Heloise to the experience of the first generations of women academics. Abelard is the ideal academic, inspiring teacher, brilliant scholar, responsive to popular culture. Heloise, his gifted pupil, suffers from the restrictions on women's scholarship: 'O God, this spider's web of woman's life, with its small panic fears and caution and obsequiousness!'

Waddell was born in Tokyo, the child of Anglo-Irish Presbyterian missionaries. Her childhood in Japan helped to foster her lifelong enthusiasm for making connections between cultures. She studied English for a BA and MA at Queens University, Belfast, then spent seven years caring for her invalid stepmother. During this period, she began to write, including the translation, *Lyrics from the Chinese* (1913). From 1920 she studied for her doctorate at Oxford, was enthralled by the medieval Latin lyrics collected in *Carmina Burana*, and from 1923 to 1925 studied in Paris on the Susette Taylor Research Award. Her doctoral thesis became *The Wandering Scholars*.

Waddell's argument in all her work concerned cultural continuities, from pagan to Christian, between Western and Eastern cultures, between scholarship and creative writing, between scholarship, high art, and popular song. Her prose style was essentially late Victorian, modelled after Walter Pater and Oscar Wilde, but her emphasis on the continuities of high and popular art was immensely congenial to ideas of artistic practice in the 1920s. Waddell was criticized for glamorizing the Vagantes, and for her very free translations of their songs in *Medieval Latin Lyrics* (1929), but her evocation of a forgotten world, where high and popular art and scholarship coexisted in intimate, dynamic relationship, had an irresistible fascination for the interwar public.

Beasts and Saints (1934) translated medieval Latin texts, 'stories of the mutual charities between saints and beasts', another cultural continuity. Another translation, *The Desert Fathers* (1936), emphasized the Fathers' 'heroic gentleness' to 'a world that has fallen to the ancient anarchs of cruelty and pride'. Waddell never held an academic post, but was much in demand on the lecture circuit, as a charismatic exponent of medieval culture. Her life thus somewhat resembled the itinerant brilliance she evoked for the Vagantes. In the 1940s she became assistant editor for the *Nineteenth Century*, and advisor for the publisher Constable. From the mid-1940s she became increasingly invalid and amnesiac, presumably from Alzheimer's. She has received little critical attention, but remains a striking example of the scholarly popularizer.

Suggested Reading
Blackett, Monica. *The Mark of the Maker: A Portrait of Helen Waddell* (London: Constable, 1973).
Corrigan, Felicitas. *Helen Waddell: A Biography* (London: Gollancz, 1986).

Anthea Trodd

War Memoirs
Women's war memoirs have always been overshadowed by those of male soldiers, canonically exemplified by Robert Graves's *Goodbye to All That* (1929) and Erich Maria Remarque's *All Quiet on the Western Front* (1929). But unlike autobiographies, memoirs are usually about only part, rather than the whole, of a life and, as such, wartime was a fertile ground for memoirs by women who, as a result of the new freedoms offered by the disruptions of war, had memorable experiences to recount. War memoirs should be read as a particular intersection of autobiography, fiction, and, especially in the case of WORLD WAR ONE, myth-making and class politics.

For those women who wished to be involved in World War One, nursing was one of the few options which was, to some degree, socially sanctioned, and women's memoirs from this war are largely concerned with nursing. Perhaps the best known of these is Vera BRITTAIN's *Testament of Youth* (1933), which details her experiences working for the Voluntary Aid Detachment. Others include Mary Borden's *The Forbidden Zone* (1929), Olive Dent's *A VAD in France* (1917), Kate Finzi's *Eighteen Months in the War Zone* (1916), Maude Onion's *A Woman at War* (1928), Flora Sandnes's *An English Woman-Sergeant in the Serbian Army* (1916), and Baroness de T'Serclaes's *The Cellar House at Pervyse* (1916). Some of these, such as the memoirs by Sandnes and T'Serclaes, were written to raise money or draw attention to parts of the war effort, while others, such as Brittain's memoirs, were PACIFIST and/or anti-war narratives.

There are fewer memoirs from WORLD WAR TWO, which can be partly ascribed to the expansion of CINEMA and photography and the role of the war correspondent. In this war, memoirs often took the form of images rather than words. A female war correspondent who did write a memoir is Iris Carpenter, who recounted her experiences in *No Woman's World* (1946). An account of the female factory worker can be found in Kate Bliss and Elsie Whiteman's diary entries in *Working for Victory* (2001). The holdings of the MASS-OBSERVATION Archive at the University of Sussex should be regarded as a repository of further memoirs.

Suggested Reading

Higonnet, Margaret R. (ed.). *Nurses at the Front: Writing the Wounds of the Great War* (Boston, MA: Northeastern University Press, 2001).
Klein, Yvonne (ed.). *Beyond the Home Front: Women's Autobiographical Writing of the Two World Wars* (Basingstoke: Macmillan – now Palgrave Macmillan, 1997).

Stacy Gillis

War Work

Total mobilization of the British population during the two world wars brought women into sectors of work where previously they had been barely represented – notably heavy industry and engineering. These advances were, however, contingent on wartime conditions; agreements between government, employers, and trade unions, as well as wider social pressures, resulted in a return to the *status quo* at the end of each war.

During WORLD WAR ONE, the State was slow to grasp the value of female labour, and it was not until problems arose in the supply of munitions (due to the poorly planned mobilization of male volunteers) that the government directed the female labour force into key areas of production. This was resisted by trade unions, concerned that the hard won status of skilled workers would be undermined. The state therefore negotiated agreements whereby the production process was broken down into repetitive tasks, assigned to women and boys, and skilled jobs such as tool setting and quality control reserved for men. The growing need to place women in skilled jobs necessitated further agreements establishing that men would be given their jobs back after the war. The numbers of women in the armaments-related metal and chemical trades expanded from 212,000 in July 1914 to 379,000 in July 1920. But the biggest growth was in transport, where the number of women workers rose from 18,200 in 1914 to 117,200 in 1918. The vast majority were conductors, ticket inspectors, cleaners, and porters, while driving was reserved for men.

Both the economy and women's labour were better managed during WORLD WAR TWO. All women between 19 and 40 had to register for work, although those with husbands in the services and merchant navy, or with children under 14, could not be conscripted. Young single women without dependents could be compelled to take 'essential work' anywhere in the country; moreover, employers had to accept them. The number of women working in industry expanded from 506,000 in 1939 to 2,000,000 by 1944. Even male bastions like shipbuilding, which had resisted women in the First World War, now took them on, although most were relegated to unskilled tasks such as painting or routing electrical cables. The state and the unions were again collaborating to preserve the skilled status of male workers.

Although most women's jobs were simple and repetitive, labour shortages meant that some women, especially those working in government-run munitions or aero factories, were trained to perform highly skilled jobs. In the auxiliary units of the armed forces, women operated sophisticated optical and communications equipment and drove and maintained vehicles. In the Second World War, women even provided valuable service as 'ferry pilots', flying military aircraft between bases in the United Kingdom.

Women rarely achieved parity in pay, except in transport, where they were granted equal pay in April 1940, and in government-run industries. During both wars, women's wages were on average half those of men, though still a great improvement on what women had received during peacetime, particularly in the sweated trades of the Edwardian era, domestic service and farming.

Women workers endured long hours: 12-hour days and 70-hour weeks were common in the 1914–18 war. During the Second World War, the situation improved slightly, with a limitation of 55 hours per week imposed in 1942. But this was still an exhausting regime, on top of travel and stints of fire watching, followed for many by childcare and domestic chores. For, contrary to the propaganda image, one-third of the female workforce were mothers, though many worked part-time. In 1939–45, levels of sickness and absenteeism caused by exhaustion led to welfare initiatives such as work-place nurseries and schemes to give workers priority when shopping – facilities rapidly withdrawn after the war. During the First World War especially, society's anxiety about the new-found freedom and independence of young women, combined with resentment generated by exaggerated claims about their wages, resulted in efforts to regulate the lives of workers, particularly women in the Land Army and those living in hostels attached to state-run munitions factories. Measures imposed included uniforms, a smoking ban, night time curfews, and restricted fraternization with men.

Many of the jobs undertaken by women were dangerous and threatening to HEALTH, particularly in munitions factories, where they were given the menial and unpleasant task of handling explosives. During a six-month period in 1916, 41 munitions workers died of TNT poisoning. Although there was greater awareness and acknowledgement of the toxicity of explosives during the Second World War, 105 women nevertheless contracted toxic jaundice and 21 died. A further 71,000 women were victims of industrial accidents.

Although women have advanced into many areas of employment since 1945, the tiny percentage working today in industry and engineering indicates the limited influence of wartime conditions. Far more significant, and often overlooked, is the fact that war accelerated women's participation in business, government, EDUCATION, and the professions. For the poorest women, war work enabled an escape from the drudgery and cruelty of employment as SERVANTS, a sector to which they never returned.

Suggested Reading

Braybon, Gail and Penny Summerfield. *Out of the Cage: Women's Experiences in Two World Wars* (London: Pandora, 1987).

Marwick, Arthur. *Women at War, 1914–1918* (London: Fontana, 1977).

Summerfield, Penny. *Reconstructing Women's Wartime Lives: Discourse and Subjectivity in Oral Histories of the Second World War* (Manchester: Manchester University Press, 1998).

Turner, Mary. *The Women's Century: A Celebration of Changing Roles, 1900–2000* (Kew: The National Archives, 2003).

Toby Haggith

Ward, Mrs Humphry 1851–1920

Translator, journalist, novelist, and first president of the Women's Anti-Suffrage League (founded 1908). Born Mary Augusta Arnold in Tasmania, she was granddaughter to Thomas Arnold of Rugby, and her father (another Thomas Arnold) was also a schoolmaster. She spent her adult life in Oxford and London, marrying Oxford academic Thomas Humphry Ward in 1872. The best known of her many novels is *Robert Elsmere* (1888). She also translated the diary of philosopher Henri Frédéric Amiel as *Amiel's Journal* (1885) and contributed articles to *The Times* and *Nineteenth Century*. Her First World War journalism included *England's Effort, Six Letters to an American Friend* (1916), explaining Britain's involvement in the hostilities.

Several of Ward's novels concentrate on the psychological make-up of a female protagonist. *Eleanor* (1900) concerns the jealousy of a mature woman towards her younger rival, whilst in *Cousin Philip* (1919), the 'type' is the postwar woman who, having worked for the war effort, no longer wants to be sheltered and chaperoned. These novels chart a growth in self-knowledge but such knowledge seldom leads to a traditional happy ending. In *The Testing of Diana Mallory* (1908), the heroine gets her man but only after he has abandoned her on account of her dead mother's sins and become dependent on morphia. Meanwhile, by the end of *Missing* (1917), war-widow Nelly has 'no precise image of the future' but is merely 'strengthened – to endure and serve'.

More startlingly, Laura in *Helbeck of Bannisdale* (1898) finds that the only way to resolve the conflict between her personal autonomy and her fiancé's suffocating brand of Roman Catholicism is suicide. As she writes in her final letter, 'the priests want my inmost will – want all that is I – and I know...that I cannot give it'. Ward also discusses Roman Catholicism in several of her other novels. *Eleanor*, set in modern-day Italy, vividly depicts both the power of the Roman

Church and the attempts of Italian politicians to create a more secular society. Ward acknowledges the grandeur, force and appeal of Catholicism but not the necessity for submission to priest and Papal Bull. Nor is Roman Catholicism the only religious system to come under Ward's scrutiny. Both *Robert Elsmere* and *The Case of Richard Maynell* (1911) critique the Anglican Church, having for their eponymous heroes clerics who doubt central tenets of Christianity.

Other novels discuss political and ethical issues. For example, *Marcella* (1894) contains affirmative discussion of political agitators and politically motivated social reformers, though its conservative closure reinscribes the values of the landed interest. Similarly ambiguous is Ward's treatment of election campaigns and parliamentary debates in *The Testing of Diana Mallory*. She never totally condemns any creed or party. Arguably, her novels reflect her own eclectic political and social preoccupations: pro-higher education for women, she was anti-suffrage; First World War propagandist, she was also a philanthropist. However, at another level we might argue that she was simply a good storyteller; one who liked to dissect human motivation and whose resistance to complete closure appealed to a very wide audience.

Suggested Reading

Trevelyan, Janet Penrose [née Ward]. *The Life of Mrs. Humphry Ward* (London: Constable, 1923).

Ward, Mary Augusta. *A Writer's Recollections* (London: Collins, 1918).

Elaine Hartnell

Warner, Sylvia Townsend 1893–1978

Novelist, poet, and socialist activist, best known for her novels, *Lolly Willowes* (1926) and *Summer Will Show* (1936). Townsend Warner was born in Harrow and educated at home. She had a 40-year relationship with the poet Valentine ACKLAND. Both joined the Communist Party and campaigned for various left-wing causes from their home in rural Dorset, visiting Spain as medical auxiliaries in the SPANISH CIVIL WAR.

Townsend Warner's first volume of poetry was *The Espalier* (1925). The subject of her long narrative pastoral poem, *Opus 7* (1931), is an old woman who ekes out a living selling flowers. *Whether a Dove or a Seagull* (1934) is a collection of 109 poems, 55 attributed to Ackland and 54 to Townsend Warner.

Townsend Warner's seven novels are disparate in content and form. *Lolly Willowes* (1926) is a fable about a middle-aged spinster who escapes patriarchal control by becoming a witch. *Summer Will Show, After the Death of Don Juan* (1938), *The Corner that Held Them* (1948), and *The Flint Anchor* (1954) are historical novels. In *Summer Will Show*, Sophia Willoughby is drawn into the revolutionary struggle in Paris in 1848 and falls in love with her husband's mistress, Minna. The novel was informed by Townsend Warner's interest in revolutionary, Marxist, and feminist ideas, and its LESBIAN sub-plot has attracted feminist critical interest. Like her other improbable liaisons – between the eponymous heroine of *Lolly Willowes* and the devil, between the missionary, Mr Fortune and his boy disciple in *Mr Fortune's Maggot* (1947), and between the orphaned Victorian servant Suky Bond and her mentally retarded husband in *The True Heart* (1949) – the liaison between Minna and Sophia dramatizes the author's conviction that personal happiness must be pursued with total disregard for convention, propriety, and sexual decorum. *After the Death of Don Juan* is a literary sequel to Mozart's opera *Don Giovanni*. Ostensibly set in eighteenth-century Spain, this is a parable on the Spanish Civil War and evokes the divisions in modern Spanish society. *The Corner that Held Them* (1948) takes place in a convent in fourteenth-century Norfolk and depicts the petty squabbles within a small, closed community where the Black Death strikes. Her final novel, *The Flint Heart* (1954), is a nineteenth-century family saga, loosely based on the life of one of Townsend Warner's ancestors.

Townsend Warner also wrote the 'Elfin' stories for children, published in *Kingdoms of Elfin* (1977), and others published in *The New Yorker*. She produced a short study, *Jane Austen*, in 1951 and a biography, *T. H. White*, in 1970.

Suggested Reading

Harman, Clare. *Sylvia Townsend Warner: A Biography* (London: Chatto & Windus, 1989).

Joannou, Maroula. 'Sylvia Townsend Warner in the 1930s', in Andy Croft (ed.), *A Weapon in the Struggle: The Cultural History of the Communist Party in Britain* (London: Pluto Press, 1998) 89–105.

Mulford, Wendy. *This Narrow Place: Sylvia Townsend Warner and Valentine Ackland: Life, Letters and Politics, 1930–1951* (London: Pandora, 1988).

Maroula Joannou

Watson, Winifred 1906–2002

Novelist, who lived in Newcastle almost all her life. Winifred Eileen Watson wrote six well-reviewed novels in the 1930s and early 1940s, and was then forgotten until, in her nineties, she came to renewed acclaim when *Miss Pettigrew Lives For A Day* (1938) was republished in 2000 by PERSEPHONE BOOKS. On its reappearance, this comic fantasy about a middle-aged governess unexpectedly encountering – and approving of – the louche London world of nightclubs, cocktails, and casual sex rapidly gained both impressive reviews and a devoted readership, and Watson herself much enjoyed the renewed attention given to this novel. Her writing career was brief and intense: she wrote all her novels in her late twenties and early thirties, and lost interest in writing when faced with the demands of marriage, motherhood, and wartime vicissitudes, publishing nothing after 1943.

Her novels are middlebrow 'library' romances: undemanding in style, they work towards a happy ending in which a balance is achieved between a woman's innate capacities and her life with a partner or in a family. These optimistic books demonstrate a genial open-mindedness about sexual matters and a strong awareness that women may need careers as much as marriage. Women are shown having second chances, moving on and changing creatively, often in spite of considerable difficulties, usually caused by the constraints of the patriarchal family, about the dark side of which Watson can be unexpectedly graphic. Companionate marriage is the ideal in these novels, and is usually attained after the experience gained in a first, less satisfactory relationship, and a Watson hero is sympathetic and intelligent rather than sexually forceful.

Watson's first book, *Fell Top* (1934), is a steamy rustic novel in which the heroine's rape and forced marriage are engineered by her stepmother, and the murder of her brutal husband by her half-brother is condoned and concealed. It caused a considerable sensation, and was successful enough to be adapted for radio. This was followed by *Odd Shoes* (1936), a historical novel set in nineteenth-century Newcastle, which deals sympathetically with adultery and elopement, while charting the course of the ill-assorted marriages of a mother who runs a shoe shop, her daughter who marries into the upper middle classes, and her son who marries a prostitute. Watson next wrote *Miss Pettigrew Lives For A Day*, but Methuen only agreed to publish it on the understanding that she would write another rustic bodice-ripper. *Upyonder* (1938) followed, and shared the setting and the theme of unhappy marriage with *Fell Top*.

Hop, Step, and Jump (1939) is perhaps the most interesting of Watson's novels apart from *Miss Pettigrew*: its working-class heroine moves through a disastrous marriage to life as a servant, a kept woman, and a bakery-shop owner before achieving a happy marriage with the man of her choice. Watson's last novel, *Leave and Bequeath* (1943), set in a wealthy home-counties family during the war, features a splendid old harridan, and is a murder-mystery involving another unhappy marriage.

Suggested Reading
Twycross-Martin, Henrietta. Introduction to *Miss Pettigrew Lives For A Day* by
    Winifred Watson (London: Persephone Books, 2000) v–xii.

Henrietta Twycross-Martin

Webb, Beatrice 1858–1943
Sociologist, political activist, pamphleteer, diarist, whose *My Apprenticeship* (1925) is among the most powerful autobiographies of the twentieth century. Webb's early 'longing to create characters and to move them to and fro among fictitious circumstances' was realized in this brilliantly engrossing analysis of a late-Victorian socialite's 'personal search for a creed', a search which became an arduous training in social investigation. Informed throughout by anxieties about 'the strain and stress of a multiple personality', it partially corrected the

legend of the ironclad politico, as caricatured by H. G. Wells in his novel *The New Machiavelli* (1911).

The eighth of nine daughters of the railway magnate, Richard Potter, Webb grew up accustomed to political debate and foreign travel. The sociologist Herbert Spencer was a family friend and personal mentor. She began her transition from society girl to social investigator in 1883 with a visit incognito, passing as a farmer's daughter, to her mother's mill-hand relatives in Yorkshire. In 1887, again incognito, she worked as a seamstress in the East End, as a researcher for Charles Booth's *The Life and Labour of the People of London* (1891–1902). In 1892 she married civil servant Sidney Webb. Their formidable partnership was immensely influential in the early days of the FABIAN SOCIETY, the London School of Economics, the *New Statesman*, and the Labour Party. They wrote many books, pamphlets, and reports together, including *The History of Trade Unionism* (1894), and *The Minority Report on the Poor Law Commission* (1909). Beatrice's solo works included *The Co-Operative Movement in Great Britain* (1891) and *The Wages of Men and Women: Should They Be Equal?* (1919), which moved away from her earlier anti-feminist opinions.

The early diaries are a powerful, often agonized, analysis of her personal dilemmas, and *My Apprenticeship* is constructed round extensive, though expurgated, quotation from them. She discusses her yearnings to be a novelist, her profound ambivalence about the women's movement, which she initially opposed, her anxieties about her 'duplex personality', and the dangers of studying inner feelings. 'It is not wise to stop the ruffianly-looking vagrant and enquire from him whence he comes and whither he goeth', she noted in one entry. Her obsessive, unrequited love for the Tory politician Joseph Chamberlain, a major topic in her diary, becomes a terse reference to a 'black thread of personal unhappiness' in the autobiography. Her personal crisis in the 1880s is subsumed within an examination of the national crisis of poverty and deprivation. A second volume, *Our Partnership*, published posthumously in 1948, almost entirely eliminates the personal element. On its own, *My Apprenticeship* is a powerful narrative of a woman, trying, as Virginia WOOLF said with guarded admiration, 'to relate all her experiences to history'. Webb's diaries were edited and published in four volumes, beginning in 1982. Read together, the autobiography and diary constitute a revealing and powerful dialogue about a woman's problems in finding her identity in political life.

Suggested Reading

Ardis, Ann. *Modernism and Cultural Conflict, 1880–1922* (Cambridge: Cambridge University Press, 2002).

Caine, Barbara. 'Beatrice Webb and her Diary', *Victorian Studies*, 27 (1983) 81–9.

Nord, Deborah. *The Apprenticeship of Beatrice Webb* (London: Macmillan, 1985).

Anthea Trodd

Webb, Mary 1881–1927

Novelist, poet, short-story writer, essayist and mystic, best known for her novel *Precious Bane* (1924), which was awarded the coveted PRIX FEMINA-VIE HEUREUSE. During her lifetime, Webb's work was admired by writers and critics, but success with the reading public eluded her. Fame came posthumously, after an eloge by Stanley Baldwin in 1928 and publication of her *Collected Works*, bestsellers throughout the 1930s. The late twentieth century saw a revival of her reputation, which continues to grow. The concerns of her work are in tune with our own times, especially her ideas about love, sexuality, religion, the development of individual consciousness, and the value of the natural world.

Celtic in ancestry, Mary Webb lived most of her life in Shropshire and the Welsh borders. Her intense, spiritual bond with this countryside is reflected everywhere in her writing, from earliest poems to her final (uncompleted) novel, *Armour Wherein He Trusted* (1929). Another profound influence was her cultured, nature-loving father, George E. Meredith, who encouraged her literary work. She was educated in his preparatory school, spent two years at a finishing school, and later studied literature with the Cambridge University Extension Society in Shrewsbury. At 20, she contracted Graves' disease (thyrotoxicosis), then incurable, which marred her appearance and would contribute to her early death. In convalescence, she wrote *The Spring of Joy* (1917), essays on the solace, joy, and healing she found in nature.

In 1912 she married Henry B. L. Webb, after which she began *The Golden Arrow* (1916), the first of six novels set in a powerfully evoked South Shropshire landscape. Autobiographical elements, folklore, legend, and superstition are finely assimilated in the service of her major themes, notably the significance of suffering and the struggle between spiritual and material values. Keenly affected by the First World War, she wrote *Gone to Earth* (1917), a novel permeated by the tragic spirit of those years, yet lit characteristically by humour. Favourably reviewed, it was selected by Rebecca WEST as 'Novel of the Year'. She then wrote *The House in Dormer Forest* (1920) and *Seven for a Secret* (1922), in which her themes include class barriers and the power of literacy, especially in women's lives. These ideas were taken further in *Precious Bane*, which is a unique blend of romantic allegory, poetic parable, and personal testament, written in an arresting lyrical style: 'So the mere was three times ringed about, as if it had been three times put in a spell.'

Living partly in London during the 1920s, Webb contributed to *The English Review* and other journals, and reviewed for the *Spectator* and *The Bookman*, writings gathered in *Mary Webb: Collected Prose and Poems* (1977). Her poetry, uncollected in her life, is available today in two editions. Her novels, classics of rural and REGIONAL WRITING, yet transcending genre and category, have been adapted for stage, radio, CINEMA, and television.

Suggested Reading
Coles, Gladys Mary. *The Flower of Light: A Biography of Mary Webb* (1978; reprint. Wirral: Headland, 1998).
Coles, Gladys Mary. *Mary Webb* (Bridgend: Seren Books, 1990).

Gladys Mary Coles

Welfare State

In the 1940s, the Welfare State was a term of abuse, particularly in the United States, for extravagant state expenditure. It was then transformed into a term of approbation by the postwar Labour government after the 'Appointed Day' of 5 July 1948, when a raft of new social services, including the National Health Service and National Insurance, was introduced. Inspired by the 1942 Beveridge Report, they complemented earlier reforms such as the 1944 Education Act and the 1945 Family Allowance Act. The term then became synonymous with government intervention in five policy areas (employment, social security, EDUCATION, HOUSING, and the personal social services). This 'core' activity was supplemented by additional services, such as legal aid, and by the establishment in the 1960s of new personal rights, such as the right to ABORTION and free CONTRACEPTION. The Beveridge Report raised early visions of 'social security' (the freedom of everyone from the historic fear of poverty, whatever its cause) and of 'social solidarity' (a greater sense of community). This led some pioneers, such as Richard Titmuss, to hope that a 'welfare state' would both create a more egalitarian society and provide a framework which naturally encouraged altruism. By the 1970s, however, the Welfare State had once again, under influence from the United States, become a term of abuse. Increasingly identified simply with cash benefits, it was seen to create a dependency culture amongst claimants which compounded the very problem it was supposed to resolve.

Women participated in this wider ideological debate, but a specific feminist critique of the Welfare State also developed. Before 1940, women were particularly disadvantaged. As household managers, for example, they often sacrificed their own needs to those of their families. Only the employed were insured and therefore the majority of women, even at their most vulnerable times of pregnancy and childbirth, had to pay the full market cost of HEALTHcare. Consequently they often went without. After 1948, therefore, the right to a minimum income and free healthcare transformed lives. However, from its Edwardian origins, welfare reform came at a perceived price. For example, the introduction in 1906 of free school meals, to mitigate the effects of poverty in children, was regarded as an intrusion into mothers' private responsibilities and a slur on their competence. Rapidly expanding numbers of mother and baby clinics, even when pioneered by women, could be regarded as 'pro-family' (encouraging and thereby reinforcing women's biological role in the national interest) rather than 'women-friendly' (empowering women in their own right, particularly to control their own bodies). The provision of help to rear, but not to limit the number of, children was significant here. So too was the growth of clinics in FASCIST states. Most seriously, after 1948 the automatic right to social security was earned through National Insurance contributions made at work. In the 1940s the majority of married women were not in paid employment and so their 'right' was earned by their husbands. Apart from the psychological cost, this also discouraged unhappy or abused wives from seeking separation or divorce. Once independent, a non-contributor's 'right' to social security could only be realized through the stigmatized means-tested system of national assistance.

Most employees in the new welfare services were women. Opportunities for economic independence were thereby enhanced, but again there was a catch. Most powerful positions, such as doctors or head teachers, were held by men and so, as an employer, the Welfare State also tended to reinforce traditional gender roles. Nevertheless, over time, it could be argued that the Welfare State, through a combination of increased employment, benefits, and services (especially education), did provide women with a platform from which they could contest both potentially coercive legislation and the power imbalance within the private sphere of the home.

Suggested Reading
Jones, Margaret and Rodney Lowe. *From Beveridge to Blair: The First Fifty Years of Britain's Welfare State* (Manchester: Manchester University Press, 2002).
Lowe, Rodney. *The Welfare State in Britain Since 1945*, 2nd edition (Basingstoke: Palgrave Macmillan, 1999).
Timmins, N. *The Five Giants* (London: HarperCollins, 2001).

Rodney Lowe

Wellesley, Dorothy 1896–1956
Poet, editor, confidante of Vita SACKVILLE-WEST (who authored Wellesley's entry in *The Dictionary of National Biography*), and protégée of W. B. Yeats, who introduced *Selections from the Poems of Dorothy Wellesley* (1936) and included some of her work in *The Oxford Book of Modern Verse*. Stepdaughter of Lord Scarborough, she grew up in privileged circumstances and was educated at home. She married Gerald, Duke of Wellesley in 1914, bearing two children; although the couple separated in 1923, as his wife she became Duchess of Marlborough in 1943. Moving in upper-class literary circles, Wellesley was known to the BLOOMSBURY GROUP and Edith SITWELL. An investor in the Hogarth Press, from 1928 she edited the First Series of the Hogarth Living Poets.

Her own poetic career began with *Early Poems* (1913); some ten further volumes concluded with *Early Light: The Collected Poems* (1955). Her work can be grim in its directness, but Wellesley's erratic but imaginative and energetic poetic style won some admiration when *Genesis* (1926) and *Deserted House* (1931) were applauded by Yeats. After the poet died, Wellesley published their correspondence. She also published a memoir, *Far Have I Travelled* (1952), but criticism of her work is scarce.

Suggested Reading
Wellesley, Dorothy. *Letters on Poetry from W. B. Yeats to Dorothy Wellesley*, new edition. ed. Kathleen Raine (Oxford: Oxford University Press, 1964).

Alice Entwistle

Welsh Language Writing
The flourishing of women's writing in Welsh during the early part of the twentieth century demonstrates a remarkable shift in the cultural and political position of the Welsh language, in spite of the systematic attempts to eradicate it on the part of English colonial powers throughout the latter half of the nineteenth century. The advent of this oppression was the publication of the *Report of the Commissioners of Inquiry into the State of Education in Wales* (1847) – better known in Wales as 'Y Llyfrau Gleision' or 'The Blue Books'. It notoriously characterized the Welsh people as dirty, lazy, ignorant, and deceitful. Women, in particular, were charged with licentiousness and immorality. Their 'flagrant want of chastity' was blamed upon their adherence to a language and culture that the Blue Books claimed prevented its people from rising to the civilized values of their English neighbours.

In response to these claims and the subsequent illegalization of Welsh in schools and public office, the magazine *Y Frythones* ('The British Woman', 1879–91), edited by Cranogwen (Sarah Jane Rees), began publishing women's writing that stressed the virtuousness of the Welsh woman with particular regard to the Puritanism of chapel culture. Although many of the contributions were morally prescriptive, the very publication of the journal was an act of proto-feminist, anti-colonial resistance.

The overtly moralistic tendencies of Welsh-language women's writing extended into the early twentieth century with writers such as Eluned Morgan (1870–1938) and Moelena (Elizabeth Mary Jones, 1878–1953). The former is perhaps best known for her travel writing and her editorship of *Y Drafod* ('The Discussion'), the newspaper of the Welsh-speaking colony of Patagonia. Moelena's *Teulu Bach Nantoer* ('The Little Family of Nantoer', 1913) and *Cwrs y Lli* ('The Current's Flow', 1927) are counted among the classics of twentieth-century Wales, and chronicle the emergence of the women's suffrage movement in poor, isolated rural Welsh communities.

Less of an earnest moralizer was Gwyneth Vaughan (Annie Harriet Vaughan, 1852–1910). Her novels identify contemporary political and social problems as emerging from key historical events in Wales's past. *Plant y Gorthrwm*

('The Children of Oppression', 1908), for instance, characterizes the 1868 General Elections (which saw the first mass revolt against the political tyranny of the land- and mine-owning class) as a kind of social epiphany that led to the early twentieth-century's near-uniform Liberal climate. It was an opinion echoed by Lloyd George that same year when he claimed – with more hyperbole – that 1868 had 'awakened the spirit of the mountains... The political power of the landlords in Wales was shattered as completely as the power of the Druids.'

One of the most influential authors working in Welsh was Winifred 'Winnie' Parry (1870–1953). Born in the Anglicized town of Welshpool, Montgomeryshire, Parry was less influenced by Welsh Nonconformism than her contemporary writers. She spoke and read French, German, and English, and lived most of her life in England. *Sioned* (1906) was the first Welsh novel to be centred on an adolescent girl. Its particular use of humour and colloquial expressions has influenced countless later writers. It was reissued by Honno, the Welsh Women's Press, in 1988.

In terms of verse, the most notable poet of the first half of the twentieth century was Dilys Cadwaldr (1902–79). For her composition '*Y Llen*' – a *pryddest*, that is, a poem that does not conform to one of the 24 metres of traditional Welsh verse – Cadwaldr became the first woman to win the Bardic Crown at the National Eisteddfod, the most prestigious prize of the festival of Welsh culture and literature.

Another Eisteddfod winner was Elena Puw Morgan (1900–73), who won the Prose Medal for her unremittingly bleak novel *Y Graith* ('The Scar', 1943). The work's austerity and occasionally cruel depictions of rural life counterbalance the romanticism of the *gwerin*, or 'folk', ideal that informs much contemporary Welsh literature in both languages – particularly the work of Allen RAINE and Kate ROBERTS.

An overtly feminist ideology can also be found in the work of Kate Bosse-Griffiths (1910–98). Although German-born, Griffiths worked in both England and Wales during a distinguished academic career, and produced several Welsh-language novels, including *Anesmwyth Haen* ('Restless Energy', 1941) which startled reviewers with its frank and challenging depictions of sex. The novel marks a major shift from the Puritanical ideal of womanhood that was necessary to resist the colonial oppressions forced upon Welsh-speaking, working-class women in the nineteenth century.

These writers all represent part of an alternative tradition to the predominantly male-orientated Welsh and Anglo-Welsh literary histories of the first half of the twentieth century: one that is less wholly concerned with the industrial landscape and one that is perhaps less obviously radical in politics. Yet it is a tradition that no less successfully challenged dominant English literary modes and imperialistic, class-driven dynamics.

Suggested Reading

Aaron, Jane. 'Finding a Voice in Two Tongues: Gender and Colonization', in Jane Aaron et al. (eds), *Our Sister's Land: The Changing Identities of Women in Wales* (Cardiff: University of Wales Press, 1994) 183–98.

Johnston, Dafydd (ed.). *A Guide to Welsh Literature, Volume 6: 1900–1996* (Cardiff: University of Wales Press, 1998).

Stephens, Meic (ed.). *The New Companion to the Literature of Wales*, 2nd edition (Cardiff: University of Wales Press, 1998).

Rob Gossedge

West, Rebecca 1892–1983

Novelist, journalist, and critic, West was a keen observer of culture and politics for much of the twentieth century. Originally called Cicily Fairfield, she felt that the primness of this name was unsuitable to her strong views and sturdy build. Her pseudonym, taken from an Ibsen heroine, betrays an early interest in acting, but she found biting feminist, SOCIALIST journalism more suited to her talents. As a teenager, West joined suffragist demonstrations and sold *Votes for Women* in the streets. Her father, Charles Fairfield, was himself a journalist, but with an opposite political agenda to his daughter's. Her mother, Isabella Mackenzie, was a gifted pianist who turned typist to support three daughters in her native Edinburgh. West's *Family Memories* (1987), *Selected Letters* (2000), and a final trio of novels inaugurated with *The Fountain Overflows* (1956) expose the lasting wound of her father's desertion, while *The Judge* (1922) takes up the challenges of single motherhood, experienced by both mother and daughter.

Family relations remained a source of anguish throughout West's long life. She argued with her gifted eldest sister, the physician Letitia Fairfield. There was reason for alarm over West's involvement with the middle-aged novelist and man of ideas, H. G. Wells. Their ten-year alliance had numerous ruptures, and their son, Anthony, would blame West for depriving him of a father for the rest of her life. In 1930, West married Henry Andrews, an international banker. Though he failed to provide the hoped-for serenity, Henry became a useful character in her travel writing, and together they refurbished an impressive manor house in Buckinghamshire.

West's early fiction, including *The Judge*, showed affinities with MODERNISM. *The Return of the Soldier* (1918) is a psychological study of combat-induced amnesia; *Harriet Hume* (1929) offers a feminist fantasy compatible with WOOLF's *Orlando*. West's interest in the corrupted lives of industrialists emerged in *The Harsh Voice* (1935), stories set largely in the United States, and *The Thinking Reed* (1936). She also began a gripping Russian historical novel, *The Birds Fall Down* (published 1966). West's later novels in *The Fountain Overflows* series sustain an element of melodrama never far from her writing; the first became a bestseller. Her literary journalism includes critical studies of Henry

James and D. H. Lawrence. The title essay of *The Strange Necessity* (1928) remains remarkable for its independent assessment of James Joyce's *Ulysses*. Elsewhere, West boldly disputed the critical authority of T. S. Eliot, and wrote appreciatively of Woolf and other women writers.

A more conservative West emerges in her writings concerning espionage, collected in *The Meaning of Treason* (1947) and *A Train of Powder* (1955). She was suspected of sympathizing with Joseph McCarthy, and fiercely denied it. Though West's work is not universally appealing, a favourite is her study of Yugoslavia on the brink of fascist invasion, *Black Lamb and Grey Falcon* (1941). By turns multicultural history, philosophical exposition, and personal travel narrative, it offers 'an inventory of a country down to its last vest-button', which has endured. Posthumous publications continue.

Suggested Reading

Glendinning, Victoria. *Rebecca West: A Life* (London: Weidenfeld & Nicolson, 1987).

Rollyson, Carl. *Rebecca West: A Saga of the Century* (London: Hodder & Stoughton, 1995).

Scott, Bonnie Kime. *Refiguring Modernism. Volume 2: Postmodern Feminist Readings of Woolf, West and Barnes* (Bloomington: Indiana University Press, 1995).

Bonnie Kime Scott

Whipple, Dorothy 1893–1966

Novelist and short-story writer, who wrote in the tradition of Mrs Gaskell, describing ordinary people with outwardly uneventful lives, and yet made her books compulsively readable because of her psychological insight. Born in Blackburn, Whipple lived most of her life in Nottingham, and she married but had no children. Nine novels appeared during the interwar years, most of which were Book Society Choices. *High Wages* (1930) is about a girl who starts a dress shop; *The Priory* (1939) traces the decline in the fortunes of the inhabitants of a large house, both upstairs and downstairs; *Someone at a Distance* (1953) evokes a happy Home Counties marriage insidiously destroyed by the egoism of the mother-in-law: 'Widowed, in the house her husband had built with day and night nurseries and a music room, as if the children would stay there for ever, instead of marrying and going off at the earliest possible moment, old Mrs North yielded one day to a long-felt desire to provide herself with company.'

Dorothy Whipple has now begun to be seen as a far better writer than, say, J. B. Priestley (who thought her work had 'a kind of North-Country Jane Austen quality'), but, unlike him, was ignored until recently, her consistently subtle style being easy to confuse with the simplistic.

Suggested Reading

Bawden, Nina. Introduction to *Someone at a Distance* by Dorothy Whipple (London: Persephone, 1999) v xi.

Macmath, Terence Handley. Afterword to *They Knew Mr Knight* by Dorothy
Whipple (London: Persephone, 2001) 471–80.

Nicola Beauman

White, Antonia 1899–1980

British novelist and translator. Born Eirene Botting, White was dominated
from childhood by her demanding, controlling father. In 1906 he converted to
Catholicism, soon followed by Antonia and her mother. This profoundly
important move resulted in a lifelong sense of ambivalence and inferiority, for
as a convert, White felt she did not truly 'belong' to the Church. In 1908, she
become a pupil of the Convent of the Sacred Heart at Roehampton; she left
aged 14, a catastrophic event that White retold in her most famous work *Frost
in May* (1933).

White subsequently held various jobs including actress, journalist, and
advertising copywriter. Her first short story, 'Strangers', was published in the
New Statesman in 1928. In 1922, following the collapse of her first, unconsummated, marriage, White had a mental breakdown and was committed to
Bethlem Hospital for nine months. Her second marriage was also annulled,
and in 1930 she married her third husband Tom Hopkinson, who encouraged
her to write her first novel.

Although it was turned down by one publisher's reader as being 'too slight to
be of interest to anyone', *Frost in May* was an instant success. Elizabeth BOWEN
praised White's style for being 'as precise, clear and unweighty as Jane
Austen's'. The story of Catholic convert Nanda Grey, and her life at the
Convent of the Five Wounds at Lippington, the book examines the ritualistic,
highly seductive world of the convent, and the nuns' attempts to systematically
break Nanda's will: 'Almost everything's a venial sin, in fact. If I don't eat my
cabbage, or if I have an extra helping of pudding when I'm not really hungry,
or if I think my hair looks really nice when it's just been washed.' The novel
also probes class consciousness; most of the other pupils are daughters of
aristocratic Catholic families, which exacerbates Nanda's alienation. White
had another mental breakdown after the book appeared, and it was 17 years
before she published another novel. Having abandoned Catholicism in 1926,
she decided to return to the Church in 1940; *The Hound and the Falcon* (1965) is
White's acclaimed account of this reconversion. Despite struggles with her
faith, White remained within the Catholic Church until her death.

White's later novels also drew on incidents from her own life, detailing her
difficult relationships with her father and her religion. *The Lost Traveller* (1950)
continues the story of Nanda (renamed Clara) after leaving Lippington. The
story of her first marriage and its aftermath is the subject of *The Sugar House*
(1952), while *Beyond the Glass* (1954) portrays White's insanity and subsequent
incarceration. But after the completion of this trilogy, a chronic mental block

descended upon White, driving her to the brink of madness. She never wrote another work of adult fiction, although she did write two children's books, *Minka and Curdy* (1957) and *Living with Minka and Curdy* (1970). She also translated over 30 novels from the French, including works by Colette and Duras. White's work was rediscovered in the 1970s when *Frost in May* became the first Virago Modern Classic in 1978. Virago have also published two volumes of her diaries. After White's death, her two daughters both wrote memoirs detailing their difficult relationship with her.

Suggested Reading

Dunn, Jane. *Antonia White: A Life* (London: Jonathan Cape, 1998).

Palmer, Paulina. 'Antonia White's *Frost in May*: A Lesbian Feminist Reading', in Susan Sellers (ed.), *Feminist Criticism: Theory and Practice* (Hemel Hempstead: Harvester Wheatsheaf, 1991) 89–108.

Louise Harrington

White, Ethel Lina 1876–1944

Mystery and suspense writer, best known for her novel *The Wheel Spins* (1936) which provided the basis for Alfred Hitchcock's 1938 thriller film, *The Lady Vanishes*. Born in Abergavenny and the fifth of 12 children, little is known of White's early life. She worked for the Ministry of Pensions before turning to professional writing in the early 1920s, becoming a semi-regular contributor to *Person's Magazine*. Her first novel, *The Wish Bone* (1927) was described by the London Evening News as a 'charming little romance', and two more mainstream novels followed before the publication of *Put Out the Light* (1931), her first mystery novel.

Having found her niche, White continued to write in this genre and became well known for her particular brand of unnerving thriller, such as *Some Must Watch* (1933) in which a girl waits in an isolated mansion as the live bait for a killer, a 'human tiger', who lurks in the darkness outside. This 'damsel-in-distress' scenario was a key feature of White's stories, and she was considered a master of the suspense story with a 'twist'. Several of her novels have been made into films, including *Some Must Watch*, filmed as *The Spiral Staircase* in 1945. White is now mostly referred to in association with these adaptations of her work, and her career as a successful mystery novelist is largely, and unjustly, forgotten.

Suggested Reading

Sutcliffe, Mark. 'Ethel Lina White: Author of *The Lady Vanishes*', *Book and Magazine Collector*, 213 (2001) 20–8.

Turnbull, Malcolm J. 'Predicaments and Premonitions: The Writing of Ethel Lina White', *Clues: A Journal of Detection*, 18.2 (1997) 99–132.

Esme Miskimmin

Wickham, Anna 1884–1947

Prolific poet with a troubled feminist voice. Before WORLD WAR ONE Wickham produced 900 poems in four years; many of these and much of her correspondence were destroyed during WORLD WAR TWO, but 1100 unpublished poems and five published collections remained. She was well known in Britain; in Paris, where she became attached to Natalie Barney and the circle of women who lived on the Left Bank; and in the United States, where her reputation was at its height after the First World War. British born, she grew up in Australia but returned to Britain in 1904. She married Patrick Hepburn in 1906, which meant relinquishing a career in opera singing. Domestically, she felt a failure: she had a stillborn child and a miscarriage before her first son, James, was born; he was followed by three more children but her third son died of scarlet fever in 1921, aged four. When her husband died in a climbing accident in 1929, she was freed from the bonds of a turbulent marriage but not from those of motherhood. Some of her guilt fuelled her social welfare work and her writing, especially that concerning the neglected needs of working-class mothers.

The publication of *The Writings of Anna Wickham* in 1984 rescued her poetry from obscurity. Her work cannot readily be categorized and she draws upon literary inheritances which are shared by all cultural echelons, such as ballad, pastoral, fairy-tale, and folk legend. Most strikingly, she exploits the opportunity for internal dialogue and for publicizing the personal in the dramatic monologue. She solved the dual demands of form and freedom by finding perfection in imperfection, through faulty rhyme, associating free verse with psychological and aesthetic liberty.

Wickham usually distances herself from the characters who often interrogate complex womanly, and sometimes male, psychology. Nevertheless, much of the poetry illuminates and can be illuminated by 'Fragment of an Autobiography: Prelude to a Spring Clean' (reprinted in *Writings*), which records how freedom of expression was her central preoccupation. Internal conflict is Wickham's signature: 'Definition' questions whether a wife's identity is anything more than that of a mother and bed partner, while tension between liberty and loyalty is replicated in the deceptively simple idioms of 'The Wife'. As in 'Dilemma', the bind was never resolved and Anna Wickham finally committed suicide at home.

Suggested Reading

Dowson, Jane. *Women, Modernism and British Poetry, 1910–39: Resisting Femininity* (Aldershot: Ashgate, 2002).

Jones, Jennifer Vaughan. *Anna Wickham: A Poet's Daring Life* (New York: Madison Books, 2003).

Rice, Nelljean McConeghey. *A New Matrix for Modernism: A Study of the Lives and Poetry of Charlotte Mew and Anna Wickham* (London: Routledge, 2003).

Jane Dowson

Wilkinson, Ellen 1891–1947

Novelist, journalist, labour activist, and Member of Parliament. Born to an upper-working-class Manchester family, Wilkinson attended grammar school and Manchester Day Teacher Training College, then earned her BA and MA from Manchester University. Victoria University of Manchester awarded her an honorary doctorate in 1946. Wilkinson was active in Manchester SUFFRAGE and SOCIALIST circles from an early age and joined the Independent Labour Party at 16. At university, she was a member of the FABIAN SOCIETY, and later she became a full-time organizer for the National Union of Women's Suffrage Societies (NUWSS). In 1915, she served as one of the few wartime female trade union officers. She contributed in these years to such journals as the *Labour Leader, Sunday Worker,* and *Time and Tide.*

In 1923, Wilkinson won a Labour seat on the Manchester City Council and in 1924 was elected MP for Middlesborough East. As Labour's youngest, and only female, MP, the outspoken and pretty redhead became known as the 'elfin fury'; she was the inspiration for Winifred HOLTBY's socialist headmistress, Sarah Burton, in the novel *South Riding.* Women's interests, including equal employment and voting rights, were always priorities for Wilkinson, but she once explained that she did 'not want to be regarded purely as a woman's MP...men voters predominate in Middlesborough East, thousands are unemployed and I mean to stand up to the gruelling work for all their sakes'. She went on to serve as MP for Jarrow in 1935; became Privy Councillor in 1945; and, as the Minister for Education in Attlee's postwar Labour Government, was responsible for raising the school leaving age to 15.

Political experience flavoured Wilkinson's two best remembered writings: the novel *Clash* (1928) and the contemporary political study *Jarrow: The Town That Was Murdered* (1939). Recent feminist scholars credit *Clash* with revising the standard romantic plot. Against the background of the 1926 General Strike, the protagonist, Joan, eventually decides against her more fascinating suitor in order to marry the man who offers to work beside her in a socialist partnership of equals. Like Wilkinson, Joan realizes that, in her Northern constituency, it is difficult to preach feminism to wives desperately concerned with their husbands' unemployment. Wilkinson's *Jarrow* was a Left BOOK CLUB volume that described the politics behind the 1936 JARROW MARCH, in which she joined as a speaker:

> In both Germany and England the real wages of the workers have had to be reduced...in order to make the profit system (based on scarcity) keep going... Nazi Germany wants to use the surplus accrued for war preparation...The English capitalists, relying on the sources of their Empire, want the profit surplus to be as big as possible. Hence they consider it better to strangle a Jarrow...in order to keep the profits...high.

Wilkinson also produced mystery fiction, political satire, and several anti-fascist texts including *Why Fascism?* (1934), *The Terror in Germany* (1938), and articles for *Time and Tide* under the pseudonym 'East Wind'.

Suggested Reading

Maslen, Elizabeth. *Political and Social Issues in British Women's Fiction, 1928–1968* (Basingstoke: Palgrave Macmillan, 2001).
Vernon, Betty D. *Ellen Wilkinson 1891–1947* (London: Croom Helm, 1982).

Ashlie Sponenberg

Women's Movement

From the mid-nineteenth century onwards, the women's movement in Britain has been a vibrant and diverse force campaigning for women's social, political, and economic equality and the enhancement of women's position in society. The movement emerged in Britain in the 1850s with the involvement of a small but significant number of women in reform campaigns such as the anti-slavery movement, the anti-Corn Law league, and Chartism. Their contribution demonstrated that despite the Victorian belief in separate spheres, which dictated that a woman's place was in the home whilst men engaged in public life, women did have the opportunity to make their opinions and voices heard in these national campaigns. Women from upper-class and middle-class backgrounds were also involved in philanthropic work, which again illustrated their ability to participate in activities outside the home. In addition, women from all classes were able to express their political preferences, long before they were granted the parliamentary vote, through their membership of auxiliary political organizations, namely the Conservative Primrose League (from 1884), the Women's Liberal Federation (1887), and the Women's Labour League (1906). Although excluded from the franchise under the 1834, 1867, and 1884 Reform Acts, by 1875 women ratepayers were entitled to vote and stand as candidates for Municipal Elections, Local School Boards, and Poor Law Guardians. By 1900 there were one million female local government electors and 270 women serving on School Boards. By 1914 there were 1546 female Poor Law Guardians.

As the century progressed, women became increasingly involved in public affairs and more vocal on a range of issues which affected women's lives. The most prominent of these campaigns was the SUFFRAGE movement, demanding the extension of the parliamentary franchise to women. In 1897 the National Union of Women's Suffrage Societies (NUWSS) was formed to unite the myriad suffrage societies which had been established by this time. Other high profile campaigns included Josephine Butler's long fight to revoke the 1860s Contagious Diseases Acts, a successful campaign which ended with their repeal in 1886. These Acts had compelled women suspected of prostitution in garrison ports and towns to submit to a medical examination and, if necessary, treatment for venereal disease. Butler's campaign reflected the lack of recognition and concern on the part of the government for women's civil rights. The civil rights of women were further compromised by their lack of legal rights within marriage. Under common law, wives were regarded as the property of their husbands and had no claim to their own wealth or the custody of their children. Individual women and women's groups highlighted these injustices and some improvement of women's status in marriage was achieved with the passing of the Married Women's Property Acts in 1870 and 1882. These reforms gave wives the right to the ownership of their earnings and to retain property on marriage.

Along with these achievements, the women's movement in Britain at the turn of the twentieth century was also celebrating greater access to EDUCATION for women. In 1870 primary education became free and compulsory for all boys and girls, and by 1914 the majority of children in Britain were educated up to 14 years of age. A small but growing number of middle-class girls were attending private schools such as Cheltenham Ladies College (1854) and women were estimated to make up 15 per cent of Britain's university population in 1900. Yet when it came to the world of work the majority of women workers were still to be found in low-paid and low-skilled jobs. Domestic work and employment in the textile industry were the major occupations undertaken by working-class women, whilst increasing numbers of lower-middle-class women were finding employment in the expanding white collar sector, most notably in clerical work, shop work, and teaching. Throughout this period and indeed up until the 1950s, only a tiny minority of women entered the higher paid professions. Moreover, the vast majority of women workers gave up work on marriage.

The suffrage campaign dominates the history of the women's movement in Britain during the years 1900 to 1918, but it is important to note that women's organizations and individual women were also involved in other campaigns at this time. Suffrage societies, most notably the NUWSS, did not limit their demands to the vote for women. They also called for an end to discrimination against women in the home, the workplace and in public life. These feminist societies recognized the imbalance of power between men and women on social, economic, and political lines, and sought to challenge such inequality by demanding equal rights, equal opportunities, and an equal moral standard for men and women. Working alongside these pressure groups were mainstream women's organizations which also wished to enhance women's position in society. The Women's Co-operative Guild (1883), an organization promoting the interests and needs of working-class housewives and mothers, was vocal on a wide range of issues affecting its members, including greater access to divorce, improved HOUSING conditions, and the right of women to birth control information. The Mothers' Union (1885), representing Anglican mothers, called on the state to provide mothers with recognition and support in areas such as housing and education. The Young Women's Christian Association (1877) provided educational and recreational opportunities to young working women and drew attention to the discrimination faced by many women workers in terms of pay and conditions.

In 1918 the parliamentary franchise was granted to women over the age of 30, and ten years later women won the vote on equal terms with men. This significant victory marked an end to the suffrage campaign, but not to the women's movement in Britain. Following the extension of the franchise, former suffrage societies had to find a new identity and purpose. In 1918 the NUWSS became the National Union of Societies for Equal Citizenship (NUSEC) and whilst continuing to demand equal rights for women, became more outspoken in calling for social and educational reforms including the payment of family allowances to mothers and access to CONTRACEPTION information. The decision to give prominence to issues relating to the role of women as wives and mothers is commonly referred to as 'new feminism'. Members of the NUSEC who disagreed with this policy left the organization and joined societies such as the Six Point Group (1921) and the Women's Freedom League (1907), which focused more on the traditional demands for equal rights and opportunities for women known as 'equal rights feminism'.

Despite these divisions over the nature of feminism, the need to continue fighting for women's equality following the extension of the franchise galvanized women's organizations throughout the interwar period. A number of important legislative reforms were introduced during the early 1920s which did improve women's position in society, including the 1923 Matrimonial Causes Act (which enabled a wife to sue for divorce on the same grounds as her husband) and the 1925 Guardianship of Infants Act. The 1919 Sex Disqualification (Removal) Act made it illegal for women to be denied employment on the grounds of marriage. Nevertheless, the Act did not prevent the implementation of the public service marriage bar throughout the 1920s and 1930s, and working women continued to be discriminated against when it came to pay and conditions. Married women were excluded from free healthcare, and women in general were underrepresented in public life, with only 38 women elected to the House of Commons during the years 1919 to 1945.

During the interwar years and throughout the 1940s, the women's movement continued to highlight the injustices faced by women in British society, although it faced many difficulties. Feminist societies failed to win much popular support, as they were often inaccurately portrayed as radical groups who wished to transform society and break up the family. The ideology of domesticity, which prevailed during these years, encouraged women to devote their time to home and family and the vast majority of women did marry and opt out of paid work in order to care for children full-time. Yet, in spite of the cult of domesticity and the unpopularity of feminism, the women's movement survived and achieved some major victories. Mainstream women's societies such as the Women's Institute Movement (1915), representing rural women, and the Mothers' Union, attracted hundreds of thousands of members and campaigned on a range of issues including housing reform and the payment of family allowances to mothers, finally introduced in 1945. After a long campaign supported by the Women's Co-operative Guild and the National Council of Women (set up in 1918), married women were provided with access to limited birth control information at local authority clinics in 1931. The Women's Institutes, along with feminist societies such as the NUSEC and the Six Point Group, supported the campaign for equal pay in the public sector and that demand was met in 1954. There is no doubt that by the 1950s considerable progress had been made. Nonetheless, women continued to face significant gender inequalities in the home, the workplace, and in public life. These inequalities would be addressed with renewed vigour with the coming of the Women's Liberation Movement in the early 1970s.

Suggested Reading
Bruley, Sue. *Women in Britain Since 1900* (London: St Martin's Press, 1989).
Caine, Barbara. *English Feminism, 1780–1980* (Oxford: Oxford University Press, 1997).
Law, Cheryl. *Suffrage and Power: The Women's Movement, 1918–1928* (London: I. B. Tauris, 2000).
Pugh, Martin. *Women and the Women's Movement in Britain, 1914–1999* (Basingstoke: Palgrave Macmillan, 2000).
Zweiniger-Bargielowska, Ina (ed.). *Women in Twentieth Century Britain* (London: Pearson Education, 2001).

Caitriona Beaumont

Women's and Girls' Magazines
Beetham and Boardman usefully characterize magazines *per se* as publications possessing heterogeneity in subject matter, variety of authorial voice, mass markets, and ephemerality, whilst describing *women's* magazines, in particular, as those additionally reflecting a supposed homogenous female experience. Such magazines centre on normative notions of femininity and domesticity and their concomitant habits of expenditure and consumption, whilst largely ignoring distinctions such as race and cultural difference. However, they also provide a wholly female space in which readers, often isolated in their everyday lives, may feel themselves to be part of a larger community of women.

Until the First World War, magazines for girls largely replicated those for women, featuring articles on cookery, health, and beauty, and some ROMANTIC

FICTION. It is therefore unsurprising that titles such as the *Monthly Packet* (1851–99) and the *Girl's Own Paper* (1880–1918) were read by both women and girls. However girls' periodicals changed entirely with the advent of the girls' comic, probably the only periodical targeting females to enjoy extensive circulation whilst not blatantly promoting femininity, domesticity, and consumer durables. Its primary ingredient was fiction, featuring adventurous and resourceful young heroines and set in girls' schools or in exotic locations; its arrant racism was less admirable. Earlier titles included *The School Friend* (first run from 1919), *Girl's Crystal Weekly* (1936–7), and *Girl* (1951–64). Other titles came and went between the 1950s and the 1970s, but by the 1980s comics had been overtaken by 'young teen' magazines, exploring relationships with boys as well as celebrating the FASHION and commercial music scene. Hence, a distinct 'girl' culture remained visible but compulsory heterosexuality and CONSUMERISM once again aligned them with more traditional women's magazines.

Women's magazines themselves are still remarkably successful in spite of competition from other kinds of publication. For example, two very different nineteenth-century purveyors of the femininity/domesticity formula – the working-class *People's Friend* (1869) and *The Lady* (1885), which targets a higher status readership – have survived into the twenty-first century, whilst the radical *Englishwoman's Journal* (1877–1910) and the explicitly feminist *Spare Rib* (1972–93) have not. Moreover, to this day, the commissioning editors for the *People's Friend* remind would-be fiction-writers that its readers 'believe in the sanctity of marriage' and the publisher of the successful *Woman's Weekly* (1911) markets the magazine as one that 'celebrates... home and family'.

The two wars inevitably had a huge impact upon the market. By 1918 the socioeconomic structure of society had changed considerably. SERVANTS were fewer and much investment income had been lost. Thus, for many women, household labour and money were in shorter supply whilst personal domestic expertise was lacking. Meanwhile, although many women war-workers were unwillingly driven back into the home, there was a renewed enthusiasm for things domestic. Publishers responded to both the need for advice and the zeal for home-making by launching a successful new range of magazines that gave detailed – even elementary – advice on practical housewifery, alongside the usual articles on fashion and beauty. These included *Good Housekeeping* (1922) and *Woman and Home* (1926). They were joined by a range of fiction periodicals aimed at the less well-educated younger working-class woman, such as *Peg's Paper*, launched in 1919.

Yet it took a second world war to establish the profile of the women's magazine we see today. During hostilities, wartime economy measures determined magazine size and circulation whilst editors ran articles about nutrition and economy and printed upbeat advice about how to 'make do and mend'. Advertisers could only frame their copy to similar ends. However, after the years of austerity, women suddenly had to deal with the new rush of consumer goods that became available. Advertisers now asserted the right to act as arbiters of taste, to educate the woman reader in what to purchase for the home and how best to adorn and beautify herself for her man. They have retained this role ever since.

Indeed, the history of women's magazines is, largely, the history of the changing relationship between editors and advertisers. By 1900, advertising revenue had become vital to both NEWSPAPERS and magazines, in order to keep cover prices down. Meanwhile, the 'feminine' focus of the magazines, on matters such as clothes, cosmetics, and cookery, both reinforced normative gender roles and created a reader anxiety which advertisers could exploit very effectively. Moreover, advertising investment had to be requited with a yielding of editorial control to the paymasters. The period 1900 to 1950 saw both a significant increase in the quantity of advertising and a greater integration of advertisements with editorial matter. By the time rationing had ended after the Second World War, advertisers had gained a total ascendancy over editors which has never since been lost.

Suggested Reading

Beetham, Margaret and Kay Boardman. *Victorian Women's Magazines* (Manchester: Manchester University Press, 2001).

White, Cynthia L. *Women's Magazines, 1693–1968* (London: Michael Joseph, 1970).

Winship, Janice. *Inside Women's Magazines* (New York: Pandora, 1987).

Elaine Hartnell

Woolf, Virginia 1882–1941

Novelist, essayist, and continuing inspiration to feminists. Novels such as *Mrs. Dalloway* (1925), *To the Lighthouse* (1927), and *The Waves* (1933) gained Woolf admittance to canonical MODERNISM, alongside T. S. Eliot (a friend whose work she published) and James Joyce. For a wider array of achievements, she is now heralded as one of the most influential novelists of the twentieth century. Her importance as a cultural critic emerged with the second wave of feminism, when *A Room of One's Own* (1929) became a basic feminist text. Her writings scrutinize EMPIRE and IMPERIALISM, advocate PACIFISM, and counter FASCISM.

Woolf self-assigned to a class of 'daughters of educated men'; her father, Sir Leslie Stephen, was editor of the *Cornhill Magazine* and the *Dictionary of National Biography*. Woolf was a precocious, voracious reader, educated at home while her brothers attended Cambridge. In 'A Sketch of the Past,' Woolf relates her experience of sexual abuse by her half-brothers, but her sister, the artist Vanessa Bell, was an enduring support and an artistic collaborator. Equally supportive was Leonard Woolf, whom she married in 1912; their Hogarth Press published avant-garde and SOCIALIST works. Vita SACKVILLE-WEST and Dame Ethel SMYTH were among Woolf's LESBIAN loves. Woolf suffered from bipolar disorder, and a lifelong series of breakdowns began at age 13, following the death of her mother, Julia Stephen, and ended with her suicide at 59, during wartime. Woolf's diaries and letters provide brilliant access to her mind, her writing projects, everyday experiences, and feelings about others, including her BLOOMSBURY circle.

Woolf's first novel, *The Voyage Out* (1915), examines the institutions of marriage and global commerce, and explores consciousness. *Night and Day* (1919) treats love and feminist enterprises in more traditional form, and *Jacob's Room* (1922) experiments with observers' perspectives ranged around the life of a young man lost in the Great War. A less extreme form of what Woolf called 'carving out caves around my characters' occurs in *Mrs. Dalloway*, in which a dual plot parallels masculine shell-shock with feminine trauma. Poetic prose claims the disruptive central section of the autobiographical novel *To the Light-house*, while *The Waves* also contains poetic natural interludes, together with soliloquies showing the mental imagery of six characters at intervals through their lives. *Orlando* (1928) ranges from the sixteeenth to the twentieth century, drawing on the ancestral history of Vita Sackville-West. Its poet-persona switches from male to female mid-way, and the novel offers a witty and cogent study of the cultural construction of gender. Generations of family life are revisited amid changing cultural conditions in *The Years* (1937), while Woolf's most radical social analysis, *Three Guineas* (1938), juxtaposes British patriarchy and fascism, proposing that women form a pacifist 'outsiders' society'. The long sweep of English culture is performed with clashes of gender and sexuality in the pageant and intervals of Woolf's last novel, *Between the Acts* (1941). Her essays and book reviews appeared often in the *TLS* and the *Nation* and were collected in *The Common Reader* (1925), and *The Common Reader, Second Series* (1932).

Suggested Reading

Hussey, Mark. *Virginia Woolf A–Z* (Oxford: Oxford University Press, 1995).
Lee, Hermione. *Virginia Woolf* (London: Chatto & Windus, 1996).
Marcus, Jane. *Virginia Woolf and the Languages of Patriarchy* (Bloomington: Indiana University Press, 1987).

Bonnie Kime Scott

World War One

World War One (1914–18), also known as the Great War, involved most of the European nations, Russia, the United States, the Middle East, and the overseas colonies in Africa, China, and the South Pacific of the European combatants. The combatants can be broadly divided into two cohesive groups: the Allies

(Great Britain and the Commonwealth, France, Russia, Italy, Japan, and the United States) and the Central Powers (Germany, Austria-Hungary, and Turkey). It ended with the defeat of the Central Powers.

The European continent had seen a number of small wars throughout the end of the nineteenth and the beginning of the twentieth centuries, which laid the political and military ground for World War One. The successive declaration of hostilities throughout the summer of 1914 is a marvel of diplomatic intricacy stretching well back into the nineteenth century. The opening of hostilities is commonly ascribed to the assassination of the heir presumptive to the Austrian Empire, Archduke Franz Ferdinand, on 28 June 1914. The archduke's death led to the Austrians presenting a territorial and political ultimatum to Serbia, relying upon German promises to prevent Russia from stepping in to protect Serbia. Serbia refused the ultimatum and on 28 July Austria-Hungary began bombing Belgrade. Russia immediately stepped into the conflict, embroiling Eastern Europe.

On 31 July Germany sent two ultimatums: one to Russia demanding that she pull out of the conflict and one to France demanding a promise of neutrality in the event of war. Both were ignored, resulting in Germany declaring war against France on 3 August. Although neither concerned with the conflict in Eastern Europe nor bound by treaty to fight for any of the involved countries, Great Britain was treaty-bound to protect Belgium. When Germany invaded Belgium, Great Britain declared war the next day. The various nations – aside from the United States – declared war on each other throughout the month of August. On 4 September, the Allied Powers – that is, Great Britain, France, and Russia – signed the Treaty of London, each promising not to make peace with the Central Powers.

The declaration of hostilities was widely regarded with confidence by the countries involved and led to an outpouring of patriotic fervour. Most imagined that the war would be over by Christmas. Although the Allied and Central Powers were largely evenly balanced, the former had greater industrial and military resources and easier access to the sea trade with such wealthy neutral countries as the United States. However, Great Britain had only a volunteer army, while the German conscript army was renowned for its discipline, leadership, and armament. This balance of power prevented either side from quickly gaining a victory in the opening months of the war.

This was an increasingly mechanized war and the planning of conflict was heavily influenced by two new weapons – the rapid-fire field artillery gun and the machine gun. These new weapons played a crucial role throughout the war and particularly in the opening months during its largest battle – the First Battle of the Marne in September 1914, involving two million troops. This battle saved Paris, but allowed the Germans to take control of much of the industrial northeast of France. By Christmas 1914, the stalemate was clear to the governments, and the generals on both sides advised that a long war was unavoidable. All involved systematically began developing national resources for a war of attrition. One result of this was the development of the tank in 1916, Great Britain's attempt to break through the trench barriers and machine guns that criss-crossed much of France.

Although the common image of World War One is the Tommy in the trench, the flurry of activity shifted back and forth several times from the Western to the Eastern Fronts. One notable engagement on the Eastern Front was the Dardanelles campaign. Imperial Russia had requested aid in the war against Turkey and Britain responded by attempting to take the Gallipoli peninsula on the western shore of the Dardanelles. Despite the successes by Australian and New Zealand troops in taking Anzac Cove in April 1915, the British were unable to hold the peninsula and troops had to be evacuated in January 1915. The campaign gained strategically very little and cost 200,000 casualties.

As a result of the heavy loss of troops in such campaigns, Great Britain introduced the Military Service Act in January 1916, replacing voluntary service with conscription. A large number of troops were needed to break the trench deadlock. This was attempted on 1 July 1916 with the Somme offensive. British commanders were convinced that the infantry would be able to move forward over the ground quickly but the Germans were extremely well prepared and that day's losses were the heaviest ever sustained by a British army. Lasting four months and accomplishing little in terms of military advancement or consolidation, the first Battle of the Somme has become a by-word for military arrogance and extreme loss of life.

The war was also being fought on the oceans. Great Britain and Germany were fairly evenly matched in terms of battleships although neither side wanted a direct confrontation. Great Britain, in particular, was more concerned with the protection of its trade routes with the United States. The navies were thus employed in interfering with the commercial strategies of the warring nations. This changed when the Germans began sinking neutral ships, having declared in February 1915 that all the waters around the British Isles were to be treated as a war zone. The sinking of the British *Lusitania* and the loss of nearly 2000 civilian lives off the coast of Ireland in May 1915 was greeted by an international outcry, particularly by the United States. The German high command was unable to see that what was really a minor tactical success – since the *Lusitania* had been carrying ammunition – was a huge public relations blunder as opinion turned against the Germans. Sea warfare came to a head in the Battle of Jutland in May 1916. Both sides claimed a victory: although Great Britain sustained greater losses, the Germans had retreated. The seaways remained largely clear after this, with the German navy staying close to its ports.

Neither side made substantial moves towards peace during the first two years of the war, despite the efforts of the American president Woodrow Wilson, who had been carefully guarding American neutrality and attempting to broker a peace deal. However, Germany's proclamation of unrestricted submarine warfare led to diplomatic relations being sundered between the United States and Germany in February 1917. Fear that the Germans would support Mexico in a war against the United States pushed the latter into declaring war on the Central Powers in April 1917. This was a turning point in the war because, logistically, it made the defeat of Germany possible. The American production of armaments and food met not only its own needs but also those of Great Britain and France.

Despite the Russian revolution of March 1917, the Russian army had continued to fight on the Eastern Front as the provisional government had feared that a German victory would be politically unhealthy for Russia. But anarchy was spreading with the appearance of previously suppressed nationalist movements. The Bolshevik Revolution of November 1917 overthrew the provisional government and brought Lenin to power. No longer wishing to fight a war which the imperial monarchy had condoned, the Bolshevik government signed an armistice with the Central Powers in December 1917.

With the closing down of the Eastern Front, the Germans were able to transfer troops to the Western Front at the beginning of 1918. This could have been decisive in a German victory, but was matched by an influx of American troops to Allied positions. This year saw the second Battle of the Somme (March) and the second Battle of the Marne (July) as Germany attempted to drive through the Allied lines. Although they made substantial headway, they used up their shock troops quickly and had difficulty in maintaining their supply lines. They lost over 800,000 troops in these offensives while the Allies were receiving 300,000 new troops each month from the United States.

The Allied Powers struck back against the Germans in August 1918, advancing steadily through the Battle of Amiens. This battle was a moral success for the Allies, and by October 1918 the German government had requested an armistice. The armistice terms demanded by the Allied Powers were hard on Germany, demanding not only that they evacuate the invaded countries but that they hand over large quantities of war materials and that they render themselves incapable of such aggression again. The armistice document was signed at 5a.m. on 11 November 1918 and at 11a.m. the war came to an end. Some Germans felt that their army had had the strength to continue and that politicians had betrayed the country in signing the armistice. Adolf Hitler was one of the foremost of the insurgents, arguing xenophobic and expansionist policies by which Germany could become the most powerful country in Europe.

World War One changed the map of Europe with new national boundaries drawn up, particularly in Eastern Europe by the Czechs, the Poles, and the

Yugoslavs. Resulting in the fall of the imperial dynasties of Germany, Russia, Austria-Hungary, and Turkey; enabling the Bolshevik Revolution in Russia; and laying the groundwork for World War Two, its impact on the geopolitical history of the twentieth century cannot be overestimated. It was also responsible for the deaths of an estimated 8,500,000 soldiers and 13,000,000 civilians.

Suggested Reading

Constantine, Stephen, Maurice W. Kirby and Mary B. Rose (eds). *The First World War in British History* (London: Edward Arnold, 1995).

Hynes, Samuel. *A War Imagined: The First World War and English Culture* (London: Pimlico, 1990).

Robb, George. *British Culture and the First World War* (Basingstoke: Palgrave Macmillan, 2002).

Strachan, Hew (ed.). *The Oxford Illustrated History of the First World War* (Oxford: Oxford University Press, 1998)

Winter, Jay. *Sites of Memory, Sites of Mourning: The Great War in European History* (Cambridge: Cambridge University Press, 1995)

Stacy Gillis

World War Two

Historians identify a number of events that preceded the outbreak of World War Two (1939–45) in Europe and the Pacific. The terms made against Germany in the Armistice at the end of World War One (loss of territory in the Saar, occupation of the Rhineland, military limitations, reparations, and the *Alleinschuld*, the exclusive war guilt clause), though not a direct cause, established a difficult economic and political environment which Hitler was able to exploit during the years of the Weimar Republic. By blaming this situation on the democratic parties of the Reichstag, the dynamic Hitler was able to take over in 1921 as leader of the German Workers' Party (DAP), which he renamed the National Socialist German Workers' Party (Nazis). By the time he was appointed Chancellor in January 1933, the Nazi Party was the largest in Germany. Hitler sought to expand German borders and to seize territory that he believed ought to be occupied by German nationals. Hitler's occupation of the Sudetenland, his assault on Czechoslovakia, and the *Anschluss* of Austria and Germany were precursors to the German invasion of Poland on 1 September 1939. In Britain, Prime Minister Chamberlain was criticized for his policy of APPEASEMENT, which had been seen as providing space for German Nazism to arise. In the days before the attack on Poland, Germany signed a non-aggression pact with the Soviet Union, and an Anglo-Polish alliance obligated Britain to come to Poland's aid in the event of an invasion. France was also positioned as a British ally. These last-minute agreements established alliances that were in place when Great Britain, in response to Hitler's refusal to leave Poland, declared war on Germany on 3 September 1939.

Tensions in the Pacific had been rising since the Japanese Kwantung Army invaded Manchuria on 18 September 1931. The invasion was criticized by world diplomats, and this led to a walkout staged by Japanese officials within the League of Nations. The Japanese created a Manchurian puppet state, Manchukuo, as the first stage in their imperialistic expansion across East Asia. In 1937, a skirmish between Japanese and Chinese troops near Peking escalated to an undeclared state of war between the two countries. The Japanese military supported the establishment of a Japanese-led East Asian 'New Order' from 1938, and in the summer of 1940 the government founded the Greater East Asia Co-Prosperity Sphere in advance of their takeover of countries across the Pacific. Thus, imperialism was a key theme in both European and Asian politics in the period preceding the start of World War Two.

In Britain, the months of late 1939 and early 1940 were referred to as the 'Phoney War' because anxious civil defence preparations (including the creation of the Home Guard), propaganda campaigns, and rationing were not followed up by any German attempt at invasion. Continental Europe saw much more activity when Germany invaded France, Belgium, and Holland on 10 May 1940. The British Expeditionary Force, sent to the French coast after the German invasion, had to be rescued at Dunkirk on 26 May 1940, a military disaster that Churchill managed to spin into an example of British determination. The British also suffered losses as German U-boats attacked in the Atlantic.

It was not until the Blitz began on 7 September 1940, with heavy raids over London, that the Phoney War came to an end. German aeroplanes attacked both industrial and civilian targets – with Coventry suffering a particularly destructive raid on 14 November – in an attempt to crush public morale prior to invasion. Any plans Hitler may have had to invade Britain were apparently foiled with the British victory in the 'Battle of Britain', the first battle to be fought entirely in the skies. The main Blitz attacks were over by May 1941, but smaller air raids continued throughout the war. Although myth represents the Blitz as a time of communality, in reality it showed up troubling class differences: while wealthy families could retire to country estates, and middle-class urban families could build Anderson shelters in their back gardens, people in more crowded areas were provided with shoddy, unsanitary, and unsafe public shelters, a situation that encouraged high levels of crime and profiteering. The occupation of London underground stations and, in other cities, the basements of public buildings were public attempts to claim safe space when the government did not provide it.

In 1941, Germany opened a second, Eastern front when it attacked the Soviet Union in June in its 'Operation Barbarossa'. From that point, the Soviet Union sided tentatively with Britain and its Allies. The Allies achieved victories against Italy at Tobruk and in Greece; German armies, however, were battling in North Africa by February, and invaded Yugoslavia and Greece in April. The war in the Pacific began officially when the Japanese, frustrated with American trade embargoes, raided the US naval base at Pearl Harbor in Hawaii; America declared war on Japan on 7 December 1941. Hitler then declared war on the United States, bringing America into the European war at last. Within a week after the attack on Pearl Harbor, Japan invaded the Philippines, Burma, and Hong Kong.

Troops from throughout the British colonies were involved in every theatre of the war, and they fought in large numbers in the Burma campaign. West and East African and Indian troops battled and were taken prisoner there, but were not allowed to qualify as officers. Throughout Africa, colonial land was turned into Allied military posts, again with colonial citizens serving military needs. English-owned companies in the African colonies profited from supplying war exports often produced by exploited African labour. Racist military policies were unofficially condoned by Churchill, who encouraged the Allies to use 'administrative means' to turn away black volunteers because the idea of even enemy white soldiers being killed by black troops was unpalatable. Eventually, the RAF allowed West Indian soldiers into its aircrews, but overall the experience of colonial forces during the war was of discrimination.

Germany experienced setbacks at Stalingrad and El Alamein (against British troops led by Montgomery) in 1942. Japan took Singapore in February of that year, and afterwards, 25,000 prisoners, including many British, were taken. The Japanese also took Borneo, Java, and Sumatra. The war in the Pacific, however, took a turn with a major American victory in June at the Battle of Midway. For the first time, Allied governments recognized the mass murders that were occurring at Auschwitz and other Nazi concentration camps. British activists and writers, including Storm JAMESON and Winifred HOLTBY, had reported on Nazi racist policies since the mid-1930s, so the official responses to Nazi atrocities were often considered to be shamefully overdue.

The first major German military defeat occurred in 1943 with their surrender at Stalingrad. Then British code breakers at Bletchley Park cracked the secret code that allowed them to intercept German messages and prevent further U-boat attacks, thus causing a turning point in the violent Battle of the Atlantic. An Allied victory in North Africa allowed them to stage an invasion of Italy from Tunisia; Italy surrendered in September but the Germans then invaded their country. The Russians recaptured Kharkov and Kiev from Germany and advanced along the Eastern Front. German cities also suffered devastation in daylight air raids. In the Pacific, British and Indian troops began a guerrilla offensive in Burma while the Americans gained victory at Guadalcanal.

In 1944, the Japanese army moved into Burma, New Guinea, Guam, and deeper into China. The Allies advanced into Italy and liberated Rome in June, one day before the D-day landings on the Normandy Coast on 6 June. Following several months of slow progress, the Allies took Cherbourg in June, and liberated Paris in August. On the Eastern Front, the Soviets moved into Warsaw, Bucharest, Budapest, and Estonia; as they progressed towards Berlin in spring 1945, the other Western Allies pushed the German armies back into Germany. The Soviets were the first to reach Berlin, on 21 April 1945, and the war in Europe ended on 7 May, 'VE Day', when the German Admiral Doeritz surrendered following Mussolini's hanging on 28 April and Hitler's suicide on 30 April. Meanwhile, the Soviets had liberated Auschwitz and the first photographs of Nazi genocide were documenting those atrocities. In the Pacific, the British advanced into Burma in early February while the Americans took Iwo Jima, the Philippines, and Okinawa. As the Japanese army began to withdraw from China, a planned American invasion of Japan was considered but President Truman, due to fears of great casualties, authorized the use of atomic bombs. The United States dropped a bomb on Hiroshima on 6 August and another on Nagasaki on 9 August. The Japanese surrendered on 14 August, bringing the world war to its close.

Globally, 50 million people died as a result of the conflicts of World War Two. Of these, 20 million were Russian civilians, four million were Poles, and six million were Jews. The four decades of Cold War that followed the official end of hostilities are indicative of the far-reaching effects that this war had on twentieth-century history.

Suggested Reading

Bergonzi, Bernard. *Wartime and Aftermath: English Literature and Its Background, 1939–1960* (Oxford: Oxford University Press, 1993).

Higonnet, Margaret Randolph et al. (eds). *Behind the Lines: Gender and The Two World Wars* (New Haven, CT, and London: Yale University Press, 1987).

Overy, R. J. *The Origins of the Second World War* (1987; rev. edn London: Longmans, 1998).

Passmore, Kevin (ed.). *Women, Gender and Fascism in Europe, 1919–1945* (Manchester: Manchester University Press, 2003).

Ashlie Sponenberg

World War One Writing

For many decades, the study of WORLD WAR ONE literature was mainly confined to readings of male writers, what Claire Tylee has called 'the "men-only" construction of the Great War'. The last 15 years, however, have seen a growth of interest in women's writing from the war years and the decade or so of its aftermath, including fiction, autobiographical writing, and memoirs. While it would be a distortion to equate women with PACIFISM, the body of women's writing does include a significant number of anti-war texts. Virginia WOOLF's *Jacob's Room* (1922), *Mrs Dalloway* (1925), and *To The Lighthouse* (1927) relate the war to an unenlightened patriarchal society. More explicitly pacifist examples include Rose MACAULAY's *Non-Combatants and Others* (1916) and Mary Agnes HAMILTON's *Dead Yesterday* (1916), which veer towards the didactic in their portrayal of pacifist activists. They are eclipsed by A. T. Fitzroy (Rose Allatini)'s *Despised and Rejected* (1918), a brave novel whose hero is a homosexual conscientious objector, copies of which were destroyed in accordance with the Defence of the Realm Act. The American-born Hilda Doolittle's *Bid Me To Live* (1960) should be included, since it was begun in the aftermath of the war and reworked over a period of years. It is an autobiographical novel, in dialogue with *Death of a Hero* (1929) by the author's estranged husband, Richard Aldington. H. D. also wrote a number of short stories on the subject of war, notably 'Asphodel'.

Real originality in the anti-war cause may be found in Vernon Lee (Violet PAGET)'s brilliant and imaginative *Ballet of the Nations* (1915), which takes the form of a pageant orchestrated by Satan in which the nations, assisted by supposed virtues, perform their mutually destructive roles. It was later republished with an accompanying exposition as *Satan the Waster* (1920). Mary BUTTS, author of 'Speed The Plough', the story of the rehabilitation of a returning soldier, produced an extraordinary and now almost forgotten novel, *Ashe of Rings* (1926), which combines the supernatural, both benign and malevolent, with a strong anti-war message. In contrast are novels such as Rebecca WEST's *Return of the Soldier* (1918), dealing with the effects of shell-shock; and May SINCLAIR's *The Tree of Heaven* (1917), charting the sacrifices of one family. Both of these come from the pens of active suffragists who gave support to the war effort, in West's case very reluctantly, while Sinclair was one of only four women to sign the 1914 Authors' Declaration in support of the war. Other novels and stories by Sinclair draw on her brief experiences as an ambulance driver in Belgium, recounted in *A Journal of Impressions in Belgium* (1915). A range of novels by the Anglo-Irish writer, Mrs Victor Rickard, notably *The Fire of Green Boughs* (1918), are broadly supportive of the war but suggest much about the complexities of its effects on both men and women. A more propagandist and xenophobic approach is taken by Mrs Belloc LOWNDES's *Good Old Anna* (1916), which describes the activities of a German spy in a small English town. There is, unsurprisingly, a wide range of patriotic fiction of the romantically sentimental variety from writers such as Berta RUCK, Ruby M. AYRES, Kate Finzi, and Olive Dent.

An obvious reason for the neglect of women's writing is their absence from military service, Flora Sandes's account of her experiences in *An English Woman Sergeant in the Serbian Army* (1916) being the only exception. Most 'battle front' texts by women recount experiences as nurses or ambulance drivers, offering a vivid and often poignant impression of the suffering associated with warfare. Like male-authored texts of the period, they range from WAR MEMOIRS to fiction, with an emphasis on autobiographical elements. An outstanding example is the

American-born Mary Borden's part-fictional collection, *The Forbidden Zone* (1929), inspired by her experience as a nurse behind the French front lines, which bears witness to the dehumanizing effects of trying to preserve life in the mutilated victims of war. Other examples include M. A. St Clair Stobart's memoir, *The Flaming Sword: In Serbia and Elsewhere* (1916); Baroness T'Serclaes's *The Cellar House at Pervyse* (1916), her account of her own and Mari Chisholm's experiences at a dressing station; Enid BAGNOLD's *The Happy Foreigner* (1920); Phyllis Campbell's vividly imagined *Back of the Front* (1915); Irene RATHBONE's ostensibly fictional *We That Were Young* (1932); as well as significant scenes from Radclyffe HALL's *The Well of Loneliness* (1928). Many of these texts carry a strongly pacifist implication, but are excelled in bitterness and hostility to both the war and the class deemed to have made it possible by Helen Zenna SMITH's *Not So Quiet* (1930), written from the war diaries of Winifred Young, as a response to *All Quiet On the Western Front* (1929).

Another kind of war experience is captured in Annie Vivanti CHARTRES's little-known *Vae Victis* (1917), an account of two Belgian women raped by German soldiers, regarded in one quarter as propaganda (a view which overlooks its anti-war message) and in another, more justifiably, as one of the best women's novels of the war. A moving war front novel, written by Cicely HAMILTON, is *William: An Englishman* (1919), the first part of which recounts the adventures of a newly married English couple caught up in the invasion of Belgium. Elizabeth VON ARNIM's *Christine* (1917, published under the name Alice Cholmondeley), another of what may be termed the 'accidental involvement' genre, is blatantly propagandist, describing the fate of the narrator's daughter who is taking music lessons in Berlin when war breaks out. Yet another range of novels and autobiography describes the often-frustrating experience of nursing at home. Best known is Vera BRITTAIN's *Testament of Youth* (1933), while BAGNOLD's *A Diary Without Dates* (1917) reputedly earned her dismissal from service as a VAD. Novels about war work range from Winifred HOLTBY's *The Crowded Street* (1924), with its insights into the liberating experience of being a land girl, through Monica Cosens's *Lloyd George's Munition Girls* (1916), based on her experience in this dangerous occupation, to E. M. DELAFIELD's satirical *The War Workers* (1918), with its officious and self-important heroine.

The publication of Catherine Reilly's anthology of First World War verse, *Scars Upon My Heart* (1981) (republished in 1997 together with her Second World War anthology, as *The Virago Book of War Poetry and Verse by Women*), awakened interest in women's war poetry, which ranges from the patriotic verse of Jessie POPE to the perceptive and elegiac poetry of Margaret Postgate COLE. While some women poets such as May SINCLAIR and May Wedderburn CANNAN write out of the experience of wartime involvement, women's poetry is largely, but not exclusively, written from the standpoint of the onlooker and is often about memory or absence. There is strong identification with the suffering male soldier, as loved individual, and with soldiers as a group. The poems of Winifred Letts and Elizabeth DARYUSH, like those of many other women writers, demonstrate an awareness of the cost of war, while the powerful anti-war stance of Helen HAMILTON is expressed with an ironic energy at times reminiscent of Sassoon. Like many of their male counterparts, women poets are strongly influenced by their pastoral inheritance, which can be seen at work, for example, in the writings of Charlotte MEW and Alice MEYNELL.

Suggested Reading

Cardinal, Agnès, Dorothy Goldman and Judith Hattaway (eds). *Women's Writing on the First World War* (Oxford: Oxford University Press, 1999).

Goldman, Dorothy (ed.). *Women and World War I: The Written Response* (London: Macmillan, 1993).

Ouditt, Sharon. *Fighting Forces, Writing Women: Identity and Ideology in the First World War* (London: Routledge, 1994).

Raitt, Suzanne and Trudi Tate (eds). *Women's Fiction and The Great War* (Oxford: Clarendon Press, 1997).

Tylee, Claire. *The Great War and Women's Consciousness: Images of Militarism and Womanhood in Women's Writing, 1914–1964* (London: Macmillan, 1990).

Terry Phillips

World War Two Writing

The Second World War is seldom considered to be a 'literary' war, and it is difficult to define a body of work that constitutes the written response to the conflict. The absence of a clear-cut canon of either male or female war writing is sometimes attributed to the rise of CINEMA and radio as passive popular distractions from the pressures of war, sometimes to a pervasive sense of *déjà vu* that stifled creativity, and sometimes to the sheer scale of the conflict. WORLD WAR TWO was 'stupefying... out of all proportion to our faculties for knowing, thinking and checking up', as Elizabeth BOWEN put it in the preface to the American edition of *The Demon Lover, and Other Stories* (1945). Perhaps for this reason, much war writing is fragmentary in form. Diaries, reportage, and short stories formed a high percentage of the literary output of the period 1939–45, and the process of writing was often presented as a means of imposing an element of control upon a world not so much chaotic as overdetermined. For British women, the war was a period of unprecedented governmental control. Some were conscripted, others evacuated, while all were subject to the physical constraints of rationing and shortages, and the psychological constraints imposed by the war environment. Within this context, writers such as Naomi MITCHISON and Frances Partridge saw diaries as a place of refuge, a potentially creative space within which doubts, anxieties, and unconstrained opinions could be expressed.

But although responses to the Second World War did not follow the paradigm of 1914–18, the period 1939–45 can nonetheless be seen as a time of remarkable creativity. After the initial shock had passed, wartime conditions created a vibrant market for books that could connect with readers' personal experiences of war's dislocation. At the forefront of the response to this demand was John Lehmann's *Penguin New Writing*, a paperback anthology of stories, poetry, and reviews that, along with Cyril Connolly's *Horizon*, has often been taken as a benchmark of wartime literary production. Unfortunately, with a few notable exceptions, such as Rosamund LEHMANN and Edith SITWELL, women writers were conspicuous by their absence from these publications. However, recent work by feminist critics has challenged the *Horizon* perspective by uncovering the work of forgotten women writers and by expanding the definition of war writing to include work previously dismissed due to its domestic preoccupations. Jenny Hartley, in her book *Millions Like Us*, resurrects a range of fiction focusing on home front life, while Phyllis Lassner identifies novels such as Betty MILLER's *On the Side of the Angels* (1945) as significant engagements with the power structures of war. Other women writers who used a domestic context for stories or novels that interrogated the assumptions of middle-class England included Mollie PANTER-DOWNES, Elizabeth Berridge and Elizabeth GOUDGE.

The picture of women's writing in the war period has been further augmented by the publication of anthologies from the MASS-OBSERVATION archive. These works supplement documentary material written for immediate publication, such as Monica DICKENS's autobiographical account of her nursing experiences, *One Pair of Feet* (1942), and Inez HOLDEN's powerful depiction of women factory workers, *Night Shift* (1941). Much of the poetry written by women in the war years was also influenced by the documentary impulse, and the poems collected in Catherine Reilly's anthology *Chaos of the Night* (1984) present snapshots of the nation at war, detailing the dislocations of Blitz and evacuation alongside the pain of grief. Women's poems, like their fiction, resist easy categorization, but the extent to which the poems in Reilly's anthology develop a trope of war as an unnatural season is nonetheless remarkable. In an attempt to find alternatives to the cycle of violence, some poets seek images of regeneration in maternity. Others, such as Sylvia Townsend WARNER in 'Road 1940', offer a more pessimistic vision in which the terror of war promotes only the instinct of self-preservation.

A number of women writers enjoyed considerable popular success in this period. Fiction as diverse as Jan STRUTHER's *Mrs Miniver* (1939), Angela THIRKELL's 'Barsetshire' novels and Nancy MITFORD's *The Pursuit of Love* (1945) all caught aspects of the changing public mood. DETECTIVE FICTION also built on its prewar popularity, and although Dorothy L. SAYERS abandoned Lord Peter Wimsey in favour of religious drama, Agatha CHRISTIE and Margery ALLINGHAM willingly deployed their popular detective figures for the good of the nation. Both writers, however, also diversified during the war years. In 1941, Allingham produced both *Traitor's Purse*, a thriller in which Albert Campion abandons comic diffidence for heroic agency, and *The Oaken Heart*, a vision of village England aimed at American readers, but more popular in Britain. Christie, meanwhile, resurrected her ageing detectives Tommy and Tuppence Beresford for *N or M?* (1941), while also producing *Absent in the Spring* (1944), a study of a woman's breakdown under the stress of isolation, written under the pseudonym Mary Westmacott.

Yet in attempting to identify a body of women's writing it is important to acknowledge that, creatively, the conflict exceeded the temporal parameters 1939–45. Women were engaging with the prospect of a second world war long before it actually broke out, and they continued to respond to its impact in their writing of the postwar period. The events of the 1930s, in particular Hitler's rise to power in Germany and the SPANISH CIVIL WAR, prompted writers such as Virginia WOOLF, Storm JAMESON and Naomi MITCHISON to produce novels and essays urging political and spiritual resistance to FASCISM. The most famous of these is Woolf's *Three Guineas* (1938). Faced with the question of why women's enfranchisement has not put an end to war, Woolf responds with an extended parody of scientific enquiry that links fascism and patriarchy in its argument that the seeds of dictatorship are rooted in domestic tyranny. Radical visions were equally evident in fiction. Storm Jameson's *In the Second Year* (1936) depicted the consolidation of a fascist dictatorship in Britain; Katherine Burdekin's *Swastika Night* (1937) created a terrifying dystopic future and Stevie SMITH's *Over the Frontier* (1938) presented a surreal indictment of the uniformed subject.

However, while writers such as Jameson continued to publish politically engaged fiction after the outbreak of war, others found themselves confronted by the difficulty of articulating the experience. In Woolf's *Between the Acts* (1941) the war figures as an oblique presence, manifesting itself only in persistent, unsettling images of violence. The prolific Naomi Mitchison, who had produced a wealth of politically engaged fiction in the 1930s, confined herself to her diary during the war years. Her epic historical novel, *The Bull Calves* (1947), was only completed after the end of the war, as was Elizabeth BOWEN's 'spy' story *The Heat of the Day* (1948). Bowen's novel interrogates gendered responses to the war situation, examining the emotional dislocations of the conflict against a superbly evocative depiction of wartime London. Other literature of the aftermath includes Rebecca WEST's extended meditation on disloyalty, *The Meaning of Treason* (1949), as well as Stevie Smith's *The Holiday* (1949) and Rose MACAULAY's *The World My Wilderness* (1950), both of which depict the loss of direction and inchoate grief of the postwar world.

Suggested Reading

Hartley, Jenny (ed.). *Hearts Undefeated: Women's Writing of the Second World War* (London: Virago, 1994).

Hartley, Jenny. *Millions Like Us: British Women's Fiction of the Second World War* (London: Virago, 1997).

Lassner, Phyllis. *British Women Writers of World War Two: Battlegrounds of their Own* (Basingstoke: Palgrave Macmillan, 1997).

Plain, Gill. *Women's Fiction of the Second World War: Gender, Power and Resistance* (Edinburgh, Edinburgh University Press, 1996).

Sheridan, Dorothy (ed.). *Wartime Women: An Anthology of Women's Wartime Writing For Mass-Observation, 1937–45* (London: Heinemann, 1990).

Gill Plain

Y

Young, E. H. 1880–1949

Author of 11 novels portraying modern struggles between male and female, law and wisdom, city and country. Emily Hilda Young was the fourth of seven children in a prosperous Northumberland family. She was educated at Gateshead High School and at Penrhos College, Wales. A passionate rock climber, she returned frequently to Wales on holiday. Young's marriage to the Bristol solicitor J. A. H. Daniell in 1902 introduced her to the complex geographical and social landscape of Bristol and Clifton that stamped her literary imagination. Although Young moved to London after Daniell's death at Ypres in 1917, she drew on this topography for all but three of her novels. In London Young lived with her lover, Ralph Henderson, along with his wife. The separate entrance to the flat of their Sydenham Hill residence enabled Henderson, headmaster at Alleyn's School, and Mrs Daniell, its librarian, to construct an edifice of respectability. Upon Henderson's retirement in 1940, Young and Henderson moved to Bradford-on-Avon.

Notwithstanding her focus on marital discord, Young valorized domesticity as a realm of rich personal relations and a forum for moral and philosophical debate. In *William* (1925) a sympathetic father defends his daughter's choice of self-fulfilment over duty, while *The Vicar's Daughter* (1928) dramatizes the intertwined nature of good and evil. Young's novels did not seek MODERNIST rupture with the past but documented a modernity of humorous, painful, and inevitable conflict. Broadminded, imaginative characters clash with those who find 'comfort in codes and creeds'. In *Miss Mole* (1930), winner of the James Tait Black Memorial Prize, *The Curate's Wife* (1934), and *Chatterton Square* (1947) they battle class prejudice and patriarchal preoccupation with female chastity. Young's unsparing realism is counterbalanced by a fundamental optimism. The high-spirited intelligence of her mature protagonists enables them to compensate for tame domestic occupations. Keen observers of human behaviour, they laugh readily at figures of authority as well as at themselves. The 40-year-old housekeeper Hannah Mole admits 'the zeal of a reformer under her thin crust of cynicism'; and the egotism of the eponymous character in *Celia* (1937) is redeemed by her ability to see her affairs as small.

Young also contributed meaningfully to a rural literary tradition. In *A Corn of Wheat* (1910), *Yonder* (1912), *Moor Fires* (1916), and *The Misses Mallett*, originally entitled *The Bridge Dividing* (1922), characters' relationship to fields, hills, and moors vies with their links to other human beings. In later novels, Young affirmed the capacity of her city dwellers to draw spiritual sustenance from a rural environment. In addition to her novels, Young published two children's books and several short stories. 'The Stream' (1932) was reprinted three times between 1933 and 1954. Young's fiction enjoyed both popular and critical success during her lifetime and in the years following her death. VIRAGO reprinted many of Young's novels in the 1980s, but she has yet to receive the sustained critical attention she deserves.

Suggested Reading

Cavaliero, Glen. *The Rural Tradition in the English Novel, 1900–1939* (Totowa, NJ: Rowman, 1977) 133–56.

Deen, Stella. ' "So Minute and Yet So Alive": Domestic Modernity in E. H. Young's *William'*, *Tulsa Studies in Women's Literature*, 22.1 (Spring 2003) 99–120.

Mezei, Kathy and Chiara Briganti. ' "She must be a very good novelist": Rereading E. H. Young (1880–1949)', *English Studies in Canada*, 27.3 (September 2001) 303–31.

Stella Deen

APPENDIXES

Appendix I
Pseudonyms

This index includes women who published under more than one name, but not those who used one pseudonym consistently. See also Appendix II Minor Writers, which gives further information on pseudonyms.

Barcynska, Countess, *see* Sandys, Oliver
Belloc, Marie, *see* Lowndes, Marie Belloc
Bland, E., *see* Nesbit, E.
Bland, Fabian, *see* Nesbit, E.
Buchan, Anna, *see* Douglas, O.
Burdekin, Kay, *see* Burdekin, Katherine
Burford, Eleanor Alice, *see* Plaidy, Jean
Burns, Sheila, *see* Bloom, Ursula
Carnie, Ethel, *see* Holdsworth, Ethel Carnie
Carr, Jolyon, *see* Pargeter, Edith
Carr, Philippa, *see* Plaidy, Jean
Cholmondeley, Alice, *see* von Arnim, Elizabeth
Constantine, Murray, *see* Burdekin, Katherine
Daviot, Gordon, *see* Tey, Josephine
Ellis, Edith, *see* Lees, Edith Oldham
Ellis, Mrs Havelock, *see* Lees, Edith Oldham
Essex, Lewis, *see* Bloom, Ursula
Essex, Mary, *see* Bloom, Ursula
Farrell, M. J., *see* Keane, Molly
Ferguson, Helen, *see* Kavan, Anna
Ford, Elbur, *see* Plaidy, Jean
Harvey, Rachel, *see* Bloom, Ursula
Holt, Victoria, *see* Plaidy, Jean
Kellow, Kathleen, *see* Plaidy, Jean
Knox, Cleone, *see* King-Hall, Magdalen
Lamb, William, *see* Jameson, Storm
Lombard, Nap, *see* Johnson, Pamela Hansford
Malet, Lucas, *see* Kingsley, Mary St Leger
Mann, Deborah, *see* Bloom, Ursula
Paget, Violet, *see* Lee, Vernon
Parker, M. E. Frances, *see* Bellerby, Frances
Peters, Ellis, *see* Pargeter, Edith
Price, Evadne, *see* Smith, Helen Zenna
Prole, Loziana, *see* Bloom, Ursula
Raimond, C. E., *see* Robins, Elizabeth
Redfern, John, *see* Pargeter, Edith
Scott, Agnes N., *see* Muir, Willa

Slone, Sara, *see* Bloom, Ursula
Strafford, Mary, *see* Mayor, F. M.
Tate, Ellalice, *see* Plaidy, Jean
Thomas, Margaret Haig, *see* Rhondda, Lady Margaret
Vivanti, Annie, *see* Chartres, Annie Vivanti

Appendix II
Minor Writers

Ashlie Sponenberg

Research into literary journals of the period 1900–50 turned up reviews and advertisements for many women writers who were successful, popular, and respected in their day, but about whom little or no critical writing has been undertaken. Their names, and what available bibliographical and biographical detail exists, have been included in this appendix. This list goes some way to indicating the amount of research waiting to be conducted on neglected women writers.

Inclusion of writers for whom I could establish no birth/death dates is based upon their frequent appearance in literary journals of the period, and upon the continued availability of their publications in British copyright libraries. Middle names and pseudonyms are contained in parentheses.

Ashton, Helen 1891–1958/9
Novels include *A Background for Caroline* (1928) and *Dr Seracold* (1930). Married name was Mrs Arthur Jordan.

Baker, Elizabeth 1876–1972
British playwright whose works, such as *Chains* (1909) and *Miss Robinson* (1918), develop feminist themes.

Bannermann, Helen B. C. W. (Brodie Cowan Watson) 1862–1946
Children's author famous for the *Little Black Sambo* novels, including *The Story of Little Black Sambo* (1899) and *The Story of Sambo and the Twins* (1937).

Batson, Henrietta M. 1859–1943
Regional (Wessex) novelist and gardening writer; titles include *The Earth Children* (1897) and *The Summer Garden of Pleasure* (1908).

Bodkin, (Amy) Maud 1875–1976
Psychoanalytic critic and author of *Archetypal Patterns in Poetry: Psychological Studies of Imagination* (1934) and *The Quest for Salvation in an Ancient and a Modern Play* (1941), amongst others.

Boyle, Nina 1866–1943
Novelist, essayist, suffragette, and founder of the Women's Police Service in 1914. Her publications include the thriller *The Rights of Mallaroche* (1927).

Brett, Dorothy Eugenie 1883–1977
Published one memoir, of her relationship with D. H. Lawrence, entitled *Lawrence and Brett: A Friendship* (1933).

Broster, D. K. (Dorothy Kathleen) 1878–1950
Popular historical novelist and poet whose works include a Jacobite Rebellion trilogy: *The Flight of the Heron* (1925), *The Gleam in the North* (1927), and *The Dark Mile* (1929).

Brown, Edith Charlotte
Novelist and grandniece of Jane Austen, her 1929 *Margaret Dashwood or Interference* was a sequel to Austen's *Sense and Sensibility*. Also wrote as Mrs Francis Brown.

Cable, Mildred (1878–1952) and Francesca French (1871–1960)
Co-authors, under the name Cable and French, of such travel and religious titles as *Despatches from North West Kansu* (1925) and *The Gobi Desert* (1942).

Caird, (Alice) Mona ('Mona Allison Caird', 'G. Noel Hatton') 1854/8–1931/2
Working in several genres, her titles include *The Morality of Marriage and Other Essays* (1897), the novel *Stones of Sacrifice* (1915), and the science fiction tale *The Great Wave* (1931).

Cam, Helen Maud 1885–1968
Historian who served as faculty at Cambridge (Girton College), Radcliffe College and Harvard University; was the second female fellow of the British Academy; and earned a CBE in 1957. Her writings include *Studies in the Hundred Rolls: Some Aspects of Thirteenth-Century Administration* (1921).

Carrington, Dora de Houghton 1893–1932
A member of the Bloomsbury Group, 'Carrington', as she was known, appeared as a character in Lawrence's *Women in Love* (1921) and Huxley's *Crome Yellow* (1921). Her collected letters and diaries were published in 1970.

Cartwright, Julia 1851–1924
Novelist, historian, art historian, journalist, and biographer whose works include *The Painters of Florence* (1901) and *Isabelle d'Este* (1903).

Clarke, Isabel C.
Novelist and literary biographer, her titles include *Stepsisters* (1930), *Haworth Parsonage: A Picture of the Bronte Family* (n.d., 2nd edn 1927), and *Six Portraits: Madame de Stael, Jane Austen, George Eliot, Mrs Oliphant, John Oliver Hobbes (Mrs Craigie), Katherine Mansfield* (1935).

Conquest, Joan
Novelist of popular romances such as *Desert Love* (1920), *The Hawk of Egypt: A Sequel to Desert Love* (1922), *Forbidden* (1927), *An Eastern Lover* (1928), and *Harem Love* (1930).

Corke, Helen 1882–1978

Novelist, autobiographer, poet, critic, and textbook author, her works include the novel *Neutral Ground* (1933) and the critical text, *Lawrence and Apocalypse* (1933).

Dickinson, Anne Hepple ('Anne Hepple')

Novelist, author of *The Untempered Wind* (1930), *Evening at the Farm* (1939), and *The House of Gow* (1948), among others.

Dixon, Ella Hepworth 1855–1932

Writer of women's advice and self-help books including *Touch the Stars: A Clue to Happiness* (1935). She was made a Dame of the British Empire in 1991.

Drew, Elizabeth

Novelist, critic, literary biographer whose works include *The Modern Novel: Some Aspects of Contemporary Fiction* (1926), *Jane Welsh and Jane Carlyle* (1928), and the novel *Six Hearts* (1930).

Ertz, Susan

Novelist, author of such works as *Now East, Now West* (1927) and the dystopic *Woman Alive* (1935).

Goddard, Constance Felicity

Her titles include *Verses Wise – and Otherwise* (1928), *Poems* (1929), and the novels *Dear Charity* (1922), *Silver Woods: The Story of Three Girls on a Farm* (1939) and *Come Wind, Come Weather* (1945).

Granville-Barker, Helen

Novelist and poet whose works include the novels *Ada* (1924) and *Traitor Angel* (1935) and the collection *Poems* (1930). Also wrote as Mrs Harley Granville-Barker.

Harraden, Beatrice 1864–1936

Suffragette and writer of the novels *Interplay* (1908), *The Guiding Thread* (1916), and the thriller *Search Will Find It Out* (1928), among others.

Harrison, Jane Ellen 1850–1928

Influential classicist and anthropologist, well-known to Virginia Woolf. Her titles include *Prologomena* (1903) and *Reminiscences of a Student's Life* (1925).

Hawkes, Jacquetta 1910–?

Cambridge-educated novelist and anthropologist whose works include *Archaeology of Jersey* (1939) and *Early Britain* (1945).

Haynes, Annie

Popular writer of such thrillers as *The Abbey Court Murder* (1924), *The Man With the Dark Beard* (1928), and *Who Killed Charmian Karslake?* (1929).

Heseltine, Olive
Critic, memoirist, essayist, and critic for *Time and Tide*, her works include *Conversation* (1927) and *Lost Content* (1948).

Holland, Ruth 1898–?
Adapted two J. B. Priestley scripts, *Laburnum Grove* (1928) and *Dangerous Corner* (1929), into novels; other works include the novels *The Lost Generation* (1930) and *Storm and Dream* (1936).

Hoult, Nora 1898–1984
Prolific, popular Irish writer whose titles include the novel *Holy Ireland* (1935) and the short-story collection *Poor Women* (1928).

Irwin, Margaret (Emma Faith) 1889–1967
Poet and bestselling historical novelist whose works include the Elizabethan trilogy *Young Bess* (1944; adapted as a film starring Jean Simmonds in 1953), *Elizabeth the Captive Princess* (1945), and *Elizabeth and the Prince of Spain* (1953).

James, Norah L. C. (Cordner) 1901–1979
Novelist and children's author, her works include *Jealousy* (1933). *The Return* (1935), *One Bright Day* (1945), and *Pay the Piper* (1950).

Knowles, Mabel Winifred ('May Wynne')
Romance novelist and children's author whose works include *A Blot on the Scutchson* (1910), *Angela Goes to School* (1922), *The Terror of the Moor* (1928), and contributions to the collections *Stories for Sunday Afternoon* (1912) and *Schoolgirls' Stories* (1939).

Lee, Mary
Her 1929 *'It's a Great War': Reality of Actual Experience* was the joint winner of a War Novel competition sponsored by publishers George Allen and Unwin in 1930.

Leverson, Ada 1862–1933
Short-story author who contributed parodies of Wilde to *Punch*. Her novels include *The Twelfth Hour* (1907) and *The Little Ottleys* trilogy: *Louis Shadow* (1908), *Tenterhooks* (1912), and *Love at Second Sight* (1916).

Linford, Madeline
Novelist, literary biographer, journalist, and editor of the *Manchester Guardian's* women's page. Her works include *Mary Wollstonecraft* (1924) and the novel *Bread and Honey* (1928), a satire on bestsellers.

Long, Marjorie ('Marjorie Bowen', 'George Preedy', 'Joseph Shearing') 1888–1952
Biographer, romance/historical novelist, and children's author whose first novel, *The Viper of Milan* (1906), was published at age 16.

Mayne, Ethel Colburn ('Frances E. Huntley') 1865–1941

Editor, novelist, translator, and literary scholar. Works include the novels *Inner Circle* (1925) and *A Regency Chapter* (1939); the biographies *Byron* (1912) and *Life and Letters of Anne Isabella, Lady Noel Byron* (1929); and translations from German and Russian such as the letters of Dostoevsky (1914). Sub-editor of the *Yellow Book* in 1896.

Milner, Marion ('Joanna Field') 1900–1998

Psychoanalyst whose writings include *An Experiment in Leisure* (1937) and *On Not Being Able to Paint* (1950).

Mitchell, Gladys ('Stephen Hockaby', 'Malcolm Torre') 1901–1983

Detective writer. Creator of sleuth Beatrice Le Strange Bradley, she also wrote children's novels. Her crime titles include *Speedy Death* (1929) and *Tom Brown's Body* (1949).

Mirless, Hope 1887?–1978

Author, scholar, and poet whose works include *Lud-in-the-Mist* (1926) and *Paris* (1919), published by the Hogarth Press.

Mort, Anne

Author of children's titles including *The Silver Fish and Other Stories* (1925), *Red Rabbit* (1927), and *Red Rabbit's Family* (1928).

Nott, Kathleen 1909/10–?1999

Poet and novelist whose works include *Landscapes and Departures* (1947), and the novel *Mile End* (1938), which is based on her experiences as a social worker.

Olivier, Edith 1875–1948

Novelist, essayist, and historian, she also helped organize the Women's Land Army in World War One. Her works include *The Love Child* (1927) and *Four Victorian Ladies of Wiltshire* (1945).

Oman, Carola 1897–1978

Novelist, poet, and historical biographer who wrote *The Menin Road and Other Poems* (1919) and, for children, *Robin Hood* (1937). Also wrote under her title, Lady Lenanton.

Orr, Christine

Scottish novelist, biographer, playwright, and poet, her works include the novels *Glorious Thing* (1919) and *Artificial Silk* (1929); *The Loud-Speaker and Other Poems* (1928); and *Clothes Do Make A Difference: A Comedy in One Act* (1934).

Pares, Winifred

Born Winifred Smith. Author of many children's titles including *An Everyday Angel: A Story for Girls* (1919), *Hens and Chickens: A Story of Girl Life in the Great War* (1920), *Through the Nursery Gate* (1927), and *The Toymakers of Trev* (1939). She published *A*

Pair of Ducks (1898) and *Peacocks: or, What Little Hands Can Do* (1899) under her maiden name.

Peterson, Margaret

Her crime novels include the titles *Fate and the Watcher* (1917), *The Unknown Hand* (1924), *Dear, Lovely One!* (1930), and *Death in Goblin Waters* (1934).

Proctor, Mary

Popular astronomy author of *Legends of the Stars* (1922), *The Romance of Comets* (1926), *The Romance of Planets* (1930), and *Everyman's Astronomy* (1939).

Rea, Lorna 1897–1978

Popular Scottish novelist and historian whose works include *Six Mrs Greenes* (1929) and *The Spanish Armada* (1933); she also contributed stories to the historical collection *Great Occasions* (1941). Also wrote under her title, Baroness Rea.

Reid, Hilda Stewart 1898–1982

Novelist, essayist, journalist, editor, and contributor to *Time and Tide* who, with Vera Brittain, co-edited Holtby's posthumous *Pavements at Anderby* (1937). Her novels include *Phillida: or, the Reluctant Adventurer* (1928) and *Ashley Hamel* (1939).

Roberts, Ursula ('Susan Miles')

Poet, anthology editor, and biographer, her titles include the collection *Dunch* (1918), *Little Mirrors, and Other Studies in Free Verse* (1924), and *An Anthology of Youth in Verse and Prose* (1925).

Robins, Denise Naomi 1897–1985

Founder, in 1960, and first president of the Romantic Novelists Association, she produced more than 200 novels during her career, including *The Marriage Bond* (1924), *Lovers of Janine* (1931), *War Marriage* (1942), and *The Feast is Finished* (1950).

Robinson, Agnes Mary Frances 1857–1944

Poet, critic, and biographer, her titles include *My Sister Henrietta* (1900), *The French Procession: A Pageant of Great Writers* (1909), and *Images and Meditations: Poems* (1923).

Salt, Sarah

Novelist and short-story author, whose works, published by Victor Gollancz, include *A Tiny Seed of Love and Other Stories* (1928), *Sense and Sensuality* (1929), and *Change Partners* (1934).

Sidgwick, Ethel 1877–1970

Her works include the novel *Jamesie* (1918) and the collection *Four Plays for Children* (1913).

Simpson, Helen 1897–1940

Born Helen de Guery. Novelist, poet, playwright, historical biographer, essayist, she immigrated from Australia to England in 1916. Her novel *Boomerang* (1932) won the

James Tait Black Memorial Prize. She wrote three collaborative novels with Clemence Dane; other works include *Cups, Wands and Swords* (1927) and *Saraband for Dead Lovers* (1935), a Book Society choice.

Smith, Constance (Isabel Stuart)

Novelist, essayist, and activist whose works include the novel *Corban* (1901), *The Case for Wage Boards* (1908), and *Children as Wage-Earners* (1908), published by the Society for Promoting Christian Knowledge.

Todd, Margaret Georgina ('Graham Travers') 1859–1918

Physician whose publications include *Mona Maclean, Medical Student* (1892, as Travers), *Growth* (1906), and *The Life of Sophia Jex-Blake* (1918).

Trevelyan, Gertrude Eileen

Her 1927 'Julia, Daughter of Claudius' was the first Newgate Prize Poem by a woman. Other works include the novels *Appius and Virginia* (1932) and *A War Without A Hero* (1935).

Walford, Lucy (Belthia) 1845–1915

Scottish author of the novel *The Matchmaker* (1893) and the memoir *Recollections of a Scottish Novelist* (1910).

Wallace, Doreen 1897–?

A journalist and lesser known Somerville College writer, her fiction includes the well-received *Latter Howe* (1935).

Ward, Barbara 1914–1981

Economist, journalist, political writer, Somerville College graduate, foreign editor of the *Economist* in 1940, and a BBC governor in the late 1940s, her non-fiction studies include *Hitler's Route to Bagdad* (1938), *The Defence of the West* (1942), and *Policy for the West* (1951). Married name was Barbara Jackson.

Weston, Jessie L. (Laidlay) 1850–1928

Medieval literary historian and translator whose works include *King Arthur and His Knights* (1899), *Morien: A Metrical Romance Rendered into English Prose from the Mediæval Dutch* (1911), *Germany's Literary Debt to France* (1915), and *From Ritual to Romance* (1920).

Williams-Ellis, Amabel 1894–1984

Born Amabel Strachey. Socialist novelist, literary biographer, sociologist, journalist, children's author, and founder/editor of *Left Review*. Works include *Women in War Factories* (1943), *The Exquisite Tragedy: An Intimate Life of John Ruskin* (1929), and *The Tank Corps* (1919), co-authored with husband Clough.

Woods, Margaret L. (Louisa) 1856–?

Her poetry includes the collections *Lyrics and Ballads* (1889), *Poems, Old and New* (1907), and *A Poet's Youth* (1923).

Appendix III
Timeline

Esme Miskimmin

Date	Literary Events	Historical Events
1900	Net Book Agreement finalized. Boots Library launched.	Salisbury becomes Prime Minister. Labour Representation Committee founded (becomes the Labour Party in 1906).
1901	World's Classics launched.	Death of Queen Victoria and succession of Edward VII. First transatlantic wireless transmissions. Census reveals population boom.
1902	Establishment of *Times Literary Supplement*. Establishment of *Daily Mirror* newspaper.	End of Boer War. Balfour succeeds Salisbury as Prime Minister. Balfour Act provides for secondary education and establishes LEAs.
1903		Emmeline Pankhurst forms Women's Social and Political Union (WSPU).
1904	Opening of the Abbey Theatre, Dublin. Establishment of the Prix Femina-Vie Heureuse. The Times Book Club launched.	'Entente Cordiale' is signed. Worker's Educational Association founded.
1905		Sinn Féin is formed. Campbell-Bannerman becomes Prime Minister. First Suffrage jailings.
1906	Foundation of the English Association. Establishment of the Anarchist magazine, *Mother Earth*. Everyman's Library launched.	Liberal government elected. Labour Representation Committee becomes the Labour Party. Foundation of Women's Labour League. Eleven members of WSPU, including Sylvia Pankhurst, jailed in Holloway Prison. Introduction of free school meals.

1907 Riots in Abbey Theatre over *The Playboy of the Western World.* *Cambridge History of English Literature* launched.

British Eugenics Education Society founded.
Women's Freedom League (WFL) established.

1908 End of the 'Book War', as *The Times* signs the Net Book Agreement.
Mills and Boon launched.
Establishment of *English Review* magazine.

Austria annexes Bosnia.
Asquith becomes Prime Minister.
Introduction of Old Age Pensions.
Emmeline and Christobel Pankhurst jailed.
Women's Anti-Suffrage League founded.
Britain stages the Olympic Games.

1909

Lloyd George's People's Budget.
Institution of old age pensions.
Suffragette hunger strikes begin.
'Younger Suffragists' founded.

1910 Establishment of *The Woman Journalist* magazine.

Death of Edward VII and succession of George V.
Miners' strike.
First Labour Exchanges Open.

1911 Establishment of *The Masses* magazine.
Establishment of *Freewoman* magazine (became the *New Freewoman* in 1913 and the *Egoist* in 1914).
Establishment of *Woman's Weekly* magazine.

National Health Insurance Bill.
Copyright Act.
First Official Secrets Act.
Parliament Act reduces powers of House of Lords.
WFL boycott the census.

1912 Death of Poet Laureate, Robert Bridges (father of Elizabeth Daryush). John Masefield becomes new Laureate.
Lady Ritchie is the first female President of the English Association.
Establishment of The Poetry Society.
Establishment of *Poetry Review* magazine.
Establishment of the *Georgian Poetry Review* magazine.

First Balkan War.
Irish Home Rule Bill.
Ulster Solemn League and Covenant drawn up.
Miners', Dockers' and, general transport strikes.
National Insurance Act.
Titanic sinks.
British Film Censor appointed.

1913 Establishment of *New Statesman* magazine.

Second Balkan War.
Ulster Volunteer Force established.
Cat and Mouse Act.
Death of Suffragette, Emily Davidson, under the King's horse.
East London Federation of Suffragettes established.
Emily Dawson is the first female magistrate.

(Continued)

Date	Literary Events	Historical Events
1914	Vorticist movement founded by Wyndham Lewis. First publication of *Blast*. First publication of the *Egoist*. Authors' Declaration in support of the war.	Germany invades Belgium. World War One begins. Battles of Ardennes, Mons, Marne, and first Battle of Ypres. Irish Home Rule Bill suspended. Panama Canal opened. Suffragettes protest at Buckingham Palace.
1915		Battles at Loos and second Battle of Ypres. Gallipoli landings. Coalition government formed under Asquith. Defence of the Realm Act. Women's Institute Movement founded. *Lusitania* sunk
1916	Establishment of *Vogue* magazine.	Battle of the Somme. Easter Rising in Dublin. Lloyd George becomes Prime Minister. Conscription introduced by the Military Service Act.
1917		Bolshevik Revolution in Russia. Battle of Passchendaele and third Battle of Ypres. United States enters war.
1918		Battle of Amiens. Armistice ends World War One. Representation of the People Act means suffrage granted to women over 30. Commons vote to allow women MPs. Influenza pandemic (to 1919).
1919	Establishment of *Peg's Paper* magazine.	Treaty of Versailles. Covenant of the League of Nations. Ministry of Health established. Sex Disqualification (Removal) Act. Nancy Astor becomes first woman MP.
1920	Cicely Hamilton, *William an Englishman* (1919) awarded the Prix Femina-Vie Heureuse. Establishment of the 'Memoir Club'. Establishment of *Time and Tide* magazine. Establishment of *The Dial* magazine.	End of Russian Civil War. Government of Ireland Act passed, separating Ulster from Eire. League of Nations founded. Formation of the Communist Party of Great Britain (CPGB). Oxford University confers its first degrees on previous women students and admits first 100 females to study for full degrees.

1921 Constance Holme, *The Splendid Fairing* (1919) awarded the Prix Femina-Vie Heureuse. Foundation of Jonathan Cape publishers.

Hitler takes over as leader of the German Workers' Party (DAP), which he renames the National Socialist German Workers' Party (Nazis).
Anglo-Irish Treaty signed and Separate Irish Parliaments established.
CPGB reformed.
The Newbolt Report, concerning the teaching of English, published.
Six Point Group established.
Marie Stopes opens first family planning clinic.
School leaving age raised to 14.

1922 Rose Macaulay, *Dangerous Ages* (1921) awarded Prix Femina-Vie Heureuse.
Establishment of *The Criterion* magazine.
Establishment of *Good Housekeeping* magazine.

Creation of the Irish Free State (Eire).
Bonar Law becomes Prime Minister.
Irish Civil War.
British Broadcasting Company begins radio transmissions (becomes the British Broadcasting Corporation in 1927).

1923

Irish Civil War ends.
Baldwin becomes Prime Minister.
British Fascisti organization founded.
Matrimonial Causes Act gives wives equality in divorce.
Establishment of the *Radio Times* magazine.

1924

First Labour government.
MacDonald becomes Prime Minister (Jan).
Conservatives win election. Baldwin becomes Prime Minister (October).
The first CPGB women's conference held.

1925 Shaw wins Nobel Prize for Literature.

Guardianship of Infants Act.
Unemployment Insurance Act.

1926 Mary Webb, *Precious Bane* (1924) awarded Prix Femina-Vie Heureuse.
Vita Sackville-West, *The Land* (1926) awarded the Hawthornden Prize.
Magdalen King-Hall, *The Diary of a Young Lady of Fashion in the Year 1764–1765* (1925) is declared a hoax by the *Daily Express*.
Mysterious disappearance of Agatha Christie.

General Strike.
Miners' Strike.

(Continued)

Date	Literary Events	Historical Events
1927	Radclyffe Hall, *Adam's Breed* (1926) awarded Prix Femina-Vie Heureuse and the James Tait Black Memorial Prize.	Trade Disputes and Trade Union Act.
1928	Virgina Woolf, *To the Lighthouse* (1927) awarded Prix Femina-Vie Heureuse. Radclyffe Hall, *The Well of Loneliness* banned as its British publishers are successfully prosecuted for obscenity. First *Oxford English Dictionary* completed.	Suffrage granted to women of 21 and over.
1929	Founding of the Book Society.	Collapse of the New York Stock Exchange. Beginning of the Depression. Second Labour Government.
1930		National Birth Council Association (later Family Planning Association) established. Amy Johnson flies solo to Australia.
1931	E. H. Young, *Miss Mole* (1930) awarded the James Tait Black Memorial Prize. Kate O'Brien, *Without My Cloak* (1931) awarded the Hawthornden Prize.	National Government formed by MacDonald. Split in Labour Party. New Party founded by Sir Oswald Mosley (renamed British Union of Fascists 1932).
1932	Stella Benson, *Tobit Transplanted* (1931) awarded Prix Femina-Vie Heureuse. Kate O'Brien, *Without My Cloak* (1931) awarded the James Tait Black Prize. Establishment of *Scrutiny* magazine. *Oxford Companion to English Literature* first published.	British Union of Fascists founded. Unemployment rises.
1933	Anne Bridge, *Peking Picnic* (1932) awarded the Atlantic Monthly Prize. Vita Sackville-West, *Collected Poems* (1933) awarded the Hawthornden Prize. Establishment of *New Verse* magazine.	Hitler becomes Chancellor of Germany. Unemployment peaks at 15 per cent.

1934	Stella Gibbons, *Cold Comfort Farm* (1932) awarded Prix Femina-Vie Heureuse. Establishment of *Left Review* magazine.	Fascist and anti-Fascist demonstrations in Hyde Park. Unemployment Act creates Assistance Boards. Peace Pledge Union Founded.
1935	Establishment of the Left. Book Club. Penguin Books launched.	Baldwin becomes Prime Minister. The Seventh Comintern Congress establishes a Popular Front against fascism, uniting the British Marxists and the Independent Labour Party.
1936	Kate O' Brien, *Mary Lavelle* banned on grounds of obscenity.	Spanish Civil War begins. Death of George V and succession of Edward VIII. Abdication of Edward VIII and succession of George VI. Jarrow March. BBC begins broadcasting its London service. First 'Butlin's' holiday camp established.
1937	Ruth Pitter, *A Trophy of Arms* (1936) awarded the Hawthornden Prize. Winifred Holtby, *South Riding* (1936) awarded the James Tait Black Memorial Prize. Launch of *Woman* magazine.	Chamberlain becomes Prime Minister. Public Order Act. Mass-Observation organization founded.
1938		Munich Agreement. Hitler's troops enter Vienna. Government committee appointed to investigate abortion laws.
1939	Book Club Proposition established.	Spanish Civil War ends. Germany occupies Czechoslovakia, signs non-aggression pact with the Soviet Union and invades Poland. End of Appeasement. Beginning of World War Two.
1940	Paper rationing instituted (continues until 1949).	Germany occupies Norway, Denmark, Benelux, and France. Dunkirk evacuation. Battle of Britain. Churchill forms national Government and becomes Prime Minister. Blitz begins. Mosley and others interned by the Security Service.

(Continued)

Date	Literary Events	Historical Events
1941	Book Production War Economy Agreement reached by The Publishers' Association. Establishment of *Our Time* magazine. Kate O'Brien, *The Land of Spices* banned on the grounds of obscenity. Around 20 million books destroyed in the Blitz.	Germany invades Soviet Union. National Service Act legalizes the conscription of British females.
1942		Beveridge Report calls for a full-scale reform of social services.
1943		Germans surrender at Stalingrad and in North Africa. Allies invade Italy.
1944		Normandy landings. Butler Act creates Ministry of Education. Education Act introduces universal selective secondary education.
1945		Hiroshima. End of World War Two. Labour Government elected and Attlee becomes Prime Minister. Family Allowance Act.
1946		National Insurance Act. Nationalization of Bank of England and mines. Creation of New Towns.
1947	F. Tennyson Jesse becomes a member of the Royal Society of Literature	Nationalization of railways. School leaving age raised to 15.
1948		Welfare State introduced. National Health Service established.
1949		Eire becomes 'Republic of Ireland'.
1950	Stella Gibbons elected a Fellow of the Royal Society of Literature.	Labour Government re-elected.

Annotated Bibliography

Faye Hammill, Louise Harrington, Ashlie Sponenberg
and Keir Waddington

The bibliography is divided into the following sections: Literary Criticism, Anthologies, Encyclopedias, Bibliographies, Key History, and Cultural Studies Books.

We have aimed to include all significant monographs and edited collections focused entirely on early twentieth-century British women's writing. Also listed are selected books with a wider remit (for example, those which also cover male-authored or American texts, or which range beyond our date limits), chosen on the basis of relevance. We have excluded studies of single writers; these will be found in the suggested reading appended to author entries. The history section of the bibliography, which is necessarily more selective than the literary sections, provides a guide to work in women's history.

The compilers have found all these books useful. However, we do not attempt to evaluate them here, but rather to summarize their contents and, where appropriate, indicate which authors are discussed. (Authors' surnames only are given, except in cases of possible ambiguity.)

Literary Criticism

Ardis, Ann. *Modernism and Cultural Conflict, 1880–1922* (Cambridge: Cambridge University Press, 2002).
Situates canonical literary modernism in relation to other cultural forces (including middlebrow art and British feminism and socialism), demonstrating the strategies used by modernists to attain a pre-eminent position. Chapters focus on: Beatrice Webb; Syrett; Lawrence; Lewis; Wilde; and the journal *New Age*. The discussion moves outwards from these case studies to trace the conservative cultural and sexual politics which underlie the radical aesthetic of writers such as Pound, Joyce and Eliot.

Ardis, Ann and Leslie W. Lewis (eds). *Women's Experience of Modernity, 1875–1945* (Baltimore, MD: Johns Hopkins University Press, 2003).
An interdisciplinary collection, amplifying literary study through reference to other cultural practices, including radical politics and activism, rural labour, and urban field-work, shopping, and selling. Analyses of the material production of modernism expand into accounts of the class-based and racially inflected discourses of the period. Authors examined include Hall, Meynell, and West, as well as several American women writers.

Ayers, David. *English Literature of the 1920s* (Edinburgh: Edinburgh University Press, 1999).
Considers high modernist alongside non-modernist and popular texts, focusing on their engagement with a shared context of social, political, and cultural issues. Chapters on:

Men and Masculinity; Ideals and Realities of the English Woman; Mass Civilization and Minority Culture; Sex, Satire, and the Jazz Age; England and its Other. Authors discussed are Conquest, Hull, Leavis, Townsend Warner, West, Wilkinson, and Woolf, alongside seven male writers.

Barker, Clive and Maggie B. Gale (eds). *British Theatre Between the Wars, 1918–1939.* **(Cambridge: Cambridge University Press, 2000).**
Essays on both mainstream and alternative British theatre, ranging from Shakespeare to thrillers, musical comedies, and revue. The essays emphasize social and cultural context, arguing against the predominant view that the theatre of that time was, in the main, conservative. Authors discussed include Kennedy, Dodie Smith, Dane, O'Brien, and Christie.

Beauman, Nicola. *A Very Great Profession: The Woman's Novel, 1914–1939* **(London: Virago, 1983).**
A pioneering survey, concentrating on the typical content of female-authored interwar fiction, and organized thematically in eight chapters (War, Surplus Women, Feminism, Domesticity, Sex, Psychoanalysis, Romance, Love). Includes brief biographical/bibliographical entries for 50 individual authors.

Bloom, Harold (ed.). *British Women Fiction Writers, 1900–1960: Volume One* **(Philadelphia: Chelsea House, 1997).**
For each author covered (Bowen, Christie, Compton-Burnett, Delafield, Du Maurier, Godden, Hall, Holtby, Hunt, Jameson, Tennyson Jesse, Hansford Johnson, Kennedy, and Mary Lavin), Bloom provides a brief biography, a bibliography of her work, and a series of critical extracts, such as contemporary reviews or essays by other writers.

Bluemel, Kristin. *George Orwell and the Radical Eccentrics: Intermodernism in Literary London* **(New York: Palgrave Macmillan, 2004).**
Concentrates on the 1930s and 1940s, examining the writings and relationships of Orwell and three of his London friends: the suburban satirist Stevie Smith, the Marxist Indian nationalist Mulk Raj Anand, and the adventuress turned socialist Inez Holden.

Bracco, Rosa Maria. *Merchants of Hope: British Middlebrow Writers and the First World War, 1919–1939* **(Oxford: Berg, 1993).**
An analysis of fictional representations of World War One in bestselling middlebrow fiction. Female authors discussed include Benson, Bottome, Brittain, Jameson, Tey, Sinclair, and Woolf.

Cadogan, Mary and Patricia Craig. *Women and Children First: The Fiction of Two World Wars* **(London: Victor Gollancz, 1978).**
Examines the two wars through the lens of bestselling fiction and periodicals, emphasizing the experiences of British women and children. Discusses both famous and little-known writers of both sexes, including Bowen, Brent-Dyer, Brazil, Brittain, Cartland, Monica Dickens, Richardson, Ruck, Stevie Smith, and West.

Cockin, Katharine. *Women and Theatre in the Age of Suffrage: The Pioneer Players, 1911–1925* **(Basingstoke: Palgrave Macmillan, 2000).**
Takes an interdisciplinary approach to women's involvement in theatre during the British women's suffrage movement, using as a focus the innovative work of The Pioneer Players, a London-based theatre society founded in 1911 by Edith Craig.

Cohen, Debra Rae. *Remapping the Home Front: Locating Citizenship in British Women's Great War Fiction* (Boston, MA: Northeastern University Press, 2002).
Discusses wartime writing from the home front, claiming difference from studies which 'reinscribe classic definitions by assuming that the war story is the story told when the battlefield conflict is over'. Examines in particular texts which defy simple categorization as pacifist or patriotic. Includes individual chapters on Benson, Hunt, Macaulay, and West.

Croft, Andy. *Red Letter Days: British Fiction in the 1930s* (London: Lawrence & Wishart, 1990).
The introduction characterizes the book as 'a study of one brief period when the Left recognized the transforming power of well-written and well-read political fiction'. Themed chapters discuss Fiction from the Coalfields, Unemployment and the Novel, Tales of Middle-Class Life, Provincial Writing, Popular Fiction for a Popular Front, Novels of the Future, Documentary Novels, Fantastic Fictions, and Anti-Fascist Novels. Approximately 300 books are surveyed, including work by 19 women.

Cunningham, Valentine. *British Writers of the Thirties* (Oxford: Oxford University Press, 1988).
A wide-ranging discussion, offering interpretations of central texts of the period in relation to social, political, historical, and personal contexts. Centres on male writers (Auden, Day Lewis, Isherwood, Spender), but a number of women are discussed, including Bowen, Christie, Gibbons, Holtby, Leavis, Lehmann, Mitchison, Sayers, and Woolf.

Deen, Stella (ed.). *Challenging Modernism: New Readings in Literature and Culture, 1914–45* (Aldershot: Ashgate, 2002).
This essay collection examines the connection between interwar Anglo-American literary production and cultural/material contexts. In particular, the 'valorization' of the modernist canon and the traditional categorization of high and low literatures are questioned. Features chapters on Bowen, Holden, Hunt, Lehmann, Stevie Smith, and Young.

Dowson, Jane. *Women, Modernism and British Poetry, 1910–1939* (Aldershot: Ashgate, 2002).
The only text which specifically addresses women and modernist poetry in Britain, though it also attends to literary exchanges with Paris and New York. A wide-ranging literary history, assessing women's participation in a range of modernist developments, including publishing initiatives and critical writing as well as poetry. Writers discussed include Ackland, Cunard, Cornford, Holtby, Loy, Mew, Mitchison, Sackville-West, Sitwell, Sinclair, Stevie Smith, Tree, Townsend Warner, and Wickham.

Gale, Maggie B. *West End Women: Women and the London Stage, 1918–1962* (London: Routledge, 1996).
Analysis of the content of women-authored plays in this period is combined with study of aspects of performance and reception; and the texts are related to the transformations in British women's lives during the period. A substantial range of playwrights is covered, including Bagnold, Dane, Kennedy, Dodie Smith, and Stern.

Garrity, Jane. *Step-Daughters of England: British Women Modernists and the National Imaginary* (Manchester: Manchester University Press, 2003).
Explores the relations between maternity, sexuality, race, and imperialism in the construction of English national culture, through readings of Richardson, Townsend

Warner, Butts, and Woolf. There is a particular focus on forms of nostalgia for the English past.

Gilbert, Sandra and Susan Gubar. *No Man's Land: The Place of the Woman Writer in the Twentieth Century.* **3 vols.** *Volume I: The War of the Words, Volume II: Sexchanges, Volume III: Letters from the Front* (New Haven, CT: Yale University Press, 1988, 1989, 1994).
This sequel to *The Madwoman in the Attic* focuses on twentieth-century women writers. Volumes I and II analyse literature and society between the 1880s and 1930s, specifically the rise of the New Woman and the suffrage movement, and the corresponding crisis of masculinity. Volume III focuses mainly on World War Two fiction. Authors mentioned include Bowen, Braddon, Broughton, Bryher, Hall, Meynell, Richardson, Sackville-West, Townsend Warner, West, and Woolf.

Goldman, Dorothy with Jane Gledhill and Judith Hattaway. *Women Writers and the Great War* (New York: Twayne Publishers, 1995).
The wartime writings of such authors as Bagnold, Brittain, Hall, Hamilton, Macaulay, Irene Rathbone, and Sinclair are contextualized within discussions of women's war work, employment, service recruitment campaigns, sexuality, authenticity of experience, suffrage, modernism, and the popularity of romances and war memoirs.

Griffin, Gabriele (ed.). *Difference in View: Women and Modernism* (London: Taylor & Francis, 1994).
A collection which highlights the diversity of women's cultural production in the modernist period, examining painting, theatre, and magazines as well as poetry and prose. Contains discussions of both male and female writings of the self in the 1930s, and of how modernist women writers represent homosexual men. Articles are devoted to Sackville-West and Leonora Carrington, and other authors discussed include Brittain, Hall, Holtby, Stevie Smith, Townsend Warner, and Woolf.

Hartley, Jenny. *Millions Like Us: British Women's Fiction of the Second World War* (London: Virago, 1997).
A wide-ranging survey, organized thematically and referring to a whole range of authors from the canonical to the forgotten. Draws comparisons also with American literature, and concludes with brief biographical notes on some 86 authors.

Hanscombe, Gillian and Virginia Smyers. *Writing for their Lives: The Modernist Women, 1910–1940* (London: The Women's Press, 1987).
Focuses on the interdependence between the writer's aesthetic theory and her personal life, emphasizing the network of support among female writers of this period. There are chapters on Bryher, Richardson, Butts, and Loy, as well as on periodical and book publishing, and a bibliography which includes archival sources.

Humble, Nicola. *The Feminine Middlebrow Novel, 1920s to 1950s: Class, Domesticity and Bohemianism* (Oxford: Oxford University Press, 2001).
A detailed study which discusses some 60 novels by about 30 authors, from the enduringly popular to the obscure. Locates the fiction in the context of other discourses of the period, including cookery and child-care manuals, magazines, literary criticism, and Mass-Observation documents.

Hynes, Samuel. *The Auden Generation: Literature and Politics in England in the 1930s* (London: Bodley Head, 1976).
A study of Auden, Day Lewis, Caudwell, Isherwood, Eliot, Forster, Greene, Orwell, Upward, Spender, and Huxley. Hynes presents a year-by-year account of their major texts of the 1930s. Women writers are mentioned briefly, including Bowen, Jameson, Lehmann, and Mitchison and Woolf.

Ingman, Heather. *Women's Fiction Between the Wars: Mothers, Daughters and Writing* (Edinburgh: Edinburgh University Press, 1998).
The opening chapter discusses women's social roles in the 1920s and 1930s, concentrating on education, careers, and maternity. Chapter 2 is on Psychoanalytic Theories of Motherhood, while the remaining chapters focus on individual authors: Macaulay, Bowen, Compton-Burnett, Rhys, Woolf, and Richardson.

Ingram, Angela and Daphne Patai (eds). *Rediscovering Forgotten Radicals: British Women Writers, 1889–1939* (Chapel Hill: University of North Carolina Press, 1993).
Influential study of neglected women writers, including essays on New Women and socialist-feminist fiction; Carnie Holdsworth and working-class women's writing; Eyles; Mannin; Stopes and marriage narratives of the 1920s; and Burdekin and utopian fiction.

Joannou, Maralou. *Ladies, Please Don't Smash These Windows: Women's Writing, Feminist Consciousness and Social Change, 1918–1939* (Oxford: Berg, 1995).
A socialist-feminist study, combining literary criticism and cultural history to examine women's political, personal, and sexual lives as represented in interwar women's writing. There are chapters on the question of gender, nation, and class in women's autobiography (Brittain); literary spinsterhood (Mansfield, Mayor); lesbian representations (Woolf, Hall); femininity and feminism (Bowen, Lehmann, West); and anti-fascist writings (Woolf, Burdekin).

Joannou, Maroula (ed.). *Women Writers of the 1930s: Gender Politics and History* (Edinburgh: Edinburgh University Press, 1999).
Contains essays on: The Woman Writer in the 1930s; Memory and Forgetting; Late Modernism and the Politics of History; Women Poets and the Political Voice; Revising the Marriage Plot; Townsend Warner; Lehmann; Von Arnim; Cunard; Jameson; Mitchison; Burdekin; Woolf; and West and Jameson.

Khan, Nosheen. *Women's Poetry of the First World War* (Brighton: Harvester Press, 1988).
A survey study organized thematically, together with a biographical appendix of all the poets discussed (about 60), and an appendix recording contemporary comments and opinions about war verse written by women.

Kime Scott, Bonnie. *Refiguring Modernism Volume I: The Women of 1928* (Bloomington: Indiana University Press, 1995).
Feminist rereading of the origins of Anglo-American modernism. Argues that the canonical 'Men of 1914' ('Edwardian Uncles', Pound, Eliot, Joyce, Lawrence, Forster, Bloomsbury group) have important affinities with an emergent female modernism dated to 1928, the year of *The Well of Loneliness* trial and of universal enfranchisement in Britain.

Lassner, Phyllis. *British Women Writers of World War II: Battlegrounds of Their Own* (Basingstoke: Macmillan – now Palgrave Macmillan, 1998).
A literary and ideological analysis of the interwar period which illustrates the complexity of women writers' attitudes to war and their challenges to the genre of war literature. Selects authors including Bowen, Bottome, Brittain, Burdekin, Cooper, Goudge, Jameson, Mannin, Manning, Mitchison, Sayers, Sackville-West, Stevie Smith, and Woolf.

Lassner, Phyllis. *Colonial Strangers: British Women Writing the End of Empire* (New Brunswick, NJ: Rutgers University Press, 2004).
Drawing on fiction, memoirs, film and contemporary reportage, this book examines how Manning, Godden, Bottome, Huxley, Muriel Spark, and Zadie Smith question their own participation in British imperialism and cultural exploitation. Also debates the connections between the ideologies of the British Empire and those of Germany under the Third Reich.

Leonardi, Susan J. *Dangerous By Degrees: Women at Oxford and the Somerville College Novelists* (New Brunswick, NJ: Rutgers University Press, 1989).
Contextualizes the work of such authors as Sayers, Kennedy, Holtby, and Brittain in terms of the degrees-for-women debate.

Light, Alison. *Forever England: Femininity, Literature and Conservatism Between the Wars* (London: Routledge, 1991).
An influential study, combining literary criticism, feminist theory, and cultural history. The four chapters focus on individual authors: Compton-Burnett, Christie, Struther, and Du Maurier.

Lucas, John. *The Radical Twenties: Aspects of Writing, Politics and Culture* (Nottingham: Five Leaves, 2000).
Lucas resists characterizations of this decade in terms of jazz and Bright Young Things, and sees the General Strike as 'the definitive moment for the 1920s'. He discusses canonical texts alongside forgotten bestsellers in an account of the socially transgressive and politically radical dimensions of 1920s literature and culture. Women authors covered include: Compton-Burnett, Cunard, Mansfield, Mew, Townsend Warner, Rhys, and Woolf.

Maslen, Elizabeth. *Political and Social Issues in British Women's Fiction, 1928–1968* (Basingstoke: Palgrave Macmillan, 2001).
Situates less well known women writers within their political and social contexts, concentrating on issues of race, class, gender, and war. Authors discussed include Bottome, Burdekin, Comyns, Dane, Ertz, Frankau, Holden, Holtby, Jameson, Mannin, Miller, Mitchison, Stevie Smith, Taylor, Townsend Warner, Wilkinson.

Miles, Peter and Malcolm Smith. *Cinema, Literature and Society: Elite and Mass Culture in Interwar Britain* (London: Croom Helm, 1987).
Actually a study of the 1930s, which combines literary criticism, film studies, cultural studies, and historical research. Chapters include: The Politics of Depression, Suburban Pastoral, The Public Schools and the Great War, Theorists of the Elite, The Working Class Writer, British Film and Hollywood, The Documentary Film Movement, the Spanish Civil War, and The Approach of War. Focuses overwhelmingly on male authors; the only women discussed are Brittain, Leavis, and Woolf.

Miller, June Eldridge. *Rebel Women: Feminism, Modernism and the Edwardian Novel* (London: Virago, 1994).
A study of fiction by men and women published between 1890 and 1914. The chapters are on Realism and the Feminization of Fiction, Women and the Marriage Problem Novel (Forster, Ada Leverson, Galsworthy, Bennett, Von Arnim), New Maids for Old (Lawrence, Hunt, Mayor, Forster, and others), Suffragette Stories (Robins, Evelyn Sharp, Gertrude Colmore, and others), and a final chapter on Wells and Sinclair.

Montefiore, Janet. *Men and Women Writers of the 1930s: The Dangerous Flood of History* (London: Routledge, 1996).
The book's main thematic focus is on gender and collective memory in the political literature of the 1930s, but it also explores issues such as mass unemployment, fascism, and appeasement. There are close readings of West, Jameson, and Woolf, and a chapter on 'neglected' women poets, including Stevie Smith, Mitchison, Townsend Warner, and Ackland.

Ouditt, Sharon. *Fighting Forces, Writing Women: Identity and Ideology in the First World War* (London: Routledge, 1994).
Examines the wartime experiences of various groups of British women, such as the Voluntary Aid Detachment nurses, the Land Army, and the munitions workers, as well as women who remained at home. The focus is on the complex ideological structures women of different classes had to confront and engage with. Authors discussed are Bagnold, Brittain, Hall, Holtby, Macaulay, Sinclair, West, and Woolf.

Parsons, Deborah. *Streetwalking the Metropolis: Women, the City and Modernity* (Oxford: Oxford University Press, 2000).
Explores women's representations of the city and feminist revisions of urban modernism. Centres on the figure of the *flâneuse*, and offers theoretically informed readings of a range of writers including Barnes, Bowen, Flanner, Lehmann, Lessing, Levy, Nin, Rhys, Richardson, and Woolf.

Plain, Gill. *Women's Fiction of the Second World War: Gender, Power and Resistance* (Edinburgh: Edinburgh University Press, 1996).
Examines the relationship between war and gender through the analysis of literary texts. Organized in two parts: Prelude to War (Sayers, Stevie Smith, Woolf) and Weathering the Storm (Woolf, Mitchison, Bowen).

Raitt, Suzanne and Trudi Tate (eds). *Women's Fiction and the Great War* (Oxford: Clarendon Press, 1997).
A collection of 12 essays on: Ward, Wharton, Sinclair, Women's Romances and Memoirs, Vernon Lee, Woolf, Bellerby, Hall, Mansfield, Butts, H. D., and Stein.

Rowland, Susan. *From Agatha Christie to Ruth Rendell* (Basingstoke: Palgrave Macmillan, 2001).
Discusses six female crime novelists, Christie, Sayers, Allingham, Marsh, Ruth Rendell, and P. D. James, in relation to social class, postcolonialism, psychoanalysis, Gothic literature, and feminism.

Sceats, Sarah, and Gail Cunningham (eds). *Image and Power: Women in Fiction in the Twentieth Century* (London: Longmans, 1996).
Focuses on the relationship between sexuality, culture and power in women's fiction. Includes an essay on Sinclair and one on women writers in the 1920s and 1930s, together with readings of feminist science fiction and Irish women writers. Authors mentioned include Bowen, Burdekin, Corelli, Du Maurier, Holtby, Jameson, Keane, Mitchison, O'Brien, Townsend Warner, and Woolf.

Schneider, Karen. *Loving Arms: British Women Writing the Second World War* (Lexington: University Press of Kentucky, 1997).
Examines how conventional definitions of gender determine traditional representations of war, and discusses women writers who redefined the genre of war literature. Focuses on Burdekin, Stevie Smith, Bowen, and Woolf.

Smith, Angela. *The Second Battlefield: Women, Modernism and the First World War* (Manchester: Manchester University Press, 2000).
Argues that women's new roles during the war years led to an experimentation with new forms of expression. Early chapters concentrate on non-fictional accounts of women's experience of the front line and wartime hospitals (diaries and letters gathered from archives), while later sections study individual authors (Sinclair, Macaulay, H. D., Rose Allatini, Mansfield, West, Bagnold).

Spender, Dale. *Time and Tide Wait for No Man* (London: Pandora, 1984).
A combination of anthology and critical study, surveying *Time and Tide* in its first decade, the 1920s. An introductory chapter describes the journal's foundation and development. Part 1, The Women Writers, introduces key 1920s contributors: Lady Rhondda, Robins, West, Cicely Hamilton, Swanwick, Holtby, Brittain, and Crystal Eastman. Selected political pieces from each author are reprinted. Part 2, The Issues, contains narrative accounts by Spender of the political and social concerns of *Time and Tide* illustrated with reprinted editorials, advertisements, and correspondence from the paper.

Trodd, Anthea. *Women's Writing in English: Britain, 1900–1945* (London: Longmans, 1998).
The most comprehensive survey study of the field. Opens with an account of women's place in early twentieth-century culture, followed by chapters on The Conditions of Women's Writing, The Forms of Women's Experience, Poetry, The Fiction of Fact, Popular Writing, and Non-Fiction. The final chapter discusses individual writers (Mansfield, Woolf, Rhys, Bowen, Townsend Warner, and West). Appendixes contain a chronology, bibliography, and biographical entries for 64 authors.

Tylee, Claire M. *The Great War and Women's Consciousness: Images of Militarism and Womanhood in Women's Writings, 1914–1964* (Basingstoke: Macmillan, 1990).
Comprises chapters on: women war correspondents, propaganda, women's war fiction, literary bestsellers, autobiography and memoir, and elegiac fictions. Also contains an extensive bibliography, appendixes with the dates of women authors and their war writings and extracts from the Defence of the Realm Act of 1914, plus a list of relevant terminology. Authors discussed include Asquith, Bagnold, Brittain, Delafield, Hall, Jameson, Macaulay, Mansfield, Sinclair, Sylvia Pankhurst, West, Antonia White, and Woolf.

Wallace, Diana. *Sisters and Rivals in British Women's Fiction, 1914–1939* (Basingstoke: Palgrave Macmillan, 2000).
Examines the historical and political context of texts featuring female rivalries by Sinclair, West, Brittain, Holtby, and Lehmann.

Williams, Merryn. *Six Women Novelists. Macmillan Modern Novelists series* (Basingstoke: Macmillan, 1987).
Individual chapters on Schreiner, Wharton, Mayor, Mansfield, Sayers, and Antonia White. Intended primarily for students, but also useful for researchers.

Anthologies

Cardinal, Agnes, Dorothy Goldman and Judith Hattaway (eds). *Women's Writing on the First World War* (Oxford: Oxford University Press, 1999).
Contains 69 stories, diary entries or articles, both contemporary and retrospective, and arranged thematically. Includes writings by British, American, and European women. Authors represented include Bagnold, Brittain, Gregory, Kaye-Smith, Mansfield, Sinclair, Townsend Warner, West, Antonia White, and Woolf.

Dowson, Jane (ed.). *Women's Poetry of the 1930s: A Critical Anthology* (London: Routledge, 1996).
Poets represented are: Ackland, Vere Arnot, Bellerby, Freda C. Bond, Cornford, Cunard, Daryush, Gibbons, Holtby, Laura (Riding) Jackson, Lynd, Bowes Lyon, Mitchison, Pitter, Raine, Ridler, Sackville-West, Scovell, Sitwell, Stevie Smith, Struther, Townsend Warner, Wellesley, Wickham, Stanley Wrench, and Winifred Welles. There are introductions to the individual authors as well as a general introduction to women's poetry in this decade.

Gardiner, Juliet (ed.). *The New Woman: Women's Voices, 1880–1918* (London: Collins & Brown, 1993).
A thematically organized anthology, in which each text is introduced by the editor. Features prose, journalism, and poetry by Asquith, Bagnold, Brittain, Wedderburn Cannan, Carrington, Cole, Corelli, Delafield, Gore-Booth, Grand, Cecily Hamilton, Tennyson Jesse, Macaulay, Mansfield, Mew, Christabel and Emmeline Pankhurst, Henry Handel Richardson, Sinclair, Smyth, Stopes, Swanwick, Webb, West, and Woolf.

Gilbert, Sandra M. and Susan Gubar (eds). *The Norton Anthology of Literature by Women: The Tradition in English* (New York: Norton, 1985).
Ranges from the medieval period to the present. The early twentieth century is well represented; authors include Meynell, Gregory, Sinclair, Mew, Richardson, Woolf, Hall, Mansfield, West, Bowen, and Stevie Smith. For each writer, there is a brief biographical and critical account together with a selected bibliography.

Giles, Judy and Tim Middleton (eds). *Writing Englishness, 1900–1950: An Introductory Sourcebook on National Identity* (London: Routledge, 1995).
Selections of literary, autobiographical, political, and journalistic writing by a range of writers. Female authors represented are du Maurier, Holtby, Pearl Jephcott, Struther, Woolf, and a female Mass-Observation diarist. Includes historical/literary timelines, suggested learning activities, and a bibliography.

Hartley, Jenny. *Hearts Undefeated: Women's Writing of the Second World War*
(London: Virago, 1994).
Includes diaries, personal letters, letters to the press, journalism, fiction, autobiography,
book reviews, and prayers. They are arranged in themed sections covering different
stages of the war and also topics such as war work, the Blitz, conscription, and sex.
Combines work by well-known authors, including Sackville-West, Stark, Cartland, and
Delafield, with the testimonies of ordinary women, among them land girls, nurses, a
refugee, a prisoner, an air-raid warden, and a bus conductor.

Kime Scott, Bonnie. *The Gender of Modernism: A Critical Anthology* **(Bloomington:
Indiana University Press, 1990).**
Aims to demonstrate how modernist writers (male and female) engage with issues of
gender in their critiques of culture. Each section has an introduction by a prominent
feminist scholar. The critical selections embrace essays, book reviews, letters, and diaries,
as well as extracts from novels. Authors represented are Cunard, Loy, Macaulay,
Mansfield, Mew, Richardson, Sinclair, Townsend Warner, West, Antonia White, and
Woolf, alongside Lawrence, Joyce, and Eliot.

Morgan, Fidelis (ed.). *The Years Between: Plays by Women on the London Stage,
1900–1950.* **Preface by Susannah York (London: Virago, 1995).**
Includes the full text of three plays: Cicely Hamilton's *Diana of Dobson's*; Dane's *Will
Shakespeare – An Invention*; and Margaret Kennedy and Basil Dean's *The Constant
Nymph*; together with the texts of wartime revue sketches by Hermione Gingold, Nina
Warner Hooke, Diana Morgan, Du Maurier, and Storm. Also includes brief introduc-
tions to each author and play, as well as a general introduction to women dramatists of
the period.

Reilly, Catherine W. (ed.). *The Virago Book of War Poetry and Verse by Women*
(London: Virago, 1997).
Combines Reilly's two previous anthologies, *Scars Upon My Heart: Women's Poetry and
Verse of the First World War* (1981) and *Chaos of the Night: Women's Poetry and Verse of the
Second World War* (1984). These books were compiled in response to modern anthologies
that tend to focus on the poetry of the frontline soldier at the expense of women poets.
Poets anthologized include Cunard, Daryush, Farjeon, Macaulay, Mitchison, Meynell,
Nesbit, Sitwell, Stevie Smith, Tynan, and Townsend Warner. Contains a brief biographical
note on each poet.

Smith, Ali, Kasia Boddy and Sarah Wood (eds). *The Virago Book of Twentieth-Century
Fiction* **(London: Virago, 2000).**
Comprises 100 extracts from authors published by Virago, one for each year of the
century, with a biographical page preceding each entry. Among the early twentieth-
century British authors included are: Comyns, Dell, Mew, Macaulay, Mayor, Mitchison,
Nesbit, Richardson, Sackville-West, Sinclair, Struther, Mary Webb, and West.

Smith, Angela. *Women's Writing of the Great War: An Anthology* **(Manchester:
Manchester University Press, 2000).**
Combines fictional extracts with diaries, letters, and journalism. Divided into themed
sections: The Outbreak of War; Belgium; Patriotism; Pacifism; Conscription; Loves,
Separation and Sexuality; The Battle Front; The Home Front; Under Fire; Medical Care;
War Work; Armistice and Aftermath.

Tate, Trudi. *Women, Men and the Great War: An Anthology of Stories* (Manchester: Manchester University Press, 1995).
Stories by Butts, Hall, Holtby, Mansfield, Townsend Warner, and Woolf. Also contains a brief biography of each writer.

Encyclopedias

Blain, Virginia, Patricia Clements and Isobel Grundy (eds). *The Feminist Companion to Literature in English: Women Writers from the Middle Ages to the Present* (London: B.T. Batsford, 1990).
Comprehensive encyclopedia which boasts over 2700 entries of about 500 words each. Includes entries on authors from around the world, together with some topic entries (women's suffrage, education, diaries, and so on), and a chronological index of names.

Buck, Claire (ed.). *The Bloomsbury Guide to Women's Literature* (London: Bloomsbury, 1992).
Entries on women writers and literary texts from all countries and periods. Includes a selection of essays that summarize women's literary endeavours in Britain, Ireland, Europe, Australasia, the Americas, Africa, and Asia, as well as an essay by Catherine Belsey on critical approaches to women's literature. The main reference section contains entries on many early twentieth-century authors, as well as relevant topics such as Bloomsbury, detective fiction, modernism, and suffrage.

Crawford, Anne et al. (eds). *The EUROPA Biographical Dictionary of British Women* (London: Europa, 1983).
The work of six editors, responsible for the various periods from the Anglo-Saxon to the contemporary, and 80 contributors, this dictionary includes over 1000 entries, among them a substantial number on early twentieth-century writers, as well as women in public life.

Janik, Vicki K. and Del Ivan Janik (eds). *Modern British Women Writers: A Sourcebook* (London: Greenwood, 2002).
Introductions to 58 twentieth-century women writers. Entries are three to six pages long and contain extensive bibliographies. Early twentieth-century writers covered are: Bowen, Brittain, Christie, Compton-Burnett, Holtby, Jameson, Hansford Johnson, Lehmann, Mansfield, Mew, Rhys, Richardson, Sackville-West, Sayers, Sinclair, Sitwell, Stevie Smith, Taylor, Thirkell, Townsend Warner, West, Woolf, and Young.

Kemp, Sandra, Charlotte Mitchell and David Trotter (eds). *Edwardian Fiction: An Oxford Companion* (Oxford: Oxford University Press, 1997).
Encyclopedia of fiction between 1900 and 1914, which contains over 800 author entries, of which almost half are on women. There are also entries on individual works, periodicals, and literary genres, together with a chronology of historical events.

Myer, Valerie G. and Steven R. Serafin (eds). *The Continuum Encyclopedia of British Literature* (New York: Continuum, 2003).
A 1200-page volume, containing 1130 entries on individual authors and 70 entries on literary topics (including genres, periods, and the national literatures of Commonwealth countries). Many early twentieth-century women writers are included, with useful, up-to-date accounts.

Sage, Lorna (ed.). *The Cambridge Guide to Women's Writing in English* **(Cambridge: Cambridge University Press, 1999).**
Contains over 2500 entries provided by a wide range of specialists. The vast majority are on individual authors and on key texts, but there are also entries for genres (fairy-tale, detective fiction, scandalous memoirs) and other relevant groupings (New Woman, modernist women).

Schlueter, Paul and June Schlueter (eds). *An Encyclopaedia of British Women Writers* **(1988; rev. edn London: Garland Publishing, 1998).**
Contains nearly 400 entries on individual authors from all periods. Entries are unusually detailed, and include full listings of works by each writer together with secondary references. There is an index which lists topics referred to in the author entries (such as abolitionism, regionalism, suffrage). Necessarily omits less well known authors.

Shattock, Joanne. *The Oxford Guide to British Women Writers* **(Oxford: Oxford University Press, 1993).**
Covers over 400 women writers, dating from the medieval period onwards, and places each writer in the context of her contemporaries, both male and female. The emphasis is on individual authors, but there are also topic entries on The New Woman, *Time and Tide*, Women Writers Suffrage League, and so on. Each entry includes secondary references, and there is also a select bibliography.

Todd, Janet (ed.). *Dictionary of British Women Writers* **(London: Routledge, 1989).**
Entries are between one and three pages long, and offer biographical details, a brief analysis of the author's most famous works, and further reading. Focuses mostly on eighteenth- and nineteenth-century writers, but does include Bowen, Brittain, Gibbons, Tey, Du Maurier, Lehmann, Mansfield, Mitchison, Sackville-West, and Woolf, amongst others.

Uglow, Jennifer (ed.). *The Macmillan Dictionary of Women's Biography.* **2nd edn (London: Macmillan, 1989).**
Offers worldwide coverage of women's biography, beginning in the Middle Ages. The index divides the women into categories: Public Life, Cultural Life, Physical Achievements, and Dynamic Characters. Contains 288 entries for writers, including a significant number from the early twentieth century, and a comprehensive bibliography of relevant reference works.

Wheeler, Kathleen M. *A Critical Guide to Twentieth-Century Women Novelists* **(Oxford: Blackwell, 1997).**
Includes substantial encyclopedia-style entries for 135 writers from all over the English-speaking world, and a discursive survey of dozens of further writers. Divided into four chronological sections, together with a final section on Theory, Further Reading, and Research.

Bibliographies

Hannam, June, Anne Hughes and Pauline Stafford. *British Women's History: A Bibliographical Guide* **(Manchester: Manchester University Press, 1996).**
Provides a guide to work on the history of women in Britain from *c*.500 AD to the present. A methodological section addresses concepts, problems, historiography, and

sources. Traditional concerns (family, education, politics, religion, feminism, and work) are covered alongside the more recent preoccupations of women's history (sexuality, crime, prostitution, travel, and autobiography).

Ouditt, Sharon. *Women Writers of the First World War: An Annotated Bibliography* (London: Routledge, 1999).
Comprehensive bibliography of texts written or published between 1914 and 1939. Part 1 lists primary sources: fiction, diaries, letters, and autobiographies. Part 2 lists secondary material, including biographies, bibliographies, reference works, literary criticism, and social and cultural history. Each entry gives a brief précis of plot or argument.

Reilly, Catherine. *English Poetry of the First World War: A Bibliography* (London: Prior, 1978).
A comprehensive list of work by British poets who experienced the war. Covers publications issued from 1914–70, in the form of books, pamphlets, cards, and broadsides. Details the contents of anthologies and identifies single-authored volumes containing war poems. There is a title index and a supplementary list of war poets of other English-speaking nations. In all, 2225 authors are covered, of whom 417 were in the Forces or uniformed services. Women poets appear on every page, though their numbers do not compare with those of the male poets.

Reilly, Catherine. *English Poetry of the Second World War: A Bibliography* (London: Mansell Publishing, 1986).
Arranged in the same way as the World War One bibliography (see above), but additionally includes biographical information, where available, for each author. An introduction analyses the patterns relating to education, profession, and war experience revealed by this biographical data. Covers 3072 separate publications issued between 1939 and 1980 and 2679 poets. Of these, 831 (including 51 women) were in the Forces or uniformed services.

Key History and Cultural Studies Books

Beddoe, Deirdre. *Back to Home and Duty: Women Between the Wars, 1918–1939* (London: Pandora Press, 1989).
A feminist history which draws on a range of primary sources including women's magazines, films, government records, novels, newspapers, diaries, and autobiographies. Chapters are entitled 'Desirable and Undesirable Images', 'Education', 'Employment', 'Home and Health', 'Leisure', and 'Politics and Issues'. Authors mentioned include Bowen, Brittain, Brazil, Delafield, Hall, Holtby, Macaulay, Mitford, and Woolf.

Braybon, Gail and Penny Summerfield. *Out of the Cage: Women's Experiences in Two World Wars* (London: Pandora Press, 1987).
Draws on oral histories, diaries, and autobiographies to show women's responses to war, men's reactions to female war workers, and how conventional views about gender roles were destabilized. Part I, written by Braybon, is on World War One, and Part II, by Summerfield, on World War Two. Chapters focus on war work, health and welfare, domestic life and marriage, and demobilization. Authors mentioned include Brittain, Holtby, and Ward.

Bruly, Sue. *Women in Britain Since 1900* (Basingstoke: Macmillan – now Palgrave Macmillan, 1999).
Examines the changing meaning of femininity in the twentieth century, combining evidence from primary research, which has an emphasis on personal testimony, with a synthesis of the work of social, economic, political, and cultural historians. Chronologically arranged chapters explore work, family sexuality, education, and feminism, within varied social, economic, and political contexts. Includes a very full annotated bibliography.

Dyhouse, Carol. *Feminism and the Family in England, 1880–1939* (Oxford: Blackwell, 1989).
Drawing upon diaries, autobiographies, pamphlets, and novels, Dyhouse considers how feminists sought to secure economic independence for women, reorganize the household, and reshape marital and sexual relations. Authors mentioned include Brittain, Grand, Holtby, Macaulay, Nesbit, Sinclair, and Woolf.

Giles, Judy. *Women, Identity and Private Life in Britain, 1900–1950* (New York: St Martin's Press, 1995).
Drawing on oral histories, autobiographical accounts, letters, magazines, and fiction, this book explores the meanings and experience of home and privacy for women who grew up in the first half of the twentieth century. It considers the extent to which gender, class, surburbanization, and 'historical moment' constructed women's understanding of domesticity. Authors mentioned include Brittain, Du Maurier, Holtby, Rathbone, and Woolf.

Giles, Judy. *The Parlour and the Suburb: Domestic Identities, Class, Femininity and Modernity* (Oxford: Berg, 2004).
Focusing on the first half of the twentieth century, Giles challenges stereotypes about domesticity, arguing that home and private life were crucial spaces in which the interrelations of class and gender impacted significantly on the formation of modern feminine subjectivities. Topics covered include Suburbia, Consumption Practices, Domestic Service, and The Housewife. Texts examined include oral narratives, women's magazines, and literary and feminist texts.

Hall, Lesley A. *Sex, Gender and Social Change in Britain Since 1880* (Basingstoke: Palgrave Macmillan, 2000).
An account of changes in sexual behaviour and attitudes, covering the social purity movement; fin-de-siècle anxieties about degeneration; early twentieth-century concerns about disease, divorce, eugenics, and contraception; and developing perceptions of marriage, reproduction, and sex education over the whole period. Considers the impact on sexuality of specific historical events, including the two wars and the emergence of the Welfare State.

Hunt, Felicity (ed.). *Lessons for Life: The Schooling of Girls and Women, 1850–1950* (Oxford: Basil Blackwell, 1987).
Hunt highlights the extent to which formal school structures (from elementary through to university) and informal socialization reflected and reinforced prevailing social practices and opinions.

Lewis, Jane (ed.). *Labour and Love: Women's Experience of Home and Family, 1850–1940* (Oxford: Blackwell, 1986).
Chapters focus on the experience of working-class childhood and motherhood; attitudes to marital sex and reproduction; domestic violence; women's economic strategies; teaching; and marital status and work. The essays suggest the extent to which the boundaries of family extended beyond immediate conjugal relations to kin and neighbours, and into the public sphere.

Lewis, Jane. *Women in England, 1870–1940: Sexual Divisions and Social Change* (London: Harvester Wheatsheaf, 1984).
Provides an account of the changing nature of English working- and middle-class women's experiences at school, home, work, and in politics from 1870 to 1950. The first section explores patterns of marriage and motherhood, addressing issues of fertility control, health and welfare, and the family economy. The second section looks at the characteristics of women's work.

Oldfield, Sybil (ed.). *This Working Day World* (London: Taylor & Francis, 1994).
Essays on aspects of British women's lives in the period 1914–45, presenting a women's cultural history that covers art, fiction, medicine, political radicalism, and the personal lives of women.

Pugh, Martin. *Women and the Women's Movement in Britain, 1914–1959* (Basingstoke: Macmillan, 1992).
Using the widest range of evidence, from the political feminist pressure groups to popular women's magazines, this book analyses the complex relationship between the organized women's movement, the majority of women outside the official women's movement, and the male political establishment in Britain.

Purvis, June (ed.). *Women's History: Britain, 1850–1945* (London: Routledge, 1995).
The introduction explores debate and controversy in British women's history, and the chapters discuss women in relation to industrialization, the family, paid work, education, popular literature, health, sexuality, politics, ethnicity, race and empire, the vote, and war.

Roberts, Elizabeth. *A Woman's Place: An Oral History of Working-Class Women, 1890–1940* (Oxford: Blackwell, 1984).
Based upon Roberts's oral history interviews in Lancashire, this book shows that many working-class women were conscious of, and secure in, the separate, private sphere of home and family, with little feeling of oppression by men, but more of class-based oppression and economic injustice. It examines the hazards of childbirth, the routines of housework and the nature of women's employment.

Summerfield, Penny. *Women Workers in the Second World War: Production and Patriarchy in Conflict* (London: Croom Helm, 1984).
Examines the impact of the war on women's employment and the contribution that women made to the war effort. Also explores the relationship between women, capital, and labour.

Tinker, Penny. *Constructing Girlhood: Popular Magazines for Girls Growing up in England, 1920–1950* (London: Taylor & Francis, 1995).
Tinker examines the contribution of magazines to the social construction of female adolescence and the role of magazines in the lives of contemporary girls. Investigates the

ways in which content was shaped by what were seen to be legitimate concerns for girls and how this was influenced by publishers' objectives and culture, reader interests, and ideologies of femininity.

Wrigley, Chris (ed.). *A Companion to Early Twentieth-Century Britain* (Oxford: Blackwell, 2002).
Most comprehensive, with 32 chapters, divided into sections: British Political Life (major parties; Wales, Scotland, and Ireland; women and politics, etc.); Britain and the World (immigrants, empire, foreign policy, and so on); Social and Economic Developments (agriculture, banking, consumers, welfare, housing medicine, education, leisure, religion, sport, culture, Britishness, and so forth). We include this book, although it is not focused on women's history, because it contains so much relevant material.

Zweininger-Bargielowska, Ina (ed.). *Women in Twentieth-Century Britain* (Harlow: Longmans, 2001).
An illustrated history of modern women's lives, work, culture and citizenship, which starts with a discussion of the development of women's history. Examines girlhood, marriage and the ageing process, the nature of women's work, crime, domestic violence, leisure, state and citizenship, the women's movement, and social policy.

INDEXES

Authors

Please note: Brief entries on 66 additional writers are provided in Appendix II Minor Writers.

Valentine Ackland

Margery Allingham

Daisy Ashford

Cynthia Asquith

Ruby M. Ayres

Enid Bagnold

Florence Barclay

Iris Barry

Frances Bellerby

Stella Benson

Phyllis Bentley

Annie Besant

Eliot Bliss

Ursula Bloom

Enid Blyton

Theodora Bosanquet

Phyllis Bottome

Elizabeth Bowen

Mary Elizabeth Braddon

Angela Brazil

Elinor M. Brent-Dyer

Ann Bridge

Vera Brittain

Rhoda Broughton

Bryher

Katherine Burdekin

Frances Hodgson Burnett

Mary Butts

May Wedderburn Cannan

Leonora Carrington

Catherine Carswell

Barbara Cartland

Annie Vivanti Chartres

Mary Cholmondeley

Agatha Christie

Margaret Postgate Cole

Ivy Compton-Burnett

Barbara Comyns

Lettice Cooper

Marie Corelli

Frances Cornford

Richmal Crompton

Nancy Cunard

Clemence Dane

Ella D'Arcy

Elizabeth Daryush

E. M. Delafield

Ethel M. Dell

Monica Dickens

O. Douglas

Daphne du Maurier

Dorothy Edwards

Margiad Evans

Leonora Eyles

Eleanor Farjeon

Rachel Ferguson

Pamela Frankau

Stella Gibbons

Elinor Glyn

Rumer Godden

Eva Gore-Booth

Elizabeth Goudge

Sarah Grand

Lady Augusta Gregory

Radclyffe Hall

Cicely Hamilton

Helen Hamilton

Mary Agnes Hamilton

Georgette Heyer

Inez Holden

Ethel Carnie Holdsworth

Constance Holme

Winifred Holtby

Mary Vivian Hughes

E. M. Hull

Violet Hunt

Elspeth Huxley

Storm Jameson

F. Tennyson Jesse

Pamela Hansford Johnson

Anna Kavan

Sheila Kaye-Smith

Molly Keane

Margaret Kennedy

Magdalen King-Hall
Mary Kingsley
Marghanita Laski
Frieda Lawrence
Q. D. Leavis
Vernon Lee
Edith Oldham Lees
Rosamund Lehmann
Marie Belloc Lowndes
Mina Loy
Sylvia Lynd
Lilian Bowes Lyon
Rose Macaulay
Ethel Mannin
Olivia Manning
Katherine Mansfield
Ngaio Marsh
Ethel Colburne
    Mayne
F. M. Mayor
Charlotte Mew
Alice Meynell
Viola Meynell
Betty Miller
Naomi Mitchison
Nancy Mitford
Olive Moore
Lady Ottoline Morrell
Willa Muir
Edith Nesbit
Kate O'Brien
Violet Paget
Emmeline Pankhurst
Sylvia Pankhurst
Mollie Panter-Downes
Edith Mary Pargeter
Ruth Pitter
Jean Plaidy
Jessie Pope
Beatrix Potter
Allen Raine
Kathleen Raine
Eleanor Rathbone
Irene Rathbone
Mary Renault
Lady Rhondda
Jean Rhys
Dorothy Richardson
Anne Ridler

Anne Thackeray Ritchie
Kate Roberts
Lynette Roberts
E. Arnot Robertson
Elizabeth Robins
Naomi Royde-Smith
Berta Ruck
Dora Russell
Vita Sackville-West
Oliver Sandys
Dorothy L. Sayers
E. J. Scovell
Margery Sharp
May Sinclair
Edith Sitwell
Dodie Smith
Helen Zenna Smith
Stevie Smith
Ethel Smyth
Somerville and Ross
Freya Stark
Flora Annie Steel
G. B. Stern
Marie Stopes
Lesley Storm
Julia Strachey
Ray Strachey
Jan Struther
Muriel Stuart
Helena M. Swanwick
Netta Syrett
Elizabeth Taylor
Josephine Tey
Angela Thirkell
Flora Thompson
Sylvia Thompson
Pamela Lyndon Travers
Iris Tree
Violet Trefusis
Katherine Tynan
Evelyn Underhill
Alison Uttley
Hilda Vaughan
Elizabeth von Arnim
Helen Waddell
Mrs Humphry Ward
Sylvia Townsend Warner
Winifred Watson
Beatrice Webb

Mary Webb
Dorothy Wellesley
Rebecca West
Dorothy Whipple
Antonia White

Ethel Lina White
Anna Wickham
Ellen Wilkinson
Virginia Woolf
E. H. Young

Topics

Please note: In the main body of the encyclopedia, these topics are arranged alphabetically, interspersed with the author entries.

Literary Terms, Genres and Movements

Auden Generation
Bloomsbury
Children's Literature
Detective Fiction (Golden Age)
Documentary Filmmakers
Georgian Poets
Historical Fiction
Modernism
Regional Writing
Revue
Romantic Fiction
Science Fiction and Fantasy
War Memoirs
Welsh Language Writing
World War One Writing
World War Two Writing

Literary Culture and Periodicals

Book Clubs
Brows (highbrow, middlebrow, lowbrow)
Censorship
Copyright Act 1911
English Association
Libraries
Little Magazines
Net Book Agreement
Newspapers and Periodical Journals
Persephone Books
Poetry Anthologies
Prix Femina-Vie Heureuse
Publishers
Society of Women Writers and
    Journalists
Virago Books
Women's and Girls' Magazines

Fashion and Culture

Broadcasting
Cinema
Consumerism
Domestic Technology
Fashion and Youth Culture
Housing
Mass-Observation
Servants

Sexuality and Health

Abortion
Contraception
Health and Medicine
Homosexuality (male)
Influenza Pandemic
Lesbianism
Prostitution
Psychoanalysis
Sexology

Historical Events

Boer War
Depression
General Strike
Jarrow March
Spanish Civil War
Titanic
World War One
World War Two

Politics in Britain

Appeasement
Communism

Education

Empire and
Imperialism

Eugenics

Fabians

Fascism

Irish Question

Pacifism

Party Politics

Socialism

Suffragism

War Work

Welfare State

Women's Movement

Printed in the United States
68030LVS00002B/243